47 $\frac{50}{}$

The Handbook of Treasury Securities

Trading and Portfolio Strategies

The Handbook of Treasury Securities

Trading and Portfolio Strategies

Edited by

Frank J. Fabozzi

Visiting Professor
Alfred P. Sloan School of Management
Massachusetts Institute of Technology
and
Managing Editor, *The Journal of
Portfolio Management*

Probus Publishing Company
Chicago, Illinois

332,632
H2362

Library of Congress Cataloging in Publication Data

The Handbook of treasury securities.

Includes index.
1. Government securities—United States—Handbooks,
manuals, etc.   I. Fabozzi, Frank J.
HG4941.H36   1987   332.63'232   86-12375
ISBN 0-917253-43-4

Library of Congress Catalog Card No. 86-12375

Printed in the United States of America

1   2   3   4   5   6   7   8   9   0

To my wife, Dessa

CONTENTS

CONTRIBUTORS

Marcelle Arak, Ph.D., Vice President, Citicorp North American Investment Bank

Jack Bernard, Financial Futures and Options Group, Merrill Lynch Capital Markets

Jackson D. Breaks, Vice President, Merrill Lynch, Pierce Fenner & Smith, Inc.

John M. Ezell, Vice President, Charter Atlantic Corporation

Frank J. Fabozzi, Ph.D., C.F.A., Visiting Professor, Alfred P. Sloan School of Management, Massachusetts Institute of Technology

H. Gifford Fong, President, Gifford Fong Associates

Kenneth D. Garbade, Ph.D., Vice President, Bankers Trust Company

Laurie Goodman, Ph.D., Vice President, Citicorp North American Investment Bank

Frank J. Jones, Ph.D., Vice President, Kidder, Peabody & Company, Inc.

James L. Kochan, Manager and Vice-President, Fixed Income Research Department, Merrill Lynch Capital Markets

Thomas J. Kluber, Senior Vice President, Wm. E. Pollock & Co., Inc.

F. Ward McCarthy, Jr., Ph.D., Senior Money Market Economist, Merrill Lynch Capital Markets

Maureen Mooney, Senior Fixed Income Research Analyst, Fixed Income Research Department, Merrill Lynch Capital Markets

Sharmin Mossavar-Rahmani, Vice President, Lehman Management Co., Inc.

Mark Pitts, Ph.D., Vice President, Shearson Lehman Brothers, Inc.

Ronald J. Ryan, C.F.A., Managing Director, Ryan Financial Strategy Group

Joseph Snailer, Assistant Vice President, Citicorp North American Investment Bank

Thomas Stauffacher, Senior Vice President, Wm. E. Pollock & Co., Inc.

Raymond W. Stone, Ph.D., Chief Financial Economist, Merrill Lynch Capital Markets

Andrea J. Trachtenberg, Vice President and Director of Marketing and Strategic Planning, Merrill Lynch Capital Markets Taxable Fixed Income Trading Group

Benjamin Wolkowitz, Ph.D., Vice President, Morgan Stanley & Co.

PREFACE

The appeal of U.S. Treasury securities is that they are viewed as free of credit risk and can be traded in a secondary market in large volume at narrow spreads between bid and asked prices. This active and highly liquid secondary market allows portfolio managers and traders, both domestic and foreign, to buy and sell Treasury securities without causing major price disruptions. With the development of the market for derivative contracts (futures and options) in which a Treasury is the underlying security, active and offensively minded portfolio management, in its broadest sense, became practicable. In effect, money managers and traders gained new degrees of freedom. The rapid development of the zero-coupon (stripped) Treasury market filled the needs of money managers, institutional investors, and individuals for a default-free security that eliminates reinvestment risk, and the needs of certain foreign investors who sought tax advantaged default-free securities.

The Handbook of Treasury Securities is designed to provide not only information about the investment characteristics of the cash securities and derivative contracts that make them attractive to a broad range of investors, but also extensive coverage on state-of-the-art strategies. To accomplish this goal, a broad perspective must be offered. The experiences of a wide range of experts is more informative than that of a single expert. I have chosen some of the best known practitioners to contribute to this book.

ACKNOWLEDGMENTS

I would like to express my appreciation to the contributors and their families. I would also like to thank the following individuals for giving generously of their time to comment on portions of the manuscript: Jack Breaks (Merrill Lynch), Teresa Garlicki (Rutgers University), Tom Kluber (Wm. E. Pollock & Co.), Sharmin Mossavar-Rahmani (Lehman Management Company), Tom Stauffacher (Wm. E. Pollock & Co.) and Vic Thompson (Gifford Fong Associates). Robin Cohen, Joe Gaziano, Tom Radwanski and David Warren provided invaluable assistance at various stages of this project. Finally, I am grateful to Probus Publishing for its encouragement and support.

Frank J. Fabozzi

CHAPTER 1

SHARMIN MOSSAVAR-RAHMANI is a vice president of Lehman Management Co., Inc., New York. A fixed income portfolio strategist, she has published extensively on the bond market as well as on international energy issues. A graduate of Princeton University (A.B. Economics) and Stanford University (M.S. Engineering-Economic Systems), she was formerly Director of Research at Ryan Financial Strategy Group, a division of Refco Partners.

FRANK J. FABOZZI is currently a Visiting Professor in the Alfred P. Sloan School of Management at MIT, on leave from Lafayette College. A magna cum laude graduate from the City College of New York with bachelor's and master's degrees, he is a member of Phi Beta Kappa. Dr. Fabozzi earned a doctorate in economics from The City University of New York and is a C.F.A. and C.P.A. He is the managing editor of *The Journal of Portfolio Management* and has authored, coauthored, and edited several widely acclaimed books in investment management.

FRANK J. JONES is currently responsible for the Research and Product Development Department of the Financial Futures Department at Kidder, Peabody & Co., Inc. Previously, Dr. Jones was Senior Vice President with the New York Stock Exchange, where he managed the Index & Options Products Division.

Dr. Jones holds a Ph.D. in Economics from Stanford University and an M.B.A. from the University of Pittsburgh. He also earned an M.S. in Nuclear Engineering from Cornell University, and B.A. and B.S. degrees from the University of Notre Dame.

BENJAMIN WOLKOWITZ is Vice President and Product Manager at Morgan Stanley & Co. His responsibilities encompass the distribution of futures and options on fixed income securities.

Prior to joining Morgan Stanley, Dr. Wolkowitz was in charge of Citibank's Futures Brokerage Operation. He also was an Economist at the New York Futures Exchange, and Section Chief of Financial Studies Section of the Federal Reserve Board of Washington, D.C.

Dr. Wolkowitz taught economics at Tulane University in New Orleans. He has a Ph.D. in Economics from Brown University in Providence, Rhode Island.

THE CASH MARKET FOR U.S. TREASURY SECURITIES

Sharmin Mossavar-Rahmani
Vice President
Lehman Management Co., Inc.

Frank J. Fabozzi, Ph.D., C.F.A.
Visiting Professor
Alfred P. Sloan School of Management
Massachusetts Institute of Technology

Frank J. Jones, Ph.D.
Vice President
Kidder, Peabody & Company, Inc.

and

Benjamin Wolkowitz, Ph.D.
Vice President
Morgan Stanley & Co.

U.S. government securities are issued by the U.S. Department of the Treasury and are backed by the full faith and credit of the United States government. Treasury securities, therefore, do not have any credit risk. They are acceptable as security for deposits of public monies and for notes discounted at Federal Reserve Banks. Interest on Treasury securities is exempt from state and local income taxes.[1]

---

[1] The federal income tax treatment of transactions involving Treasury securities is explained in the appendix to this book.

The interest rates on Treasury securities are the benchmark interest rates throughout the U.S. economy as well as in the international capital markets. Two factors account for the prominent role of Treasury securities: volume (in terms of dollars outstanding) and liquidity. The U.S. Department of the Treasury is the largest single issuer of debt in the world, with Treasury securities accounting for $1.5 trillion, consisting of over 180 Treasury notes and bonds and 30 Treasury bills. In contrast, the entire U.S. corporate bond market accounts for about $750 billion and over ten thousand issues; the U.S. municipal bond market similarly accounts for about $720 billion, more than 70,000 separate issuers, and millions of individual issues. Therefore, the dollar amount outstanding of any single Treasury security dwarfs that of any other fixed income security. The large volume of total debt and the large size of any single issue have contributed to making the Treasury market the most active and hence most liquid market in the world. The spread between bid and asked prices is considerably narrower than other sectors of the fixed income market, and most issues can be readily purchased. In contrast, most issues in the corporate and municipal market are somewhat illiquid and cannot be readily located.

In this chapter, the primary and secondary markets for Treasury securities are described. Chapters 11 and 12 describe zero coupon securities collateralized by Treasury securities. Options and futures on Treasury securities are described in Chapters 14 and 15.

U.S. GOVERNMENT SECURITIES

There are two categories of government securities—discount and coupon securities. The fundamental difference between these two types of securities is the form in which the holder receives interest and, as a result, the prices at which they are issued. On coupon securities, specific interest payments are periodically (usually every six months) made by the Treasury during the life of the securities. Discount securities do not make periodic interest payments. Instead, the security holder realizes interest at the maturity date, the interest being the difference between the face value received at maturity and the purchase price.

According to current Treasury practices, all Treasury securities with maturities of one year or less are issued as discount securities; and all securities with maturities of two years or more are issued as coupon securities. Treasury discount securities are called *bills*. Treasury coupon securities issued with original maturities between two and 10 years are called *notes,* and those with maturities greater than 10 years are called *bonds*.

On coupon securities, an amount equal to half the annual coupon is paid to the holder every six months. For example, if a Treasury security is issued with a 10 percent coupon, a $50 payment is made every six months for every $1,000 face value.

Since the coupon payment of the coupon securities represents the payment of interest during the time the security is outstanding, the initial issue price of a Treasury coupon security is approximately the same as its maturity value. Thus, Treasury coupon securities are issued at about par. If interest rates subsequently increase, the coupons of newly issued bonds will be higher; and thus the price of the bonds previously issued at lower coupons will sell at a price below its maturity value, that is, "at a discount" to par. If interest rates subsequently decrease, the coupons of newly issued bonds will be lower than the coupons of the previously issued bonds; and thus the price of the bonds previously issued at higher coupons will sell at a price above its maturity value, that is, at a premium to par.

Because no specific interest is paid on a discount security, the security must be issued at a price less than its maturity value, such that the difference between the initial discount price and the final maturity price represents the return to the holder of the security. For example, if a one-year Treasury bill with a maturity value of $1,000 is sold "at a discount" of $900, the $100 difference is the interest payment and it is approximately equivalent to a 11 percent rate of interest.

The Treasury issues marketable and nonmarketable securities. The former can be sold prior to maturity in the secondary market (discussed below). Marketable securities currently consist of bills, notes, and bonds. Nonmarketable securities cannot be sold in the secondary market; instead, an investor who wants to cash in the security before the stated maturity date must redeem it at a predetermined price at any Federal Reserve Bank or branch. Nonmarketable securities include U.S. Savings Bonds (Series EE Savings Bonds and Series HH Current Income Bonds) and special issues to Treasury trust funds, state and local governments, and foreign monetary authorities. The focus of this book is marketable securities which in 1985 represented about 75 percent of total interest-bearing public debt.

Treasury bills are issued in minimum denominations of $10,000 with multiples of $5,000 thereafter. Currently, Treasury notes with original maturities of three years or less are available in denominations of $5,000, $10,000, $100,000, $1 million, $100 million, and $500 million. Prior to the latter part of 1974, $1,000 denominations were available on Treasury note issues with a maturity of less than four years. Treasury notes longer than three years and Treasury bonds come in denominations of $1,000, $5,000, $100,000 and $1 million. Bonds with a $500 denomination were eliminated on new issues since mid-1971.

All marketable securities are available in book-entry form at the Federal Reserve Bank System (Fed). This means that the investor receives only a receipt that evidences ownership instead of an engraved certificate. Treasury bills come only in book-entry form. Treasury notes and bonds that were issued prior to January 1, 1983 are available in both registered and bearer form. Treasury notes and bonds issued after January 1, 1983 are required to be in book-entry form.

Although Treasury notes are not callable, many Treasury bond issues are. Typically, the call date is five years before maturity. Notice of a call must be given four months prior to the call date. Issues that are callable are denoted by two dates in the financial press and on some dealer quote sheets. The first date is the date that the issue can first be called and the second date is the maturity date. For example, the Treasury bond issue denoted May 2000–05 means that the issue matures in May 2005 but is callable beginning May 2000.

There are a number of Treasury bonds that have a favorable tax treatment for federal estate tax purposes. When tendered for payment of federal estate taxes these bonds are valued at par value regardless of their market price. Thus, if $100,000 of par value of these special bonds is held in an individual's portfolio who has died and the deceased's estate owes $100,000 of federal estate taxes, these bonds can be tendered to satisfy the tax liability. It does not make a difference if the market price of the bonds at the time that they are tendered is less than $100,000.

These bonds are nicknamed "flower bonds" because they are suggestive of funerals. Flower bonds were issued by the Treasury between 1953 and 1963. The following Treasury issues are flower bonds.

Coupon Rate (%)	Maturity
$4^1/_4$	August 15, 1987–92
4	February 15, 1988–93
$4^1/_8$	May 15, 1989–94
$3^1/_2$	February 15, 1990
3	February 15, 1995
$3^1/_2$	November 15, 1998

Since these bonds carry a coupon rate between 3 and $4^1/_4$ percent, they sell at a discount (that is, below par). For example, on April 14, 1986, the 3 percent coupon issue due on February 1995 sold for 91.5 percent of its par value. Thus, $100,000 of par value of these bonds had a market value of $91,500 but could be used to satisfy a $100,000 federal estate tax liability. In fact, the only reason for holding flower bonds is for federal estate tax planning purposes. The yields on these bonds reflect this feature and consequently are lower than the yields on similar maturity Treasury issues. For example, the $10^1/_2$ percent coupon issue due in February 1995 was priced to yield 7.31 percent on April 14, 1986. The flower bond maturing in February 1995 was priced to yield only 4.16 percent.

In October 1984, the first Treasury notes targeted for the foreign market were issued. Subsequently the Treasury has sold additional issues of foreign targeted investor notes (TINs) (during November 1984, May 1985, and February 1986). There are two features that differentiate TINs from domestic issues. First, the conventional practice in the Euromarket of annual coupon payments rather than semiannual coupon payments in the case of domestic issues has been adopted for TINs. Second, domestic issues are registered in the name of the owner. However, TINs are not registered in the name of the owner; instead, the security is registered in the name of an international financial organization[2] which need only certify that the ultimate owner of the securities has declared itself to be a non-U.S. citizen.[3] Thus anonymity sought by a foreign investor is maintained.

At the option of the holder, foreign targeted securities can be converted into domestic securities 45 days after the auction. The conversion into a domestic issue will not usually be swapped par for par but based on a Treasury-specified formula. TINs usually trade at a lower yield than domestic issues, on rare occasions by as much as 90 basis points. A more detailed discussion of TINs is presented in Chapter 5.

PRIMARY MARKET

Marketable Treasury securities are initially issued into the primary government securities market. These securities are typically issued on an auction basis by the Treasury with the assistance of the Federal Reserve System.

The Treasury has found that it can reduce the interest cost of its

---

[2] An international financial organization is defined in the offering circular as a "central bank or monetary authority of a foreign government or a public international organization of which the United States is a member that is characterized as a foreign corporation for U.S. federal income tax purposes to the extent that such central bank, authority, or organization holds Notes solely for its own account and is exempt from U.S. federal income tax under sections of 892 or 895 of the Internal Revenue Code."

[3] A U.S. alien is defined as a "corporation, partnership, individual, or fiduciary that for U.S. federal income tax purposes, as to the United States (including its territories, possessions, all areas subject to its jurisdiction and the Commonwealth of Puerto Rico), is a foreign corporation, a nonresident alien individual, a nonresident fiduciary of a foreign estate or trust; a foreign partnership one or more of the members of which is, for U.S. federal income tax purposes, a foreign corporation, a nonresident alien individual, or a nonresident alien fiduciary of a foreign estate or trust; or an International Financial Organization."

debt, particularly when issuing substantial amounts to fund large budget deficits, by issuing Treasury securities on a regular basis (i.e., by having a stable schedule for auctioning securities with specific maturities). This scheduling provides the purchasers of Treasury debt with certainty regarding the timing of issuances of the various types of Treasury securities. The schedule of the Treasury funding process has developed so that there are now several regular cycles on which the Treasury auctions and issues specific maturities. A description of these cycles is provided in Exhibit 1. Exhibits 2 and 3 provide examples of Treasury announcements for the auctions and issues of Treasury coupon and discount securities, respectively.

As indicated in Exhibit 1 there are three discount security (Treasury bill) cycles. Every Monday the Treasury auctions 91-day Treasury bills. These bills are issued on the following Thursday and mature on the Thursday 13-weeks (91 days) later. On the same cycle, every Monday the Treasury also auctions 182-day bills, which are issued on the following Thursday and mature on the Thursday 26 weeks, or 182 days, after their issue date. The third Treasury bill cycle is the "year bill" cycle. On this cycle, every fourth Thursday the Treasury auctions a 52-week Treasury bill, which is issued on the following Thursday and matures on the Thursday 52 weeks, or 364 days, later.

The initial 91-day and 182-day Treasury bills mature every Thursday, and the initial 364-day Treasury bills mature every fourth Thursday. Note also that during the last 91 days of its maturity, an initial 182-day Treasury bill is indistinguishable from an initial 91-day Treasury bill issued 91 days after it. Similarly, during the last 182 days of its maturity, a 364-day Treasury bill is indistinguishable from an initial 182-day Treasury bill issued 182 days later.

At irregular intervals the Treasury also issues *cash management bills* with maturities ranging from a few days to about six months. They are occasionally issued a few days or weeks before a large tax payment is due in March, April, June and September to tide the Treasury over a brief period of cash shortfall. The Treasury sets the maturity date so that it coincides with a seasoned Treasury bill. This facilitates trading of cash management bills in the secondary market. Typically the announcement of a cash management bill auction is a few days prior to the auction date. On rare occasions,

EXHIBIT 1
Treasury Auction Cycles

Discount securities:

Three-month (91-day) Treasury bills — Auctioned every Monday; issued on the following Thursday

Six-month (182-day) Treasury bills — Same auction and issue cycle as for three-month Treasury bills (auctioned on Monday; issued on Thursday). Thus, 182-day Treasury bills eventually trade in consonance with 91-day Treasury bills.

Fifty-two week (364-day) Treasury bills — Auctioned every fourth Thursday; issued on the following Thursday. Thus, 364-day Treasury bills eventually trade in consonance with 182-day and then 91-day Treasury bills.

Coupon securities:

Two-year — Two-year Treasury notes are auctioned every month, normally near the end of the month, for settlement on the last business day of the month and mature on the last business day of the month two-years hence.

Five-year — Five-year Treasury notes are auctioned on a quarterly cycle near the end of the February, May, August and November months for settlement at the beginning of the March, June, September and December months. These issues mature on the 15th of the February, May, August and November months approximately five years and two months after their settlement date (these notes are, thus, five-year, two-month notes and their first coupon is a long coupon, that is, the first coupon represents approximately eight months interest).

Mini-Refunding (Four-year/seven-year) — The mini-refunding is a quarterly cycle issue of, typically, a four-year note, and a seven-year note. These issues are an-

EXHIBIT 1—*Continued*
Treasury Auction Cycles

Mini-Refunding— *Continued*	nounced at the same time, typically during the middle of the auction month. They are then typically auctioned on consecutive business days late during the March, June, September and December months for settlement at the beginning of the January, April, July, and October months. The four-year note matures on the last business day of the March, June, September, and December months four years after settlement; the seven-year note matures on the 15th day of the January, April, July, and October months seven years after settlement.
Refunding (Three-year/ten-year/ thirty-year)	The refunding cycle is a quarterly cycle issue of notes and bonds which are issued on the 15th day of the February, May, August and November quarterly cycle months and are typically auctioned on the Tuesday, Wednesday and Thursday during the second week prior to the issue. Each refunding typically contains three issues: (1) a 3-year note, (2) a 10-year note, and (3) a 30-year bond. These issues mature on the 15th day of the February, May, August or November months, the appropriate number of years (3, 10 or 30) after their issue. The issues in the refunding cycle have, however, been subject to some variations.
Summary of Maturity *Schedule*	15th day of February, May, August and November months: 3-year; 5-year; 10-year; and 30-year.
	15th day of January, April, July, and October: 7-year.
	End of Month: 2-year (monthly); 4-year (March, June, September, and December).

EXHIBIT 2

FEDERAL RESERVE BANK
OF NEW YORK

Fiscal Agent of the United States

TREASURY AUCTION OF 4-YEAR AND 7-YEAR NOTES
TOTALING $13,500 MILLION

To All Banking Institutions, and Others Concerned,
in the Second Federal Reserve District:

The following statement has been issued by the Treasury Department:

The Treasury will raise about $9,750 million of new cash by issuing $7,000 million of 4-year notes and $6,500 million of 7-year notes. This offering will also refund $3,746 million of 4-year notes maturing March 31, 1986. The $3,746 million of maturing 4-year notes are those held by the public, including $437 million currently held by Federal Reserve Banks as agents for foreign and international monetary authorities.

In addition to the maturing 4-year notes, there are $8,348 million of maturing 2-year notes held by the public. The disposition of this latter amount was announced last week. Federal Reserve Banks, as agents for foreign and international monetary authorities, currently hold $1,035 million, and Government accounts and Federal Reserve Banks for their own accounts hold $1,458 million of maturing 2-year and 4-year notes. The maturing securities held by Federal Reserve Banks for their own account may be refunded by issuing additional amounts of the new 2-year and 4-year notes at the average prices of accepted competitive tenders.

The $13,500 million is being offered to the public, and any amounts tendered by Federal Reserve Banks as agents for foreign and international monetary authorities will be added to that amount. Tenders for such accounts will be accepted at the average prices of accepted competitive tenders.

The Treasury Department announced that it will not offer the 20-year bond usually announced at this time in the quarter. In the absence of sufficient certainty that Congress will act soon on pending legislation to increase Treasury's bond authority, the Treasury decided to preserve its remaining authority for the 30-year bond tentatively scheduled for announcement on April 30. Treasury has used $191.6 billion of the present $200 billion authority to issue bonds (maturities over 10 years) without regard to the 4¼ percent ceiling on such issues. The remaining $8.4 billion is not enough to provide for reasonable amounts of both a 20-year bond and a 30-year bond; and the 30-year bond has been the more attractive issue in the market and thus less costly to the Treasury.

Printed on the reverse side is a table summarizing the highlights of the offerings. Copies of the official offering circulars will be furnished upon request directed to our Government Bond Division (Tel. No. 212-791-6619). In addition, enclosed are copies of the forms to be used in submitting tenders.

This Bank will receive tenders at the Securities Department of its Head Office and at its Buffalo Branch on the dates and times specified on the reverse side of this circular as the deadlines for receipt of tenders. *All competitive tenders*, whether transmitted by mail or by other means, must reach this Bank or its Branch by that time on the specified dates. However, for investors who wish to submit noncompetitive tenders and who find it more convenient to mail their tenders than to present them in person, the official offering circular for each offering provides that *noncompetitive* tenders will be considered timely received if they are mailed to this Bank or its Branch under a postmark no later than the date preceding the date specified for receipt of tenders.

Bidders submitting noncompetitive tenders should realize that it is possible that the average price may be above par, in which case they would have to pay more than the face value for the securities.

Payment with a tender may be made in cash, by check, in Treasury securities maturing on or before the issue date of the securities being purchased, by a charge to an institution's reserve account at this Bank, or, in the case of Treasury Tax and Loan Note Option Depositaries, by credit to a Treasury Tax and Loan Note Account. Payment by check must be in the form of an official bank check, a Federal funds check (a check drawn by a depository institution on its Federal Reserve account), or a personal check, which need not be certified. All checks must be drawn payable to the Federal Reserve Bank of New York; *checks endorsed to this Bank will not be accepted.*

Recorded messages provide information about Treasury offerings and about auction results: at the Head Office — Tel. No. 212-791-7773 (offerings) and Tel. No. 212-791-5823 (results); at the Buffalo Branch — Tel. No. 716-849-5158 (offerings) and Tel. No. 716-849-5046 (results). Additional inquiries regarding this offering may be made by calling, at the Head Office, Tel. No. 212-791-6619, or, at the Buffalo Branch, Tel. No. 716-849-5016.

E. GERALD CORRIGAN,
President.

EXHIBIT 2—*Continued*

HIGHLIGHTS OF TREASURY
OFFERINGS TO THE PUBLIC
OF 4-YEAR AND 7-YEAR NOTES

	4-Year Notes	7-Year Notes
Amount Offered:		
To the public..............	$7,000 million	$6,500 million
Description of Security:		
Term and type of security	4-year notes	7-year notes
Series and CUSIP designation......	Series N-1990 (CUSIP No. 912827 TL6)	Series F-1993 (CUSIP No. 912827 TM4)
Issue date.................	March 31, 1986	April 3, 1986
Maturity date	March 31, 1990	April 15, 1993
Call date.................	No provision	No provision
Interest rate.................	To be determined, based on the average of accepted bids	To be determined, based on the average of accepted bids
Investment yield	To be determined at auction	To be determined at auction
Premium or discount	To be determined after auction	To be determined after auction
Interest payment dates.............	September 30 and March 31	October 15 and April 15 (first payment on October 15, 1986)
Minimum denomination available ..$1,000		$1,000

Terms of Sale:

Method of sale	Yield auction	Yield auction
Competitive tenders	Must be expressed as an annual yield, with two decimals, e.g., 7.10%	Must be expressed as an annual yield, with two decimals, e.g., 7.10%
Noncompetitive tenders	Accepted in full at the average price up to $1,000,000	Accepted in full at the average price up to $1,000,000
Accrued interest payable by investor . .	None	None
Payment through Treasury Tax and Loan (TT&L) Note Accounts	Acceptable for TT&L Note Option Depositaries	Acceptable for TT&L Note Option Depositaries
Payment by non-institutional investors	Full payment to be submitted with tender	Full payment to be submitted with tender
Deposit guarantee by designated institutions	Acceptable	Acceptable

Key Dates:

Receipt of tenders	Tuesday, March 25, 1986, prior to 1:00 p.m., EST	Wednesday, March 26, 1986, prior to 1:00 p.m., EST
Settlement (final payment due from institutions)		
a) cash or Federal funds	Monday, March 31, 1986	Thursday, April 3, 1986
b) readily collectible check	Thursday, March 27, 1986	Tuesday, April 1, 1986

EXHIBIT 3

FEDERAL RESERVE BANK OF NEW YORK

Fiscal Agent of the United States

Circular No. 10,021
April 4, 1986

Offering of $9,250,000,000 of 364-Day Treasury Bills

Dated April 17, 1986

Due April 16, 1987

To All Banking Institutions, and Others Concerned,
in the Second Federal Reserve District:

Following is the text of a notice issued by the Treasury Department:

The Department of the Treasury, by this public notice, invites tenders for approximately $9,250 million of 364-day Treasury bills to be dated April 17, 1986, and to mature April 16, 1987 (CUSIP No. 912794 MF8). This issue will provide about $900 million of new cash for the Treasury, as the maturing 52-week bill is outstanding in the amount of $8,362 million. Tenders will be received at the Federal Reserve Banks and Branches and at the Bureau of the Public Debt, Washington, D.C. 20239, prior to 1:00 p.m., Eastern Standard time, Thursday, April 10, 1986.

The bills will be issued on a discount basis under competitive and non-competitive bidding, and at maturity their par amount will be payable without interest. This series of bills will be issued entirely in book-entry form in a minimum amount of $10,000 and in any higher $5,000 multiple, on the records either of the Federal Reserve Banks and Branches, or of the Department of the Treasury.

The bills will be issued for cash and in exchange for Treasury bills maturing April 17, 1986. In addition to the maturing 52-week bills, there are $14,550 million of maturing bills which were originally issued as 13-week and 26-week bills. The disposition of this latter amount will be announced next week. Federal Reserve Banks currently hold $1,687 million as agents for foreign and international monetary authorities, and $5,360 million for their own account. These amounts represent the combined holdings of such accounts for the three issues of maturing bills. Tenders from Federal Reserve Banks for their own account and as agents for foreign and international monetary authorities will be accepted at the weighted average bank discount rate of accepted competitive tenders. Ad-

tenders for customers, must submit a separate tender for each customer whose net long position in the bill being offered exceeds $200 million.

A noncompetitive bidder may not have entered into an agreement, nor make an agreement to purchase or sell or otherwise dispose of any non-competitive awards of this issue being auctioned prior to the designated closing time for receipt of tenders.

Payment for the full par amount of the bills applied for must accompany all tenders submitted for bills to be maintained on the book-entry records of the Department of the Treasury. A cash adjustment will be made on all accepted tenders for the difference between the par payment submitted and the actual issue price as determined in the auction.

No deposit need accompany tenders from incorporated banks and trust companies and from responsible and recognized dealers in investment securities for bills to be maintained on the book-entry records of Federal Reserve Banks and Branches. A deposit of 2 percent of the par amount of the bills applied for must accompany tenders for such bills from others, unless an express guaranty of payment by an incorporated bank or trust company accompanies the tenders.

Public announcement will be made by the Department of the Treasury of the amount and yield range of accepted bids. Competitive bidders will be advised of the acceptance or rejection of their tenders. The Secretary of the Treasury expressly reserves the right to accept or reject any or all tenders, in whole or in part, and the Secretary's action shall be final. Subject to these reservations, noncompetitive tenders for each issue for $1,000,000 or less without stated yield from any one bidder will be ac-

ditional amounts of the bills may be issued to Federal Reserve Banks, as agents for foreign and international monetary authorities, to the extent that the aggregate amount of tenders for such accounts exceeds the aggregate amount of maturing bills held by them. For purposes of determining such additional amounts, foreign and international monetary authorities are considered to hold $125 million of the original 52-week issue. Tenders for bills to be maintained on the book-entry records of the Department of the Treasury should be submitted on Form PD 4632-1.

Each tender must state the par amount of bills bid for, which must be a minimum of $10,000. Tenders over $10,000 must be in multiples of $5,000. Competitive tenders must also show the yield desired, expressed on a bank discount rate basis with two decimals, e.g., 7.15%. Fractions may not be used. A single bidder, as defined in Treasury's single bidder guidelines, shall not submit noncompetitive tenders totaling more than $1,000,000.

Banking institutions and dealers who make primary markets in Government securities and report daily to the Federal Reserve Bank of New York their positions in and borrowings on such securities may submit tenders for account of customers, if the names of the customers and the amount for each customer are furnished. Others are only permitted to submit tenders for their own account. Each tender must state the amount of any net long position in the bills being offered if such position is in excess of $200 million. This information should reflect positions held as of 12:30 p.m., Eastern time, on the day of the auction. Such positions would include bills acquired through "when issued" trading, and futures and forward transactions as well as holdings of outstanding bills with the same maturity date as the new offering, e.g., bills with three months to maturity previously offered as six-month bills. Dealers, who make primary markets in Government securities and report daily to the Federal Reserve Bank of New York their positions in and borrowings on such securities, when submitting

cepted in full at the weighted average bank discount rate (in two decimals) of accepted competitive bids for the respective issues. The calculation of purchase prices for accepted bids will be carried to three decimal places on the basis of price per hundred, e.g., 99.923, and the determinations of the Secretary of the Treasury shall be final.

Settlement for accepted tenders for bills to be maintained on the book-entry records of Federal Reserve Banks and Branches must be made or completed at the Federal Reserve Bank or Branch on the issue date, in cash or other immediately-available funds or in Treasury bills maturing on that date. Cash adjustments will be made for differences between the par value of the maturing bills accepted in exchange and the issue price of the new bills. In addition, Treasury Tax and Loan Note Option Depositaries may make payment for allotments of bills for their own accounts and for account of customers by credit to their Treasury Tax and Loan Note Accounts on the settlement date.

In general, if a bill is purchased at issue after July 18, 1984, and held to maturity, the amount of discount is reportable as ordinary income in the Federal income tax return of the owner at the time of redemption. Accrual-basis taxpayers, banks, and other persons designated in section 1281 of the Internal Revenue Code must include in income the portion of the discount for the period during the taxable year such holder held the bill. If the bill is sold or otherwise disposed of before maturity, the portion of the gain equal to the accrued discount will be treated as ordinary income. Any excess may be treated as capital gain.

Department of the Treasury Circulars, Public Debt Series—Nos. 26-76 and 27-76, Treasury's single bidder guidelines, and this notice prescribe the terms of these Treasury bills and govern the conditions of their issue. Copies of the circulars, guidelines, and tender forms may be obtained from any Federal Reserve Bank or Branch, or from the Bureau of the Public Debt.

Tenders will be received prior to 1:00 p.m., Eastern Standard time, Thursday, April 10, 1986 at the Securities Department of this Bank's Head Office, at our Buffalo Branch, or at the Bureau of the Public Debt. A tender form is enclosed. Please be sure to use that form to submit the tender and return it in the enclosed envelope. Forms for submitting tenders directly to the Treasury are available from the Government Bond Division of this Bank. Tenders not requiring a deposit may be submitted by telegraph, subject to written confirmation; no tenders may be submitted by telephone. Settlement must be made in cash or other immediately available funds or in Treasury securities maturing on or before the issue date. Treasury Tax and Loan Note Option Depositaries may make payment for Treasury bills by credit to their Treasury Tax and Loan Note Accounts.

Results of the previous 52-week bill offering are shown on the reverse side of this circular.

E. GERALD CORRIGAN, *President.*

EXHIBIT 3 *(Continued)*
**Results of Previous 52-Week Offering of Treasury Bills
(Issued March 20, 1986)**

	Range of Accepted Competitive Bids		
	Discount Rate	Investment Rate (Equivalent Coupon-Issue Yield)	Price
Low –	6.59%	7.03%	93.337
High –	6.63%	7.08%	93.296
Average–	6.61%	7.06%	93.317

Tenders at the high discount rate were allotted 59%.

	Tenders Received and Accepted (In Thousands)	
Location	Received	Accepted
Boston	$ 19,150	$ 19,150
New York	19,264,070	7,522,120
Philadelphia	7,200	7,200
Cleveland	15,960	15,960
Richmond	60,960	60,960
Atlanta	32,970	28,870
Chicago	1,550,485	377,835
St. Louis	79,110	53,110
Minneapolis	13,865	13,865
Kansas City	44,720	44,720
Dallas	6,705	6,705
San Francisco	1,278,270	737,850
Treasury	125,595	125,595
TOTALS	$22,499,060	$9,013,940
Type		
Competitive	$19,500,275	$6,015,155
Noncompetitive	548,785	548,785
Subtotal, Public	$20,049,060	$6,563,940
Federal Reserve	2,250,000	2,250,000
Foreign Official Institutions	200,000	200,000
TOTALS	$22,499,060	$9,013,940

An additional $200,000 thousand of the bills will be issued to foreign official institutions for new cash.

cash management bills have been announced and auctioned on the same day.

As indicated in Exhibit 1, there are several auction cycles for Treasury coupon issues. Although none of these cycles is immutable, the auction cycles for the two-year notes and the refunding cycle have been fairly stable. In addition, there has been a five-year and a mini-refunding auction cycle consisting of two notes and prior to April 1986, a 20-year bond.

The refunding cycle is most important, since it contains the Treasury long bond, which typically has 30 years to maturity. The Treasury refunding cycle involves the issue of three coupon securities, typically a short note, a long note, and a long bond, during the February, May, August, and November quarterly cycle months. The securities to be auctioned and issued on the Treasury refunding cycle are usually announced late in the month prior to the auction. The three securities are auctioned on different days early in the refunding month and issued on the 15th day of the month.

Auction Process

The Public Debt Act of 1942 grants the Treasury considerable discretion in deciding on the terms for a marketable security. An issue may be sold on an interest-bearing or discount basis and may be sold on a competitive or other basis, at whatever prices the Secretary of the Treasury may establish. There are two restrictions imposed on the sale of Treasury bonds. First, the coupon rate may not exceed $4^1/4$ percent. Second, Congress imposes a restriction on the total amount of bonds outstanding. Although Congress granted exemption to these two restrictions, there have been times when the failure of Congress to extend the exemption has resulted in the delay or cancellation of a Treasury bond offering.

Both Treasury bills and Treasury coupon issues are sold on an auction basis. Prior to April 18, 1983, Treasury bills were auctioned on the basis of price (e.g., 97.865). Since April 18, 1983, bids submitted at auction must be expressed on a bank discount basis with no more than two decimals (e.g., 8.45 percent). Bids are taken by the Treasury and securities allocated from the lowest yield to the highest yield accepted by the Treasury. Those who have submitted a bid higher than the stop-out yield are not allocated bills. The highest yield accepted by the Treasury is referred to by dealers as the *stop*. The difference between the average and the stop is called the *tail*. A tender form for submitting bids for 52-week Treasury bills is shown in Exhibit 4.

Tenders may also be submitted on a noncompetitive basis (see Exhibit 4). Such tenders include no bid yield, only a quantity. These bids are completely allocated at the average price of the successful bids. Noncompetitive bids are usually made by small, noninstitutional investors. Currently, noncompetitive bids are accepted for amounts up to $1 million. Noncompetitive bids are not accepted for cash management bills.

Auction results for a $9.0 billion issue might be determined as follows:

Total issue	= $9.0 billion
Less noncompetitive bids	= .5 billion
Left for competitive bidders	= $8.5 billion

Total competitive bids might have been received as follows:

amount	bid
$0.9 billion	8.21 (high or top bid)
2.1	8.22
3.5	8.23
4.0	8.24
7.0	8.25
	etc.

$6.5 billion was awarded to bidders from 8.21 to 8.23, leaving $2.0 billion to be awarded. Each of the bidders at 8.24 would be awarded one-half his bid. The results would show 8.21 high, 8.23 average and 8.24 the stop, with 50 percent awarded at the stop. Bidders higher in yield than 8.24 "missed" or were "shut out." The auction had a tail of .01 (8.24 minus 8.23).

Different auction methods have been used by the Treasury for auctioning coupon issues. The most common auction method is to require the bids to be made on a *yield* basis, to two decimal points, for example 11.27 percent. The Treasury then allocates the securities, beginning with the lowest yield bid to the highest yield until the announced amount is fully subscribed. The average yield of those

EXHIBIT 4

TB-12 (Rev. 9/85)

IMPORTANT — This is a standard form. Its terms are subject to change at any time by the Treasury. This tender will be construed as a bid to purchase the securities for which the Treasury has outstanding an invitation for tenders. *(See reverse side for further instructions.)*

TENDER FOR 12-MONTH BOOK-ENTRY TREASURY BILLS
(For Use in Subscribing Through a Financial Institution)
Do Not Use This Form for Direct Subscriptions to the Treasury

Dated at ....

.... , 19........

To FEDERAL RESERVE BANK OF NEW YORK
   Fiscal Agent of the United States
   New York, N.Y. 10045

Pursuant and subject to the provisions of Treasury Department Circulars No. 26-76 and No. 27-76, Public Debt Series, and to the provisions of the public notice issued by the Treasury Department inviting tenders for the current offering of 12-month Treasury bills, the undersigned hereby offers to purchase such currently offered Treasury bills in the amount indicated below, and agrees to make payment therefor at your Bank on or before the issue date in accordance with the provisions of the official offering circular.

COMPETITIVE TENDER	*Do not fill in both Competitive and Noncompetitive tenders on one form*	NONCOMPETITIVE TENDER

$.................................... (maturity value) or any lesser amount that may be awarded.

Rate: .... (Bank Discount Basis)

(Rate must be expressed in two decimal places, for example, 7.15 percent. See reverse side of form for additional explanation.)

$.................................... (maturity value) *(Not to exceed $1,000,000 for one bidder through all sources)* at the average of accepted competitive bids.

A noncompetitive bidder may not have entered into an agreement, or may not make an agreement with respect to the purchase or sale or other disposition of any noncompetitive awards of this issue in this auction prior to the designated closing time for receipt of tenders.

EXHIBIT 4—Continued

Certification by Competitive Bidders: The Bidder's ☐ Customer's ☐ net long position in these bills (including bills acquired through "when issued" trading, and futures and forward transactions, as well as holdings of outstanding bills with the same maturity date as the new offering) as of 12:30 p.m. Eastern time on the day of this auction, was —

☐ Not in excess of $200 million.
☐ In excess of $200 million, amounting to $ . . . . million.

Subject to allotment, please issue and accept payment for the bills as indicated below:

Safekeeping or Delivery Instructions
(No changes will be accepted)

Book-Entry—
☐ 1. Hold in safekeeping at FRBNY in-
  ☐ Investment Account (4)
  ☐ General Account (5)
  ☐ Trust Account (6)
☐ 2. Hold as collateral for Treasury Tax and Loan Note Account*(7)
☐ 3. Wire to . . . . (8)
  (Exact Receiving Bank Wire Address / Account)

Payment Instructions

Payment will be made as follows:
☐ By charge to our reserve account
☐ By credit to the Treasury Tax and Loan Note Account
☐ By check in *immediately available funds*
☐ By surrender of eligible maturing securities
☐ By charge to my correspondent bank
. . . .
  (Name of Correspondent)

*The undersigned certifies that the alloted securities will be owned solely by the undersigned.

Name of Subscriber (Please Print or Type)		
Address		
City	State	Zip Code
Phone (Include Area Code)	Signature of Subscriber or Authorized Signature	
Title of Authorized Signer		

Insert this tender in envelope marked "Tender for Treasury Securities"

(Banking institutions submitting tenders for customer account must list customers' names on lines below or on an attached rider)

INSTRUCTIONS:

1. No tender for less than $10,000 will be considered, and each tender must be for a multiple of $5,000 (maturity value).

2. Only banking institutions and dealers who make primary markets in Government securities and report daily to this Bank their positions with respect to Government securities and borrowings thereon, may submit tenders for customer account; in doing so, they may consolidate competitive tenders *at the same rate* (except that a separate tender must be submitted for each customer whose net long position in the bill being offered exceeds $200 million) and may consolidate noncompetitive tenders, provided a list is attached showing the name of each bidder and the amount bid for his account. Others will not be permitted to submit tenders except for their own account.

3. If the person making the tender is a corporation, the tender should be signed by an officer of the corporation authorized to make the tender, and the signing of the tender by an officer of the corporation will be construed as a representation that such officer has been so authorized. If the tender is made by a partnership, it should be signed by a member of the firm, who should sign in the form "................................., a member of the firm".

4. Tenders will be received without deposit from incorporated banks and trust companies and from responsible and recognized dealers in investment securities. Tenders from others must be accompanied by payment of 2 percent of the face amount of Treasury bills applied for, unless the tenders are accompanied by an express guaranty of payment by an incorporated bank or trust company. All checks must be drawn to the order of the Federal Reserve Bank of New York; and personal checks must be certified. Checks endorsed to this Bank will not be accepted.

5. The Bank Discount Basis is the difference between the dollar price of a Treasury bill and the maturity value for a given number of days based on a 360-day year. (The investment return or annualized bond-equivalent yield on a Treasury bill is at a higher rate than the bank discount basis.)

6. If the language of this tender is changed in any respect, which, in the opinion of the Secretary of the Treasury, is material, the tender may be disregarded.

receiving an allocation is used to determine the coupon of the newly issued bonds. The coupon is usually set slightly less than the average yield so that the new bonds or notes are issued at a slight discount to par. The price paid by each successful bidder is determined from the coupon on the issue established by the Treasury and the yield bid by the particular bidder.

If the current yield on an outstanding bond or note of approximately the same maturity as that which the Treasury plans to auction is approximately the same as the coupon on the outstanding issue (that is, the issue is trading at about par), the Treasury may announce the reopening of this outstanding security (i.e., an additional amount of this outstanding security is auctioned). In this case, since the coupon is predetermined, the auction is done on a price basis rather than on a yield basis.

The Treasury also accepts noncompetitive bids for coupon issues. However, noncompetitive bids are not accepted for TINs. Each of the 12 Federal Reserve Banks has its own tender form for submitting noncompetitive bids. Exhibit 5 is an example of a tender offer for a coupon issue.

The auction process relies on the participation of the primary government securities dealers. The primary dealers are expected to participate in every auction and typically bid for about three percent of every issue that is auctioned. The primary dealers subsequently redistribute the issue, at a profit or a loss, to both other non-primary dealers and institutional investors. The primary dealers are also expected to maintain a certain level of trading activity in the secondary market. Primary dealers must report their financial status to the Federal Reserve Bank of New York every day, hence the name reporting Fed dealers. A current list of primary reporting dealers as specified by the Federal Reserve Bank of New York (FRBNY) is provided in Exhibit 6.[4]

---

[4] At the time of this writing, the following 16 dealers had applied to the FRBNY to become primary government dealers:

Alex Brown & Sons Inc.	Nomura Securities International Inc.
CRT Government Securities	Security Pacific National Bank
Daiwa Securities America Inc.	A. E. Staley Financial Services Inc.
Dillon, Read & Co.	Thomson McKinnon Securities Inc.
L. F. Rothschild, Unterberg, Towbin Inc.	UBS Securities Inc.
Lloyds Bank P.L.C.	S. G. Warburg & Co.
Mosley Securities Corp.	Wertheim & Co.
Nikko Securities Company International Inc.	Yamaichi International (America) Inc.

EXHIBIT 5

IMPORTANT — This tender must be received prior to 1:00 p.m., Tuesday, March 25, 1986

TENDER FOR 4-YEAR TREASURY NOTES OF SERIES N-1990

TO FEDERAL RESERVE BANK OF NEW YORK
Fiscal Agent of the United States
New York, N.Y. 10045

Dated at ....

.... 19 ..

The undersigned hereby offers to purchase the above-described securities in the amount indicated below, and agrees to make payment therefor at your Bank in accordance with the provisions of the official offering circular.

COMPETITIVE TENDER	Do not fill in both Competitive and Noncompetitive tenders on one form	NONCOMPETITIVE TENDER

$ .... (maturity value)
or any lesser amount that may be awarded.

Yield:.................
(Yield must be expressed with two decimal places, for example, 7.10)

$ .... (maturity value)
(Not to exceed $1,000,000 for one bidder through all sources)
at the average price of accepted competitive bids.

A noncompetitive bidder may not have entered into an agreement, or may not make an agreement with respect to the purchase or sale or other disposition of any noncompetitive awards of this issue in this auction prior to the designated closing time for receipt of tenders.

Certification by Competitive Bidders: The Bidder's ☐ Customer's ☐ net long position in these securities (including those acquired through "when issued" trading, and futures and forward transactions, as well as holdings of outstanding securities of the same series as the new offering) as of 12:30 pm Eastern time on the day of this auction, was —
   ☐ Not in excess of $200 million.
   ☐ In excess of $200 million, amounting to $ .... million.

Subject to allotment, please issue, deliver, and accept payment for the book-entry securities indicated below and/or the registered securities indicated on the reverse side *(if only registered securities are desired, please only complete schedule on the reverse side):*

Safekeeping or Delivery Instructions
(No changes will be accepted)

Book-Entry—
☐ 1. Hold in safekeeping at FRBNY in-
   ☐ Investment Account (4)
   ☐ General Account (5)
   ☐ Trust Account (6)
☐ 2. Hold as collateral for Treasury Tax and Loan Note Account*(7)
☐ 3. Wire to .... (8)
   (Exact Receiving Bank Wire Address/Account)

Payment Instructions for Institutions

Payment will be made as follows:
   ☐ By charge to our reserve account
   ☐ By credit to the Treasury Tax and Loan Note Account
   ☐ By check in *immediately available funds*
   ☐ By surrender of eligible maturing securities
   ☐ By charge to my correspondent bank

....
(Name of Correspondent)

EXHIBIT 5—Continued

*The undersigned certifies that the allotted securities be owned solely by the undersigned. (If a commercial bank or dealer is subscribing for its own account or for account of customers, the following certifications are made a part of this tender.)

WE HEREBY CERTIFY that we have received tenders from customers in the amounts set forth opposite their names on the list which is made a part of this tender and that we have received and are holding for the Treasury, or that we guarantee payment to the Treasury of, the payments required by the official offering circular.

WE FURTHER CERTIFY that tenders received by us, if any, from other commercial banks or primary dealers for their own account, and for the account of their customers, have been entered with us under the same conditions, agreements, and certifications set forth in this form.

Name of Subscriber (Please Print or Type)		
Address		
City	State	Zip Code
Phone (Include Area Code)	Signature of Subscriber or Authorized Signature	
Title of Authorized Signer		

Insert this tender in envelope marked "Tender for Treasury Securities"

(Institutions submitting tenders for customer account must list customers' names on lines below or on an attached rider)

_____
(Name of customer)

_____
(Name of customer)

See Reverse Side For Further Instructions

SCHEDULE FOR ISSUE OF REGISTERED TREASURY SECURITIES

SUBSCRIPTION NO.

FOR FRB USE ONLY

TRANS. ACCOUNTING DATE

ISSUE AGENT 12 | LOAN CODE

110-01

SUBSCRIBER'S NAME

ADDRESS

CITY _____ STATE _____ ZIP _____

SIGNATURE _____

DELIVERY INSTRUCTIONS

☐ DELIVER OVER THE COUNTER   ☐ OTHER INSTRUCTIONS:

☐ SHIP TO SUBSCRIBER

PAYMENT INSTRUCTIONS FOR INSTITUTIONS

☐ BY CHARGE TO OUR RESERVE ACCOUNT
☐ BY CREDIT TO THE TREASURY TAX AND LOAN NOTE ACCOUNT
☐ BY CASH OR CHECK IN IMMEDIATELY AVAILABLE FUNDS
☐ BY SURRENDER OF MATURING SECURITIES
☐ BY CHARGE TO MY CORRESPONDENT BANK

REGISTRATION INSTRUCTIONS	NO. OF PIECES	DENOM	AMOUNT	SERIAL NOS. (LEAVE BLANK)
NAME(S)		1,000		
		5,000		
		10,000		
ID OR S.S. NO.		100,000		
ADDRESS		1,000,000		
CITY STATE ZIP		TOTAL		
NAME(S)		1,000		
		5,000		
		10,000		
ID OR S.S. NO.		100,000		

EXHIBIT 5—Concluded

ADDRESS			1,000,000
CITY	STATE	ZIP	TOTAL
NAME(S)			1,000
			5,000
			10,000
ID OR S.S. NO.			100,000
ADDRESS			1,000,000
CITY	STATE	ZIP	TOTAL

INSTRUCTIONS

1. No tender for less than $1,000 will be considered; and each tender must be for a multiple of $1,000 (maturity value).

2. Only banking institutions, and dealers who make primary markets in Government securities and report daily to this Bank their positions with respect to Government securities and borrowings thereon, may submit tenders for customer account; in doing so, they may consolidate competitive tenders at the same yield or at the same price and may consolidate noncompetitive tenders, provided a list is attached showing the name of each bidder and the amount bid for his or her account. Others will not be permitted to submit tenders except for their own account.

3. Tenders will be received without deposit from commercial and other banks for their own account, federally insured savings and loan associations, States, political subdivisions or instrumentalities thereof, public pension and retirement and other public funds, international organizations in which the United States holds membership, foreign central banks and foreign states, dealers who make primary markets in Government securities and report daily to the Federal Reserve Bank of New York their positions with respect to Government securities and borrowings thereon, and Government accounts. Tenders from others must be accompanied by full payment of the face amount of the securities applied for.

4. Payment with a tender may be in the form of a personal check, which need not be certified, an official bank check, or a Federal funds check (a check drawn by a commercial bank on its Federal Reserve account). All checks must be drawn payable to the Federal Reserve Bank of New York; checks endorsed to this Bank will not be accepted. Payment may also be made in cash or Treasury securities maturing on or before the issue date of the securities being purchased. Treasury Tax and Loan Note Option Depositaries may make payment for Treasury securities by credit to their Treasury Tax and Loan Note Accounts.

5. For information on currently available Treasury offerings, call our 24-hour recorded message at (212) 791-7773 at the Head Office or (716) 849-5046 at the Buffalo Branch. For results of recent Treasury auctions, call (212) 791-5823 at the Head Office or (716) 849-5046 at the Buffalo Branch. For other information about Treasury securities, call (212) 791-6619 at the Head Office or (716) 849-5016 at the Buffalo Branch during normal business hours.

6. If the language of this tender is changed in any respect that, in the opinion of the Secretary of the Treasury, is material, the tender may be disregarded.

SECONDARY MARKET

The secondary market for Treasury securities is the most liquid financial market in the world. Daily trading volume in mid-1985 was about $100 billion. This market is "made" by a group of U.S. government securities dealers who continually provide bids and offers on outstanding Treasuries. In the secondary market, the most recently auctioned issues are referred to as "on-the-run" or "current coupon" issues. Issues auctioned prior to the current coupons are typically referred to as "off-the-run" issues and are not as liquid as on-the-run issues.

Dealers

Dealers continuously provide bids and offers on specific outstanding government securities, buying for and selling from their inventories. Dealers' earnings are derived from three sources. First, dealers profit from their market making through the difference in their bid/ask quotes, the spread. The bid/ask spread is a measure of the liquidity of the market for the issue, as discussed below. Second, to the extent that dealers hold inventories, they also profit from price appreciation of their inventories (or price depreciation of securities they have shorted) but experience a loss from their inventory positions if prices decline. Finally, dealers may profit on the basis of "carry," the difference between the interest return on the securities they hold and the financing costs of these securities. Dealers, typically, do not have sufficient capital to own outright the securities they hold in their inventory, so their inventories are financed. When the interest return on the securities they hold is greater than the financing cost, a "positive carry" exists, and thus a profit results from this differential. In the opposite case of "negative carry," dealers experience a loss from carrying their inventory.

Since dealer financing is of a very short maturity and the securities held in inventory are almost always of a longer maturity, the carry is positive when long-term interest rates are higher than short-term interest rates and negative when short-term interest rates are higher than long-term interest rates. Obviously, when carry is negative, the dealers generate a loss on carrying their

EXHIBIT 6
Primary Government Securities Dealers*

Bank of America
Bankers Trust Co.
Bear, Stearns & Co.
Carroll McEntee & McGinley Inc.
Chase Manhattan Government Securities Inc.
Chemical Bank
Citibank
Continental Illinois Nat'l Bank and Trust Co. of Chicago
Crocker National Bank
Dean Witter Reynolds Inc.
Discount Corporation of New York
Donaldson, Lufkin & Jenrette Securities Corp.
Drexel Burnham Lambert Government Securities Inc.
First Boston Corp.
First Interstate Bank of California
First National Bank of Chicago
Goldman, Sachs & Co.
Greenwich Capital Markets Inc.
Harris Trust and Savings Bank
E.F. Hutton & Co.
Irving Securities Inc.
J.P. Morgan Securities Holdings Inc.
Kidder, Peabody & Co.
Kleinwort Benson Government Securities Inc.
Aubrey G. Lanston & Co.
Lehman Government Securities Inc.
Manufacturers Hanover Trust Co.
Merrill Lynch Government Securities Inc.
Morgan Stanley & Co.
Northern Trust Co.
Paine Webber Inc.
Wm. E. Pollock Government Securities Inc.
Prudential-Bache Securities Inc.
Refco Partners
Salomon Brothers Inc.
Smith Barney Government Securities Inc.

*As of March 1986

inventories and attempt to minimize the size of their inventory for this reason.

The typical mechanism for financing Treasury securities is the repurchase agreement, or "repo," which is basically a collaterized loan wherein the Treasury securities owned by the dealer are used as collateral to the lender on the loan to the dealer. Repurchase agreements are typically of very short maturity, commonly one day. Longer repurchase agreements are called term repos. The market for term repos becomes quite thin as the maturity lengthens. A more detailed discussion of repurchase agreements is presented in Chapter 7.

The government securities dealers work closely with the Federal Reserve System and the Treasury in several ways. First and most importantly, the FRBNY, on behalf of the Board of Governors of the Federal Reserve System conducts its open-market operations and its repo and reverse repo transactions through auctions with the primary dealers. Such activities are conducted by the FRBNY among the dealers on an auction basis in a matter of minutes. Second, as a basis of its conduct of monetary policy, the FRBNY gets information on a frequent basis from the primary dealers about the condition of the financial markets.

Brokers

Treasury dealers trade with each other through intermediaries known as government bond brokers. Dealers leave firm bids and offers with brokers who display the highest bid and lowest offer in a computer network tied to each trading desk and displayed on a monitor. The dealer responding to a bid or offer by "hitting" or "taking" pays a commission to the broker.[5] The size and prices of these transactions are highly visible to all dealers at once.

Brokers are used by dealers because of the speed and efficiency with which trades can be accomplished. Brokers never trade for

---

[5] Prior to October 1985, commissions were roughly 1/128 point, or $78.12 per million trade of coupon securities. For bills, the commission was about $25 per million trade. Competitive pressure from a government brokerage firm formed by a majority of the primary government dealers, Liberty Brokerage Inc., has forced commissions to roughly one-half the pre-October 1985 level.

their own account and keep confidential the names of the dealers involved in trades. Five major brokers handle about 50 percent of the daily trading volume. They include Fundamental Brokers Inc., RMJ Securities Corp., Garban Ltd., Cantor, Fitzgerald Securities Corp., and Chapdelaine & Company Government Securities Inc. These five brokers service the primary government dealers and a dozen or so other large government dealers aspiring to be primary dealers. Cantor, Fitzgerald Securities Corp. also serves as a broker for about 200 nonprimary dealers.

When-Issued Market

Another component of the governments market is the "when-issued market," or "W/I market," wherein Treasury securities are traded prior to the time they are issued by the Treasury. The when-issued trading for both Treasury bills and Treasury coupon issues extends from the day the auction is announced until the issue day. All deliveries on when-issued trades occur on the issue day of the Treasury security traded.

Bid and Offer Quotes

Bids and offers in the dealer market for Treasury bills are made on a bank discount basis, not a price basis, in basis points. A basis point is $1/100$th of 1 percent in discount return; for example, the difference between 10.00 percent and 10.01 is one basis point. Thus a bid/offer quote may be 11.63 percent/11.61 percent. This discount is converted into a price for delivery.

Bids and offers for coupon securities are made on the basis of yield to a basis point prior to the auction and after the auction, until issue day, are made on the basis of price to $1/32$ of 1 percent of par (par is taken to be $100). For example, a quote of 97-19 refers to a price of 97 and $19/32$.[6] Thus, on the basis of $100,000 par value, a change in price of 1 percent is consistent with $1,000 and $1/32$ with $31.25. A *plus* sign following the number of 32nds means that a 64th is added to the price. For example 97-19 + refers to a price

---

[6] In newspapers, the number of 32nds is shown after a decimal point. For example, 97-19 would be shown as 97.19.

of 97 and $^{39}/_{64}$. Exhibit 7 provides the decimal equivalents of 32nds and 64ths per $100 of par value. A quote of 97-19 + means 97.609375 percent of par value.

EXHIBIT 7
Decimal Equivalents of 32nds and 64ths per $100

32nds	64ths	Per $100	32nds	64ths	Per $100
+	1	$.015625	16 +	33	$.515625
1	2	.031250	17	34	.531250
1 +	3	.046875	17 +	35	.546875
2	4	.062500	18	36	.562500
2 +	5	.078125	18 +	37	.578125
3	6	.093750	19	38	.593750
3 +	7	.109375	19 +	39	.609375
4	8	.125000	20	40	.625000
4 +	9	.140625	20 +	41	.640625
5	10	.156250	21	42	.656250
5 +	11	.171875	21 +	43	.671875
6	12	.187500	22	44	.687500
6 +	13	.203125	22 +	45	.703125
7	14	.218750	23	46	.718750
7 +	15	.234375	23 +	47	.734375
8	16	.250000	24	48	.750000
8 +	17	.265625	24 +	49	.765625
9	18	.281250	25	50	.781250
9 +	19	.296875	25 +	51	.796875
10	20	.312500	26	52	.812500
10 +	21	.328125	26 +	53	.828125
11	22	.343750	27	54	.843750
11 +	23	.359375	27 +	55	.859375
12	24	.375000	28	56	.875000
12 +	25	.390625	28 +	57	.890625
13	26	.406250	29	58	.906250
13 +	27	.421875	29 +	59	.921875
14	28	.437500	30	60	.937500
14 +	29	.453125	30 +	61	.953125
15	30	.468750	31	62	.968750
15 +	31	.484375	31 +	63	.984375
16	32	.500000	32	64	1.000000

SUMMARY

This chapter has provided an overview of U.S. government securities and the primary and secondary markets for these securities. For ease of exposition, we have limited our discussion to cash securities, leaving the options and futures markets in which Treasury securities are the underlying instrument for Chapters 14 and 15. In practice, however, the options and futures markets are frequently viewed as facets of the same market. Hedgers, by implication, are involved with cash, futures and options markets. Traders typically consult all three markets even if they are involved in only one. Only the most limited or specialized market participants will focus on just one of these markets.

CHAPTER 2

RONALD J. RYAN founded Ryan Financial Strategy Group (RFSG) in October 1982 as the first bond strategy firm.

RFSG has developed several innovations for the bond market including the first daily index (Treasury yield curve) (February 1983); the first bond analysis network on smart terminals (October 1983); the first color bond network (October 1984); and Market Watch, the first graphic/analytical system vs "the market" (January 1986).

From June 1977 to 1982, Mr. Ryan was the director of research and strategy for Lehman Brothers where he designed and supervised most of the Lehman bond indices.

From June 1973 to 1977, he was manager of the bond effort for the advisory company spinoff of the First National Bank of Dallas (F.I.I.M.).

From 1966 to 1973, Mr. Ryan was security analyst and mortgage supervisor for Pan-American Life Insurance Co.

THE TREASURY DEBT STORY

Ronald J. Ryan, C.F.A.
Managing Director
Ryan Financial Strategy Group

Blessed are the youth, for they shall inherit the national debt.

Herbert Hoover

President Hoover showed a touch of clairvoyance when he made this comment several decades ago. But he could not have realized how enormous the national debt would become in so short a time. Nor could he have envisioned the structural refunding dilemma that has resulted.

HISTORICAL GROWTH PATTERN

The United States is experiencing the fastest growth in interest bearing debt in history. The 1970s was a decade of unparalleled increases in all areas of debt, except longer maturity bonds which were either exchanged for non-marketable securities or redeemed (i.e., flower bonds redeemable at par upon death of owner of record). To date, the 1980s will surpass the 1970s in every category but non-marketable securities. (See Table 2-1.)

Due to the interest rate environment and/or the political environ-

TABLE 2-1
Historical Growth of Treasury Debt ($ Millions)

Fiscal Year	Interest Bearing Debt	Treasury Bills	Treasury Notes	Treasury Bonds	Total Marketable Securities	Non-Marketable Securities
1969	$ 351,729	$ 68,356	$ 78,496	$ 78,805	$ 226,107	$125,623
1970	369,026	76,154	93,489	62,956	232,599	136,426
1971	396,289	86,677	104,807	53,989	245,473	150,816
1972	425,360	94,648	113,419	49,135	257,202	168,158
1973	456,353	100,061	117,840	45,071	262,971	193,382
1974	473,238	105,019	128,419	33,137	266,575	206,663
1975	532,122	128,569	150,257	36,779	315,606	216,516
1976	619,254	161,198	191,758	39,626	392,581	226,673
1977	697,629	156,091	241,692	45,724	443,508	254,121
1978	766,971	160,936	267,865	56,355	485,155	281,816
1979	819,007	161,378	274,242	71,073	506,693	312,314
1980	906,402	199,832	310,903	83,772	594,506	311,896
1981	996,495	223,388	363,643	96,178	683,209	313,286
1982	1,140,883	277,900	442,890	103,631	824,422	316,461
1983	1,375,751	340,733	557,525	125,742	1,024,000	351,751
1984	1,559,570	356,798	661,687	158,070	1,176,556	383,015
Percent growth						
1969–1979	132.85%	136.08%	249.37%	–9.8%	124.09%	148.61%
1979–1984	90.42	121.09	141.28	122.41	132.20	22.64

Source: Treasury Bulletins

ment, Treasury financing has changed radically in this decade particularly when compared to Treasury financing in the 1970s. The 1970s are, however, best thought of as a transitional period that experienced the creation of two new auction series that continued as a trend into the 1980s:

Treasury thirty-year auction started in 1973;
Treasury ten-year auction started in 1976;
Treasury fifteen-year auction started in 1980 (ended 1980);
Treasury twenty-year auction started in 1981 (ended 1986).

In 1976 by an act of Congress the definition of a Treasury note was changed from a seven-year maximum maturity to ten years. This change allowed for a greater issuance of notes to avoid the debt ceiling set at that time on the amount of bonds outstanding (longer than seven-year original maturity and not including flower bonds). Moreover, it served to extend the average maturity of Treasury debt outstanding, which in 1976 was reduced to one of the shortest levels in the post war period. The average length of Treasury debt went from four years, two months at the end of fiscal 1969 to a low of two years, seven months for fiscal 1976. By the end of fiscal 1984, the average maturity was lengthened to four years, six months.

The ten-year, twenty-year and thirty-year issues have now become regular quarterly auctions in the 1980s. Since 1979, these three maturities have accounted for 23 percent of all Treasury financings. This is quite remarkable considering the historical trend towards very short maturity issuance, plus the fact that the twenty-year issue was first issued in 1981.

SURPLUS VS. DEFICIT

Federal debt is a direct result of Federal deficits: When the national budget is imbalanced, having spent more than we received, we borrow the difference. A key therefore to reducing and eliminating debt is to reduce and eliminate deficits. Most of America has become so complacent about deficit financing that we have accepted it as a permanent part of the operations of our Federal government. Actu-

TABLE 2-2
Historical Relationship between Federal Spending and Federal Revenue

	Balance Years	Total Surplus Years	Huge Surplus Years	Total Deficit Years	Huge Deficit Years
1791–1810	3	12	10	5	5
1811–1830	0	13	11	7	4
1831–1850	0	11	7	9	9
1851–1870	1	11	4	8	7
1871–1890	1	19	12	0	0
1891–1910	1	8	0	11	1
1911–1930	4	12	5	4	3
1931–1950	1	2	1	17	16
1951–1970	6	3	0	11	0
1971–1984	1	0	0	13	3
	18 (9%)	91 (47%)	50 (26%)	85 (44%)	48 (25%)
1971–1990 (as projected)	1	0	0	19	8

Notes: *Balance Years* are years where Federal Income and outgo were within 2% of each other. *Surplus Years* are years where revenues exceeded spending by 3% or more. *Huge Surplus Years* are years where revenues exceeded spending by 25% (surplus typically was used to reduce debt). *Deficit Years* are years where spending was 103% or more of revenues. *Huge Deficit Years* are years where spending exceeded revenues by 20% or more.

Source: *Deficits on the Red Sea*, Special Research Study by Levthold Group (associated with Lynch, Jones, & Ryan, September 1984).

ally, in the 194 years of U.S. economic history from 1791 to 1984, there have been more years of surpluses (47 percent) than balanced budgets (9 percent) or deficits (44 percent).

Table 2–2 tracks the relationship between federal spending and federal revenue by twenty-year periods (except for the most recent period where only 14 years are now known). Unfortunately, no historical twenty-year period matches the consistent deficit record of the most recent fourteen-year period (1971–1984) in which thirteen of fourteen years (93 percent) were clear cut deficit years. If projections now being made by the Office of Management and Budget (OMB) for the rest of the decade become reality, nine-

TABLE 2-3
Interest Expense on Federal Budget ($ Millions)

	New Budget Outlays	Interest on Public Debt	Interest as Percent of Budget
1969	$184,548	$ 16,588	9.0%
1970	196,588	19,304	9.8
1971	211,425	20,959	9.9
1972	232,021	21,849	9.4
1973	247,074	24,167	9.8
1974	269,621	29,319	10.9
1975	326,105	32,665	10.0
1976	365,648	37,063	10.1
1977	402,836	41,900	10.4
1978	450,836	48,695	10.8
1979	493,221	59,837	12.1
1980	579,603	74,860	12.9
1981	657,204	95,589	14.5
1982	728,424	117,404	16.1
1983	795,916	128,813	16.2
1984	841,800	153,838	18.3

teen out of the last twenty years (95 percent) would be deficit years.

THE DEBT SERVICE BUILD UP

In 1970, $20 billion was paid out by the government as interest on the debt. In 1984 $154 billion was paid out as interest. This amounted to a 683 percent increase in fourteen years in absolute dollars and about a 600 percent increase on a per capita basis. As can be seen in Table 2-3, since 1969, interest on the public debt has grown from 9.0 percent of budget outlays to 18.3 percent in 1984 and is escalating.

If current deficit trends continue, by 1989 the Federal debt will approximate $2.5 trillion. Assuming a 10 percent interest rate, the interest on the 1989 debt would be about $250 billion or a 63 percent increase from the 1984 level. Recently revised OMB forecasts are slightly more optimistic, if you can call it that, suggesting that the budget deficit for the years 1985 through 1989 should be:

1985	= $	211.3	Billion
1986	=	177.8	
1987	=	139.3	
1988	=	99.8	
1989	=	53.6	
Total	= $	681.8	
1984 Level	= $1,559.6		
1989 Level	= $2,241.4 Billion		

Previous OMB forecasts would have pushed Federal debt over the $2.6 trillion mark by 1989. Given an average interest cost of 10 percent, Federal debt service would be $224 to $260 billion per year by 1989. More importantly, the relative cost of debt service compared to the GNP is alarming.

Prior to World War I, debt service as a percent of GNP remained below 1 percent, rising briefly above 2 percent with World War II. Debt service costs did not rise again above 2 percent of GNP until 1974. Since then, this ratio has exploded, exceeding 3 percent in 1980 and above 4 percent in 1983. Assuming a steady and optimistic 6 percent growth in GNP, this ratio would rise above 6 percent in 1989.

THE REFUNDING DILEMMA

What few people seem to realize or pay enough attention to is the financing of existing debt at its maturity—refunding. Unlike corporate debt, Treasury debt is almost always rolled over or refinanced. It is seldom allowed to mature and never called by virtue of its call protection for life (an exception is the thirty-year bond that, prior to 1985, had twenty-five years of call protection with all issues still protected).

Since refundings are simply refinancings, the going rate at the date of refunding will play a major role in determining future debt-service cost. As mentioned earlier, Treasury debt had an average maturity of 4.5 years at the end of fiscal 1984, suggesting we will turnover the entire debt burden at least once by the end of fiscal

1989. A 10 to 20 percent increase in interest rates over the next few years would have a significant impact since it would become an additional deficit to be financed and thus become additional debt. This structural weakness has become known as a "structural deficit," where America's debt burden grows by compound interest similar to a zero-coupon bond.

A highly salient example of our structural or refunding dilemma is the now-prominent Senate joint resolution of January 26, 1983, calling for a balanced budget amendment to the Constitution. Basically, it calls for total outlays never to exceed total receipts. It all sounds so promising until one examines Section 4, which defines total receipts as "all receipts of the United States except those derived from borrowing and total outlays shall include all outlays of the United States except those for repayment of debt principal." So once again there is no provision made to reduce or pay off the government debt burden and the refunding problem.

As a result, refundings will grow unrestricted as a major part of Treasury financing and our budget. Based on the OMB budget forecast for the years 1985 to 1989, plus the known maturities as of the end of calendar 1984, there is a massive Treasury refunding schedule ahead. This can be seen in Table 2–4. Note that the num-

TABLE 2–4
Treasury Refunding Dilemma ($ Billions)

Maturity	1984	1985	1986	1987	1988	1989
3 Month	$ 84.7	$ 95.4	$102.5	$108.0	$112.0	$114.1
6 Month	166.3	181.9	189.1	194.7	198.7	200.9
1 Year	101.6	109.0	118.1	125.8	131.8	136.1
2 Year	74.6	106.2	115.7	156.7	158.0	189.8
3 Year	24.7	27.3	32.0	39.5	37.3	40.4
4 Year	21.3	14.6	17.7	19.5	27.9	22.8
5 Year	2.6	11.6	13.3	16.4	22.8	25.1
7 Year	11.3	8.9	0	8.7	12.6	15.8
10 Year	2.2	0	14.7	2.4	7.6	8.4
20 Year	0	0	0	0	0	0
30 Year	0	1.0	1.2	0	0	0
Total	$489.3	$555.9	$604.30	$671.70	$708.7	$753.40

bers in Table 2–4 are without any growth due to interest cost or the rate at time of refunding.

Since the auction process is comprised of two components (refunding plus new cash), let's now take a look at the total financing picture or the total dilemma through 1989.

SUPPLY AND DEMAND

No matter how large our debt burden becomes it has always been financed incrementally and mostly through the routine auction process. Counting bills, we now have eleven maturities auctioned over 156 routine auctions from a three-month bill to a thirty-year bond. (See Table 2–5.) The size of these individual auctions are a key factor in the direction and level of interest rates. If there is not enough demand for an issue(s) there is usually a price concession (higher yield) to attract buyers. Since this is an open auction, such

TABLE 2–5
Treasury Auction Issue Size ($ Billions)

Maturity	Actual 1984	1985	1986	1987	1988	1989	1989/ 1984
3 Month	$ 6.85	$ 7.57	$ 7.96	$ 8.46	$ 8.70	$ 8.81	28.6%
6 Month	6.83	7.33	7.56	7.70	7.98	7.81	14.3
1 Year	8.59	9.85	10.49	10.98	11.35	11.53	34.2
2 Year	10.10	13.05	13.18	15.83	15.16	16.89	67.2
3 Year	8.18	9.34	10.12	11.53	10.52	10.75	31.4
4 Year	6.81	5.69	6.14	6.29	8.33	6.21	− 8.8
5 Year	7.95	10.37	9.61	9.03	9.23	8.18	2.9
7 Year	5.75	4.38	1.81	3.60	4.18	4.50	− 21.7
10 Year	6.66	7.04	9.60	5.24	5.22	3.88	− 41.7
20 Year	4.02	4.82	4.05	3.18	2.28	1.22	− 69.7
30 Year	6.01	6.83	5.83	4.33	3.10	1.67	− 72.8

Notes: 1984 = size of last auction issued per maturity

1955–1989 = sum of refundings plus OMB deficit forecasts
OMB deficit financed at same maturity percent distribution as 1984.

a price concession comes in the form of a lower bid being accepted and/or a wider distribution between best bid and lowest bid accepted.

If the OMB is correct and future deficit financing will be reduced dramatically (from $211 billion in 1985 to $54 billion in 1989), then the Treasury auction process will be mostly refundings (from $556 billion in 1985 to $753 billion in 1989). As you can see in Table 2–5, the short maturities from the three-month bill to the three-year note will be the Treasury auction mainstay.

Looking back it is hard to remember that no single auction exceeded $2.5 billion in 1975. Moreover, the first $5.0 billion auction was the two-year note in 1980 and the first $10.0 billion issue was again the two-year note in 1984. 1986 will be a real test of the supply-demand mechanism for Treasuries particularly as three, and possibly five, maturities could come into being with $10 billion routine auctions.

In conclusion there seems to be only three things you can count on in your future: death, taxes, and more Treasuries.

CHAPTER 3

SHARMIN MOSSAVAR-RAHMANI is a vice president of Lehman Management Co., Inc., New York. A fixed income portfolio strategist, she has published extensively on the bond market as well as on international energy issues. A graduate of Princeton University (A.B. Economics) and Stanford University (M.S. Engineering-Economic Systems), she was formerly Director of Research at Ryan Financial Strategy Group, a division of Refco Partners.

PERFORMANCE OF THE TREASURY MARKET IN THE 1980s

Sharmin Mossavar-Rahmani
Vice President
Lehman Management Co., Inc.
New York

Since 1980 the Treasury market has grown several-fold in size as well as in diversity. The volume of marketable Treasury securities has more than doubled to over one trillion dollars. New maturities such as 20-year Treasuries and new securities such as zero-coupon Treasuries have been introduced. Attractive investment opportunities are now available that rival those found not only in other sectors of the fixed income market but also in the equity market. In December 1985, for example, long-term zero-coupon Treasuries produced returns of over 20 percent, matching some of the highest monthly returns in the equity market.

The purpose of this chapter is to examine the performance of the Treasury market over the six-year period from January 1, 1980 to December 31, 1985. What have been the returns in Treasuries? What have been the risks associated with those returns? What have been the major market cycles? And finally, what have been some of the rewarding investment strategies in this market?

Historical risk and returns are measured using the following indices: the Ryan Index, an equal-weighted average of the most re-

49

cently auctioned and hence, most actively traded, Treasury securities; the Ryan Index maturity subsectors which include the 2-, 3-, 4-, 5-, 7-, 10-, 20-, and 30-year maturities; the Ryan Financial Strategy Group STRIPS and Treasury Bill Indices; the Payden and Rygel Money Market Performance Indices; and, finally, the Ibbotson Associates' *Stocks, Bonds, Bills and Inflation* bond series.

HISTORICAL RETURNS

Coupon Treasuries have produced very competitive returns in the recent past. In 1982, for example, the Ryan Index measured a total return of 32.50 percent, the highest annual return in bond history. Three years later, in 1985, the Ryan Index measured a total return of 24.24 percent, representing the second highest annual return in bond history.

Needless to say, performance within the Treasury market has been far from uniform. Among Treasury notes and bonds (maturities between 2 and 30 years), the returns of short maturities have differed from those of long maturities by a factor of seven. In 1980, for example, the 2-year note produced a total return of 8.34 percent while the 30-year bond produced a negative return of 1.39 percent (see Exhibit 3–1).

EXHIBIT 3–1
Annual Total Returns of Treasury Notes and Bonds

Issue	1980 (%)	1981 (%)	1982 (%)	1983 (%)	1984 (%)	1985 (%)
2 Year	8.34	13.08	21.42	8.94	14.85	14.64
3 Year	5.96	11.56	24.75	7.83	14.23	16.22
4 Year	4.53	9.40	28.02	7.18	14.10	19.29
5 Year	3.98	8.11	29.40	6.08	15.31	22.46
7 Year	3.09	6.62	33.71	4.66	14.92	25.22
10 Year	− 0.59	7.35	34.80	4.37	14.06	29.12
15 Year	− 3.42	2.82	38.19	—	—	—
20 Year	—	− 1.91	41.75	2.53	16.02	33.85
30 Year	− 1.39	2.97	40.94	− 0.43	17.07	34.30
Ryan Index	2.65	6.93	32.50	5.27	15.11	24.24

Note: 20-year was first auctioned on 1/06/81. 15-year returns end 4/14/83. Last 15-year was auctioned on 10/07/80.

EXHIBIT 3-2
Annual Total Returns of Treasury Bills

Issue	1980 (%)	1981 (%)	1982 (%)	1983 (%)	1984 (%)	1985 (%)
3 Month	12.23	16.59	12.49	9.17	10.78	8.51
6 Month	12.18	17.14	14.90	9.21	11.65	8.81
1 Year	10.79	16.19	17.70	8.64	12.40	10.66

Note: 1980–1984 data are based on Payden and Rygel Indices.
1985 data are based on Ryan Financial Strategy Group Treasury Bill Indices.

Among Treasury securities without coupons, i.e., Treasury bills and zero-coupon Treasury securities, the returns of short and long maturities have differed significantly as well. In 1985, the 3-month bill produced a total return of 8.51 percent, whereas long-term zero-coupon Treasuries produced a return of 51.53 percent (see Exhibits 3–2 and 3–3). Exhibit 3–3 provides annual returns of zero-coupon Treasuries for 1984 and 1985; even though introduced as early as September 1981, the zero-coupon Treasury market has grown significantly only since 1984.

EXHIBIT 3-3
Annual Total Returns of Zero-Coupon
Treasury Securities

Issue	1984 (%)	1985 (%)
2 Year	15.83	16.22
3 Year	15.54	20.09
4 Year	15.15	23.59
5 Year	14.47	27.83
7 Year	13.98	31.43
10 Year	14.88	37.40
20 Year	15.09	51.23
25 Year	11.65	51.53

Note: 30-year zero-coupon Treasuries were available only after February 1985 when the 25-year call feature was removed from the 30-year Treasury bond.

EXHIBIT 3–4
Total Returns of Treasury Notes and Bonds: 1/1/80 to 12/31/85

Issue	Price Return (%)	Income Return (%)	Reinvestment Return (%)	Total Return (%)	Annualized Total (%)
2 Year	6.04	69.93	37.39	113.36	13.46
3 Year	5.02	69.83	36.24	111.09	13.26
4 Year	5.03	70.99	37.55	113.56	13.48
5 Year	7.04	71.10	39.76	117.90	13.86
7 Year	8.18	71.59	41.54	121.32	14.16
10 Year	8.51	71.20	41.41	121.12	14.14
20 Year	21.65	59.89	39.84	121.38	14.16
30 Year	11.10	70.16	42.80	124.06	14.39
Ryan Index	8.09	70.61	40.27	118.97	13.95

Note: 20-year was first auctioned on 1/06/81. Totals may not add up due to rounding.

The difference in the performance of bills and zero coupons, however, is not as large as the duration of the two securities would imply. The duration of long-term zero coupons is over 100 times as large as that of a 3-month bill, while their returns are only about six times as large.

The historical data clearly indicate that the difference in returns within the Treasury market is substantial over short-time horizons. Moreover, maturity has been the single most important factor in determining the difference in returns within this market. Over long-time horizons, however, the difference in returns is smaller and maturity is less significant. Since 1980, for example, the 2-year note has underperformed the 30-year bond by a total 10.71 percent, or 1.71 percent on an annualized basis. In 1985 alone, the difference in returns between the two securities was 19.66 percent.

Total return consists of three components: price return due to changes in interest rate, income return from coupon and accrued interest or from amortization, and reinvestment return from the reinvestment of income. Over short-time horizons, price return is the largest component of total return, particularly in securities with long maturities. Price return therefore accounts for most of the difference in returns within the Treasury market over short-time horizons. Over long-time horizons, income return and reinvestment return are the overriding components of total return. As illustrated in Exhibit 3–4, income and reinvestment have accounted for 93 percent of total return since 1980, even though 1982 and 1985 witnessed the strongest price rallies in bond market history. Exhibit 3–5 further compares the contribution of price and income return since 1980. Changing economic and, hence, bond market cycles have diminished the role of price return while a steady stream of income has increased the role of income return.

Returns in the Treasury market increasingly match those of the corporate bond market. In 1985, long-term coupon Treasuries produced a return of over 33 percent, compared to less than 30 percent for long-term corporate bonds. Between 1980 and 1985, long-term Treasuries produced a return of over 123 percent, compared with 129 percent for long-term corporates, a difference of less than one percent on an annualized basis. Thus contrary to widespread belief, the total return spread between the Treasury and the corporate bond markets

EXHIBIT 3–5
Cumulative Returns of the Ryan Index

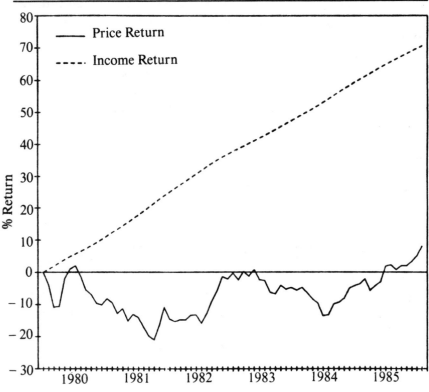

has not been very wide. Indeed, this spread historically has been relatively narrow; between 1926 and 1979 long-term Treasuries underperformed long-term corporates by 0.7 percent on an annualized basis. The spread between the Treasury and the corporate bond markets
partly offsets the credit and liquidity risks of corporate bonds.

A similar pattern of strong Treasury market performance exists in
the money market as well. Treasury bills, for example, have outperformed certificates of deposits (CDs) in recent years. Between 1980
and 1985, the 6-month Treasury bill produced a return of 100.32
percent (see Exhibit 3–6), compared to a return of 98.95 percent in
6-month CDs.

EXHIBIT 3-6
Total Returns of Treasury Bills:
1/1/80 to 12/31/85

Issue	Total (%)	Annualized (%)
3 Month	93.16	11.60
6 Month	100.32	12.28
1 Year	104.74	12.68

Note: 1980–1984 data are based on Payden and Rygel Indices. 1985 data are based on Ryan Financial Strategy Group Treasury Bill Indices.

HISTORICAL RISK

The risk profile of the Treasury market has changed considerably since 1980. In 1980 and 1981, the Treasury market exhibited the greatest volatility of any period in its history. In 1980, total return volatility, measured by the standard deviation of monthly total returns, stood at 4.25 percent, falling slightly to 3.65 percent in 1981. Such a volatility level was more than four times the average level of the late 1970s. Daily interest rate volatility, measured by the standard deviation of daily yield changes, was also very high in 1980 and 1981; the 30-year bellwether Treasury bond averaged a daily interest rate volatility of 15 basis points, reaching a high of 18 basis points in the fourth quarter of 1981.

Several factors account for the greater volatility of the early 1980s. The Federal Reserve Bank shifted its operating procedures to target reserves instead of interest rates. Meanwhile, interest rates and inflation were at historically high levels, resulting in wide daily interest rate swings. Finally, 1982 witnessed a transition period from rapid inflation to disinflation, leading to strong market sentiment at both ends of the bullish-bearish spectrum.

By the end of 1985, total return volatility had reached a low of 2.02 percent, and interest rate volatility, a low of 5 basis points. Conflicting economic data and widespread uncertainty regarding

EXHIBIT 3–7
Monthly Total Return Volatility of Treasury Notes and Bonds (by Year)

Issue	1980 (%)	1981 (%)	1982 (%)	1983 (%)	1984 (%)	1985 (%)
2 Year	2.89	2.02	1.17	0.79	0.98	0.73
3 Year	3.55	2.54	1.53	1.09	1.29	1.02
4 Year	3.85	2.78	1.75	1.36	1.66	1.35
5 Year	4.45	3.13	2.09	1.60	1.98	1.66
7 Year	4.42	3.62	2.44	2.04	2.42	2.16
10 Year	4.84	4.31	2.53	2.60	2.83	2.68
15 Year	5.14	4.90	3.27	—	—	—
20 Year	—	5.35	3.27	3.34	3.45	3.35
30 Year	5.74	5.49	3.17	3.44	3.53	3.59
Ryan Index	4.25	3.65	2.26	2.07	2.19	2.02

Note: 20-year was first auctioned on 1/06/81. 15-year returns end 4/14/83. Last 15-year was auctioned on 10/07/80.

the direction of both the economy and Federal Reserve Bank credit policy led to such low volatility. Similar uncertainty contributed to very low volatility in late 1983 and early 1984. (See Exhibits 3–7 and 3–8.)

The zero-coupon Treasury market has been the most volatile sector of the Treasury market, and indeed of the entire fixed income market. Due to the absence of coupon payments, the duration (an approximate measure of price volatility) of zero-coupon bonds is equivalent to their maturity. The duration of a 25-year zero-coupon bond is therefore 25 years, compared to a duration of 8 to 12 years for long-term Treasury bonds.

As shown in Exhibit 3–9, in 1985 long-term zero-coupon Treasuries had a total return volatility of 8.72 percent, compared to a total return volatility of 3.59 percent in long-term Treasury bonds. The longer duration of zero-coupon Treasury bonds partly accounts for their greater volatility. In addition, unpredictable but still very significant foreign demand—notably Japanese demand—for zero-coupon Treasuries has contributed to their volatility.

EXHIBIT 3-8
Daily Interest Rate Volatility of the 30-Year Bond Index (by Quarter)

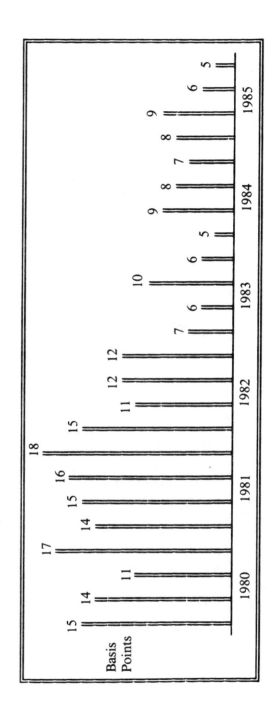

EXHIBIT 3–9
Monthly Total Return Volatility of Zero-Coupon
Treasury Securities (by Year)

Issue	1984 (%)	1985 (%)
2 Year	1.14	0.71
3 Year	1.51	1.21
4 Year	1.88	1.82
5 Year	2.34	2.07
7 Year	3.07	3.12
10 Year	4.44	4.44
20 Year	8.25	8.31
25 Year	10.85	8.72

Note: 30-year zero-coupon Treasuries were available only after February 1985 when the 25-year call feature was removed from the 30-year Treasury Bond.

MARKET CYCLES

The Treasury market has registered four major market cycles in the last decade. (See Exhibit 3–10.) The first was the bear market cycle that began at the end of December 1976, and lasted through the end of September 1981. This bear market cycle was one of the longest such cycles on record in spite of a 3-month market rally that began in April 1980.

The bull market cycle that followed lasted until May 1983 and produced spectacular returns. Total return measured 56.20 percent and the Treasury yield curve dropped an average of 600 basis points.

Next came a short and uneventful bear market cycle that lasted about a year. Returns were negative at minus 3.94 percent, interest rates rose nearly 400 basis points, and volatility was a low 1.8 percent.

As the economic recovery slowed, the Treasury market took off on another strong bull market cycle in late May 1984. Even though the cycle had not yet ended by the end of 1985, the Treasury market had returned 49.14 percent. Long-term Treasuries had returned over 73.87 percent and long-term zero-coupon Treasuries had

EXHIBIT 3–10
Market Cycles of Treasury Notes and Bonds

Major Cycles	Start Date	End Date	Total Returns (%)	Interest Rate Move (Basis Points)	Percent Change in Rates (%)
Bear market	12/31/76	9/30/81	−6.24	952	146.24
Bull market	9/30/81	5/04/83	56.20	−618	38.56
Bear market	5/04/83	5/30/84	−3.94	383	38.87
Bull market	5/30/84	12/31/85*	49.14	−497	36.32

*The bull market cycle had not yet ended by 12/31/85.

EXHIBIT 3–11
Historical Yield Levels of the Ryan Index

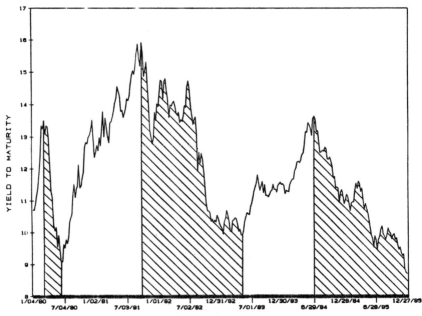

Peaks and troughs in historical yield levels:

9/30/81 = 16.03%
5/04/83 = 9.85%
5/30/84 = 13.68%
12/31/85 = 8.71%

returned 91.43 percent. Interest rates had dropped nearly 500 basis points to their lowest level in over six years as shown in Exhibit 3–11.

ATTRACTIVE INVESTMENT STRATEGIES

Maturity is the single most important factor in determining total return over short-time horizons. However, once the maturity selection has been made, further value can be added to a portfolio by taking advantage of specific investment opportunities within the

Treasury market. Such opportunities are usually a result of either the shape of the Treasury yield curve, of supply and demand imbalances, or of risk and reward characteristics of specific securities at any point in time.

The slope of the Treasury yield curve offered several attractive investment strategies in 1985. As illustrated in Exhibit 3–12, the slope of the curve, measured by the spread between the 2- and 30-year Treasuries, was at historically wide levels in June 1985. In fact, the spread between the 2- and 30-year Treasuries was over 180 basis points, the widest since November 1976. Nearly three-quarters of this spread occurred between the 2- and 7-year Treasuries. An effective strategy would have been to swap out of both ends of the yield curve by selling the 2- and 30-year Treasuries, moving instead into the middle of the curve by buying the 7-year Treasury for a similar duration, greater yield, and better performance in all inter-

EXHIBIT 3–12
Historical Yield Curve Spreads between 30- and 2-Year Treasuries

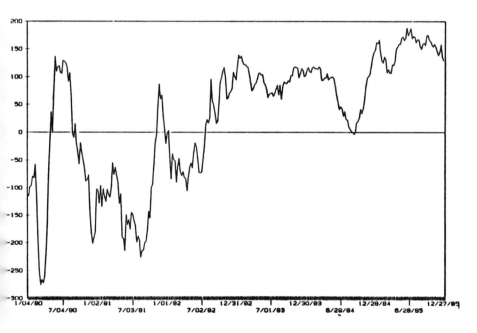

est rate scenarios. Such a strategy would have improved returns by 0.75 percent in 1985.

The risk and reward characteristics of intermediate Treasuries relative to intermediate zero-coupon Treasuries have also offered attractive investment strategies. In 1985, for example, a duration swap out of 7-year Treasuries and into 5-year zero-coupon Treasuries improved returns by 2.61 percent. Intermediate zero-coupon Treasuries had higher yields than their current coupon counterparts and enjoyed a stronger roll down the yield curve.

It is important to realize that a portfolio's returns can be significantly enhanced by taking advantage of investment strategies within the Treasury market. Such strategies can be implemented without sidestepping the maturity or duration constraints of a portfolio.

CONCLUSION

In recent years, the Treasury market has produced spectacular returns, rivaling other sectors of the fixed income market such as the corporate bond market and other sectors of the capital markets such as the equity market. With higher rewards have come higher price risks. The Treasury market now offers zero-coupon bonds, one of the most volatile investment vehicles with large price appreciation potential. Furthermore, the growing size and diversity of the Treasury market has also provided an environment where effective investment strategies can be implemented. These strategies can increase returns without increasing the credit or interest rate risk of a portfolio. As the Treasury market continues to grow, so will such investment opportunities.

CHAPTER 4

SHARMIN MOSSAVAR-RAHMANI is a vice president of Lehman Management Co., Inc., New York. A fixed income portfolio strategist, she has published extensively on the bond market as well as on international energy issues. A graduate of Princeton University (A.B. Economics) and Stanford University (M.S. Engineering-Economic Systems), she was formerly Director of Research at Ryan Financial Strategy Group, a division of Refco Partners.

MEASURING RISK AND REWARD IN THE TREASURY MARKET

Sharmin Mossavar-Rahmani
Vice President,
Lehman Management Co., Inc.

The mathematics of all fixed-income securities is driven by one fundamental concept: the time value of money. Money received at an early date has more value than the same money received at a later date, since money received earlier can be invested and hence increased. Time value of money can be evaluated in one or more of the following ways: the present value of a lump sum investment, the future value of a lump sum investment, the present value of an annuity, and the future value of an annuity. These four evaluation tools are used to derive the risk and reward measurements of all fixed-income securities.

This chapter focuses on methods of calculating risk and reward of marketable U.S. Treasury securities, namely Treasury bills, Treasury notes and bonds, and zero-coupon Treasuries. Each of these securities has its own particular risk and reward measurements. The risk exposure of Treasury bills, for example, is expressed in terms of the value of an 01 basis point, while the risk exposure of Treasury notes and bonds is expressed in terms of duration or of the yield value of a $1/32$nd change in price. Thus, the chapter will begin with a discussion of the reward measurements of each type of Treasury security, including the bank discount rate, price, yield-to-maturity and realized compound yield, and total return. The risk measurements, including the value of an 01, Macaulay's duration and modified duration, convexity, value of $1/32$, and volatility, are then addressed. The chapter will conclude with a review of the drawbacks that currently exist in the risk and reward measurements of Treasury securities.

REWARD MEASUREMENTS

Treasury Bills

Treasury bills are discount securities that are issued with maturities of one year or less at a price below face value. Three distinct maturities are issued on a regular basis: a 91-day bill auctioned weekly (usually on Monday and issued the following Thursday), a 182-day bill similarly auctioned weekly on Monday and issued on Thursday; and a one-year (364-day) bill, auctioned monthly (usually every fourth Thursday and issued the following Thursday). The U. S. Department of the Treasury (the Treasury) also issues other bills with varying maturities on a need basis; these bills are called cash management bills.

As discount securities, Treasury bills do not pay interest. Instead, Treasury bills are issued at a discount from face value; the return to the investor is the difference between the purchase price and face value redeemed at maturity. The purchase price is determined by three variables: the bank discount rate (quoted as a percentage of face value on a 360-day year basis), the face or redemption value (usually 100 with a minimum trading denomination of $10,000), and the term-to-maturity (number of days between settlement date of a transaction and maturity date of a bill).

Let d = bank discount rate (expressed in decimals)

   RV = redemption value (expressed in dollars)

   DSM = term to maturity (expressed in number of days)

DV = discount value (expressed in dollars)

PV = present value (expressed in dollars)

TR = total return (expressed in percent)

APR = annual percentage rate (expressed in percent)

The present value of a bill is the redemption value less the discount value:

$$PV = RV - DV$$

where

$$DV = (d)(RV)\left(\frac{DSM}{360}\right)$$

The present value of a bill is equal to its price since accrued interest is zero in discount securities that do not make coupon payments.

For example, to determine the price of a 91-day bill issued at a discount rate of 7.00 percent, the discount value is first determined as follows:

$$DV = (0.07)(\$100)\left(\frac{91}{360}\right)$$
$$= \$1.769$$

The price can then be determined as follows:

$$PV = \$100 - \$1.769$$
$$= \$98.231$$

Once the price and discount value have been determined, the actual reward to the investor can be measured. First, the dollar value of the return is expressed as a percentage of the initial investment PV:

$$TR = \left(\frac{DV}{PV}\right)100$$
$$= \left(\frac{(RV - PV)}{PV}\right)100$$
$$= \left[\left(\frac{RV}{PV}\right) - 1\right]100$$

In the example above, the percent total return is

$$TR = \left(\frac{\$\ 1.769}{\$98.231}\right)100$$

$$= 1.801\%$$

The 1.80 percent total return represents the reward to an investor over a 91-day holding period; the reward can be annualized on the basis of a 365-day year as follows:

$$APR = TR\left(\frac{365}{DSM}\right)$$

The annualized percentage rate is thus 7.225 percent.

The annual percentage rate can also be expressed in terms of bond equivalent yield (called yield-to-maturity in notes and bonds) to provide a benchmark comparable to reward measurements of other Treasury securities. A key difference between Treasury bills and Treasury notes and bonds is that the latter pay interest semi-annually, thereby allowing for the compounding of interest. Treasury bills, on the other hand, do not pay interest until maturity and therefore do not offer the opportunity of reinvesting interest payments. Restating the annual percentage rate in terms of the bond equivalent yield requires a downward adjustment of the annual percentage rate to reflect the absence of a reinvestment opportunity.

A downward adjustment is only necessary for Treasury bills with terms-to-maturity greater than six months. Treasury bills with terms-to-maturity less than or equal to six months offer the same compounding opportunity as Treasury notes and bonds with terms-to-maturity less than six months. Thus, the bond equivalent yield of a Treasury bill with a term-to-maturity less than or equal to six months is equal to its annual percentage rate. Treasury bills with terms-to-maturity greater than six months, however, entail the opportunity cost of foregoing reinvestment of any interest payments. This opportunity cost can be measured by examining the cash flows to an investor if semi-annual compounding were available.

Let bey = bond equivalent yield or interest rate with semi-annual compounding (expressed in decimals)

DY = number of days in a year (365 or 366 days)

DSM = number of days from settlement to maturity

DSC = number of days from settlement to the six-month mark

The hypothetical cash flows of a Treasury bill with a term-to-maturity greater than six months and with reinvestment opportunities at the six-month mark can be expressed as follows:

Cash Flow 1.   Interest on the bill at the six-month mark equal to

$$PV\left(\frac{bey}{DY}\right)(DSC)$$

Cash Flow 2.   Interest on the bill between the six-month mark and maturity equal to $PV\left(\frac{bey}{2}\right)$

Cash Flow 3.   Interest on Cash Flow 1 equal to

$$PV\left(\frac{bey}{DY}\right)(DSC)\left(\frac{bey}{2}\right)$$

It is important to note that the six-month mark can be determined by moving back six months from maturity date or by going forward six months from settlement date; the implied bond equivalent yield is the same in both cases. The sum of the initial investment of PV and the three cash flows equals the redemption value of the bill at maturity as follows:

$$RV = PV + PV\left(\frac{bey}{DY}\right)(DSC) + PV\left(\frac{bey}{2}\right) + PV\left(\frac{bey}{DY}\right)(DSC)\left(\frac{bey}{2}\right)$$

The bond equivalent yield, bey, can be shown to be:[1]

$$bey = \frac{\dfrac{-DSM}{DY} + \sqrt{\left(\dfrac{DSM}{DY}\right)^2 - 4\left(\dfrac{DSM}{2DY} - \dfrac{1}{4}\right)\left(\dfrac{PV-100}{PV}\right)}}{2\left(\dfrac{DSM}{2DY} - \dfrac{1}{4}\right)}$$

[1] The formula is derived as follows. The expression for RV can be simplified into a quadratic equation given a redemption value of $100. Substituting DSM − DY/2

For example, a 364-day Treasury bill sold at a discount rate of 7.00 percent has a bond equivalent yield of 7.498 percent, as shown below.

$$\text{bey} = \frac{-\dfrac{364}{365} + \sqrt{\left(\dfrac{364}{365}\right)^2 - 4\left(\dfrac{364}{2(365)} - \dfrac{1}{4}\right)\left(\dfrac{92.922 - 100}{92.922}\right)}}{2\left(\dfrac{364}{2(365)} - \dfrac{1}{4}\right)}$$

$$= .07498 \text{ or } 7.498 \text{ percent}$$

While the bank discount rate is the key reward measurement for trading Treasury bills, the annual percentage rate and bond equivalent yield are the critical reward measurements for evaluating and

---

for DSC and $100 for the RV, the expression can be rewritten as follows:

$$100 = \text{PV}\left[1 + \left(\text{DSM} - \frac{\text{DY}}{2}\right)\left(\frac{\text{bey}}{\text{DY}}\right)\right]\left[1 + \frac{\text{bey}}{2}\right]$$

then

$$\frac{100}{\text{PV}} = \left[1 + \frac{\text{bey}(2\text{DSM} - \text{DY})}{2\text{DY}}\right]\left[1 + \frac{\text{bey}}{2}\right]$$

$$= 1 + \frac{\text{bey}(2\text{DSM} - \text{DY})}{2\text{DY}} + \frac{\text{bey}}{2} + \frac{(\text{bey})^2(2\text{DSM} - \text{DY})}{4\text{DY}}$$

Rearranging the terms

$$\frac{100}{\text{PV}} - 1 = \frac{\text{bey}(2\text{DSM} - \text{DY}) + \text{DY}}{2\text{DY}} + \frac{(\text{bey}^2)(2\text{DSM} - \text{DY})}{4\text{DY}}$$

$$\frac{100 - \text{PV}}{\text{PV}} = \text{bey}\left(\frac{\text{DSM}}{\text{DY}}\right) + (\text{bey})^2\left(\frac{2\text{DSM}}{4\text{DY}} - \frac{\text{DY}}{4\text{DY}}\right)$$

$$0 = (\text{bey})^2\left(\frac{\text{DSM}}{2\text{DY}} - \frac{\text{DY}}{4\text{DY}}\right) + \text{bey}\left(\frac{\text{DSM}}{\text{DY}}\right) + \left(\frac{\text{PV} - 100}{\text{PV}}\right)$$

the expression is simplified into a quadratic equation in the form of

$$0 = ax^2 + bx + c$$

where one can solve for x as

$$x = \frac{-b + \sqrt{b^2 - 4ac}}{2a}$$

Similarly, one can then solve for the bond equivalent yield bey.

hence investing in Treasury bills. The former measures the actual return to an investor on an annualized 365-day year basis and the latter provides a benchmark to measure the risk and return trade-offs between Treasury bills and Treasury notes and bonds.

Treasury Notes and Bonds

Treasury notes and bonds are interest-bearing instruments that pay interest semi-annually; notes are securities with maturities greater than one year but not more than 10 years, and bonds are securities with maturities greater than 10 years. The Treasury auctions six different notes—2-, 3-, 4-, 5-, 7-, and 10-year notes, and one bond—a 30-year bond. The Treasury regularly auctioned a 15-year bond prior to October 1980 and a 20-year bond prior to April 1986; the Treasury ceased to auction both maturities in the absence of market interest.

The Treasury's auction process follows a regular schedule. The 2-year maturity is auctioned every month, the 3-, 10-, and 30-year maturities are generally auctioned the second month of every quarter (in February, May, August, and November), and the 4- and 7-year maturities are usually auctioned on the third month of every quarter (in March, June, September, and December). The 5-year is typically auctioned after the 3-, 10-, and 30-year maturities, and before the 4- and 7-year maturities.

Three reward measurements are used to evaluate Treasury notes and bonds: yield-to-maturity, realized compound yield, and total return. Unlike the discount rate of Treasury bills which is based on a 360-day year, the rewards measurements of Treasury notes and bonds are based on the actual number of days in any year and the actual number of days in any month; an "actual/actual" day count compares with a "30/360" day count for corporate bonds. Yield-to-maturity, the most widely used of the three measurements, is the discount rate that equates the present value of all cash flows of a security (semi-annual interest payments plus redemption value at maturity) to the purchase price of that security.

Let PV = present value of cash flows (expressed in dollars)
    n = number of remaining full compounding periods

C = annual coupon rate (expressed in dollars)

y = yield-to-maturity with semi-annual compounding (expressed in decimals)

RV = redemption value at maturity (expressed in dollars)

Then the present value of the security is

$$PV = \sum_{t-1}^{n} \frac{C/2}{(1 + y/2)^n} + \frac{RV}{(1 + y/2)^n}$$

For example, The present value of a 2-year Treasury note with a 10 percent coupon at a yield-to-maturity of 8 percent can be obtained as follows:

$$PV = \frac{10/2}{\left(1 + \frac{.08}{2}\right)} + \frac{10/2}{\left(1 + \frac{.08}{2}\right)^2} + \frac{10/2}{\left(1 + \frac{.08}{2}\right)^3} + \frac{10/2}{\left(1 + \frac{.08}{2}\right)^4} + \frac{100}{\left(1 + \frac{.08}{2}\right)^4}$$

$$= \$103.630$$

Treasury notes and bonds are generally traded on a price basis rather than on a yield-to-maturity basis. Deriving the yield-to-maturity from the price requires a first approximation of the yield-to-maturity followed by one of several iteration methods that will converge onto a yield-to-maturity that, in turn, corresponds to the quoted price.

The present value formula is the general formula for the yield-to-maturity of a Treasury note or bond; however, the formula only applies to cases where the next coupon payment is six months away from the settlement date of a transaction. Three other cases must be considered: Case I where settlement date falls between two coupon payment dates; Case II where settlement date falls in the last coupon payment period; and Case III where the first coupon payment is either greater or less than six months from the issue date of a security.

In Case I, settlement date falls between two coupon payment dates; the cash flows, therefore, must be discounted back to a settlement date that falls between two coupon payment dates. The time line diagram shown as Figure 4–1(a) below clarifies the sequence of cash flows and the discounting procedures that are necessary to derive the present value and price of a security.

Let DCD = days between coupon payment dates
   DSC = days between settlement date and next coupon payment date
   FR = DSC/DCD
   SD = settlement date
   CD = coupon payment date
   N = number of remaining coupons payments which, in this case, equals n plus one

and recall that

   PV = present value (expressed in dollars)
   RV = redemption value (expressed in dollars)
   C = annual coupon payment (expressed in dollars)
   y = yield-to-maturity (expressed in decimals)

As illustrated in Figure 4-1(a), the coupon payments and the redemption value of a security must be discounted back to the settle-

FIGURE 4-1
Time Line Diagram for Case I
Settlement data falls between two coupon payment dates

(a)

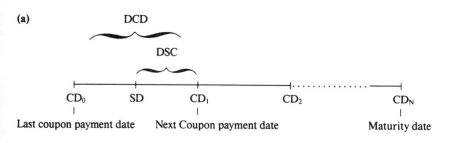

(b)

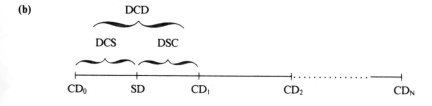

ment date by the sum of the remaining number of whole coupon periods and the remaining fraction of a coupon period. The remaining number of whole coupon periods is, by definition, equal to the number of remaining coupon payments minus one (i.e. $N - 1$). The remaining fraction of a coupon period is the number of days between settlement date and next coupon payment date as a fraction of the total number of days between coupon payment dates (i.e. DSC/DCD). The present value of the cash flows can thus be calculated as follows:

$$PV = \sum_{t=1}^{N} \frac{\frac{C}{2}}{(1 + y/2)^{t-1+FR}} + \frac{RV}{(1 + y/2)^{N-1+FR}}$$

Using the 2-year note example, let

Issue Date   = 12/31/85
Maturity Date = 12/31/87
Settlement Date = 3/31/86

The maturity date implies that coupon payments will be made twice a year, once on the anniversary date of the maturity (i.e. 12/31/86 and 12/31/87) and once on the six-month anniversary date of the maturity (i.e. 6/30/86 and 6/30/87). The settlement date falls between two anniversary dates; therefore the cash flows of the 2-year note must be discounted back to 3/31/86 as follows:

DCD = days between 12/31/85 and 6/30/86
    = 181
DSC = days between 3/31/86 and 6/30/86
    = 91
FR = 91/181

The present value of the 2-year note can then be calculated as follows:

$$PV = \frac{\frac{10}{2}}{\left(1 + \frac{.08}{2}\right)^{\frac{91}{181}}} + \frac{\frac{10}{2}}{\left(1 + \frac{.08}{2}\right)^{1+\frac{91}{181}}} + \frac{\frac{10}{2}}{\left(1 + \frac{.08}{2}\right)^{2+\frac{91}{181}}}$$

$$+ \frac{\frac{10}{2}}{\left(1 + \frac{.08}{2}\right)^{3+\frac{91}{181}}} + \frac{100}{\left(1 + \frac{.08}{2}\right)^{3+\frac{91}{181}}}$$

$$= \$105.671$$

Alternatively, all cash flows can be first discounted to 6/30/86 using whole coupon period; the value obtained at 6/30/86 can be then discounted to 3/31/86 using the fractional period.

Since settlement date falls between two coupon payment dates, the present value term includes the interest that has accrued on the security since the last coupon payment date. The daily interest that accrues on Treasury notes and bonds is a fixed sum that is a function of the coupon payment and the number of days between the two coupon payment dates. (See Figure 4–1(b).)

Let AI = accrued interest (expressed in dollars)

DCS = number of days from last coupon payment date to settlement date which equals DCD minus DSC

P = price (expressed in dollars)

Using the notation presented earlier, accrued interest can be calculated as follows:

$$AI = \left[\frac{\frac{C}{2}}{DCD} \right] DCS$$

Returning to the 2-year note example:

$$DCS = DCD - DSC$$
$$= 181 - 91 = 90$$

Therefore accrued interest can be calculated as

$$AI = \left(\frac{\frac{10}{2}}{181} \right) (90)$$

$$= \$2.486$$

and given accrued interest, the price of the security can be expressed as

$$
\begin{aligned}
P &= PV - AI \\
&= \$105.671 - \$2.486 \\
&= \$103.185
\end{aligned}
$$

In Case II, settlement date falls in the last coupon payment period of a security. In the last coupon payment period, the present value of the cash flows (the last coupon payment plus redemption value) is calculated on a simple interest or straight line basis compared with an exponential basis in other coupon payment periods. The present value of the Treasury note or bond in its last coupon period is derived as follows:

$$
PV = \frac{\dfrac{C}{2}}{1 + \dfrac{y}{2} \cdot FR} + \frac{RV}{1 + \dfrac{y}{2} \cdot FR}
$$

$$
= \frac{\dfrac{C}{2} + RV}{1 + \dfrac{y}{2} \cdot FR}
$$

Therefore, on 10/31/87, the present value of the 2-year note discussed above can be calculated as

$$
PV = \frac{\dfrac{10}{2}}{1 + \left(\dfrac{.08}{2} \times \dfrac{61}{184}\right)} + \frac{100}{1 + \left(\dfrac{.08}{2} \times \dfrac{61}{184}\right)}
$$

$$
= \$103.626
$$

and
$$
\begin{aligned}
P &= \$103.626 - \$3.342 \\
&= \$100.283 \text{ (totals do not add up due to rounding)}
\end{aligned}
$$

The accrued interest and price calculations for Treasury notes and bonds in their last coupon period is identical to the accrued interest and price calculations for other coupon periods.

Case III is that of odd first coupons. The Treasury often issues securities that have either greater or less than six months between the issue date and the first coupon payment date. If the first coupon payment date is more than six months away from issue date, the security is a long first coupon security; if the first coupon payment date is less than six months away from issue date, the security is a short first coupon security. The 5-year note, for example, is usually auctioned with a long first coupon. The logic in the calculations for long and short first coupons is identical; therefore only long first coupons will be examined here.

The fixed income market currently uses two different methods to determine the price and yield of odd first coupons: the Treasury method and the "Street" method. The only difference between the two methods is the manner in which cash flows are discounted before the first coupon payment date. In the Treasury method, cash flows are discounted on a simple interest or straight line basis while in the "Street" method, cash flows are discounted on an exponential basis.

Let ID = issue date of security

PD = pseudo-coupon date or the coupon payment date for the security assuming it were a normal bond. This date is also referred to as the quasi-coupon date

DPD1 = number of days between pseudo-coupon dates

DPD2 = number of days from next pseudo-coupon date to first coupon payment date

DIS = number of days from issue date to settlement date

DSP = number of days from settlement date to next pseudo-coupon date

DIP = number of days from issue date to next pseudo-coupon date

DPS = number of days from previous pseudo-coupon date to settlement date

DSC = number of days from settlement date to first coupon payment date

---

FIGURE 4–2
Time Line Diagram for Case III

(a) Settlement data falls between two pseudo-coupon dates

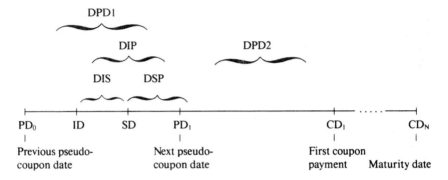

(b) Settlement date falls between a pseudo-coupon and the first coupon date

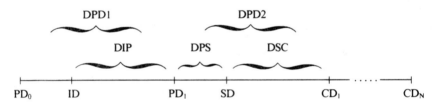

Figure 4–2(a) illustrates the time line diagram for the cash flows if the settlement date falls between two pseudo-coupon dates. Figure 4–2(b) illustrates the time line diagram for the cash flows if the settlement date falls between a pseudo-coupon date and the first coupon date.

Before proceeding to the price and yield calculations, the size of the first coupon payment must be determined. Since the first coupon payment is more than six months away from issue date, the first coupon is proportionately larger than the normal coupon payment. The Treasury and the "Street" both use the same method for determining the size of the first coupon.

Let C1 = size of first coupon (expressed in dollars)

Using the notation from above, C1 is calculated as follows:

$$C1 = \left(\frac{C}{2}\right)\left(1 + \frac{DIP}{DPD1}\right)$$

The Treasury and the "Street" also use the same method to calculate accrued interest for settlement dates before the first coupon payment date. The method for calculating accrued interest depends on whether settlement date falls before or after the pseudo-coupon date (PD_1). If settlement date falls before the pseudo-coupon date, accrued interest is calculated as follows:

$$AI = \left(\frac{C}{2}\right)\left(\frac{DIS}{DPD1}\right)$$

If settlement date falls after the pseudo-coupon date, accrued interest is calculated thus:

$$AI = \left(\frac{C}{2}\right)\left[\left(\frac{DIP}{DPD1}\right) + \left(\frac{DPS}{DPD2}\right)\right]$$

An example will clarify the calculation involved. Assume a 5-year note has been auctioned with a long first coupon:

Issue Date	= 6/15/86
Maturity Date	= 8/15/91
Coupon	= 10%
Yield-to-maturity	= 8%

If this security were a normal bond, its issue date would fall on a sixth-month anniversary of its maturity date and its first coupon payment date would be six months away from issue date. This security, however, is a long first coupon. Its issue date is only two months away from the six-month anniversary of its maturity and a coupon payment is not made on this six-month anniversary date. This six-month anniversary date when the coupon payment is skipped is known as the pseudo-coupon date—8/15/86 in this example. The first coupon payment date is, therefore, 2/15/87, and the size of the first coupon is determined as

$$Cl = \left(\frac{10}{2}\right)\left(1 + \frac{61}{181}\right)$$

$$= \$6.685$$

where

181 days   184 days

61 days

30 days   31 days   32 days   152 days

2/15/86   6/15/86   7/15/86   8/15/86   9/16/86   2/15/87
PD_0 ID   SD PD_1

On 7/15/86, the accrued interest is determined as follows:

$$AI = \left(\frac{10}{2}\right)\left(\frac{30}{181}\right)$$

$$= \$0.829$$

On 9/16/86, after the pseudo-coupon date, accrued interest is determined as follows:

$$AI = \left(\frac{10}{2}\right)\left[\frac{61}{181} + \frac{32}{184}\right]$$

$$= \$2.555$$

Given the size of the first coupon payment and the accrued interest calculations, one can now proceed to examine the Treasury and "Street" methods of calculating the price and yield of odd first coupon securities. As stated earlier, the only difference between the two methods is the discounting procedure used in the period before the first coupon payment; after the first coupon payment, the securities are treated like normal bonds.

In the Treasury method, cash flows are discounted using simple interest when settlement date is before the first coupon payment date. Again, let FR represent the fractional period between settlement date and the next coupon payment date. If settlement date falls before the pseudo-coupon date, the fractional period is the days between settlement date and the pseudo-coupon date divided by the number of days between pseudo-coupon dates:

$$FR = \frac{DSP}{DPD1}$$

If settlement date falls after the pseudo-coupon date, the fractional period is the days between settlement date and the first coupon payment date divided by the number of days between the pseudo-coupon date and the first coupon payment date:

$$FR = \frac{DSC}{DPD2}$$

Thus, if settlement date falls before the pseudo-coupon date, the present value of a long first coupon security can be calculated as follows:

$$PV = \frac{C1}{(1 + \frac{y}{2} \cdot FR)(1 + \frac{y}{2})} + \sum_{t=2}^{N} \frac{\frac{C}{2}}{(1 + \frac{y}{2} \cdot FR)(1 + \frac{y}{2})^t}$$

$$+ \frac{RV}{(1 + \frac{y}{2} \cdot FR)(1 + \frac{y}{2})^N}$$

Using the 5-year note example, and a settlement date of 7/15/86, the present value is calculated as follows:

$$PV = \frac{6.685}{\left(1+\frac{.08}{2}\times\frac{31}{181}\right)\left(1+\frac{.08}{2}\right)} + \frac{5}{\left(1+\frac{.08}{2}\times\frac{31}{181}\right)\left(1+\frac{.08}{2}\right)^2} + \cdots$$

$$+ \frac{5}{\left(1+\frac{.08}{2}\times\frac{31}{181}\right)\left(1+\frac{.08}{2}\right)^{10}} + \frac{100}{\left(1+\frac{.08}{2}\times\frac{31}{181}\right)\left(1+\frac{.08}{2}\right)^{10}}$$

$$= \$108.985$$

If settlement date falls after the pseudo-coupon date but before the first coupon payment date, the present value of a long first coupon security can be calculated as follows:

$$PV = \frac{C1}{1+\frac{y}{2}\cdot FR} + \sum_{t=2}^{N}\frac{\frac{C}{2}}{\left(1+\frac{y}{2}\cdot FR\right)\left(1+\frac{y}{2}\right)^{t-1}} + \frac{RV}{\left(1+\frac{y}{2}\cdot FR\right)\left(1+\frac{y}{2}\right)^{N-1}}$$

On a 9/16/86 settlement date, the present value is

$$PV = \frac{6.685}{\left(1+\frac{.08}{2}\times\frac{152}{184}\right)} + \frac{5}{\left(1+\frac{.08}{2}\times\frac{152}{184}\right)\left(1+\frac{.08}{2}\right)} + \cdots$$

$$+ \frac{5}{\left(1+\frac{.08}{2}\times\frac{152}{184}\right)\left(+\frac{.08}{2}\right)^{9}} + \frac{100}{\left(1+\frac{.08}{2}\times\frac{152}{184}\right)\left(1+\frac{.08}{2}\right)^{9}}$$

$$= \$110.470$$

In the "Street" method, the cash flows are discounted exponentially when settlement date is before the first coupon payment date. If settlement falls before the pseudo-coupon date, the present value of a long first coupon security can be calculated using the "Street" method as follows:

$$PV = \frac{C1}{\left(1+\frac{y}{2}\right)^{FR}\left(1+\frac{y}{2}\right)} + \sum_{t=2}^{\lfloor N\rfloor}\frac{\frac{C}{2}}{\left(1+\frac{y}{2}\right)^{FR}\left(1+\frac{y}{2}\right)^{t}} + \frac{RV}{\left(1+\frac{y}{2}\right)^{FR}\left(1+\frac{y}{2}\right)^{N}}$$

If settlement falls after the pseudo-coupon date but before the first coupon payment date, the present value of a long first coupon security can be calculated using the "Street" method as follows:

$$PV = \frac{C1}{\left(1+\frac{y}{2}\right)^{FR}} + \sum_{t=2}^{N} \frac{\frac{C}{2}}{\left(1+\frac{y}{2}\right)^{FR}\left(1+\frac{y}{2}\right)^{t-1}} + \frac{RV}{\left(1+\frac{y}{2}\right)^{FR}\left(1+\frac{y}{2}\right)^{N-1}}$$

Returning to the 5-year note example, the present value of the note is \$108.997 on 7/15/86, and \$108.482 on 9/16/86. In these two cases the first term in the denominator has been changed from a simple interest or straight-line basis of $(1 + y/2 \cdot FR)$ to an exponential basis of $(1 + y/2)^{FR}$. It is important to note that the "Street" method results in a higher price for an FR of less than one.

In both the Treasury and the "Street" method, the price of a long first coupon is the present value minus the accrued interest.

The price and yield-to-maturity calculations discussed above are the key reward measurements used in the Treasury note and bond market. These reward measurements, however, reflect a security's value only at one point in time given certain assumptions about market conditions over the life of the security. In fact, the yield-to-maturity reflects the actual reward to an investor only if two assumptions are realized. The first assumption is that all coupon payments are reinvested at a rate equal to the yield-to-maturity; if the reinvestment rates are higher, the actual reward to the investor is higher, and if the reinvestment rates are lower, the actual reward to the investor is lower. The second assumption is that the bond is either held to maturity and therefore redeemed at par or that the bond is sold prior to maturity at the same yield-to-maturity that prevailed at purchase time.

Two additional measures have been developed to address the restrictive assumptions of the yield-to-maturity measurement: realized compound yield which allows for any reinvestment rate, and total return which incorporates a given reinvestment rate as well as a different yield-to-maturity at the end of a holding period.

Let RT = reinvestment rate with semi-annual compounding (expressed in decimals)

FV = future value of coupon payments plus redemption value (expressed in dollars)

RY = realized compound yield with semi-annual compounding (expressed in decimals)

Then the future value of a security with a redemption value RV is:

$$FV = \left[\sum_{t=1}^{N} \frac{C}{2}\left(1 + \frac{RT}{2}\right)^{N-t}\right] + RV$$

where each coupon payment C/2 is reinvested at the rate RT with semi-annual compounding. The realized compound yield is the discount rate that equates the present value of FV to the price plus accrued interest of the security. First, the future value of the investment must be discounted to the present:

$$PV = \frac{FV}{(1 + RY/2)^{N-1+FR}}$$

Substituting for FV, and solving for the realized compound yield:

$$RY = 2\left[\frac{\left[\sum_{t=1}^{N} C/2\left(1 + RT/2\right)^{N-t}\right] + RV}{PV}\right]^{\frac{1}{N-1+FR}} - 2$$

In our earlier example of a 2-year note maturing on 12/31/87 with a coupon of 10%, the security was purchased at a yield-to-maturity of 8%. If, however, all coupons are reinvested at a reinvestment rate of 6%, the realized compound yield is 7.865% as shown below:

$$RY = 2\left[\frac{\left[\sum_{t=1}^{4} C/2\left(1 + .06/2\right)^{4-t}\right] + 100}{103.630}\right]^{\frac{1}{4-1+1}} - 2$$

In this example, FR is equal to one, and the redemption value is equal to 100.

Thus, with an externally specified reinvestment rate, the realized compound yield (also called the external rate of return) is a more appropriate measure of the potential reward to an investor. The yield-to-maturity (or the internal rate of return) is a useful measure of reward to the investor only if the internally specified reinvestment rate (i.e., the yield-to-maturity) is available during the investor's holding period.

The concept of total return addresses the actual return to the investor over a specific holding period given a reinvestment rate or rates and given an ending price and yield-to-maturity. Total return consists of three components: price return which measures the percentage change in price due to the change in interest rates, income return which measures interest payments as a percent of the initial investment, and the reinvestment return which measures the cash flow from the reinvestment of interest as a percent of the initial investment. The initial investment is defined as the beginning price plus accrued interest at the time of purchase.

An example will best illustrate the derivation of the components of return. Consider a Treasury security under the following conditions:

Coupon	= 8%
Maturity Date	= 2/15/96
Purchase Date	= 12/31/85
Purchase Price (yield-to-maturity)	= 95.014 (8.75%)
Sale Date	= 12/31/86
Sale Price (yield-to-maturity)	= 98.404 (8.25%)
Reinvestment Rate	= 6%

and let TR = total return (expressed in percent)
    PR = price return (expressed in percent)
    IR = income return (expressed in percent)
    RR = reinvestment return (expressed in percent)
    PP = purchase price (expressed in dollars)
    SP = sale price (expressed in dollars)
    II = initial investment (expressed in dollars)
    EI = ending investment (expressed in dollars)
    AIP = accrued interest at purchase (expressed in dollars)
    AIS = accrued interest at sale (expressed in dollars)

CI = coupon income (expressed in dollars)

RI = reinvestment income (expressed in dollars)

Total return is simply the change in the value of an investment as a percentage of the initial investment:

$$TR = \left[\frac{(EI - II)}{II}\right]100$$

where

$$II = PP + AIP$$

$$EI = SP + AIS + CI + RI$$

In the Treasury security above

$$II = \$95.014 + \$3.00$$

$$= \$98.014$$

$$EI = \$98.404 + \$3.00 + \$8.00 + \$0.302$$

$$= \$109.706$$

Total return is therefore

$$TR = \left[\frac{(\$109.706 - \$98.014)}{\$98.014}\right]100$$

$$= 11.929\%$$

Price return is measured as

$$PR = \left[\frac{(SP - PP)}{II}\right]100$$

which in this example is

$$PR = \left[\frac{(\$98.404 - \$95.014)}{\$98.014}\right]100$$

$$= 3.459\%$$

Income return is measured as

$$IR = \left(\frac{CI}{II}\right)100$$

which in this example is

$$IR = \left(\frac{\$8.00}{\$98.014}\right)100$$

$$= 8.162\%$$

And reinvestment return is measured as

$$RR = \left(\frac{RI}{II}\right)100$$

which in this example is

$$RR = \left(\frac{\$0.302}{\$98.014}\right)100$$

$$= 0.308\%$$

It should be noted that

$$TR = PR + IR + RR$$

which in this example is

$$11.929\% = 3.459\% + 8.162\% + 0.308\%$$

The total return measure is mostly used by the investment community to evaluate the historical performance of various securities and portfolios, and also to compare the expected total return of specific securities under different interest rate scenarios.

Zero Coupon Treasuries

The mathematics of the reward measures of zero coupon Treasuries is the most straightforward of the reward measures of the Treasury market.[2] Zero coupon Treasuries are discount bonds with no coupon payments; the return to the investor is, therefore, the difference between purchase price and the redemption value at maturity. The purchase price is simply the present value of a single payment at maturity:

$$PV = \frac{RV}{(1 + y/2)^{N-1+FR}}$$

[2] Zero coupon Treasuries are discussed in Chapters 11 and 12.

This expression is identical to the second term of the present value expression for Treasury notes and bonds. It is important to note that the reinvestment of coupon payments is not a consideration with zero coupon bonds and that the realized compound yield is equal to the yield-to-maturity. Furthermore, since there are no coupon payments, accrued interest is always zero.

The total return of zero coupon Treasuries is the difference between the purchase price of a security and the sale price (or redemption value if the security is held to maturity) as a percentage of the purchase price:

$$TR = \left[\frac{(SP - PP)}{PP}\right] 100$$

Income return is the change in the purchase price of a security due to the passage of time and the consequent amortization of the discount security.

Let PP = Purchase price at a yield-to-maturity y at time t

AP = Amortized price at a yield-to-maturity y at time t + 1

Then income return is

$$IR = \left[\frac{(AP - PP)}{PP}\right] 100$$

Price return is the change in the price of a security due to the change in interest rates; it is the component of total return that is not explained by the accretion of the zero coupon bond:

$$PR = \left[\frac{(SP - AP)}{PP}\right] 100$$

Again

$$TR = IR + PR$$

RISK MEASURES

Treasury Bills

The conventional risk measure used for Treasury bills is the value of an 01. The value of an 01 measures the change in the price of a

Treasury bill due to a one basis point change in its bank discount rate. Mathematically, the value of an 01 is the first derivative of the present value function of a Treasury bill with respect to its discount rate.[3] The value of an 01 is usually expressed in terms of a face value of $1,000,000. For example, the value of an 01 for a 90-day Treasury bill is quoted as $25, for a 180-day bill as $50, and a 360-day bill as $100.

Treasury Notes and Bonds and Zero-Coupon Treasuries

Three risk measures are used both for Treasury notes and bonds and also for zero-coupon Treasuries: duration, yield value of $1/32$, and volatility. Duration and yield value of $1/32$ measure a security's risk exposure at any point in time while volatility measures the historical risk exposure of a security given the historical pattern of interest rates.

Duration is an approximate measure of the price sensitivity of a security to changes in its yield-to-maturity. Two measures of duration are currently used: Macaulay's duration and modified duration. Frederick Macaulay introduced the duration measure in 1938 as a weighted average maturity where each cash flow is weighted by the ratio of the present value of that cash flow to the present value of all cash flows.[4]

---

[3] This can be seen as follows: as presented earlier in the chapter, the price of a Treasury bill is

$$PV = RV - (d)(RV)\left(\frac{DSM}{360}\right)$$

Let δP = value of an 01 or the change in price due to a one basis point change in the bank discount rate

δd = one basis point or unit change in the bank discount rate

Then

$$\delta P = \delta PV = -RV\left(\frac{DSM}{360}\right)\delta d$$

[4] Frederick R. Macaulay, *Some Theoretical Problems Suggested by the Movement of Interest Rates, Bond Yields, and Stock Prices in the United States Since 1985* (New York: National Bureau of Economic Research, 1938).

Let t = time of cash flow (expressed in half years)
Ct = cash flow at time t (expressed in dollars)
CN = cash flow at maturity equal to coupon payment plus re-
demption value (expressed in dollars)
MD = Macaulay's duration (expressed in half years)

Then

$$MD = \frac{\dfrac{C1}{(1+y/2)^{FR}} \cdot FR + \dfrac{C2}{(1+y/2)^{2-1+FR}} \cdot (2-1+FR) + \ldots}{PV}$$

$$+ \frac{\dfrac{CN}{(1+y/2)^{N-1+FR}} \cdot (N-1+FR)}{PV}$$

The duration of the two-year note maturing on 12/31/87 can be calculated as follows:

$$MD = \frac{\dfrac{5}{\left(1+\dfrac{.08}{2}\right)}(1) + \dfrac{5}{\left(1+\dfrac{.08}{2}\right)^2}(2) + \dfrac{5}{\left(1+\dfrac{.08}{2}\right)^3}(3) + \dfrac{105}{\left(1+\dfrac{.08}{2}\right)^4}(4)}{103.630}$$

$$= 3.729$$

The above expression can be rewritten as:

$$MD = \frac{\displaystyle\sum_{t=1}^{N} \frac{Ct}{(1+y/2)^{t-1+FR}} \cdot (t-1+FR)}{\displaystyle\sum_{t=1}^{N} \frac{Ct}{(1+y/2)^{t-1+FR}}}$$

The duration measure from this formulation is in half years; the measure is divided by two to express duration in full years. The duration of the two-year note in the example above is 1.86 years when expressed in full years. The above formulation is different from the original expression introduced by Macaulay. The original expression ignores both accrued interest and the time between settlement date and the next coupon payment date, and is therefore valid only when settlement date falls on a coupon payment date.

Modified duration is Macaulay's duration divided by $(1+y/2)$. Mathematically, it is also the negative of the first derivative of the present value expression with respect to yield divided by the present value of the security. Modified duration, therefore, measures the percentage change in the price of a security per unit of change in its yield-to-maturity; that is:[5]

$$\left(\begin{array}{c}\text{percentage change in price} \\ \text{plus accrued interest}\end{array}\right) = -\left(\frac{MD}{1 + y/2}\right)\left(\frac{\text{change in basis points}}{100}\right)$$

Several conclusions can be drawn from examining Macaulay's duration. First, the duration of zero coupon bonds is equal to their maturity. Due to the absence of coupon payments, the payment of a

[5] This relationship can be demonstrated as follows. Using the present value and yield-to-maturity relationship derived earlier, one can take the first derivative of the present value with respect to yield-to-maturity as follows:

$$\frac{\delta PV}{\delta y/2} = -(t - 1 + FR)\sum_{t=1}^{N} \frac{C/2}{(1 + y/2)^{t+FR}} - (N - 1 + FR)\frac{RV}{(1 + y/2)^{N+FR}}$$

$$= \frac{-1}{1 + y/2}\left[\left(\sum_{t=1}^{N} \frac{C/2}{(1 + y/2)^{t-1+FR}}\right) \cdot (t - 1 + FR)\right.$$

$$\left. + \frac{RV}{(1 + y/2)^{N-1+FR}} \cdot (N - 1 + FR)\right]$$

The redemption value RV can be added to the last coupon payment $C/2$ and represented as CN. The first derivative can then be rewritten as:

$$\frac{\delta PV}{\delta y/2} = \frac{-1}{1 + y/2}\left(\sum_{t=1}^{N} \frac{Ct}{(1 + y/2)^{t-1+FR}} \cdot (t - 1 + FR)\right)$$

where $Ct = C/2$ for all $t < N$
    $= C/2 + RV$ for $t = N$

The expression in parentheses is equivalent to the expression for Macaulay's duration multiplied by the present value of the security. Therefore, the term can be further simplied to

$$\frac{\delta PV}{\delta y/2} = \frac{-1}{1 + y/2}(MD)(PV)$$

and

$$\frac{\delta PV}{PV} = \frac{-MD}{1 + y/2}\delta\frac{y}{2}$$

single cash flow at maturity receives 100 percent of the weighting; hence, duration will equal the maturity.

Second, duration of coupon-bearing instruments decreases as coupon size increases. Intuitively, given two bonds with the same maturity and yield but different coupon rates, the return of the bond with the higher coupon is less sensitive to price changes simply because a larger component of the return is driven by income. Similarly, the bond with a higher coupon produces a larger component of the total return sooner rather than later.

Third, duration is inversely related to yield-to-maturity; as yield-to-maturity increases, duration decreases. Again, intuitively, if the discount rate is higher, cash flows that are further out into the future become less significant, thereby lowering the duration. Mathematically, one can show this inverse relationship by examining the second derivative of the present value function. As indicated earlier, the first derivative of the present value function measures the sensitivity of the present value to changes in yield-to-maturity, hence the negative of modified duration. The second derivative of the present value function with respect to yield-to-maturity, also known as *convexity,* measures the sensitivity of modified duration to changes in yield-to-maturity.

Figure 4–3 depicts a graphic illustration of duration and convexity that is useful in understanding the derivation of these risk measurements. The curve P represents the present value function: as the yield level increases, the present value of the bond decreases. The slope of the curve at any yield level is measured by the slope of a line tg that is tangent to the curve at that point. This slope is the negative of modified duration. The change in the slope of the tangent line represents the change in modified duration due to changes in yield levels; as yield levels increase from y to y', the slope of the curve flattens and becomes less negative. Similarly, as yield levels increase, modified duration decreases. The change in the slope of the curve reflects the curvature of the present value curve; the greater the change in the slope of the curve, the greater its curvature or convexity.

The yield value of $1/32$ is another measure of risk in Treasury notes and bonds and zero coupon Treasuries. It is used more widely by the broker/dealer community than by the portfolio man-

FIGURE 4–3
Graphic Illustration of Duration and Convexity

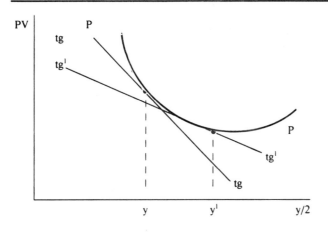

agement community. The yield value of $1/32$ is the change in the yield-to-maturity of a security given a change in price of $1/32$ or .03125 per $100.

The formula for the change in yield for a given change in price plus accrued interest is:[6]

---

[6] From footnote 5 we concluded with the following expression

$$\frac{\delta PV}{PV} = \frac{-MD}{1 + y/2} \delta\frac{y}{2}$$

where MD = Macaulay's duration in half years
       PV = present value equal to price and accrued interest

The terms of this expression can be rearranged to obtain the change in yield for a $1/32$ change in price:

$$\delta\frac{y}{2} = \left(\frac{-\delta PV}{PV}\right)\left(\frac{1 + y/2}{MD}\right)$$

and since δPV is equal to $\delta(P + AI)$ which is equal to δP the expression can be further simplified to

$$\delta y = 2\left(\frac{-\delta P}{PV}\right)\left(\frac{1 + y/2}{MD}\right)$$

$$\begin{pmatrix} \text{change in} \\ \text{yield} \end{pmatrix} = -2 \begin{pmatrix} \text{percentage change in price} \\ \text{plus accrued interest} \end{pmatrix} \left(\frac{1 + y/2}{MD} \right)$$

For example, on December 31, 1985, the yield value of $1/32$ of an 8 percent coupon Treasury bond maturing on 11/15/86 and purchased at a price of $98 can be measured as follows:

current price   = 98
accrued interest   = 1.01657
change in price of $1/32$ = .03125
yield-to-maturity (y)   = .10433
Macaulay's duration in half years (MD) = 1.708

then

$$\begin{pmatrix} \text{yield value} \\ \text{of } 1/32 \end{pmatrix} = -2 \left(\frac{.03125}{98 + 1.01657} \right) \left(\frac{1 + .10433/2}{1.708} \right)$$

$$= .000388 \text{ or } .0388\%$$

Smaller yield values of $1/32$ imply greater price risk while larger yield values of $1/32$ imply lesser price risk. If the yield value of $1/32$ is small, then a small change in interest rates has a large impact on the yield for a $1/32$ change in the price of the security; in other words, the price has to move many 32nds for a noticeable change in the yield level. If, on the other hand, the yield value of $1/32$ is large, then a large change in interest rates has a small impact on prices.

The risk measures discussed above are useful indications of the expected price and yield-to-maturity sensitivity of a security at any one point in time. The historical risk pattern of a security is measured by its historical volatility. Volatility can be used to measure price risk, total return risk, or interest rate risk. Total return volatility is commonly used by the portfolio management community to measure the risk of a portfolio relative to the risk of various market benchmarks. Price and interest rate volatility are commonly used in pricing options.

Volatility is defined as the historical fluctuation of a variable about its historical mean, and is measured by the standard deviation of the variable. The variable may represent price levels, price changes, interest rate levels, interest rate changes, or total return. The data can have daily, weekly, monthly, or even quarterly frequency. For example, the historical risk pattern of a portfolio is usually measured by the standard deviation of its quarterly returns.

CONCLUSION

Each type of marketable Treasury security has its own particular risk and reward measurements. While these measurements provide a useful range of tools for traders, brokers, investors, and analysts, they do have certain drawbacks. Some measurements such as yield-to-maturity are too restrictive. Some measurements such as price and yield-to-maturity calculations for odd first coupons securities are not standardized and uniformly accepted in the fixed-income market. And some such as price and yield-to-maturity calculations for Treasury securities in their last coupon payment period are inconsistent with the same calculations in other coupon payment periods. It is, therefore, important to understand and evaluate the advantages and drawbacks of each risk and reward measurement used in the Treasury market.

CHAPTER 5

KENNETH D. GARBADE is Vice President of
Fixed Income Research for Banker's Trust
Company. Formerly he was Professor of
Economics and Finance at New York University.
He also was Research Officer of the Federal
Reserve Bank of New York.

Dr. Garbade has a Bachelor of Science in
Physics and History from the California Institute
of Technology. He also has a Ph.D. in Economics
from Princeton University.

FOREIGN-TARGETED TREASURY SECURITIES*

Kenneth D. Garbade, Ph.D.
Vice President
Bankers Trust Company

On Wednesday, October 24, 1984, the United States Treasury sold $7 billion of 4-year notes in two separate auctions. It sold $6 billion of conventional notes at yields ranging between 11.38% and 11.44% per annum. The balance of the notes were offered as "Foreign-Targeted" securities, and sold at much lower yields, between 11.00% and 11.15% per annum.

The October offering of Foreign-Targeted ("Targeted") notes represented an innovation of some significance in Treasury financing. The notes were designed in two specific respects to attract the interest of foreign buyers. First, following the convention of the Eurobond market, they pay interest annually. Second, they have tax disclosure provisions which offer more anonymity to foreign investors than conventional Treasury securities. As a result, foreign securities dealers and investors were willing to acquire the Targeted notes at yields approximately 30 basis points lower than yields on conventional 4-year notes.

The 30 basis point difference between the auction yield on the Targeted 4-year note and the yield on conventional 4-year notes

99

saved the Treasury about $9 million. It is, therefore, hardly surprising that the Treasury followed up its initial success with an offering of $1 billion of Targeted 5-year notes in late November, 1984. This second offering was not as well received by the market, but nevertheless resulted in a savings of 7 basis points, or about $2\frac{3}{4}$ million.

This chapter discusses the major characteristics of Foreign-Targeted Treasury securities, using the October 4-year note as a specific example. The first section describes their basic features, including most especially the unique tax disclosure provisions. The second section examines price and yield calculations for Targeted securities. These vary from traditional market practices, because of the annual coupon, and also because accrued interest is computed on a calendar with 30-day months and 360-day years (a so-called "30/360" calendar), rather than an actual calendar. Finally, the third section describes the special provisions for exchanging a Targeted security into a conventional Treasury issue. This exchange option is important, because it links Targeted securities directly to the larger and more liquid markets for conventional Treasury notes and bonds.

CHARACTERISTICS OF TARGETED SECURITIES

This section describes the special tax disclosure provisions for Targeted securities, some restrictions on their initial distribution, and the provision for exchanging a Targeted security into a conventional Treasury issue.

In What Sense Are Targeted Securities Targeted?

The most important features of Targeted securities are those that lead a foreign investor to view them more favorably than ordinary Treasury bonds. It is these features which enhance the value of Targeted issues, and reduce the debt management costs of the Treasury.

Annual Coupon. Interest payments are the most obvious difference between Targeted securities and conventional Treasury issues. The

October, 1984 Targeted 4-year note pays an $11\frac{3}{8}$% *annual* coupon every September 30 to maturity. In contrast, the ordinary 4-year note auctioned at the same time pays an $11\frac{3}{8}$% *semi-annual* coupon, or 5.6875% of principal every March 31 and September 30. The annual coupon payment on the Targeted note parallels the Eurobond convention on interest payments, and differs from the American practice of semi-annual payments.

Tax Disclosure.   The most important aspect of Targeted bonds concerns U.S. taxation of interest payments made to foreigners. This aspect can best be described by reviewing first the taxation of interest on conventional Treasury bonds.

Except as noted below, interest paid to foreigners, including foreign corporations, on U.S. Treasury bonds issued prior to July 18, 1984 is subject to a 30 percent U.S. tax. To enforce this tax, U.S. persons who pay to foreigners interest on such "old" bonds are required to withhold, and remit to the Treasury, 30 percent of the amounts of those payments. In the alternative, the payor can obtain a Form 1001 from the payee, stating the name and address of the beneficial owner of the securities, and withhold whatever lower amount might be required by tax treaty between the United States and the country of residence of that beneficial owner. These amounts are, for example, zero for the Federal Republic of Germany and the United Kingdom, and five percent for Switzerland.

In mid-1984 Congress changed the tax laws to encourage foreign ownership of Treasury debt. In particular, it provided that there would be no taxation of, and hence no withholding on, an interest payment made to a foreigner who discloses the name and address of the beneficial owner of the security paying the interest. (Disclosure is made on Form W-8). The exemption from taxation and withholding via disclosure of beneficial ownership eliminates taxation of interest payments made to foreigners, while preventing tax evasion by Americans who might otherwise hold bonds offshore.

Foreigners obviously view Treasury notes and bonds issued after July 18, 1984 at least as favorably as older securities, because, upon disclosure of the beneficial owner, there is neither taxation nor withholding of any interest payment from the more recent issues, regardless of the country of residence of the beneficial owner. However, many foreigners find objectionable the disclosure requirement itself, and remain reluctant to acquire conventional Treasury securities.

Targeted Treasury notes and bonds carry a significantly different provision for escaping the foreign withholding tax. A person making an interest payment to a foreign financial institution and certain other foreign payees on a Targeted security can omit any withholding simply by obtaining certification from the payee that the beneficial owner is a "United States Alien." (A U.S. Alien is defined as a foreign corporation, a nonresident alien individual, a nonresident fiduciary of a foreign estate or trust, and certain related foreign partnerships.) In particular, there is no requirement for disclosure of the actual identify of the beneficial owner of a Targeted security.

The novel disclosure provision on Targeted issues offers foreign investors more anonymity than conventional, registered, Treasury securities. A registered bond is transferable only by changing the identity of the owner recorded on the books of the U.S. Treasury. Interest on a registered bond is paid directly, by check or wire transfer, to the owner of record on the payment date. Thus, the Treasury always knows the identity of the person to whom it is paying interest on a registered bond. More particularly, it knows when it is paying interest directly to a foreigner, and it requires a domestic financial institution, as a registered owner, to identify any foreign beneficial owner to whom it passes an interest payment. Based on this information, the Treasury can, as a practical matter, monitor compliance with its conventional tax and withholding requirements.

With respect to Targeted securities, mere certification by a foreign payee that the beneficial owner is a U.S. Alien suffices to avoid any foreign withholding tax. Since Targeted bonds are registered, the Treasury can monitor compliance with the *certification* requirement. It would obviously have more difficulty *verifying* foreign beneficial ownership, since the identity of the beneficial owner need not be disclosed by a foreign payee. It is in this sense that Targeted bonds offer foreign investors more anonymity than conventional Treasury bonds, even though both types of bonds are registered securities.

It should be noted, however, that Targeted securities do not guarantee the nearly complete anonymity associated with bearer bonds. Interest on a bearer bond is paid upon presentation of an engraved coupon clipped from the original bond. Since a bearer bond is transferable by simple physical delivery, there is no practical way for the Treasury to identify whether it has paid interest on a bearer bond to an American, to a foreign, or to an American acting through a foreigner.

**Restrictions on the Initial Distribution of
Targeted Securities**

Paralleling the intent that Targeted securities should be of special interest to foreigners, sales of those securities are restricted during an initial distribution period. We will explain these restrictions using the Targeted 4-year notes sold in October, 1984 as a concrete example.

Prior to December 9, 1984, only U.S. Aliens and foreign branches of U.S. financial institutions qualified as holders of the Targeted 4-year notes. The Treasury stipulated that it would sell the notes only to such qualified holders, and required that they, in turn, agree to acquire the notes only for their own account or as agent for other similarly qualified holders. Moreover, a buyer had to agree that if he sold Targeted 4-year notes before December 9, he would sell only to other similarly qualified holders. Thus, as a practical matter, ownership of the notes was limited to U.S. Aliens and foreign branches of U.S. financial institutions during a distribution period lasting about six weeks. After December 8, 1984, anybody could acquire the Targeted notes.

The Treasury adopted two provisions to enforce the restrictions on the initial marketability of the Targeted 4-year notes. First, it announced that definitive notes would not be issued before December 9, 1984, and that the only device for establishing registered ownership of the notes would be a book-entry account at the Federal Reserve Bank of New York. Second, it provided that, prior to December 9, the notes could be held only in special "International" book-entry accounts, and could not be transferred into ordinary book-entry accounts until after December 8. International accounts were defined as book-entry accounts at the New York Fed which identify either a foreign financial institution or a foreign branch of a U.S. financial institution. Thus, for example, prior to December 9 Bankers Trust Company could not own the Targeted securities in its own name or as agent, although Bankers Trust Company (London Branch), or Bankers Trust Company International Limited (a wholly-owned investment bank subsidiary) could own the notes—in their respective International book-entry accounts.

Relation to Tax Disclosure Requirements. The International book-entry accounts have a role in addition to serving as a device to limit ownership during the initial distribution period. The special tax disclosure provisions for Targeted securities are available *only* for book-entry securities recorded in International accounts and for definitive securities registered to foreign owners. Any institution paying interest to a foreign payee on a Targeted security held in a conventional book-entry account, or registered in definitive form to a domestic owner, must either obtain a Form W-8 or withhold part of the payment. Thus, International book-entry accounts serve as a continuing means of identifying those Targeted securities held in book-entry form which are eligible for the special tax certification provisions.

The Exchange Option

The Targeted 4-year note sold in October, 1984 has an unusual exchange option which has not been seen for many decades on U.S. Treasury securities. Specifically, a holder of the Targeted note has the option to exchange it, at any time after December 8, 1984, for the conventional 4-year note auctioned in October, 1984. As described more fully below, an exchange will usually involve a payment to or from the Treasury as a consequence of the difference in interest payments on the two notes.

The exchange option is an important device for enhancing the marketability, or liquidity, of the Targeted note. Given the relatively small, $1 billion, size of the Targeted 4-year issue, it is not inconceivable that a seller of a significant amount of Targeted notes could encounter difficulty in obtaining an acceptable bid. (Discounted bids stemming from illiquidity are certainly known in the Federal agency and corporate debt markets.) The exchange provision gives a seller the option of selling his notes by first converting them into conventional notes and then selling the conventional notes. Presumably, the market for the conventional notes should be at least as liquid as the market for the Targeted notes, since the Treasury issued $6 billion of the former notes.

A decision to exchange the Targeted 4-year note for the conventional note is irreversible. Thus, while the stock of outstanding Targeted notes may decline as a result of conversions, it can never increase. This is similar to convertible corporate debt, where the debt can be converted into common stock, but the resulting stock can not be converted back into debt.

INVOICE PRICES, CASH FLOWS, AND YIELDS ON TARGETED SECURITIES

The preceding section described attributes which enhance the value of Targeted securities relative to conventional notes and bonds. In this section we put aside those special attributes, and analyze the primary characteristics of a Targeted issue. More specifically, we examine the cash flows from a Targeted security, including periodic interest payments and return of principal at maturity; the price of a Targeted bond, including both the quoted price and any accrued interest; and the yield on a Targeted bond.

Figuring the cash flow, invoice price, and yield on a Targeted security differs from comparable calculations for an ordinary Treasury issue, because Targeted securities pay interest annually (instead of semi-annually) and because they use a 30/360 calendar (instead of an actual calendar).

Cash Flows

Four pieces of information are needed to describe the cash flow on a Targeted bond:

1. maturity date, at which time a final interest payment is made and principal repaid,
2. coupon rate, indicating the amount of interest paid annually, on an anniversary date of the bond,
3. issue date, and
4. date of first coupon payment.

TABLE 5-1.
**Future Cash Flows from the
Foreign-Targeted 11³/₈% Note of
September 30, 1988.**

Payment Date	Payment Amount
9/30/1985	10.39549*
9/30/1986	11.375
9/30/1987	11.375
9/30/1988	111.375

*Short-first-coupon, figured as
  $10.39549 = 11.375 \cdot (329/360)$,
where there are 329 days from 10/31/1984 to
9/30/1985, and 360 days from 9/30/1984 to 9/
30/1985, where both day-counts use a 30/360
calendar.

The issue date and date of first coupon payment are needed to compute the size of the first coupon payment.

To appreciate how the cash flow on a Targeted security is specified, consider the 4-year note sold in October, 1984. The parameters of the note are:

September 30, 1988 maturity date
$11\frac{3}{8}\%$ annual coupon
October 31, 1984 issue date
September 30, 1985 first coupon date

The note will pay regular coupons, equal to 11.375% of principal, on September 30, 1986, 1987, and 1988, and it will repay principal on September 30, 1988.

The first coupon on the Targeted 4-year note is a short coupon, because it is paid less than 1 year after the issue date of the note. The size of that coupon is figured with a 30/360 calendar.

To calculate the size of the first coupon, we need to count the number of days from the issue date to the September 30, 1985 coupon payment date. Assuming 30-day months, we first move the October 31, 1984 issue date to November 1, 1984, and then figure 10 full months of 30 days each to September 1, 1985. Adding 29 days to September 30, 1985 gives a total day-count of 329 days. Since the Targeted note pays an 11.375% annual coupon, and since there are assumed to be 360 days in one year, the first coupon on the note will be for 10.39549% of principal ($10.39549 = 11.375 \cdot (\frac{329}{360})$).

Table 5–1 shows the fully specified cash flows on the Targeted 4-year note. We now have to calculate the purchase price of those future cash flows.

Invoice Price

The quoted price of a Targeted bond is expressed as a percent of principal value, with fractions of a percent expressed either in decimal form (the European convention) or in 32nds (the American convention). The *invoice price* of a Targeted bond is its quoted price plus accrued interest on the next coupon, where interest is accrued from the last coupon date, or from the issue date, to the settlement date of the transaction.

Accrued Interest. Accrued interest on a Targeted bond is computed using a 30/360 calendar. Consider, for example, the accrued interest on the Targeted 4-year note for settlement on May 10, 1985. Using a calendar with 30-day months, we first move the October 31, 1984 issue date to November 1, 1984, and then figure six full months of 30 days each to May 1, 1985. Adding 9 days to May 10, 1985 gives a total day-count of 189 days between original issue and the settlement date. Since the Targeted note pays an 11.375% annual coupon, and since there are assumed to be 360 days in a year, the accrued interest from issue to May 10, 1985 is 5.97188% of principal ($5.97188 = 11.375 \cdot (\frac{189}{360})$).

Yield

We now know how to describe the cash flows on a Targeted security, and we know how to compute its invoice price. In principle, this is all we need to know: the amounts and dates of the cash payment for, and the receipts on, the security. However, market participants often want a simple measure of the value of a bond to compare with other bonds. In particular, they often want to know the yield to maturity on a bond.

The yield on a bond is defined generally as the discount rate which makes the present value of the bond's future payments equal to the invoice price of the bond. This broad definition does not, however, suffice to calculate a yield. An analyst must also specify a choice for the compounding period, a method of calculating the length of a fractional compounding period, and how payments are discounted over fractional periods.

Unlike conventional Treasury bonds, the basic yield on a Targeted bond is figured with an *annual* compounding period (to match the frequency of its interest payments) and a 30/360 calendar (to match the interest accrual convention). We first describe this basic yield, and then examine two ways to compute a semi-annually compounded yield on a Targeted bond. The latter is important for comparing Targeted bonds to conventional Treasury bonds.

The Annually Compounded Yield on a Targeted Bond. Consider a Targeted bond with n annual coupons remaining to be paid, and with coupon rate Rcp. Let P denote the quoted price of the bond, A the accrued interest to the settlement date, and Q the size of the next coupon. (Q will be equal to Rcp if the next coupon is a full coupon, and it will be less than Rcp if the bond has a short first coupon which has not yet been paid.)

The annually compounded yield on the Targeted bond is the value of R_m^a which satisfies the equation:

$$P + A = \frac{Q}{(1 + R_m^a)^w} + \frac{Rcp}{(1 + R_m^a)^{1+w}} + \cdots$$

$$+ \frac{Rcp}{(1 + R_m^a)^{n-1+w}} + \frac{100}{(1 + R_m^a)^{n-1+w}} \tag{1}$$

The fraction w is the fraction of a year between settlement and payment of the next coupon, computed with a 30/360 calendar.

To illustrate the application of equation (1), consider the yield on the Targeted 4-year note priced at $99\frac{7}{32}$ for settlement on May 10, 1985. We have already described in Table 1 the payments on the note subsequent to May 10, 1985, and we have calculated accrued interest of 5.97188 to a May 10 settlement date. The invoice price of the bond is, therefore, P + A = 105.19063 (105.19063 = $99\frac{7}{32}$ + 5.97188).

The only other piece of information needed to apply equation (1) is the value of w, the fraction of a year between settlement and the next interest payment date. There are four months and 20 days between the May 10, 1985 settlement date and the next, September 30, 1985, coupon date. Assuming 30-day months and 360-day years, this interval is 140 days or w = .38889 years (.38889 = 140/360).

Using this value of w, equation (1) becomes:

$$105.19063 = \frac{10.39549}{(1 + R_m^a)^{.38889}} + \frac{11.375}{(1 + R_m^a)^{1.38889}}$$

$$+ \frac{11.375}{(1 + R_m^a)^{2.38889}} + \frac{111.375}{(1 + R_m^a)^{3.38889}} \qquad (2)$$

This implies R_m^a = .11626, or 11.626% per annum, compounded annually.

It should be noted that the definition of the yield on a Targeted bond in equation (1) uses compound interest, and not simple interest, in discounting future payments over a fractional period. This parallels the method of computing the yield on most conventional Treasury bonds used by all market participants except the U.S. Treasury. The Treasury has, however, announced that, for Targeted bonds, it also will use equation (1).

A Simply Computed Semi-Annually Compounded Yield on a Targeted Bond. Knowing the annually compounded yield on a Targeted security is useful if that yield is to be compared with other annually compounded yields, but it is not particularly useful for comparison with semi-annually compounded yields. For such comparisons it is important to develop a semi-annual yield on a Targeted bond.

Suppose the annually compounded yield on a Targeted bond is 11.00% per annum. In crude terms, this means that $1 will grow to $1.11 after one year. The same result would follow from investing $1 for two semi-annual periods at a yield of 10.71% per annum, compounded semi-annually ($1.11 = $1.00 · (1 + $\frac{1}{2}$(.1071))^2). More specifically, a yield of 11.00% compounded annually is equivalent to a yield of 10.71% compounded semi-annually.

The semi-annually compounded yield R_m^s which is equivalent in a simple way to the annually compounded yield R_m^a can be found from the equation:

$$(1 + R_m^a) = (1 + \tfrac{1}{2}R_m^s)^2 \qquad (3)$$

Using this equation, an annually compounded yield of 11.626% on the Targeted 4-year note is equivalent to a yield of 11.306% per annum, compounded semi-annually $(1 + .11626 = (1 + \tfrac{1}{2}(.11306))^2)$.

A More Accurate Semi-Annually Compounded Yield on a Targeted Bond. Equation (3) would appear to state an accurate equivalence between the annually compounded yield and the semi-annually compounded yield on a Targeted security. However, the latter yield is not precisely equivalent to the yield on a Targeted bond which would be calculated from the conventions of the market in ordinary Treasury bonds.

To appreciate this claim, let us rewrite equation (1) using the semi-annually compounded yield defined in equation (3):

$$P + A = \frac{Q}{(1 + \tfrac{1}{2}R_m^s)^{2w}} + \frac{Rcp}{(1 + \tfrac{1}{2}R_m^s)^{2+2w}} + \cdots$$

$$+ \frac{Rcp}{(1 + \tfrac{1}{2}R_m^s)^{2n-2+2w}} + \frac{100}{(1 + \tfrac{1}{2}R_m^s)^{2n-2+2w}} \qquad (4)$$

Equation (4) defines a semi-annually compounded yield R_m^s under the assumption that the interval to the next coupon payment is 2w semi-annual periods, and where each subsequent coupon is 2 semi-annual periods further in the future.

In this form the semi-annually compounded yield on the Targeted 4-year note at a price of $99\tfrac{7}{32}$ for settlement on May 10, 1985 would be calculated as the value of R_m^s which solves the equation:

$$105.19063 = \frac{10.39549}{(1 + \tfrac{1}{2}R_m^s)^{.77778}} + \frac{11.375}{(1 + \tfrac{1}{2}R_m^s)^{2.77778}}$$

$$\frac{11.375}{(1 + \tfrac{1}{2}R_m^s)^{4.77778}} + \frac{111.375}{(1 + \tfrac{1}{2}R_m^s)^{6.77778}} \qquad (5)$$

This implies $R_m^a = .11306$, or 11.306% per annum, compounded semi-annually. (We derived the same result above, in a two-step procedure, by using equation (2) to figure the annually compounded yield $R_m^a = 11.626\%$, and then using equation (3) to convert to a semi-annually compounded yield. Equation (5) combines the two steps into a single calculation.)

Now consider the problem of defining, from first principles, the semi-annually compounded yield on a Targeted bond, using the conventions of ordinary Treasury securities. As before, let P be the quoted price of the bond, A the accrued interest, Rcp the coupon rate, Q the size of the next coupon, and n the number of remaining coupons.

The semi-annually compounded yield which is truly equivalent to conventional Treasury yields is the value of R_m which solves the equation:

$$P + A = \frac{Q}{(1 + \frac{1}{2}R_m)^v} + \frac{Rcp}{(1 + \frac{1}{2}R_m)^{2+v}} + \cdots$$

$$+ \frac{Rcp}{(1 + \frac{1}{2}R_m)^{2n-2+v}} + \frac{100}{(1 + \frac{1}{2}R_m)^{2n-2+v}} \qquad (6)$$

The fraction v is the number of semi-annual periods from settlement to the next coupon payment.

If the next coupon payment date is less than six calendar months after settlement, v is the *actual* number of days from settlement to coupon payment, divided by the *actual* number of days in the six calendar months preceding the coupon payment. For example, for a May 10, 1985 settlement, v would be .78571 (.78571 = $\frac{143}{182}$, where there are 143 days between May 10, 1985 and September 30, 1985, and where there are 182 days between March 31, 1985 and September 30, 1985. Note that the 6-month interval begins on March 31, and not on March 30, because 4-year notes pay interest on the last day of a month, rather than on a particular calendar date like the 15th or the 30th.)

If the next coupon payment date is more than six calendar months after settlement, v is 1.0 plus a fraction, where the fraction is the *actual* number of days from settlement to the date six months before the next coupon, divided by the *actual* number of days from the date twelve months before the next coupon to the date six months before the next coupon. (A similar convention is used for long-first-coupon bonds in the ordinary Treasury bond market.) For example, v would be 1.55191 for a December 20, 1984 settlement date (1. for the inter-

val from March 31, 1985 to the September 30, 1985 coupon, plus
.55191, where, .55191 = $\frac{101}{183}$, and where there are 101 days between
December 20, 1984 and March 31, 1985, and 183 days between September 30, 1984 and March 31, 1985.)

Using these actual day-count conventions, the semi-annually
compounded yield on the Targeted 4-year note at a price of $99\frac{7}{32}$ for
settlement on May 10, 1985 is the value of R_m which solves the
equation:

$$105.19063 = \frac{10.39549}{(1 + \frac{1}{2}R_m)^{.78571}} + \frac{11.375}{(1 + \frac{1}{2}R_m)^{2.78571}}$$

$$+ \frac{11.375}{(1 + \frac{1}{2}R_m)^{4.78571}} + \frac{111.375}{(1 + \frac{1}{2}R_m)^{6.78571}} \qquad (7)$$

This implies $R_m = .11299$, or 11.299% per annum, compounded
semi-annually.

It is worth spending a moment to understand how equations (4)
and (6) differ. Both define a semi-annually compounded yield.
However, equation (4) is based on a 30/360 calendar, because the
fraction w was defined originally in equation (1) with such a calendar. Equation (6), on the other hand, is based on an actual calendar.

The difference between equations (4) and (6) is illustrated numerically in equations (5) and (7). Equation (5) uses a 30/360 calendar
convention, and says there are .77778 semi-annual periods between
a May 10, 1985 settlement date and a September 30, 1985 coupon
payment date. Using an actual calendar convention, equation (7)
says there are .78571 semi-annual periods between May 10, 1985
and September 30, 1985. The longer length of time between settlement and the next coupon payment is the basis for figuring the
lower semi-annually compounded yield of 11.299% on the Targeted
bond in equation (7).

Since yields on ordinary Treasury securities are computed with
an actual calendar, equation (6) provides a definition of the semi-annually compounded yield on a Targeted security which is appropriate for comparing with the yield on a conventional Treasury security.
As a practical matter, however, this yield will rarely differ from the
yield defined in equation (4) by more than 1 or 2 basis points.

THE EXCHANGE OPTION

The only feature of a Targeted security remaining to be examined is the option to exchange it for a conventional Treasury issue. There are two parts to analyzing the exchange option. We first describe the adjustment payment made to or by the Treasury in the course of effecting an exchange. We then analyze the price relationship between a Targeted issue and a conventional issue consistent with a decision to exchange the former for the latter. This is a matter of computing the "intrinsic value" of the Targeted issue, given the market price of the conventional security. (The actual price of a Targeted security will likely exceed its contemporaneous intrinsic value, because of the special tax disclosure provisions for Targeted securities.)

The Net Cash Adjustment Upon Exchange

The option to exchange a Targeted security for a conventional issue can be appreciated by examining an actual example. The Treasury sold $1 billion of the Targeted $11\frac{3}{8}$% notes of September 30, 1988 in October, 1984. Holders of the notes have a continuing option to convert them into the conventional $11\frac{3}{8}$% notes of September 30, 1988 at a price relationship which leaves the Treasury indifferent as to whether it is paying on the Targeted notes or on the conventional notes.

The price relationship defining the indifference point of the Treasury is derived from the average annually compounded *auction* yield of the Targeted notes. For a given exchange date, the Treasury computes the value of the Targeted note at this yield, and the value of the conventional note at an equivalent semi-annually compounded yield. If the latter value exceeds the former, the Treasury is due a cash adjustment payment (because it is issuing a "more valuable" security than what it is receiving in exchange). If the former exceeds the latter, the Treasury will make a cash payment.

To complete the explanation of the adjustment payment, we have to specify precisely how the Treasury calculates the values of the Targeted and conventional notes.

Valuing the Targeted Note. The Treasury values a Targeted note for exchange purposes using equation (1). For an exchange date of May 10, 1985, the Treasury will value the Targeted 4-year note at 105.77154 percent of principal value. This figure, denoted V_t, is calculated from equation (1) using the cash flow schedule in Table 1, $w = .38889$, and the average auction yield of $R_m^a = 11.41\%$ per annum, compounded annually:

$$V_t = \frac{10.39549}{(1.+.1141)^{.38889}} + \frac{11.375}{(1.+.1141)^{1.38889}}$$

$$+ \frac{11.375}{(1.+.1141)^{2.38889}} + \frac{111.375}{(1.+.1141)^{3.38889}} \tag{8}$$

or:

$$V_t = 105.77154$$

It should be noted that this "value" is equivalent to an invoice price, and includes accrued interest as well as principal. It should also be noted that this "value" has no necessary relation to the price at which the Targeted note is trading in the secondary markets at the time of exchange. It is a function only of the average auction yield on the note.

Valuing the Conventional Note. The Treasury values a conventional note for exchange purposes using an equation which has no analog in any other sector of the Treasury market.

Consider a conventional note which has n semi-annual coupons remaining to be paid, an annual coupon rate of Rcp, and which will pay Q on its next coupon. (Q will equal $\frac{1}{2}$Rcp if the next coupon is a regular coupon, and will be less than $\frac{1}{2}$Rcp if the note has a short-first-coupon which has not yet been paid.)

The value V_c of the conventional note for exchange purposes is given by the equation:

$$V_c = \frac{Q}{(1+\frac{1}{2}R_m^s)^u} + \frac{\frac{1}{2}Rcp}{(1+\frac{1}{2}R_m^s)^{1+u}} + \cdots$$

$$+ \frac{\frac{1}{2}Rcp}{(1+R_m^s)^{n-1+u}} + \frac{100}{(1+R_m^s)^{n-1+u}} \tag{9}$$

The fraction u is the fraction of a semi-annual period between the exchange date and the date of payment of the next coupon, figured using a 30/360 calendar. The yield R_m^s is the semi-annually compounded yield which is equivalent, *in the sense of equation (3),* to the annually compounded average auction yield on the Targeted note. This computation is unique in the Treasury markets, because it is the only instance where a conventional Treasury security is valued with a 30/360 calendar.

To illustrate the use of equation (9), consider valuing the $11\frac{3}{8}\%$ conventional note of September 30, 1988 for exchange on May 10, 1985. The cash flows from that note are shown in Table 5–2.

There are four months and 20 days between the May 10, 1985 exchange date and the September 30, 1985 date of payment of the next coupon. (Observe that the first coupon, due March 31, 1985, was paid before the exchange.) Using a 30/360 calendar, this is 140 days, or .77778 semi-annual periods ($.77778 = \frac{140}{180}$, where there are assumed to be 180 days in a single six month interval).

Using this fraction for u, and using the payment schedule in Table 2, equation (9) becomes:

TABLE 5–2.
**Future Cash Flows from the Conventional
$11^3/_8\%$ Note of September 30, 1985.**

Payment Date	Payment Amount
3/31/1985	4.71875*
9/30/1985	5.6875
3/31/1986	5.6875
9/30/1986	5.6875
3/31/1987	5.6875
9/30/1987	5.6875
3/31/1988	5.6875
9/30/1988	105.6875

* Short-first-coupon, figured as
    $4.71875 = 5.6875 \cdot (^{151}/_{182})$,
where there are 151 days from 10/31/1984 to
3/31/1985, and 182 days from 9/30/1984 to
3/31/1985.

$$V_c = \frac{5.6875}{(1 + \frac{1}{2}R_m^s)^{.77778}} + \frac{5.6875}{(1 + \frac{1}{2}R_m^s)^{1.77778}} + \cdots$$

$$+ \frac{5.6875}{(1 + \frac{1}{2}R_m^s)^{6.77778}} + \frac{100}{(1 + \frac{1}{2}R_m^s)^{6.77778}} \tag{10}$$

The average auction yield on the Targeted note was 11.41% per annum, compounded annually, so we have from equation (3) that $R_m^s = 11.10\%$. Using this yield in equation (10) gives a value for the conventional 4-year note of $V_c = 101.99698$ percent of principal value.

The Net Adjustment Payment. Since the Treasury values the Targeted 4-year note at 105.77154 and the conventional 4-year note at 101.99698, it will pay 3.77455 percent of principal upon an exchange of the notes on May 10, 1985. Against receiving $10 million principal amount of the Targeted notes, it will issue $10 million of conventional notes, and pay a $377,455 cash adjustment.

Table 5–3 shows cash adjustments for converting the Targeted 4-year note at various date during its lifetime. (The dates are month-end

TABLE 5–3.
Adjustment Payments for Converting the Foreign-Targeted 11³/₈% Note of September 30, 1988 Into the Conventional 11³/₈% Note of September 30, 1988.

Exchange Date	Adjustment Payment[a]
1/31/1985	.94127
2/28/1985	.94879
4/ 1/1985	− 3.73044
4/30/1985	− 3.76319
5/31/1985	− 3.79853
7/ 1/1985	− 3.83303
7/31/1985	− 3.86786
9/ 2/1985	− 3.90417
9/30/1985	.77072
10/31/1985	.74728
12/ 2/1985	.75411
12/31/1985	.76055
1/31/1986	.76728

TABLE 5-3—*Continued*
Adjustment Payments for Converting the Foreign-Targeted 11³/₈% Note of September 30, 1988 Into the Conventional 11³/₈% Note of September 30, 1988.

Exchange Date	Adjustment Payment[a]
2/28/1986	.77338
3/31/1986	− 4.90660
4/30/1986	− 4.91918
6/ 2/1986	− 4.96681
6/30/1986	− 5.00887
7/31/1986	− 5.05585
9/ 1/1986	− 5.10174
9/30/1986	.54102
10/31/1986	.51549
12/ 1/1986	.52000
12/31/1986	.52455
2/ 2/1987	.52929
3/ 2/1987	.53392
3/31/1987	− 5.14906
4/30/1987	− 5.16383
6/ 1/1987	− 5.21225
6/30/1987	− 5.25796
7/31/1987	− 5.30727
8/31/1987	− 5.35543
9/30/1987	.28510
11/ 2/1987	.25733
11/30/1987	.25936
12/31/1987	.26163
2/ 1/1988	.26384
2/29/1988	.26592
3/31/1988	− 5.41918
5/ 2/1988	− 5.43966
5/31/1988	− 5.48736
6/30/1988	− 5.53547
8/ 1/1988	− 5.58737
8/31/1988	− 5.63806

[a] Positive values are payments *to* the Treasury, negative values are payments *from* the Treasury.

dates, or the first weekday thereafter.) Two characteristics are evident. First, exchanges effected between March 31 and September 29, inclusive, result in a payment *from* the Treasury, while exchanges between September 30 and March 30 require a payment *to* the Treasury.

The payments *from* the Treasury for exchange between March 31 and September 29 reflect the different frequency of interest payments on the Targeted and conventional notes. For example, an exchange on April 30 involves giving up a note with 7 months of accrued interest and receiving a note with only 1 month of accrued interest. The adjustment payment by the Treasury for an April 30 exchange is largely compensation for the 6 month difference in accrued interest.

Exchanges executed between September 30 and March 30 involve swapping securities with comparable amounts of accrued interest. Payments *to* the Treasury for these exchanges reflect the value of getting interest semi-annually instead of annually.

If we look at the September 30 exchanges in Table 3 (for which neither note carries any accrued interest), we can isolate the second important characteristic of the adjustment payments:

Exchange Date	Adjustment Payment
9/30/1985	.77072
9/30/1986	.54102
9/30/1987	.28510

These payments *to* the Treasury reflect *only* the value of going from a note paying $11\frac{3}{8}$% annual interest to a note paying $11\frac{3}{8}$% semi-annual interest. While the latter note is always more valuable, because it pays the same dollars sooner, the added value declines as the notes approach maturity. This is why exchange payments *to* the Treasury decrease, and exchange payments *from* the Treasury increase, as in the notes in Table 3 age.

The Intrinsic Value of a Targeted Security

Having described in detail the adjustment payments associated with exchange of a Targeted security, we are ready to define the "intrinsic value" of the security. Intrinsic value is most easily defined as the answer to the following question: for settlement and exchange on a given date, at what price does it make sense to buy the Targeted security, exchange it, and sell the conventional security obtained in the exchange, recognizing the adjustment payment in the exchange and the market price of the conventional security.

Suppose we examine this question for the Targeted 4-year note for a May 10, 1985 settlement and exchange date. On that date the accrued interest on the Targeted note is 5.97188 percent of principal, the accrued interest on the conventional 4-year note is 1.24317 percent of principal, and (as shown earlier) exchange results in a payment of 3.77455 from the Treasury. Against selling the conventional note at a quoted price of P, a dealer could, as a breakeven proposition, buy (and convert) the Targeted note at a quoted price of P – .954, computed as:

P	quoted sale price of the conventional 4-year note
+1.24317	accrued interest received on the conventional 4-year note
+3.77455	exchange payment received from the Treasury
−5.97188	accrued interest paid on the Targeted 4-year note
P – .954	breakeven quoted purchase price of the Targeted 4-year note.

This means that the Targeted note has an intrinsic value on May 10, 1985 equal to the quoted market price of the conventional note, less .954. If the Targeted note is quoted cheaper than this value, it is profitable (and riskless) to buy the Targeted note, convert it into the conventional note, and sell the conventional note.

Table 5–4 shows the parity price spread, or maximum price spread, between the Targeted 4-year note and the conventional 4-year note at various dates. Note that the parity spread is in terms of quoted prices, after accounting for interest accruals and exchange adjustment payments.

As shown in the table, the parity price spread is always negative. This follows because a note paying interest of $11\frac{3}{8}\%$ annually is not as valuable as a note paying half that amount twice as frequently. The spread goes towards zero as the notes age, because the value of

TABLE 5-4.
Parity Price Spread of the
Foreign-Targeted 11³/8% Note of
September 30, 1988 Compared to the
Conventional 11³/8% Note of
September 30, 1988.

Settlement and Exchange Date	Parity Price Spread
1/1/1985	-.891
7/1/1985	-.891
1/1/1986	-.730
7/1/1986	-.693
1/1/1987	-.494
7/1/1987	-.444
1/1/1988	-.247
7/1/1988	-.166

swapping out of an annual coupon into a semi-annual coupon declines as the number of coupons remaining to be paid gets smaller.

Why the Targeted Note Can Trade Above Its Intrinsic Value

There are two reasons why the Targeted 4-year note can trade at a price in excess of its intrinsic value. First, exchanging the Targeted note for the conventional note can sometimes produce a sacrifice in yield, when the yields on the notes are computed at intrinsic value and market price, respectively. In these cases a U.S. investor might offer to "pay" more than the Treasury for the Targeted note in order to pick up yield. Second, and more important, the price of the Targeted note will likely be enhanced by the special tax disclosure provisions on the note. The value of these provisions are not included in the computation of intrinsic value. We will discuss each of these reasons.

A Yield Analysis of the Exchange Option. Table 5-5 shows an array of prices and yields on the conventional and Targeted 4-year

TABLE 5-5.
Intrinsic Value, and Yield at Intrinsic Value, of the Foreign-Targeted
11³/₈% Note of September 30, 1988 for Settlement and Exchange on
May 10, 1985.

Conventional Note		Foreign-Targeted Note		
Quoted Price	Yield	Intrinsic Value	Yield	Yield Spread
105	9.604%	104 ¹/₃₂	9.645%	− 4.1 bp.
104	9.948	103 ¹/₃₂	9.981	− 3.3
103	10.296	102 ¹/₃₂	10.321	− 2.5
102	10.648	101 ¹/₃₂	10.665	− 1.7
101	11.004	100 ¹/₃₂	11.013	− .9
100	11.365	99 ¹/₃₂	11.366	− .1
99	11.731	98 ¹/₃₂	11.723	.8
98	12.101	97 ¹/₃₂	12.084	1.7
97	12.476	96 ¹/₃₂	12.450	2.6
96	12.856	95 ¹/₃₂	12.821	3.5
95	13.241	94 ¹/₃₂	13.197	4.4

notes for settlement and exchange on May 10, 1985. The prices for the conventional note were chosen arbitrarily, and the yield on that note was computed at each price. The intrinsic value of the Targeted note was then computed at each price for the conventional note, and the yield on the Targeted note was computed at each intrinsic value.

To appreciate the significance of Table 5-5, consider the position of a seller of the Targeted note when the conventional note is trading at 105, or at a yield of 9.604% per annum, compounded semi-annually. If he exchanges his Targeted note (receiving 3.77455 points from the Treasury as described above) and then sells the conventional note at 105, he will have effectively sold the Targeted note at a quoted price equal to its intrinsic value: $104\frac{1}{32}$.

On the other hand, suppose other investors are willing to swap out of the conventional note and into the Targeted note at anything better than an even yield. Against selling the conventional note at 105 (or at a yield of 9.604%), they would buy the Targeted note at any yield above 9.604%, or at any price below $104\frac{5}{32}$. In this case they would be willing to "outbid" the effective price of $104\frac{1}{32}$ offered by the Treasury.

Generalizing this argument, the Targeted 4-year note will trade above its intrinsic value as long as two conditions are satisfied:

1. investors are willing to swap out of the conventional note into the Targeted note at anything better than an even yield spread, and
2. the conventional note is trading above par.

Of course, there is nothing to guarantee that the Targeted note will never trade cheaper, on a yield basis, than the conventional note, but it is probably a reasonable working hypothesis, given the similarity of the two notes.

Looking at Table 5–5 shows that, if the conventional note is trading at a discount, the Targeted note can trade at its intrinsic value and still be more expensive, on a yield basis, than the conventional note. For example, if the conventional note is priced at 95, for a 13.241% yield, the intrinsic value of the Targeted note is $94\frac{1}{32}$. At this price the Targeted note yields 13.197%, or about $4\frac{1}{2}$ basis points *less* than the conventional note. This implies that yield pickup swaps will not support the price of the Targeted note above its intrinsic value if yields are above about $11\frac{3}{8}$%.

The Value of the Special Tax Disclosure Feature on the Targeted Note.   Thus far we have examined the value of the Targeted 4-year note relative to the price of the conventional 4-year note in terms of the exchange option and in terms of yield swaps in the secondary market. Of course, the primary difference between the two notes is the different tax disclosure provisions.

Following the October 24, 1984 auctions, the Targeted 4-year note traded at yields 15 to 30 basis points lower than the yields on the conventional 4-year note. This yield spread is far in excess of anything that comes out of an intrinsic value or yield swap analysis, and most likely reflects the value of the tax disclosure provisions. As long as foreign investors continue to be willing to give up 15 to 30 basis points of yield to preserve their anonymity, Targeted securities can be expected to trade well above their intrinsic value.

CONCLUSION

This chapter examined three characteristics of Foreign-Targeted Treasury securities. Their pricing and cash flow characteristics were analyzed, including calculation of accrued interest and the size of an odd first coupon using a 30/360 calendar, and calculation of annually and semi-annually compounded yields. The more qualitative aspects of the securities were examined, including their special tax disclosure provisions. The option to exchange a Targeted issue for a conventional Treasury bond was analyzed, and the notion of the intrinsic value of a Targeted bond was developed. This last feature is important, because it links Targeted bonds directly to the conventional markets, and provides a benchmark for estimating the value of the special disclosure provisions of a Targeted security.

CHAPTER 6

F. WARD MCCARTHY, JR. In 1982, as Senior Economist for the Federal Reserve Bank of Richmond, VA., Mr. McCarthy supervised its Bank Studies Division and was a member of the policy committee that briefed the bank president for federal open market committee meetings. In June of 1984 he became Senior Money Market Economist for Merrill Lynch Capital Markets.

Mr. McCarthy earned his Ph.D. in Economics in 1982 at Rutgers University, where he has also taught Econometrics and Financial & Monetary Economics.

RAYMOND W. STONE. From 1974–1976, Mr. Stone was in the research department of the Federal Reserve Bank of New York. Subsequently, he served two years (1979–1981) as Senior Economist for Fidelity Bank in Philadelphia. In January 1982, he became Vice President, Fixed Income Research, for McCarthy, Crisanty & Maffei, where he remained until March, 1984. Currently, Mr. Stone is Chief Financial Economist for Merrill Lynch Capital Markets.

Mr. Stone earned his Ph.D. in 1980 from Rutgers University.

BASICS OF FED WATCHING

F. Ward McCarthy, Jr., Ph. D.
Senior Money Market Economist
Merrill Lynch Capital Markets

and

Raymond W. Stone, Ph. D.
Chief Financial Economist
Merrill Lynch Capital Markets

INTRODUCTION

As the nation's central bank, the Federal Reserve System (Fed) plays a critical role in the U.S. credit markets. The Fed affects the general direction and level of short-term interest rates in the conduct of monetary policy. Depending on economic conditions and market psychology, the Fed also exerts a degree of influence on medium-term and longer-term rates as well. As a consequence, an understanding of the formulation and implementation of monetary policy is essential for participants in the market for Treasury securities.

There is much confusion about the way the Federal Reserve formulates and implements monetary policy. Policy deliberations are held in private, and policy decisions are not formally released to the general public until several weeks after policy decisions are made. In addition, the implementation of monetary policy is a sophisticated

127

process that is not always readily decipherable but is often obscured in a barrage of Federal Reserve data and jargon.

Because of the importance of understanding the Federal Reserve, a specialized industry called "Fed watching" has developed to reduce the uncertainty surrounding Fed actions. "Fed watchers" carefully study the behavior of the policymakers and the entrails of Fed data for hints of Fed policy intentions, and provide projections of Fed open market activity and monetary data that are important factors in the determination of interest rates.

THE FORMULATION OF MONETARY POLICY

Monetary policy is formulated jointly by the Board of Governors of the Federal Reserve System and the 12 Reserve Banks. The objective of monetary policy is to control monetary and credit aggregates in an attempt to promote full employment, price stability and orderly foreign exchange and financial markets. The Fed utilizes three primary instruments in implementing monetary policy. First, the Board of Governors and the twelve regional Reserve Banks jointly determine the thrust of open market transactions in securities markets through the Federal Open-Market Committee (FOMC). Open-market operations are conducted by the domestic trading desk of the Federal Reserve Bank of New York and are the most frequently utilized and the most flexible of the policy tools of the Fed. Second, the Directors of the Reserve Banks can petition the Board of Governors to consider changes in the discount rate. Finally, the Board of Governors sets reserve requirements that deposit-taking institutions must meet. The structure of the Federal Reserve System is presented in Exhibit 6–1.

The FOMC

The Federal Open-Market Committee directs the formulation and implementation of monetary policy through open market operations in the securities markets. The FOMC is comprised of all seven Governors from the Board of Governors and the twelve Reserve

EXHIBIT 6-1
Structure of the Federal Reserve System

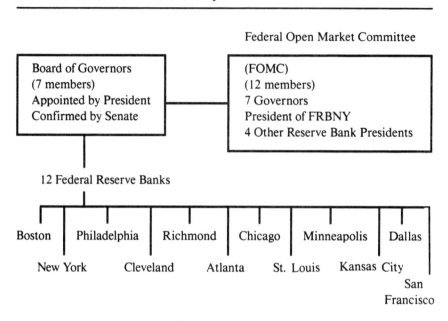

Bank Presidents. The Committee meets eight times a year to assess economic developments and determine the thrust of monetary policy until the next FOMC meeting. All members of the FOMC participate in policy discussions at each meeting, but only twelve members vote on policy matters at any one meeting. The seven Governors and the President of the Federal Reserve Bank of New York vote on policy decisions at each meeting, with the other Reserve Bank Presidents serving as voting members on a rotating basis. The Chairman of the Board of Governors presides at each meeting and lays the ground rules under which policy discussions and the ensuing decisions are made.

FOMC deliberations are directed primarily at the determination of the appropriate thrust of open market operations, but occasionally also include discussion of the discount rate and reserve requirements when it is appropriate.

Factors Affecting Policy Decisions

Exhibit 6–2 lists several factors that influence monetary policy decisions. According to the Humphrey-Hawkins Act of 1978, the FOMC must set annual growth objectives for money and credit that are consistent with the attainment of long-run economic growth and price stability. The FOMC attempts to set a monetary course that balances the growth/inflation trade-off. That is, to provide sufficient stimulation that the pace of economic activity will generate more jobs, higher incomes and greater purchasing power, but to provide sufficient restraint that inflation remains subdued and does not erode the purchasing power of income, the value of the financial assets and the general standard of living.

Other financial considerations are important, however. For example, the foreign exchange value of the dollar plays an increasing role in monetary policy decisions because of the advances in communication and transportation technologies that increased the interdependencies of national economies. The value of the dollar is a major determinant of the prices of and, therefore, the demand for goods imported into this country and also the nature and volume of foreign capital flows into U.S. financial markets. Because of the importance of financial institutions to the overall health of the economy, the FOMC is also quite sensitive to any financial strains, such as bank failure, that may occur in the financial sector. While the Fed's role as lender of last resort is the primary tool for alleviating widespread financial distress, a degree of accommodation on monetary policy may at times be the ounce of prevention that precludes a more serious set of circumstances.

EXHIBIT 6–2
Factors Influencing Policy Decisions

- Growth of the Various Monetary Aggregates
- Pace of Economic Expansion
- Behavior of Measures of Inflation
- Foreign Exchange Developments
- Strains in the Financial Sector
- Political Setting

Finally, the political setting can exert an important influence on policy in spite of institutional safeguards against political manipulation. Each of the members of the Board of Governors is appointed by the President subject to the review and approval of the Senate Banking Committee. In order to prevent any presidential administration from exerting undue influence on the Board of Governors, the Governors are appointed for fourteen-year terms and the terms are staggered so that a new appointment is made every two years. These safeguards are effective, however, only if each appointee serves the full term of appointment since vacancies caused by premature departures from office are filled by presidential appointment. Because of the obvious importance of economic developments to the political arena, the Fed is subject to other forms of political pressure periodically. Political figures often resort to "jaw-boning" either to affect policy decisions or to place the mantle of blame on the Fed for economic and financial developments that are considered to be political liabilities. Finally, since the Fed's authority as central bank is granted by an act of Congress, the threat of loss of power or even dissolution can be used to influence monetary policy decisions.

FOMC Decisions

As indicated in Exhibit 6–3, there are two types of decisions that the FOMC must make: long-term and short-term.

EXHIBIT 6–3
Types of Decisions

	Long-Term
Set in February and Reviewed in July	Annual Targets for Monetary Aggregates
	Short-Term
Determined at Each of the 8 FOMC Meetings including February and July	Short-Run Objectives for Monetary Aggregates Degree of Reserve Restraint Consultation Range for Federal Funds Rate

EXHIBIT 6–4
Ranges of Monetary Growth 1985 and 1986
(in Percent)

	1985 Ranges Set in February	1985 Ranges Set in July	1986 Tentative	1985 Actual QIV 1984 to QII 1985
M1	4 to 7	3 to 8*	4 to 7	10.5
M2	6 to 9	6 to 9	6 to 9	8.8
M3	6 to 9½	6 to 9½	6 to 9	7.9
Total Domestic Nonfinancial Sector Debt	9 to 12	9 to 12	8 to 11	12.8*

*Annual rate of growth from the second quarter to fourth quarter 1985.

Source: Board of Governors, The Federal Reserve System.

At the February and July meetings, the FOMC addresses the annual objectives for the growth rates of various monetary and credit aggregates in the current calendar year, as required by the Humphrey-Hawkins Act. To meet this requirement, the FOMC sets annual target ranges for the monetary aggregates M1, M2 and M3, as well as a broader credit aggregate.[1] The Chairman of the Board of Governors reports these growth objectives to the House and Senate Banking Committees every February. Exhibit 6–4 presents the annual target ranges for the monetary and credit aggregates from previous Humphrey-Hawkins testimony. At the Mid-Year Review in July, the Chairman discusses any revisions that are made to the annual target ranges for the current year and presents preliminary target ranges for the upcoming year. Over the course of the year, monetary policy is intended to be consistent with the

[1] M1 is comprised of travelers checks, currency, demand deposits and other checkable deposits such as NOW and ATS accounts. M2 is comprised of M1 plus overnight RP's and Eurodollars, savings deposits, small time deposits, money market deposit accounts and general purpose money market funds. M3 is comprised of M2 plus large certificates of deposit, term RP's, and term Eurodollars and institutional money market funds.

EXHIBIT 6-5
M1 Growth Ranges and Actual M1 (Billions of Dollars)

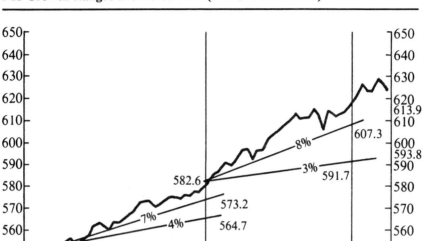

attainment of these growth objectives for the monetary and credit aggregates subject to the performance of the economy and developments in foreign exchange and financial markets.

Exhibits 6-5, 6 and 7 illustrate the behavior of the primary monetary aggregates M1, M2 and M3 relative to their respective annual target ranges in recent years.

At each of the eight meetings a year, the FOMC makes short-run decisions on the implementation of policy and directs the trading desk at the Federal Reserve Bank of New York on the thrust of open market operations in the intermeeting period. Specifically, the FOMC sets short-run objectives for the monetary aggregates, an initial level of short-term adjustment borrowing from the Federal Reserve discount window that is the key to the open market desk's management of bank reserves, and a consultation range for the federal funds rate. The FOMC's intention is to set a short-run strategy

EXHIBIT 6–6
M2 Growth Ranges and Actual M2 (Billions of Dollars)

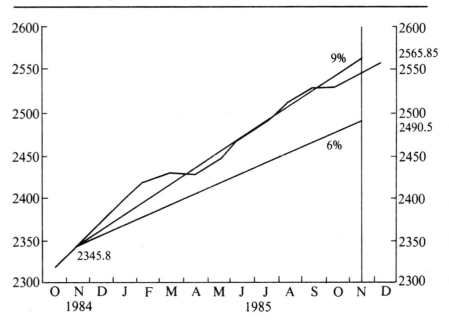

for pursuing the annual objectives for monetary and credit growth, but these decisions are considered against the backdrop of developments in the economy, foreign exchange markets and the prospective inflationary pressures.

The short-run monetary objectives for the monetary aggregates are quarterly objectives that are set at the beginning of each quarter against the backdrop of economic and financial developments. These targets are reviewed during the quarter. The growth objectives are stated in terms of seasonally adjusted annual rates, using the monthly average of the aggregate at the end of each quarter as the basis for comparison. For example, fourth quarter growth is expressed as growth in the September through December period with the growth rate being expressed as:

EXHIBIT 6-7
M3 Growth Ranges and Actual M3 (Billions of Dollars)

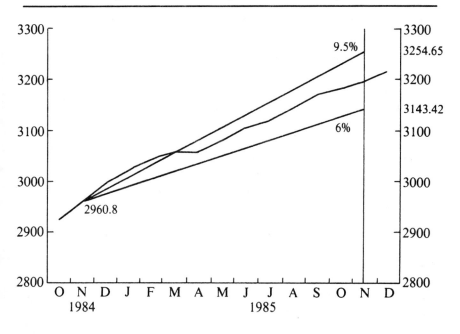

$$\text{Quarterly growth rate} = \left[\left(\frac{\text{December level}}{\text{September level}}\right) - 1\right] \times 4$$

In attempting to meet these short-term objectives, the Fed will not necessarily assume that the growth will be distributed evenly over the course of the quarter. The Fed will take into account seasonal factors that may affect money growth, such as the IRA season or tax refunds, that may not be fully accounted for by seasonal adjustment factors. Furthermore, the FOMC reviews the monetary aggregates against the backdrop of developments in the economy and financial markets and the relative growth of all the monetary aggregates. M1 growth has typically been given the greatest weight in policy deliberations, but the Fed has, at times, disregarded M1 growth that exceeded specified objectives when a tighter policy appeared to be inappropriate in the economic and inflation environment.[2] In the past, when the FOMC has been uncertain about the proper interpretation of M1, it has weighed M1 growth against the behavior of the broader aggregates, M2 and M3, or placed greater emphasis on the behavior of these aggregates.

The initial borrowings level specified in the directive determines the nature of the open market desk's reserve management in the period directly following the FOMC meeting. The Committee has three choices: It can raise, lower or leave unchanged the borrowings assumption as it wishes to tighten, ease or leave policy implementation unchanged. The time frame for any borrowings level is unspecified. An initial borrowings assumption may remain unchanged for an entire intermeeting period or it may be adjusted as economic and financial developments unfold. "Open-ended" directives permit adjustments in policy implementation between FOMC meetings.

To facilitate the decision process, the FOMC is presented with a thorough analysis of financial and economic developments and a menu of policy alternatives regarding the monetary aggregates, bank reserves and the funds rate that are prepared by the staff of the Board of Governors. Each of the alternatives represents a strategy for the implementation of short-term policy that is consistent with the long-term policy objectives. Exhibit 6–8 serves as a useful demonstration.

Alternatives "A," "B" and "C" represent strategies for an "easier," "unchanged," and "tighter" policy implementation respectively. For example, alternative "A" provides for the fastest money growth and

[2] The Fed's willingness to rigorously target M1 often depends on the behavior of M1 velocity, the ratio of gross national product (GNP) to M1. M1 is a reliable indicator of economic activity and, therefore, should be targeted rigorously when M1 velocity is stable. If velocity is unstable, rigorous targeting of M1 would be inappropriate. Volumes of research address the velocity issue. Velocity is often an issue at FOMC meetings and a factor of FOMC policy decisions. For example, at the FOMC held October 5, 1982, the FOMC de-emphasized M1 and established a "monitoring range" rather than a target range for the aggregate because of aberrant velocity behavior. In July 1984, the M1 target range was informally reinstated as velocity returned to normal behavior. In July 1985, the Fed again responded to aberrant velocity. This time the decision was made to raise the base for the target and expand the growth range from a 4% to 8% range to a 3% to 7% range.

EXHIBIT 6–8
Short-Run Menu of Policy Alternatives

	Alternative "A" (Easier)	Alternative "B" (Unchanged)	Alternative "C" (Tighter)
M1 December–September	7%	6%	5%
M2 December–September	9%	9%	7%
M3 December–September	9%	8%	7%
Funds Consultation Range	6 to 10%	6 to 10%	6 to 10%
Initial Borrowings Assumption	$400 min.	$600 min.	$800 min.

the lowest initial level for short-term adjustment borrowing from the Fed. The borrowing target is a key variable in the open market desk's management of bank reserves; the lower the borrowing objective, the more generous the open market desk's provision of nonborrowed reserves to the banking system.[3]

Alternative "A" might be the appropriate choice for short-term policy implementation if money growth were below target, the pace of economic activity were substandard, inflation were subdued and conditions in foreign exchange and financial markets were appropriate. At the other extreme is Alternative "C" which provides for a "tighter" policy implementation as evidenced by slower growth in the monetary aggregates and a higher initial level of borrowing from the discount window of $800 million—the latter indicating a more stingy provision of reserves in the open market desk's management of bank reserves through open market operations. A tighter policy implementation might be appropriate were the monetary aggregates above target, the economy growing rapidly and inflation accelerating. Finally, for Alternative "B" the monetary growth targets are slower than Alternative "A," but faster than Alternative "C." The initial borrowing level is higher than Alternative "A," but lower than Alternative "C" and unchanged from the previous FOMC

---

[3] The mechanics of the open market desk's reserve management will be discussed in greater detail in the following section.

meeting. Therefore, Alternative "B" is consistent with the reserve provision by the open market desk that is unchanged from the previous meeting, less generous than that provided by Alternative "A" but more generous than Alternative "C." A selection of Alternative "B" suggests satisfaction with the general nature of economic and financial developments.

Before reaching a decision on the implementation of policy, each of the members of the FOMC presents his or her view on economic and financial developments in light of the analyses and projections that the Board of Governors' staff prepared as the basis for the menu of policy alternatives. Perceptions of economic and financial developments may vary widely among the FOMC members because of different individual backgrounds, experiences and economic indoctrination, but also because economic and financial trends are usually difficult to decipher without the advantage of hindsight. During this go-around, each FOMC member focuses on the economic developments which the individual believes should be key to the policy decision.

Following the discussion of current economic and financial conditions, the FOMC must decide on the appropriate directive. The voting members vote for a choice of policy alternatives and, in the process, articulate a view that each member hopes will draw support for his or her favored alternative. Because the FOMC wants to maintain the support and confidence of the financial markets, a concerted attempt is made to gain a unanimity of opinion. To that end, adjustments are sometimes made to a policy alternative that is favored by the majority of members, but not all, in the hope of gaining support from one or more members who object to specific aspects of the favored alternative or, perhaps, favor another alternative altogether. For example, an FOMC member who is satisfied with the economy's performance but concerned about money growth might be persuaded to vote for no change in policy implementation rather than a tightening if the monetary targets were lowered. Many times a persuasive Chairman can suggest adjustments to policy alternatives that will satisfy all the voting members. One means of doing so is to choose a conditional policy directive that makes implementation "open-ended" depending on future developments. Even so, on occasion one or more members may dissent from the majority decision. When this occurs, the voting member must state the reason for doing so.

When the FOMC finally agrees on a policy implementation alternative, it sends a policy directive to the New York trading desk. This policy directive determines the thrust of monetary policy until the following FOMC meeting. The results of the current FOMC meeting are not released to the public until the Friday following the next FOMC meeting. At that time, the Fed releases a record of the current FOMC meeting that includes a summary of the discussion of the economy and the main policy discussion, a copy of the directive to the trading desk and the voting record, including reasons for dissent. In spite of the delay between the FOMC meeting and the release of the record of the meeting, market participants study these records in great detail for explanations of past developments as well as for clues about the future direction of Fed policy.

THE IMPLEMENTATION OF POLICY

The Directive to the Open Market Desk

The formulation of the appropriate policy decision begins with the FOMC's assessment of economic and financial developments and ends with a vote on a policy alternative. The implementation of the appropriate policy begins with the directive to the open market desk and ends with an adjustment to the trading desk's management of bank reserves through open market operations. The directive is the link between policy decisions and policy implementation. The language used in the directives is very specialized and stylized, but has very specific meaning. Exhibits 6–9 and 6–10 present excerpts from policy directives of two FOMC meetings, March 26–27, 1984 when policy was tightened and December 17–18, 1984 when policy was eased.

In each of the directives, the FOMC set specific short-term targets for the monetary aggregates and related it with a specific strategy for reserve management or "reserve pressures" through an initial discount window borrowing objective. In March of 1984, the

---

EXHIBIT 6-9
Directive Issues to Open Market Desk Following the March 26–27, 1984
FOMC Meeting When Policy Was Tightened

"[In the short run the committee seeks to maintain pressures on bank reserve positions judged to be consistent with growth in M1, M2, and M3 at annual rates of around $6\frac{1}{2}$, 8, and $8\frac{1}{2}$ percent, respectively, during the period from March to June.]* Greater reserve restraint *would* be acceptable somewhat lesser restraint *might* be acceptable if growth of the monetary aggregates slowed significantly; in either case, such a change would be considered in the context of appraisals of the continuing strength of the business expansion, inflationary pressures, and the rate of credit growth.**

The Chairman may call for Committee consultation if it appears to the Manager of Domestic Operations that pursuit of the monetary objectives and related reserve paths during the period before the next meeting is likely to be associated with federal funds rate persistently outside of range of $7\frac{1}{2}$ to $11\frac{1}{2}$ percent.***

Votes for this action: Messrs. Volcker, Solomon, Boehne, Boykin, Corrigan, Mrs. Horn, Messrs. Partee, Rice, and Mrs. Teeters. Votes against this action: Messrs. Gramley, Martin, and Wallick.****

---

*This sentence sets guidelines for each monetary aggregate and makes reference indirectly to the initial borrowings assumption . . . i.e., pressures on bank reserve positions. At this meeting, the borrowings assumption was raised from $650 million to $1,000 million.

**Note: The use of the word "would" vs. "might." This implies that the Fed would be more prompt in further tightening in the intra-meeting period than easing.

***Consultation range for funds rate.

****Split vote 9 to 3; Gramley and Wallich wanted still tighter policy, while Martin argued against tightening.

FOMC lowered the growth targets for the monetary aggregates and tightened policy implementation by increasing the "degree of reserve restraint" by raising the initial level of adjustment borrowing from the discount window. In December of 1984, the FOMC raised the growth targets for the monetary aggregates and implemented an easier policy and an easier "degree of reserve restraint" by lowering the initial borrowings assumption. Both directives also include

EXHIBIT 6–10
**Directive Issued Following December 17–18, 1984 When
Policy Was Eased**

"[In the implementation of policy in the short run, the Committee seeks
to reduce pressures on reserve positions consistent with growth of M1,
M2, and M3 at annual rates of around 7, 9, and 9 percent, respectively,
during the period from November to March.]* Somewhat more rapid
growth of M1 would be acceptable in light of the currently estimated
shortfall in growth for the fourth quarter relative to the Committee's expectations at the beginning of the period, particularly in the context of
sluggish growth in economic activity and continued strength of the dollar
in exchange markets. Greater restraint ob reserve positions *might* be acceptable in the event of strengthening of economic activity and inflationary pressures.** The Chairman may call for Committee consultation if it
appears to the Manager for Domestic Operations that pursuit of the monetary oejectives and related reserve paths during the period before the next
meeting is likely to be associated with federal funds rate persistently outside a range of 6 to 10 percent.***

Votes for this action: Messrs. Volcker, Boehne, Boykin, Corrigan, Mrs.
Horn, Messrs. Partee, Rice, Ms. Seger, and Mr. Wallick. Votes against
this action: Messrs. Solomon and Gramley.****

*Initial borrowings assumption reduced to $300 million from $575 million estab-
lished at previous meeting . . . Note: The November to March M1 objective was
set at 7% which implies growth at the upper bound of the annual 45 to 7% target.

**Note: The reversal of the usage of the words "would" and "might." In other
words, the directive was asymmetric on the easier side.

***Consultation range dropped from 7% to 11% range established at previous
meeting . . . significant because old range was not a constraint to small changes
in the funds rate which was trading around $8\frac{1}{2}$%.

****Vote 10 to 2. Solomon dissented because he wanted more a cautious approach
to easing. Gramley wanted to keep policy unchanged.

options for additional changes in policy implementation under
specified circumstances, and, therefore, are "open-ended." In
March of 1984, the directive specified greater weight to the possibility of additional tightening. In December, 1984, the directive
gave greater weight to the likelihood of additional easing. On some

occasions, the FOMC may issue an open-ended directive that is symmetrical, giving equal weight to changes in policy implementation in either direction.

Discount Window Borrowings and Reserve Management

The key variable in the directive in terms of policy implementation is the level of discount window borrowing. The level of borrowings is a barometer of the degree to which the open market desk is being generous or restrained in the provision of reserves through open market operations. By controlling borrowings, the Fed influences the spread between the funds rate and the discount rate. In general, the higher the level of adjustment credit from the discount window, the tighter money market conditions are and the higher the funds rate is. The converse is also true.

The open market desk's bank reserve management determines the relative proportion of total bank reserves that are nonborrowed and borrowed from the Federal Reserve discount window. The lower the level of borrowed reserves that the Fed targets, the more generous the open market desk is in the provision of nonborrowed reserves and, therefore, the narrower the spread between the prevailing discount rate and the funds rate. Theoretically, if the Fed set the borrowings objective at zero, the funds rate would collapse to the discount rate.[4] The higher the borrowings objective, the less generous is the open market desk in the provision of nonborrowed reserves, the tighter are bank reserve positions and, therefore, the wider is the spread between the discount rate and the funds rate. It is important to understand that the higher borrowings are the consequence of the less generous nonborrowed reserve provision. At the end of every reserve maintenance period, banks must settle their reserve positions to meet reserve requirements. Banks with reserve surpluses will sell reserves to banks with deficits. The less generous has been the provision of nonborrowed reserves, the more

---

[4] No matter how liberal the degree of reserve restraint, the discount window will generally attract a "frictional level" of borrowing that will occur because of market imperfections, temporary reserve dislocations or misjudgment on the part of bank reserve managers.

aggressive is the bidding by the deficit banks and the wider the funds rate/discount rate spread.

Banks, then, will borrow reserves for one of two reasons. First, the wider is the funds rate/discount rate spread, the greater is the incentive to borrow at the lower discount rate. Second, there is a finite level of nonborrowed reserves available at the end of a maintenance period, and, if the available reserves are not sufficient to meet bank reserve needs, banks must borrow at the discount window. The relationship between the funds rate and the level of discount window borrowing is presented in Exhibit 6–11 on the following page.

In order to appreciate the significance of discount window borrowing, it is necessary to understand the nonborrowed reserve objective targeting procedure under which the open market desk operates.

OPEN-MARKET OPERATING PROCEDURES

The process begins with the formulation of a reserve path from the short-term monetary targets adopted in the policy directive. First, the staff calculates seasonally-adjusted levels of M1 and M2 that are consistent with the specified short-term targets and then deseasonalizes the data to obtain the appropriate levels of unadjusted deposits. This is necessary because the reserve requirements of financial institutions are based on unadjusted deposit balances. Taking into consideration the composition of M1 and M2, the relevant required reserve ratios for reservable deposits[5] of the components and growth of unadjusted deposits that are consistent with the seasonally-adjusted growth targets, Fed staff members make projections of required reserves. Recall that the money growth need not be distributed evenly over the projection horizon.

By incorporating an additional allowance for excess reserves, the open market desk estimates a path for total reserves that is consistent with monetary growth targets set in the directive. To arrive at a nonborrowed reserve path, the staff simply subtracts the initial level of adjustment credit specified in the policy directive. The

[5] Reserve requirements are not uniform.

EXHIBIT 6-11
Money Market Conditions and Borrowed Reserves

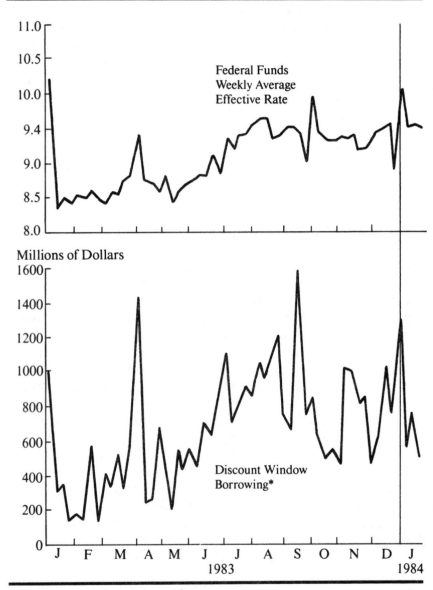

Federal Funds
Weekly Average
Effective Rate

Millions of Dollars

Discount Window
Borrowing*

J F M A M J J A S O N D J
1983   1984

*Excludes extended credit borrowing.

EXHIBIT 6–12
Projecting a Reserve Path

Two-Week Reserve Period Ending	Path Assumptions (1) Required Reserves	(2) Excess Reserves	(3) Borrowing	NBR Path (4) = (1) + (2) – (3)	Projected Supply NBR (5)	Open Market Operations to Hit Path (6) = (4) – (5)
June 20	36.650e	600	1.000	36.250	35.050	+ 1.200
July 4	36.100e	700	1.000	35.800	34.375	+ 1.425
July 18	37.200e	600	1.000	36.800	33.850	+ 2.950

process of estimating a nonborrowed reserve path is presented in Exhibit 6–12. Please note that all data in Exhibit 6–12 reflect calculations of average balances over a two-week reserve maintenance period. Under contemporaneous reserve accounting established in 1984, financial institutions must meet required reserves over a two-week period ending on alternate Wednesdays. As a consequence, the reserve path is divided into three or four two-week periods depending on the length of time between FOMC meetings.

The next step in the process is to project reserve availability (column 5) and subtract the projected supply of nonborrowed reserves from the nonborrowed reserve path (column 4) in order to arrive at the reserves balances that must be added to or drained from the banking system in order to hit the nonborrowed reserve path. It is important to stress that the higher the level of discount window borrowings, the lower the level of reserves provided by the Fed through open market operations and, therefore, the greater the pressure on bank reserve positions.

The projection of the available supply of nonborrowed reserves is an involved process that essentially involves predicting changes in bank reserve balances and other entries on the Fed's balance sheet. Increases in assets of the Federal Reserve increase reserve availability, while increases in liabilities, other than bank reserve balances themselves, decrease reserve availability. Exhibit 6–13 is a copy of the weekly "Worksheet for H.4.1 Factors Affecting Reserve Balances

EXHIBIT 6-13

FEDERAL RESERVE

Factors Affecting Reserve Balances of Depository Institutions and
Condition Statement of F.R. Banks

Worksheet for H.4.1.

For release at 4:30 p.m. Eastern time
December 27, 1985

REPRODUCED AT THE FEDERAL RESERVE BANK OF NEW YORK

	Averages of daily figures (millions)			
Reserve balances at F.R. Banks. Reserve Bank Credit, and related items	Week ended Dec. 24-25 1985	Changes from week ended		Wednesday Dec. 24-25 1985
		December 18, 1985	December 26, 1984	
Reserve Bank Credit: 1/ 2/	204,576	+ 1,455	+20,572	204,384
U.S. government securities-- Bought outright--system account	177,887	+ 13	+17,052	177,730
Held under repurchase agreements	1,024	+ 695	+ 1,024	--
Federal agency obligations-- Bought outright	8,227	--	- 162	8,227
Held under repurchase agreements	476	+ 378	+ 476	--
Acceptances--Bought outright	--	--	--	--
Held under repurchase agreements	--	--	--	--
Loans to depository institutions	948	- 53	- 896	1,362
Includes: seasonal borrowing of	56	+ 1	- 18	50
extended credit of	498	- 32	- 1,179	489
Float	1,347	+ 210	+ 120	2,219
Other F.R. Assets	14,667	+ 213	+ 2,958	14,846
Gold stock	11,090	--	- 6	11,090
Special Draw. Rights Certif. Acct.	4,718	--	+ 100	4,718
Treasury currency outstanding	17,063	+ 14	+ 660	17,075
Total factors supplying reserves	237,447	+ 1,469	+21,326	237,267
Currency in circulation*	195,964	+ 1,204	+13,151	196,697
Treasury cash holdings*	557	- 3	+ 44	557
Deposits, other than res. bal., at FRBs: Treasury	3,577	- 199	- 92	3,286
Foreign	251	- 3	+ 37	209
Service-related balances and adj. 3/	2,055	- 229	+ 277	1,492
Other	449	- 81	- 6	413
Other F.R. liabilities and capital	6,334	+ 3	+ 4	6,385
Total factors, other than res. balances, absorbing reserves	209,187	+ 693	+13,416	209,039
Reserve balances with F.R. banks 4/	28,260	+ 776	+ 7,909	28,228

On December 24-25, 1985, marketable U.S. government securities held in custody by the Federal Reserve Banks for foreign official and international accounts were $ 125,161 million a decrease of $ 774 million for the week.

1/ Net of $ 3,730 million, daily avg., matched sale-purchase transactions outstanding during the latest statement week, of which a net of $ 3,730 million was with foreign official and international accounts. Includes securities loaned--fully secured by U.S. govt. securities.

2/ Net of $ 3,899 million matched sale-purchase transactions outstanding at the end of the latest statement week, of which a net of $ 3,899 million was with foreign official and international accounts. Includes $ 624 million securities loaned--fully secured by U.S. govt. securities.

3/ Consists of required clearing balances of $ 1,492 million and adjustments of $ 563 million to compensate for float.

4/ Excludes required clearing balances and adjustments to compensate for float.

* Estimated (Treasury's figures)

of Depository Institutions and Condition Statement of Federal Reserve Banks."

For simplicity, it is useful to rearrange the Fed's balance sheet into the system open market (SOMA) and other factors "supplying reserves" in the asset side and bank reserve balances and other factors "draining reserves" on the liability side. Exhibit 6–14 presents the simplified balance sheet and identifies the most important "supplying factors" as float, discount window borrowings and other assets, and the most important "draining factors" as currency in circulation, Treasury deposits held at the Federal Reserve and other liabilities. Simple manipulation of these definitions permits us to express changes in the Federal Reserve Open Market Account in terms of changes in bank reserve balances and factors that drain reserves and factors that supply reserves. This identity is expressed as:

$$SOMA = RB + DF - SF$$

By utilizing this simple identity and accounting for the reserve effect of maturing operations, both internal and through the open market, it is possible to get an estimate of the reserve add or drain requirement that the open market desk must address through open market operations in order to hit the nonborrowed reserve path which is column 6 in Exhibit 6–12.

One method of projecting this open market add/drain requirement is demonstrated in Exhibit 6–15. Projections of the average

---

EXHIBIT 6–14
Fed's Balance Sheet

Federal Reserve	
System Open Market Account (SOMA)	Bank Reserve Balances (RB)
Supplying Factors (SF):	Draining Factors (DF):
Float	Currency in Circulation
Discount Window Borrowings	Treasury Deposits
Other Assets	Other Liabilities & Capital

$$SOMA + SF = RB + DF$$
$$SOMA = RB + DF - SF$$

EXHIBIT 6-15
A Method of Projecting Open Market Operations (in Millions of Dollars)

Reserve Projections	Oct 2	Oct 9	2-wk avg 10/2– 10/9	Oct 16	Oct 23	2-wk avg 10/16– 10/23	Oct 30
+ Required Reserves			670			200	
+ Excess Reserves			33			– 126	
+ Vault Cash			177			532	
(Changes in Reserve Balances)			526			– 458	
= Reserve Balances	25880	25147	25540	24390	25774	25082	26032
+ Float	803	– 417		– 356	0		0
+ Loans	178	– 91		– 414	350		0
+ Other	– 18	359		344	150		150
(Change in Supplying Factors	963	– 149		– 426	500		150
= Supplying Factors	48174	48025	48099.5	47599	48099	47849	48249
+ Currency in Circulation	– 46	1276		1041	– 600		– 500
+ Treasury Deposits at Fed	– 2929	– 763		36	0		– 300
+ / – Other	66	9		161	0		0
(Change in Draining Factors)	– 2909	522		1238	– 600		– 800
= Draining Factors	200344	200866	200605	202104	201504	201804	200704
System Open Market Account	178050	177988	178045.5	178895	179179	179037	
Change (Res Eff OMO)	– 3692	– 62	– 2242	907	284	991.5	
Maturing OMO	913	5041	2266	5102	4194	5071.5	
Internal Matched Sales	– 5041	– 4717	– 4879	– 4623	– 4650	– 4636.5	– 4600
Add/Drain Requirements	436	– 386	371	428	740	556.5	
System Repurchase	0	0	0	0	0	0	
Customer Repurchase	0	214	107	429	740	556	
Matched Sales	0	– 599	– 299.5	0	0	0	
Out right	432	1	541	0	0	0	

level of the open market desk's add/drain requirement for six two-week maintenance periods are made by projecting changes in reserve balances and factors that affect reserves, and accounting for the reserve effect of internal and open market operations of the previous period. The maintenance period for the week ended October 23 is a

EXHIBIT 6-15—*Continued*
A Method of Projecting Open Market Operations (in Millions of Dollars)

2-wk avg 10/30-11/6	Nov 13	Nov 20	2-wk avg 11/13-11/20	Nov 27	Dec 4	2-wk avg 11/27-12/4	Dec 11	Dec 18	2-wk avg 12/11-12/18
- 35			837			- 200			1030
150			66			0			0
- 835			710			- 350			215
950			193			150			815
26032	26225	26225	26225	26375	26375	26375	27190	27190	27190
	0	0		0	0		0	0	
	0	0		0	0		0	0	
	150	- 1800		150	150		150	150	
	150	- 1800		150	150		150	150	
48324	48549	46749	47649	46899	47049	46974	47199	47349	47274
	1600	500		750	- 150		1070	600	
	1400	0		0	0		0	0	
	0	0		0	0		0	0	
	3000	500		750	- 150		1070	600	
200779	203854	204354	204104	205104	204954	205029	206024	206624	206324
178487			182680			184430			186240
- 550			4193			1750			1810
4080.5			4600			3207			3457
- 4600	- 4500	- 4500	- 4500	- 4500	- 4500	- 4500	- 4500	- 4500	- 4500
- 30.5			4093			3043			2853
0			0			0			1853
0			1293			1043			0
0			0			0			0
- 30.5			2800			2000			2000

good example. Projections on reserve balances and reserve factors give the necessary change in the system open market account, or

$$SOMA = RB + DF - SF$$

$$\$179,037m = \$25,082m + \$201,804m - \$47,849m$$

which is the level of the system open market account necessary to offset projected changes in reserve balances and the factors that may affect these balances.

Three final adjustments must be made. First, the reserve effect of the change in the system open market account from the previous maintenance period must be calculated. In the current example, the change is $991.5 million. Second, the reserve effect of maturing open market operations must be calculated. In the current example, previous operations in the earlier maintenance period that drained reserves internally (internal matched sales = $4,879 million) and through the open market (matched sales = $299.5 million) mature in the current period to add an additional $5,178.5 million on an average daily basis in the period ending October 23. This is only partially offset by the maturing of operations that added reserves in the previous period (customer RP = $100 million) and, therefore, drains an equal amount in the current period. So far, then, we have:

$$
\begin{array}{ll}
\text{Change in SOMA} = & +\$991.5 \text{ million} \\
\text{Maturing OMO} = & +\$5,071.5 \text{ million} \\
\hline
& \$6,063.0 \text{ million}
\end{array}
$$

The final step requires estimating internal matched sales. All or only a fraction of internal matched sales may be rolled over into the next period. Internal matched sales that are rolled over, of course, again drain reserves from the banking system. Internal matched sales can also become larger depending on the needs of foreign central banks. In the current example, $4,636.5 million is rolled over, leaving an open market requirement of:

$$
\begin{array}{ll}
\text{Change in SOMA} & = +\$991.5 \text{ million} \\
\text{Maturing OMO} & = +\$5,071.5 \text{ million} \\
\text{Internal Matched Sales} & = -\$4,636.5 \text{ million} \\
\hline
\text{Add/Drain Requirement} = & \$556.5 \text{ million}
\end{array}
$$

In the current example, the open market desk must add an average of $556.5 million per day over the course of the two-week maintenance period in order to hit the appropriate nonborrowed reserve path.

Notice the effect that a change in the level of discount window borrowing will have on the level of nonborrowed reserves that the open market desk will provide through open market operations. In the current example, the level of discount window borrowing increased by an average of $267 million (first week = $344 million, second week = $150 million) over the maintenance period. Without this increase in borrowing, the open market desk would have added an additional $267 million through open market operations and added a total of $823.5 million per day in nonborrowed reserves. This higher level of discount window borrowing resulted in a less liberal provision of nonborrowed reserves. If this increase in borrowing is representative of a change in policy implementation, then the banking system is faced with a shortfall in nonborrowed reserves at the end of the maintenance period that would result in tighter bank reserve positions. It is this tightening of reserve conditions that causes a bidding up of the funds rate and forced discount window borrowings at the end of a bank reserve maintenance period.

Open Market Operations

Once the open market desk has estimated the average reserve need necessary to meet the nonborrowed reserve path, the desk has a number of options it may use to address the add or drain need.

Exhibit 6–16 presents the options available to the open market desk when it is necessary to add reserves. First is the system RP, or system repurchase agreement, which is arranged with nonbank dealer firms or bank dealers. When the open market desk conducts

---

EXHIBIT 6–16
The Fed Can Add Reserves Via: (Increase the Level of System Open Market Account)

- System RP
- Customer RP
  Outright Purchases
    With Dealers:
      Bill Pass
      Coupon Pass
      Agency Pass
      Internal with Foreign Customer

---

a system RP, it simply temporarily borrows securities from dealer firms for the system open market account and, therefore, temporarily increases the level of reserves in the banking system either directly through bank dealers or through clearing banks for the nonbank dealers. The open market desk typically conducts a system RP when the add requirement is in excess of $3 billion per day. However, the Fed does not announce the size of a system RP.[6] A system RP may be an overnight operation or a term operation that typically matures in two to fourteen days. The open market desk will conduct a term operation if it is clear that a specific add requirement will have to be adhered to for a specific number of days. The estimated duration of the add need determines the term of the RP. When conducting a term system RP, the open market desk may stipulate terms on the RP that are at a variable or a fixed rate. Fixed-rate term RPs may be subject to collateral pullback when market rates change.

The open market desk may also add reserves temporarily by conducting a customer RP. The major difference between a system RP and a customer RP is that transaction is conducted through the accounts of foreign central banks held at the Fed. The accounting is more convoluted, but a customer RP and a system RP have the same reserve effect dollar for dollar. Because of limitations imposed by the level of internal matched sales, the open market desk rarely conducts a customer RP that is larger than $2.5 billion. The Fed announces the size of customer RPs. It is unusual for the open market desk to arrange term customer RPs. However, the Fed has arranged a customer RP for as long as fifteen days.

The open market desk may also make permanent additions of reserves by making outright purchases through the open market with dealers or internally with foreign customers. The open market desk typically conducts outright purchases or "passes" when the add requirement is anticipated to be of either a long duration or so large that available collateral may be in short supply which would impose operational difficulties adding reserves temporarily. A bill pass, in which the Fed agrees to purchase all Treasury bills at the

[6] The reserve effect of the open market desk's operations such as RP's can be calculated from the weekly H.4.1.

EXHIBIT 6–17
The Fed Can Drain Reserves Via: (Reduce the
System Open Market Account)

- Matched Sales
  Outright Sales
     Dealer
     Foreign Customer
- Redemptions at Weekly T-Bill Auctions

---

best available price, is usually the largest of the outright operations. Recent bill purchases have exceeded $2.5 billion. The open market desk may also purchase all coupons, conduct a coupon pass, when a permanent add need is not so large and the open market desk needs coupon issues for the proper management of system open market account. Recent coupon purchases have been as large as $1.5 billion. Finally, on rare occasions, the desk may also announce an agency pass in which only agency securities are purchased on a competitive basis through the open market. In addition, the open market desk may also make outright purchases internally with foreign customers. These purchases are not always announced to the market, and can only be detected by market participants through scrutiny of changes in the Fed's balance sheet when the H.4.1 is released.[7]

Exhibit 6–17 lists the options that the Fed has when it is necessary to drain reserves from the banking system in order to hit the specified nonborrowed reserve path. When draining is necessary on a temporary basis, the open market desk will engage in matched sales or reverse repurchase agreements. When the Fed conducts matched sales it lends out securities and, therefore, causes a temporary decline in the system open market account and an equal decline in bank reserves. Like a system RP, a matched sales agreement can be arranged on an overnight or a term basis, depending on the size of the drain requirement, the flow of reserve factors and the time frame that it is estimated the drain requirement will persist.

---

[7] The size of outright purchases can also be calculated from the weekly H.4.1.

When a more permanent draining of reserves is necessary, the open market desk can sell securities outright, either in the open market or to foreign customers, or redeem Treasury bills in the regular scheduled weekly three and six month bill auctions, or the 52 week T-bill auctions.

The open market desk does not engage in outright sales to the market very often for two reasons. First, an outright sales tends to have a strong negative impact on market psychology. As a consequence, the desk usually prefers other alternatives. Second, it is unusual for the open market desk to face a large enough drain that an outright sale is the only alternative. Most frequently, the open market desk will address a large drain with a combination of matched sales and internal operations, sales to foreign customers and redemption of holdings at weekly bill auctions. Sales to foreign customers have the advantage of bringing about the desired change in the system open market account and, therefore, have the same reserve effect without causing a negative announcement effect on the market prices and psychology. Finally, the open market desk may also drain reserves reducing the system open market account holdings of Treasury bills by redeeming a fraction of the maturing holdings, rather than rolling-over all of the bill holdings.

When the Fed engages in temporary operations such as RP's and matched-sales, the open market desk will typically announce the operation to the market between 11:30 A.M. and 12:00 noon, with most activity taking place between 11:35 A.M. and 11:45 A.M. Permanent operations, such as "passes" or "sales," are usually announced early in the afternoon. There are no hard and fast rules, however, as the open market desk must be able to be flexible enough to adjust to changes in reserve factors. The open market desk has "come in early" to announce either temporary or permanent operations, and sometimes pre-announces operations a day early when it appears that there may be some difficulty, such as a collateral shortage, in addressing a reserve need.

WATCHING THE FED

Fed watching involves anticipating, projecting and interpreting open-market interventions, changes in policy implementation, money supply and reserve releases, minutes to previous FOMC meetings, changes in discount rate policy and even public statements by Fed officials.

Fed Intervention and Changes in Policy Implementation

One of the most visible and important functions in Fed watching is projecting and interpreting open market intervention. Projecting open market intervention essentially involves duplicating the open market desk's projection of the open market requirement that was demonstrated in Exhibit 6–15. The object is to project the same open market requirement that the open market desk projects as the basis for predicting daily open market intervention.

There are two major obstacles; the information flow and open market desk discretion. The first obstacle is simply that the open market desk has a better flow of information on changes in reserve factors and the system open market account than does anyone not priviledged to daily information on changes in the Fed's balance sheet. For example, information regarding Treasury balances at the Fed is an important factor in reserve projections that is released to the public on a daily basis with a day lag, but is available to the open market desk on a daily basis. As a consequence, the open market desk may revise its projections and alter its open market operations before market participants are aware of the information that caused the reactions by the market desk. The lag between the availability of information on other changes in the system open market account, such as float, or the size of reserve operations is even longer since these data are released to the public only on a weekly basis with the release of the H.4.1. As a consequence, reserve projections may be perfectly accurate at the beginning of a maintenance period, but lose accuracy over the course of the period due to changes in reserve factors that can be accounted for only with a lag. Changes in reserve factors are the most frequent cause of unexpected open market intervention. It is for this reason that the market often responds to daily releases on Treasury balances or rumors regarding reserve factors because of the possible implications for upcoming open market operations or interpretations of previous operations.

It is also important to note that errors in projections are magnified as the end of the maintenance period approaches. For example, if projections underestimate the size of the add requirement of the open market desk by $500 million at the beginning of the period, it represents a projection miss of a total of $7 billion ($500 million times 14) over the entire period. As such, a projection miss of $500 million per day on the first day of the maintenance period is an error of $3.5 billion per day by the middle of the period and is a $7 billion error by the last day of the period. As a consequence, projections of open market operations based on reserve projections alone are subject to the greatest margin of error at the end of a maintenance period.

The second major pitfall of projecting daily open market intervention is the degree of discretion that the open market desk may exercise in addressing any specific open market requirement. Reserve projections yield an average daily level of reserve balances that the open market desk must add or drain over the course of the entire maintenance period. Any given add requirement may be addressed over a two-week maintenance period in any of a number of ways in regard to the type of open market operations utilized and the timing of the chosen operations.

Exhibit 6–18 illustrates two examples of open market operations in a maintenance period in which the open market desk faces an add requirement of $2.0 billion/day on average, or a total add of $28 billion over the course of the entire maintenance period.

In Example 1, the open market desk provides nonborrowed reserves almost evenly over the course of the maintenance period. In the second example, the Fed "front-loads" the add requirement by adding over 70% of the reserve requirement in the first two days and completing the add requirement before the end of the maintenance period. In reality, it is difficult to assess how aggressive the desk has been since the open market desk does not announce the size of system RP operations.

There are several factors that affect the timing and nature of open market operations over the course of a maintenance period. Among the most important are the distribution of the add/drain requirement based on the flow of reserve factors, current market conditions and perceptions, new information and finally, policy changes.

The distribution of reserve factors can have an important impact on the timing and aggressiveness of open market intervention. Refer

EXHIBIT 6-18
Examples of Open Market Operations
(Figures are in Billions of Dollars)

	Example 1			Example 2		
Day	Open Market Operations	Reserve Effect	Cumulative Reserve Effect	Open Market Operations	Reserve Effect	Cumulative Reserve Effect
Thu	$2.0 CRP	$2.0	$ 2.0	$3.5 4-day SRP	$14	$14
Fri	2.5 CRP	7.5	9.5	2.0 CRP	6	20
Mon	No Fed	—	9.5	No Fed	—	20
Tue	2.0 CRP	2.0	11.5	No Fed	—	20
Wed	2.5 CRP	2.5	14.0	No Fed	—	20
Thu	2.0 CRP	2.0	16.0	2.0 4-day SRP	8	28
Fri	2.0 CRP	6.0	22.0	No Fed	—	28
Mon	2.0 CRP	2.0	24.0	No Fed	—	28
Tue	2.0 CRP	2.0	26.0	No Fed	—	28
Wed	2.0 CRP	2.0	28.0	No Fed	—	28

back to the examples in Exhibit 6-18. The evenly distributed provision of reserves, Example 1, would be appropriate if reserve factors drained reserves evenly throughout the period. Reserves would be provided as they are needed so that no major reserve dislocations should occur, and the funds rate should be relatively stable. Example 2 might be an extreme case where the add requirement may be skewed heavily toward the second week of the maintenance period. Such a case might arise if reserve factors drained $3 billion in the first week but only $1 billion in the second week, for an average add requirement of $2 billion over the course of the period. In this case, a "front-loading" would be appropriate in order to provide reserves as they are needed and to prevent severe money market pressures from arising early in the maintenance period.

Current market perceptions and conditions are another important consideration in the open market desk's decision on daily intervention. The manager of the open market desk conducts daily meetings with members of the dealer community in order to gather information on market conditions and perceptions of the current thrust of Fed policy. If market performance is being unduly affected by misconceptions of Fed intentions, the open market desk may adjust the timing and nature of operations in order to calm fears or deflate euphoria that is misplaced. Sometimes this may involve making "a funds rate protest," adding reserves if the funds rate is at a level that is above that which is consistent with the thrust of Fed policy, or draining reserves if the funds rate is aberrantly low. For example, the open market desk is not generally willing to "stray from the path," engage in open market operations that are inconsistent with the nonborrowed reserve path and the projected add/drain requirement, every time the funds rate shows some volatility. However, the open market desk is sensitive to misleading the market especially if it disrupts the Treasury's financing calendar.

New information on reserve factors may also alter open market operations. For example, if a snow storm in the Midwest causes airports in major cities to close, the open market desk may be less aggressive in adding reserves or be more aggressive in draining reserves than projections suggest is appropriate until it can quantify the reserve effect of any float that may have resulted from the storm. The desk has displayed an aversion for "coming in on both sides of the market," adding and draining reserves in the same maintenance period, but if it is necessary the desk will do so in order to hit the reserve projections.

The most important type of new information that the open market desk will consider is a policy directive from the FOMC that specifies new short-term monetary growth targets and a new initial level of discount window adjustment credit. Adjustments to the borrowings assumption tends to be small, $250 million is common, and, therefore, does not cause major alterations in the open market requirement for a maintenance period. For example, if the FOMC lowered the borrowings objective by $250 million, then the $2 billion per day add requirement would increase to an add requirement of $2.25 billion per day. Given the uncertainty and imprecision of reserve projections, it would be very difficult to discern this adjustment to the open market desk's bank reserve management simply by observing open market operations, especially if the desk distributed the add requirement evenly throughout the maintenance period. Of course, the switch in policy implementation would generally be evident at the end of the maintenance period because of an average level of discount window borrowings that is about $250 million below that of the previous period and a funds rate that is about 50 basis points lower on average. Sometimes the open market desk will send the market a signal. One way of doing this is to "front-load" the add requirement. Unless done to offset draining by reserve factors, "front-loading" the add requirement creates a surplus bank reserve position that will generally cause the funds rate to move lower. Against the appropriate economic backdrop, the combination of aggressive open market intervention and a lower funds rate will send the desired signal to the market. In general, any combination of apparently aggressive open market intervention and a funds rate that is below the prevailing rate will generate expectations of an easing of policy. There is always the risk of misinterpretation, however, until perceptions are validated by the borrowing data and a funds rate that persistently trades below the previous prevailing rate.

The opposite is true when the open market desk is implementing a tighter policy. If the open market desk faces an add requirement, the desk will address this need less aggressively and later in the maintenance period than if policy implementation were unchanged. As a consequence, money market conditions will become tighter, resulting in a firmer funds rate. Frequently, the tighter reserve positions will not be evident until the end of the maintenance period when banks must settle reserve positions. The result of the open market desk's less generous provision of nonborrowed reserves is that banks are unable to meet reserve needs through the funds market and, therefore, are "forced" to meet these needs at the discount window. In general, when the Fed is tightening, open market desk reserve provision is less responsive to a firming trend in the funds rate and reserve draining is more responsive to a softening trend in the funds rate.

It is important to understand that the overwhelming majority of open market operations are intended strictly to meet reserve needs and have no policy significance. Market interpretations of open market intervention will vary depending upon the current economic setting and the behavior of the funds rate. Market perceptions of Fed intervention are not always correct because both the Fed and "Fed watchers" make errors in reserve projections and because the funds rate is subject to temporary aberrations that may be misleading. For every change in Fed policy implementation, the market may speculate several times that a policy change is "imminent."

Money Supply Projections

Another important and visible function is projecting the weekly and monthly changes in the monetary aggregates. Changes in M1 and in some of the components of M2 and M3 are released on a weekly basis in the Federal Reserve Statistical Release "Money Stock, Liquid Assets, and Debt Measures," the H.6 release.

M1 is released every Thursday at 4:30 P.M. with a lag of 10 days. The weekly M1 numbers are calculated on a Tuesday-to-Monday basis, but are released on the Thursday of the following week because of the time that is necessary to compile the data. The H.6 also includes weekly data on the components of the broader aggregates M2 and M3. The actual M2 and M3 are released on a monthly rather than a weekly basis.

Money supply projections are important because money supply has been institutionalized as a factor that influences FOMC policy decisions and open market desk policy implementation. As a consequence, both projections and actual releases of the monetary aggregates are very important.

Weekly M1

Projecting weekly changes in M1 is a very difficult task that requires an understanding of unadjusted deposit flows, seasonal adjustment factors, institutional factors, deposit deregulation and interest rates. Weekly changes in M1 can be quite volatile, so that no single week-to-week change is likely to have a significant change on monetary policy, but any weekly M1 release can have an important effect on market psychology.

There are several ways of projecting weekly M1 changes. One common way is to make projections of the individual components of M1. Using this method, the most important but most difficult task in projecting weekly changes in M1 is projecting the demand deposits. Exhibit 6–19 presents a representative composition of M1. The largest component is demand deposits, with currency and other

EXHIBIT 6-19
Components of M1

	Percentage of Seasonally Adjusted M1
Currency	25
Travelers Checks	1
Demand Deposits	45
Other Checkable Deposits	29

checkable deposits accounting for similar shares. Based just on size, then, projections of demand deposits would be the most important with other checkables and currency being about equal in importance.

What is of even greater importance than the relative composition is the volatility of the individual components. The more volatile is a component, the greater is the contribution of that component to the weekly changes in M1. From a volatility standpoint, demand deposits are by far the most volatile of the components of M1, with other checkables being the second most volatile component. The relative volatilities are demonstrated in Exhibit 6-20 which simply shows the weekly changes in the components of M1 over an eight week period. Over this period, changes in demand deposits accounted for about 73% of the weekly changes in M1.

The process of making weekly M1 projections involves first, projecting changes in unadjusted data and second, seasonally adjusting this data to arrive at the seasonally adjusted changes. In projecting changes in the unadjusted data, analysts rely on two general sources, historical time series and surveys of bank deposits.

Historical time series provide a good starting point for projecting unadjusted changes in the individual components of M1. Exhibit 6-21 presents weekly changes in demand deposits over a three year period. There is a similarity in the pattern of changes, in terms of direction and magnitude, that can be useful in projecting weekly changes. Charts of the other components would show an even stronger correlation between calendar weeks in different years and less volatility on a weekly basis. This again illustrates that demand

EXHIBIT 6–20
Change in Components of M1 (in Billions of Dollars)

Date	M1	Currency	Travelers' Checks	Demand Deposits	Other Checkable Deposits
Nov 11	+ $ 1.6	+ $0.2	—	– $ 1.0	– $0.4
18	+ 2.8	– 0.3	—	2.8	– 0.3
25	+ 4.4	+ 0.1	—	+ 4.5	– 0.2
Dec 2	+ 4.4	+ 0.1	—	+ 3.2	+ 1.3
9	– 2.2	+ 0.1	—	– 3.3	– 1.6
16	+ 1.5	+ 0.2	—	– 0.3	+ 1.6
23	+ 3.2	+ 0.2	—	+ 3.4	– 0.4
30	– 3.3	UNC	—	– 2.3	– 1.0

deposits are the most difficult component but also the most important component of M1 to project.

In using historical data to project demand deposits, there are a number of factors that can affect weekly changes. For example, notice that the correlation of weekly changes in Exhibit 6–21 is less reliable around the end of the month. One of the reasons for the inconsistency is the timing of social security payments which are made by the third day of every month. When these payments are made, most of them through automatic transfer, demand deposits rise sharply and then diminish as funds are spent or transferred to other accounts. If the social security payments are made on Friday, then the balances remain high over the weekend and, therefore, bloat the weekly average because Friday balances account for 3/7 of the weekly average. If the payments are made earlier in the week, then the effect on the weekly average is significantly less. Other factors that are extremely important include the timing and size of Treasury interest payments and auction settlements, the effect of holidays and other developments on corporate cash management practices, deposit deregulation and movements in interest rates.

The same principles apply to analysis of historical data of the other components. However, the weekly changes in currency and other

EXHIBIT 6-21
Level of Demand Deposits (Millions of Dollars)
December-February, 1983-1985

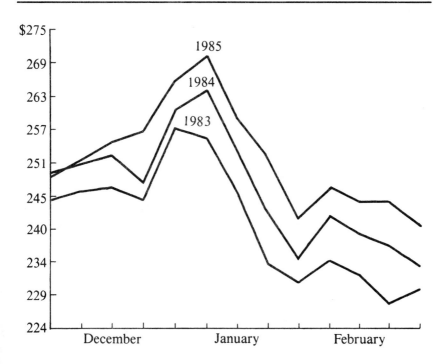

checkable deposits are less volatile than are demand deposits but more predictable based on historical patterns. As a consequence, these components are somewhat easier to project on a regular basis.

Another source of information that can be useful is bank deposit surveys that are conducted by private analysts. These surveys give information on percentage changes in demand deposits and other checkable deposits in a sample of banks. These surveys can be very useful in terms of assessing the risk of projections based on historical data analysis. Some forecasters even rely solely on the deposit survey data for projections. While the surveys are useful, they can also be misleading because of problems with sampling techniques.

For example, the samples are, by necessity, only a fraction of the banking system and the samples typically are comprised of a high proportion of large and money center banks. As a consequence, the surveys are sometimes misleading if the behavior of deposits at large and small banks differ.

Seasonal Adjustment Factors

Once projections are made for the changes in the unadjusted deposits, these numbers must be seasonally adjusted using the seasonal adjustment factors provided by the Federal Reserve. Exhibit 6–22 presents an example of the weekly seasonal factors provided by the Fed.

There are two basic approaches that can be used to get the final estimate of a weekly seasonally adjusted M1. The first involves using the seasonal adjustment factors for currency and transactions deposits. The second involves using the seasonal adjustment factors for currency and demand deposits and creating an "implied" seasonal adjustment factor for other checkable deposits.

In the first case, the final change is simply derived by dividing the projected levels of unadjusted currency and combined demand and other checkable deposits by the appropriate seasonal adjustment factor to get the projected level of seasonally adjusted M1. The difference between the projected level and the previous actual level is the forecast for the change in M1.

The second method is only slightly more involved because it requires the intermediate step of calculating an implied seasonal adjustment factor for other checkable deposits. Rather than using a combined transaction deposit component for projecting the M1 level, each component is adjusted by the component-specific seasonal adjustment factor.

Both of these methods should give similar results, but each has advantages depending on the relative volatility and predictability of demand deposits and other checkable deposits. Using either procedure, the ability to project weekly M1 changes amounts to being able to assess when the seasonal adjustment factors are appropriate and when they are inappropriate. The ability to "outguess" the seasonals involves an understanding of fundamental and institutional factors that affect deposit flows. Over time statistical models

EXHIBIT 6-22
Seasonal Factors for Currency and Deposit Components of M1 and
Selected Commercial Bank Components of M2 and M3,
December 1983-December 1984

Week Ended	Currency	Transactions Deposits*	Demand Deposits*	Savings	Commercial Bank Deposits Small Denomination Time	Large Denomination Time
	1	2	3	4	5	6
1983						
Dec. 5	1.0090	1.0210	1.0240	.9792	.9926	1.0153
12	1.0210	1.0260	1.0280	.9808	.9918	1.0149
19	1.0197	1.0280	1.0320	.9815	.9935	1.0130
26	1.0260	1.0130	1.0145	.9822	.9962	1.0133
1984						
Jan. 2	1.0050	1.0530	1.0750	.9808	.9959	1.0197
9	1.0050	1.0690	1.0680	.9928	.9983	1.0139
16	.9930	1.0575	1.0360	.9946	1.0021	1.0072
23	.9840	.9950	.9900	.9936	1.0040	1.0048
30	.9740	.9640	.9720	.9935	1.0048	1.0075
Feb. 6	.9880	.9920	.9910	.9972	1.0069	1.0080
13	.9905	.9810	.9820	.9990	1.0071	1.0070
20	.9885	.9690	.9640	.9986	1.0073	1.0046
27	.9785	.9610	.9630	.9994	1.0066	1.0031
Mar. 5	.9935	.9955	.9880	1.0045	1.0083	1.0041
12	.9980	.9880	.9860	1.0085	1.0080	1.0008
19	.9933	.9830	.9840	1.0099	1.0071	.9984
26	.9884	.9620	.9600	1.0111	1.0065	1.0011
Apr. 2	.9925	1.000	.9955	1.0163	1.0043	1.0015
9	1.0080	1.0310	1.0239	1.0201	1.0025	.9946
16	1.0009	1.0400	1.0300	1.0166	1.0021	.9887
23	.9950	1.0300	1.0080	1.0123	1.0015	.9855
30	.9880	.9920	.9850	1.0107	1.0014	.9840
May 7	1.0030	.9990	.9930	1.0121	1.0000	.9892
14	1.0018	.9930	.9930	1.0132	1.0000	.9894
21	.9975	.9770	.9800	1.0132	1.0000	.9912
28	.9930	.9580	.9610	1.0125	.9998	.9933
June 4	1.0030	1.0030	1.0010	1.0153	1.0003	.9933
11	1.0110	1.0050	1.0040	1.0160	.9997	.9915
18	1.0050	1.0050	1.0040	1.0119	.9992	.9886

EXHIBIT 6-22—*Continued*
Seasonal Factors for Currency and Deposit Components of M1 and
Selected Commercial Bank Components of M2 and M3,
December 1983–December 1984

					Commercial Bank Deposits	
					Small	Large
Week		Transactions	Demand		Denomination	Denomin
Ended	Currency	Deposits*	Deposits*	Savings	Time	Time
	1	2	3	4	5	6
June 25	.9975	.9710	.9740	1.0092	.9987	.988
July 2	1.0050	.9980	.9970	1.0136	.9971	.989
9	1.0180	1.0220	1.0228	1.0159	.9968	.986
16	1.0106	1.0120	1.0160	1.0143	.9968	.984
23	1.0045	.9870	.9860	1.0111	.9970	.986
30	.9970	.9780	.9850	1.0071	.9973	.989
Aug. 6	1.0080	.9990	.9990	1.0048	.9985	.997
13	1.0100	.9980	1.0030	1.0029	.9990	.999
20	1.0043	.9860	.9870	.9996	.9994	1.000
27	.9930	.9650	.9670	.9964	.9996	1.002
Sept. 3	1.0010	.9920	.9960	.9945	.9979	1.006
10	1.0100	1.0065	1.0110	.9931	.9981	1.004
17	1.0008	1.0050	1.0100	.9906	.9984	1.001
24	.9940	.9750	.9770	.9884	.9986	1.00:
Oct. 1	.9870	.9850	.9850	.9911	.9968	1.00:
8	1.0065	1.0150	1.0170	.9937	.9970	1.00.
15	1.0000	1.0160	1.0200	.9918	.9978	1.00:
22	.9951	.9955	.9980	.9878	.9986	1.00:
29	.9870	.9840	.9845	.9838	.9987	1.00-
Nov. 5	1.0045	1.0150	1.0160	.9838	.9982	1.00
12	1.0115	1.0200	1.0170	.9831	.9980	1.00
19	1.0072	1.0100	1.0130	.9809	.9976	1.00
26	1.0045	.9650	.9910	.9791	.9966	1.00
Dec. 3	1.0050	1.0150	1.0164	.9776	.9935	1.01
10	1.0220	1.0260	1.0240	.9781	.9922	1.01
17	1.0200	1.0290	1.0320	.9782	.9927	1.01
24	1.0260	1.0170	1.0250	.9795	.9949	1.01
31	1.0090	1.0450	1.0560	.9809	.9966	1.01

*In constructing M1 the seasonal factors for "transactions deposits" are used to der
seasonally adjusted sum of demand deposits and other checkable deposits. The dema
posits seasonal factors are used to construct seasonally adjusted demand deposits. Sea
adjusted other checkable deposits is derived as the difference between these two series.

have proven to be no match for good judgment and understanding of institutional factors.

M2 and M3

The Fed releases M2 and M3 on a monthly basis. However, information on the components of M2 and M3 is available on a weekly basis in the H.6 release. The weekly data can be monitored over the course of the month to get an assessment of the growth in these broader aggregates. One method of assessing M2 and M3 is to estimate monthly changes to date in each of the components. Exhibit 6-23 presents such an "on-line" estimate.

Notice that the available data are incomplete. For example, no data on term Eurodollars, a component of M3, is released on a weekly basis. In addition, the data on savings deposits, small time deposits, money market deposit accounts and large certificates of deposit are strictly from bank deposits. Data from thrift institutions are not released on a weekly basis. As a consequence, estimates of all thrift components and term Eurodollars must be estimated to complement the information compiled on bank data.

EXHIBIT 6-23
Weekly Components of the Monetary Aggregates

	Nov.	Dec. 2	Dec. 9	Dec. 16	Dec. 23	Dec. 30	Avg	Change
M1	617.7	626.1	623.2	622.2	627.9		624.6	+ 6.9
O/N RP's	55.5	55.8	58.7	56.9	57.9		57.7	+ 2.1
O/N Euro's	14.1	13.6	17.3	15.7	16.1		16.1	+ 2.0
Savings	125.3	125.2	124.9	124.7	124.6		124.7	− 0.6
Small Time	381.6	382.5	384.0	384.4	384.6		384.0	+ 2.4
MMDA's	329.8	331.6	333.1	333.9	333.4		333.5	+ 3.7
Gen. MMG's	176.8	177.2	177.6	176.9	176.6		177.2	+ 0.4
M2								+ 16.9
Large CD's	280.0	280.4	281.6	281.6	280.6		281.2	+ 1.2
Term RP's	33.7	39.9	30.9	33.2	35.8		31.8	− 1.9
Term Euro's	N/A	N/A	N/A	N/A	N/A		N/A	N/A
Inst. MMF's	64.6	64.7	64.3	63.9	65.1		64.0	− 0.6
M3								+ 15.6

Note: The Monthly changes are in monthly S.A.A. levels.

Because much of the data on M2 and M3 is available before the actual numbers are released by the Fed, estimates of those aggregates are usually fairly accurate.

CONCLUSION

In addition to all of the above, Fed watchers have to be keenly aware of many other factors that could alter the thrust of monetary policy. Most Fed watchers are economists by training and many were employed within the Federal Reserve System at one time. With this training as economists and a keen sensitivity to the demands of policy-makers, Fed watchers closely monitor domestic and international economic developments that could warrant a change in the thrust of Fed policy. It is important for the Fed watcher to do more than analyze statistics. What is most important and the key to success, is an ability to assess real world development in a fashion similar to policy-makers. To do this properly the Fed watcher has to constantly be aware of the political and economic bias of individual Fed officials. Solid understanding of the dynamics of the formulation and implementation of policy can at times be a critical ingredient to interpreting and anticipating fluctuations in prices of fixed income securities.

Most Fed watcher responsibilities are somewhat more broadbased than simply monitoring the Federal Reserve. These responsibilities generally include the analysis of the cash management and debt management of the Treasury Department, and the analysis and prediction of a variety of economic indicators released each month. Of critical importance, the Fed watcher serves as a conduit of information that serves as a constant resource to the trading and sales operations which they support.

The Fed watching industry expanded sharply following the Federal Reserve's move in October 1979 towards reserve management and away from targeting the funds rate. The volatility introduced into the market by this operational change, and the ensuing substantial and forceful changes in Fed policy that triggered major market moves, created a need for careful analysis of the credit markets. Today intense competition among security firms, banks and other sell-side participants requires high quality information and forecasts. The horizons of market participants and the analysis of economists have to be transactions oriented to impact the bottomline. These demands have created an industry for Fed watching.

Fed watchers are employed by securities firms, banks, insurance companies, investment advisors and other institutions. The thrust of Fed watching information has created a market for video transmission of analyses and forecasts. Currently TeleRate, Reuters and SPMI offer Fed watching analyses by third-party vendors. Timely electronic transmission of this form of information has become an important resource to market participants. Although opinions always differ regarding the significance of a particular desk transaction, set of money supply statistics, or public statement by a Fed official, the dissemination of Fed watching analysis has provided for a more efficient and informed marketplace.

CHAPTER 7

ANDREA J. TRACHTENBERG is currently a
Vice President and Manager of Marketing and
Planning for Taxable Debt Products at Merrill
Lynch Capital Markets. Previously, she was a
Product Manager for the Merrill Lynch Cash
Management Account.

Andrea started her career at EF Hutton and was
responsible for the introduction of money market
funds and unit investment trusts. She received an
MBA and a registered representative license in
1978.

REPURCHASE AGREEMENT

Andrea J. Trachtenberg
Vice President and Director of Marketing and
Strategic Planning
Merrill Lynch Capital Markets Taxable Fixed
Income Trading Group

The market for repurchase agreements (repo) has undergone dramatic growth both in dollar volume and range of products in the last decade. A number of key factors has stimulated this growth. These include the increasing government debt, enhanced use of arbitrage and other sophisticated investment strategies that use repo or reverse repo in a pivotal role. The overnight repo market has been around since shortly after World War II. In the last decade, however, it has soared in popularity, with volume in the overnight market surpassing $200 billion, and an additional $200–$300 billion traded in the term market.

The terms "repurchase agreement," "repo," "RP," and "reverse repo" are all used to describe the same transaction. In practice a repo is a loan of cash backed by collateral of securities. In a repo transaction the borrower (such as a government securities dealer) receives cash and, in turn, provides securities as collateral, to the lender of funds. The borrower pays the lender interest for use of the cash.

There is some disagreement as to the legal definition of a repurchase agreement. The contract may refer to the transaction as a

173

"purchase and sale" of the securities, but in reality, the transaction is a financing. The borrower remains the beneficial owner of the collateral even though he may temporarily place the collateral in the lender's possession. And the borrower retains the right to all coupon interest accruing on the collateral.

MECHANICS OF REPOS

Suppose that a government dealer has $1 million worth of U.S. government bonds. Suppose also that an investor such as a corporation, a bank trust department or a local government has $980,000 in cash to invest for one day's time. What are the investment alternatives to this investor?

The investor has the following four investment alternatives available: (1) the investor can make an overnight deposit at a commercial bank; (2) the investor can buy a security for a day and sell it the next morning; (3) the investor can look for an investment maturing in one day, or; (4) the investor can enter into a repo with the government dealer.

With the last alternative, the government dealer agrees to deliver the $1 million worth of U.S. government bonds to the investor and to pay the investor the prevailing repo rate (usually less than the Federal Funds rate) for the use of the $980,000 overnight. The $1 million in U.S. government securities is to be returned in the morning by the investor to the government dealer. Fed Funds are to be wired by the government dealer to the investor for the use of $980,000 lent plus the interest earned for one day. This is the repo in its simplest, but essential form.

The mirror image of a repo is called a reverse repurchase agreement. When a reverse repo is transacted, the dealer lends funds and receives specified securities from the investor as collateral for the loan. Reverse repos enable investors to take advantage of arbitrage opportunities using securities they already own. This provides a readily accessible source of cash for reinvestment into higher yielding instruments. Reverse repos also provide a source of liquidity, since they can be used to meet short-term cash needs at low cost without actually selling the underlying securities.

Repo Collateral

The most popular forms of securities used in the repo market are government or mortgage-backed securities, and money market instruments. The market value of these securities when used as collateral should always exceed the principal dollars invested. The lender of money, because it has the more liquid asset, receives the additional margin to provide a safeguard against market price fluctuation and the potential risk of default. Margin, also called "haircut," is defined as the amount by which the market value of the securities collateralizing the transaction exceeds the dollar amount lent. It usually ranges from 101 percent to 103 percent of the actual dollars lent. For example, if a corporation invests $10 million in overnight repo it will receive securities with a current market value of $10.1 to $10.3 million as collateral. When pricing the securities as collateral, both principal plus accrued interest is included in calculating the current market value.[1]

TYPES OF REPO

There are basically *four* types of repo. The most common is an *overnight repo,* a 24-hour loan of cash secured by specific collateral. Anything longer than overnight (one week, one month, etc.) is a *term repo.* The third type of repo is an *open repo* where there is no pre-determined maturity and is terminable on demand. In an open repo, the rate varies daily and the repo is rolled daily until terminated either by the borrower or lender. Finally, there is a *flex repo,* a loan at a rate agreed upon by the parties for a specified time period providing, however, that the lender may withdraw all or part of the cash lent before the originally agreed expiration date.

DETERMINATION OF REPO RATES

A number of factors influence overnight and term repo rates. In the overnight market, the Fed Funds rate, quality of collateral, supply

[1] An exception is mortgage-backed securities used as collateral. Because mortgage-backed securities pay interest on a monthly basis, the pricing formula is the face

and demand for collateral and delivery mechanism all have an impact on rates. Treasury bill rates and short-term money market rates affect the term market. However, the most visible rate used as a benchmark for repo levels is the Federal Funds rate. A typical overnight government repo rate usually falls slightly below ($\frac{1}{8}$ percent to $\frac{1}{2}$ percent) overnight Fed Funds because repo is a secured transaction. The purchase and sale of Fed Funds, in comparison, are done on an unsecured basis. Additionally many investors, including dealers, municipalities and corporations, do not have direct access to the Fed Funds market.

The supply of money or securities also affects rates. For example, normally there is a large supply of securities for the dealer to finance after a Treasury auction, causing the dealer to bid more aggressively for the money to finance its inventory position. In this case, the spread between repo and Fed Funds rates narrows and in some cases the repo rate may be at the same level or higher than the Fed Funds rate. If the opposite situation occurs, and collateral dries up, the spread widens because dealers have less of a need for money, because they have fewer securities to finance. When a particular issue is in demand it is called a "hot" or special issue. This frequently occurs when dealers have large short positions that they must cover, usually around auction time or when they must deliver on a futures contract. This creates a "specials" market where the reverse repo rate is low. The party owning the issue can lend the specific security that the broker/dealer needs and borrow money at a cheap, attractive rate.

Timing in a repo transaction is an additional determinant of rate. The bulk of all repo business is transacted between 8:00 and 10:00 A.M. Eastern time. As the day wears on dealers generally become less flexible and competitive in rates, since their major financing need has been met.

Quality and delivery method are the final ingredients affecting rate. Government securities, the most popular form of collateral used, provide the highest level of safety and liquidity, and therefore the lowest repo rate. Government-backed, mortgage-backed securi-

---

amount (par) times a mortgage factor times the current market value. Larger haircuts are also taken on mortgage-backed securities.

ties come next in safety and rate, followed by money market instruments. Depending on spreads in the market and supply of these securities, at certain times the difference in repo rates between the securities may widen or narrow.

Delivery of Repo

Most repo transactions are executed on a deliverable basis whereby collateral is delivered directly to the investor's custodian bank. This is the safest way to execute a repo, since the investor is in physical possession of the collateral. If technical glitches (e.g., faulty delivery instructions, problems with the Fedwire) prevent delivery, it is considered a collateral "fail". Fails are costly to the lender of securities, since they must still pay interest on the transaction.

Another method developed for overnight repo is the *Tri Party Repo.* In a Tri Party Repo, collateral is delivered and held by a third party bank in the investor's name. This saves delivery costs, cuts down on collateral "fails" and provides attractive returns. In a Tri Party Repo, the investor maintains a perfected lien (first call in the event of bankruptcy) on securities pledged as collateral. A contract between the customer, custodian bank and dealer is required to establish a Tri Party Agreement.

The third method is on a *due bill* or *letter basis,* whereby a promissory note/letter is issued in lieu of the delivery of securities. The due bill takes the form of a letter setting forth the collateral used and the dealer's method, if any, of segregating the collateral. This method is commonly used for overnight repo of non-wireable securities. This is the least safe method of repo.

The calculation for determining repo rates is based on a 360 day basis using simple interest. Interest is payable on the termination date of the transaction. Because repo is a loan, not an actual purchase and sale, all coupon interest on the underlying collateral is passed back to the actual owner of the security. The calculation is shown below:

$$\text{Interest} = (\text{dollar principal}) \times (\text{Repo rate}) \times \left(\frac{\text{Repo term}}{360}\right)$$

For example, if the dollar principal is for $1 million and the repo rate is 8 percent, the interest for an overnight repo is $222.22 as shown below:

$$\$1,000,000 \times .08 \times (\tfrac{1}{360}) = \$222.22$$

RECENT DEVELOPMENTS IN
THE REPO MARKET

The repo market was little noticed until the Spring of 1982. At that time a few inadequately capitalized government bond dealers with repos outstanding experienced severe financial stress. These firms were Drysdale Securities Corporation, Comark Securities, Inc., and Lombard-Wall, Inc.

Drysdale Government Securities built massive government trading positions with minimal cash. The scandal became highly publicized, in part, because major money center banks were involved. Using reverse repos, Drysdale borrowed securities from the money center bank to cover short sales. Following standard practice at that time, the value of the accrued interest payments was not included in the market value of the securities lent. However, Drysdale had received the accrued interest when it sold the securities short and reinvested the difference. When the coupons came due, the owners of the securities called for their interest payments, from the money center banks to whom they had lent. Drysdale could not, in turn, cover its payment to the money center banks because its investments had lost money in the meantime. An impasse resulted until the money center banks honored their obligations to the parties from whom they borrowed.

The results of Drysdale's bankruptcy were twofold. The securities industry instituted changes to more closely regulate repo transactions, stipulating that accrued interest must be counted in repos. Perhaps more importantly, investors in repos began to study the creditworthiness of the ultimate borrower more carefully and to demand to know if a bank was acting as a principal or undisclosed agent.

However, just a few months later Lombard-Wall went bankrupt putting many municipalities and other investors at risk. The bankruptcy court's restraining order prevented the sale or disposition of securities received from Lombard-Wall under repurchase or investment agreements without court approval. Additionally, the court considered the collateral used in the repos to be secured loans to Lombard-Wall. Thus, the courts decided on the terms of the liquidation and disposition of the proceeds.

These events, coupled with pressure from major broker/dealers in the repo market, led to the passage of an Amendment to the Bankruptcy Act signed into law by the President on July 10, 1984.

THE BANKRUPTCY AMENDMENT

The Bankruptcy Amendment exempts certain repurchase and reverse repurchase agreements from an otherwise automatic stay (freeze) on a bankrupt's assets. Under this law, underlying collateral in a repo or reverse repo agreement is no longer frozen and may be liquidated directly by the repo participant (the entity that has an outstanding repo or reverse repo agreement with the bankrupt). This ability to liquidate the underlying collateral in a timely and effective manner greatly lessened the perceived risk in repo/ reverse transactions which prevailed in the repo market after the Lombard-Wall case in September 1982. The collateral must of course be in the possession and control of the liquidating party.

It should be noted that the amendments exempt repo and reverse repo agreements only where underlying collateral consists of either certificates of deposit, eligible bankers' acceptances, or securities that are direct obligations of, or that are fully guaranteed as to principal and interest by the United States government. The amendments apply only to repo or reverse repo with a maturity of one year or less. The amendments do not define repo or reverse repo agreements as the purchase and sale of securities or as a loan but as a simultaneous transfer of cash versus securities. Although these amendments were welcome clarification for the financial markets, they did not relieve investors of the responsibility to see that the appropriate margining of collateral and the possession of the collateral be secured.

The liquidation provisions are applicable only to those situations where a petition in bankruptcy has been filed. The new amendments do not yet apply if a SIPC member is the bankrupt. The amendment applies only to those institutions coming under Chapter 11.

BANKRUPTCIES AFTER THE AMENDMENT
AND SUGGESTED GUIDELINES

Three major bankruptcies have occurred since the passage of the Repo Amendment. Lion Capital, RTD Securities, and ESM Securities caused additional shock waves for the repo market. In these cases the problem was not the liquidation of the collateral but the fact that the investors, mainly municipalities, did not have possession of the collateral to liquidate. Securities being held as collateral by the bankrupt's clearing bank were being pledged in duplicate and sometimes triplicate. These incidents again highlight the need to adhere to strict procedural guidelines when doing repo.

To minimize the level of risk on repurchase transactions the following guidelines should be considered by all market participants:

1. *Evaluation of Customer Creditworthiness.* Even though repurchase agreements are fully collateralized by high quality, liquid assets, participants (whether borrowers or lenders of funds) should always evaluate customer creditworthiness to ensure the highest possible degree of safety.

2. *Delivery of Collateral.* As was highlighted in the bankruptcy of Lion Capital, investors in repos must ensure possession of collateral pledged to them. If an entity invests in a due bill repo, the safety of the transaction is solely a function of the creditworthiness of the borrower. If a municipality, for example, is unable to arrange securities safekeeping services from a local bank, a dealer can alternatively arrange delivery of collateral to a third-party bank. In this case, the customer must receive independent confirmation from the third-party bank of the receipt of collateral into his account.

3. *Margining of Repurchase Agreements.* Standard practice in the repo market dictates that the provider of funds is entitled to receive some amount of margin on the transaction (generally 1–2 percent on government repo transaction). In addition, the investor may request additional margin if the collateral is insufficient during the term of the repurchase agreement. Most major firms now mark to the market (i.e., reprice the collateral to

reflect current market value) and make margin calls on repo positions daily. Similarly, it would be in a lender's best interest to make margin calls regularly. If investors do not have the necessary resources to price collateral on an ongoing basis, their custodian banks should be able to perform this service for them. The margin is determined by customer creditworthiness, quality of collateral, maturity and term of the transaction.

PARTICIPATION IN THE REPO MARKET

In addition to dealers, the major participants in the repo market include bank trust departments, municipalities, money market funds and corporations. These entities use repurchase agreements as a flexible, low-risk short-term investment vehicle. It provides an overnight investment alternative for non-banking institutions that do not have direct access to the Federal Funds market.

Financial institutions such as securities dealers use repo as the primary mechanism to finance their long trading inventory positions, or reverse repo to finance their short positions. Repo provides a lower cost financing vehicle than either Federal Funds (which they do not have direct access to) or bank loans, the most expensive way to finance inventory. The secondary use of repo is for running a matched book. A dealer maintains a matched book taking on repo and reverse repo of equal maturity earning the spread between both as its profit.

The Federal Reserve is also a major user of repurchase agreements. The Fed uses repo as a vehicle through its open market committee to either temporarily withdraw or inject reserves into the market. For example, the Fed does a repo by buying government securities from dealers that it agrees to sell back to them after a predetermined period, usually overnight. With a reverse repo (technically called a matched sale-purchase transaction), the Fed sells government securities to drain reserves temporarily, which it agrees to buy back at a later date.

Investors use reverse repos to liquefy a security portfolio, and to take advantage of arbitrage opportunities by providing a source of cash for reinvestment into higher yielding instruments.

SPECIALIZED REPO PRODUCTS

There are many specialized repo products that have been developed over the last few years in response to customer needs and technological advancements in the market place. In addition to the Tri-Party Repo, discussed earlier, there are also the following two products.

Bonds Borrowed/Securities Lending

The bonds borrowed program was originally developed as a way of maximizing a portfolio's current return and was targeted to those institutions which cannot do repo because of legal or investment restrictions. It involves the lending of government and government agencies by institutions to dealers. Borrowed securities are collateralized with acceptable securities, normally other governments. For this the customer receives fee income. An additional benefit of the program is the accounting treatment of the transaction. The transaction is recorded as a contingent liability and therefore does not inflate the balance sheet. The borrowed government securities are used by securities dealers primarily to cover short inventory positions or to re-lend to other brokers or dealers who have a need to borrow a specific security.

Reverse to Maturity and Repo to Maturity

Reverse to maturity is a reverse repo in which the termination of the transaction coincides with the maturity date of the reversed security. Reverse to maturity transactions provide an alternative to customers restricted from selling securities positions at a loss. It provides a way to enhance a security's return or to take advantage of higher yielding investment opportunities. Repo to maturity, on the other hand, provides an investment alternative to investors who are restricted from purchasing a specific type of security. Repo to maturity is principally used for money market securities.

CHAPTER 8

JACKSON D. BREAKS began his career in the
bond business at The First Boston Corporation in
1968 as a money market salesman. By the end of his
twelve-year experience at FBC his duties included
sales training and co-manager of the Government
Securities Department. He left the firm in April,
1980, to do yield curve arbitrage. He joined Merrill
Lynch in March, 1983, where he is a Vice President
and Account Executive in MLGSI. He attended
Purdue University for his undergraduate and
graduate work, receiving his M.A. in 1964.

YIELD CURVE ARBITRAGE AND TRADING

Jackson D. Breaks
Vice President
Merrill Lynch, Pierce Fenner & Smith, Inc.

Yield curve arbitrage and yield curve trading are similar bond trading activities which attempt to profit from an expected change in the yield spread(s) between two or more points along the yield curve. Arbitrage is a form of trading with one or more short positions against one or more contra positions long. Yield curve trading, on the other hand, is simply swapping one or more long positions for one or more new long positions. Our discussion will deal mostly with yield curve arbitrage.

Yield curve arbitrage is conducted almost exclusively in the U.S. Treasury market because the market has the following characteristics necessary to encourage this form of trading.

1. U.S. Treasuries are of uniform and high quality credit.
2. U.S. Treasuries trade in a highly liquid market where each issue is so large and so easy to borrow that the securities can be sold short as easily as bought long.
3. The U.S. Treasury Department has established a regular financing pattern which allows all market participants to know

185

when the Treasury is going to issue securities at particular points along the yield curve.

Thus yield curve arbitrageurs usually limit their concentration to those points along the yield curve where the Treasury regularly finances. If an arbitrageur sells short a five-year note because it seems expensive, he knows that on a specific date in the future the Treasury will issue a new five-year note, creating supply pressure which should cheapen that point on the curve. The points along the yield curve where the Treasury regularly finances and the frequency of the financings are as follows:

three-month bills—weekly
six-month bills—weekly
one-year bills—every four weeks
two-year notes—monthly
three-year notes—quarterly
four-year notes—quarterly
five-year notes—quarterly
seven-year notes—quarterly
ten-year notes—quarterly
twenty-year bonds—quarterly (eliminated 5/1/86)
thirty-year bonds—quarterly

The three-year, ten-year, and thirty-year issues comprise the mid-quarter financing auctioned in early February, May, August, and November. The four-year, seven-year, and twenty-year issues comprise the quarter-end financing and are auctioned late in March, June, September, and December. The five-year note is auctioned in late February, May, August, and November.

FORCES THAT SHAPE THE YIELD CURVE

We will now examine some yield curves to demonstrate the forces that shape the curve and to see how differently they can be shaped.

EXHIBIT 8-1
Sample Yield Curves

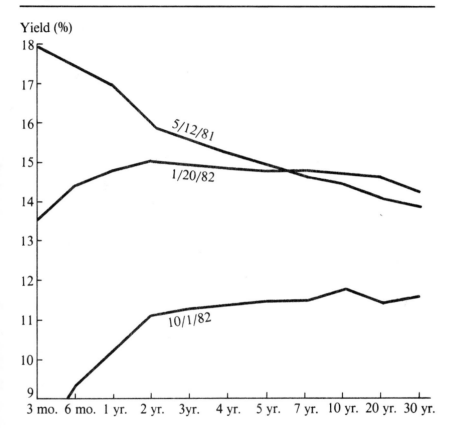

Yield (%)

We will define the yield curve as yield levels (the vertical axis) for each point in the Treasury's financing schedule (the horizontal axis). Exhibit 8-1 shows three yield curves which occurred during the volatile interest rate climate from early 1981 to late 1982. May 1981 marks the extreme point in the Federal Reserve's tight money policy of the early 1980s. January of 1982 shows a less tight period, and October of 1982 shows the period during which the Federal Reserve was engaged in an aggressive easing policy.

These three yield curves dramatically demonstrate the basic rule that governs yield curve arbitrage: short-term interest rates are usually more volatile than long-term interest rates. The period May 1981 to October 1982 was marked by a general lowering of interest rates, but short-term rates fell approximately ten percentage points while long-term rates fell only about three percentage points.

The factors that influence the shape of the yield curve are as follows:

1. Current Federal Reserve Bank policy or expected changes in Federal Reserve Bank policy.
2. Bullish or bearish moves in the bond market.
3. Extraordinary activity in the market by various institutional participants.
4. Abrupt supply/demand imbalances.
5. Coupon disparities among issues comprising the yield curve.

Changes in Federal Reserve Policy

No other factor so influences the basic shape of the yield curve or the speed with which it changes as Federal Reserve Bank policy. When the Fed tightens or eases, it often changes short-term rates so much and so quickly that the longer term bond market cannot "catch up" with the rate change. The longer term rates usually lag, and the yield curve flattens (even inverts in extreme cases) or steepens.

From October 1979 to August 1982, the Fed was engaged in what has been called mechanical monetarism. During this period the Fed reacted quickly to changes in money supply growth with abrupt and extreme changes in short-term rates. As a result, short-term rates were usually so high that the yield curve was inverted. Since the late summer of 1982, the Federal Reserve has changed policy more gradually and has eased more consistently than it has tightened. The yield curve has therefore been more positively sloped, changed shape more subtly and slowly than in the 1979 to 1982 period, and has less often followed the general rule that "short rates are more volatile than long rates."

Bullish or Bearish Moves in the Bond Market

The bond market, however, moves up and down even during periods of stable monetary policy. During normal bullish and bearish moves, short-term rate changes are usually greater than long-term rate changes. Market participants usually get much more excited about the 10 3/8 of '12 going from 99 to 100 than the two-year note rising 7/32, but in this common bull move the yield curve will have steepened. Because we tend to measure profit in terms of price change per $1 million unit, we can easily lose track of yield changes as we focus more on price changes.

Extraordinary Activity in the Market by Various Institutional Participants

Major shifts in the economy or financial structure can also influence the activities of various institutions in the bond market, and in turn influence the shape of the yield curve.

Money market mutual funds are natural investors in short-term money market instruments. They may be invested in overnight repurchase agreements (RPs), three-month T-bills or CDs, one-year T-bills, or a combination. Should most money market mutual funds at once become bearish and move into RPs or become bullish and move into six-month or one-year T-bills, that shift in investment emphasis would show up as a change in slope of the short end of the yield curve.

Commercial banks invest in securities as well as extend loans to individuals and businesses. When investing in Treasury securities, banks tend to buy one-year to five-year maturities. When a steep yield curve makes the interest rate on deposits much less than can be earned on intermediate Treasury securities, banks are sizable buyers, causing a drop in the yield levels in intermediate-term maturities.

Exhibit 8–2 shows an extreme example of a change in institutional activity dramatically changing the shape of the yield curve. By late September of 1982, the Federal Reserve had been aggressively easing monetary policy. Three-month bill rates dropped 184 basis points from 9.91 percent on August 2, 1982. Long-term rates dropped 136 basis points from 13.21 percent on August 2, 1982. Two-year notes,

EXHIBIT 8-2
Yield Curve Influence of Banks

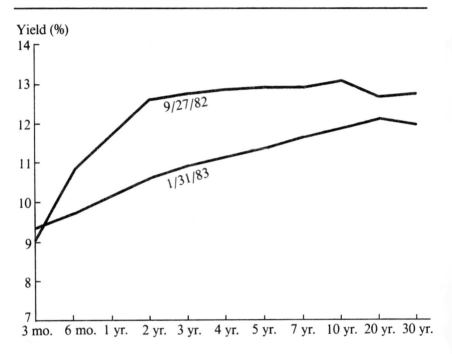

Yield (%)

however, had lagged in the general interest rate decline. By September 27, 1982, the three-month to two-year yield spread was 362 basis points while the two-year to thirty-year spread was almost flat. The banking system, the natural buyer of two-year notes, was about to engage in an unprecented buying spree.

The steepening front half of the yield curve invited banks to spend their now relatively inexpensive deposits on much higher-yielding intermediate Treasuries, profiting from the 3 to 4 percent rate advantage. At the same time the banking laws were to change by early December to permit banks to pay competitive interest rates on new accounts known as money market deposit accounts. Banks marketed this new product by offering extraordinarily high yields, increasing their deposits much at the expense of money market mutual funds. The only market in which to quickly invest such large

EXHIBIT 8-3
Treasury Securities at Commercial Banks

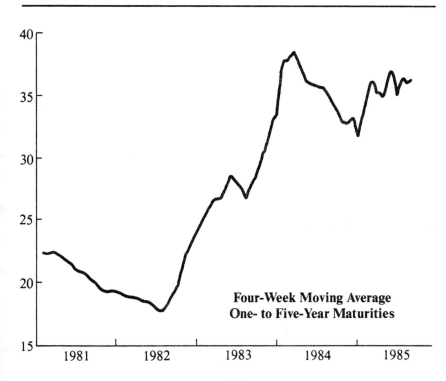

Four-Week Moving Average
One- to Five-Year Maturities

amounts of new funds was intermediate Treasury securities. By January 31, 1983, the buying programs of the commercial banks had dropped two-year note rates 210 basis points while three-month bill rates actually rose and 30-year Treasury rates dropped only 83 basis points. Exhibit 8-3 shows the moribund activity of bank portfolios during the flat yield curve period of early 1982 and the explosive growth beginning in August with a much steeper yield curve and deposit law changes late in the year.

Abrupt Supply/Demand Imbalances

Another factor that influences the shape of the yield curve is supply/demand imbalances. Treasury financing is a classic example of sizable supply potentially putting pressure on a specific point on the yield curve. If the Treasury is about to auction $7 billion new-money five-year notes, it is likely that the five-year point of the yield curve will bend up in yield relative to the rest of the curve. Such a concession on the yield curve may be small or nil if the market atmosphere is bullish and quite substantial if the climate is bearish. The amount of concession can be an acid test of a market's true depth and breadth.

Financing pressures in other markets may also influence the shape of the Treasury yield curve. If the long-term corporate financing calendar and/or municipal calendar is heavy, underwriters may hedge their commitments by selling short long-term Treasuries or bond futures contracts. In the absence of other yield curve influences, these hedging activities may steepen the back half of the yield curve.

Financial futures contract price changes can lead up or down sectors of the cash market that include deliverable securities for those contracts, namely Treasury bills and Treasury bonds. The front and back ends of the yield curve can therefore be more volatile. Contract prices may hit critical chart points that trigger buy or sell stops. These futures price changes translate to cash securities price changes through the activities of basis arbitrageurs.

In 1982, securities dealers began an activity known as "stripping," whereby a Treasury issue, usually long term, was separated into individual coupon payments and the final principal payment known as the corpus. In late 1984, the Treasury facilitated the further development of this product by allowing separate delivery of individual interest payments and the corpus over the Federal Reserve's wire transfer system for selected securities.

These zero-coupon securities appealed to corporations defeasing debt, to pension funds cash matching future liability payments, and to foreign investors who wanted to invest in Treasury or near-Treasury securities with minimum currency risk. When demand for these securities, usually the corpus, is strong, dealers buy strippable conventional long-term bonds, sell the large corpus for a sizable premium to a retail buyer and attempt to sell the various coupons at the best price possible. The supply of conventional long-term Treasuries is reduced; the intermediate- and long-intermediate part of the yield curve are under pressure of the coupon strips; and the result is a flat or inverted yield curve from seven-year or ten-year notes out to long-term bonds.

When demand for zero-coupon issues is weak, the yield curve from seven-year notes to long bonds is usually positively sloped.

Coupon Disparities among Issues Comprising the Yield Curve

Exhibit 8–4 demonstrates another factor that can affect the shape of the yield curve. Notice that the ten-year point represented by 13 3/4's

EXHIBIT 8–4
Yield Curve in Early Bull Market

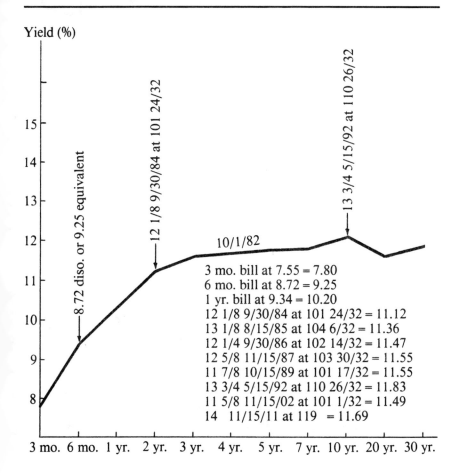

Yield (%)

8.72 diso. or 9.25 equivalent

12 1/8 9/30/84 at 101 24/32

13 3/4 5/15/92 at 110 26/32

10/1/82

3 mo. bill at 7.55 = 7.80
6 mo. bill at 8.72 = 9.25
1 yr. bill at 9.34 = 10.20
12 1/8 9/30/84 at 101 24/32 = 11.12
13 1/8 8/15/85 at 104 6/32 = 11.36
12 1/4 9/30/86 at 102 14/32 = 11.47
12 5/8 11/15/87 at 103 30/32 = 11.55
11 7/8 10/15/89 at 101 17/32 = 11.55
13 3/4 5/15/92 at 110 26/32 = 11.83
11 5/8 11/15/02 at 101 1/32 = 11.49
14   11/15/11 at 119   = 11.69

3 mo. 6 mo. 1 yr. 2 yr. 3 yr. 4 yr. 5 yr. 7 yr. 10 yr. 20 yr. 30 yr.

EXHIBIT 8–5
Coupon Disparity Influence of Yield Curve

Yield (%)

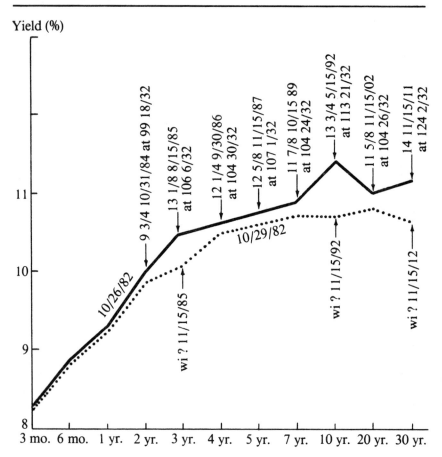

of 5/15/92 and the thirty-year point represented by 14's of 11/15/11 jump up in yield from other points along the back end of the yield curve. Both issues are trading at a substantial price premium compared to the seven-year and twenty-year issues near them. It is common for premium-priced issues with high coupons to trade at higher yields than par-priced or discount-priced issues with current or discount coupons. Arbitrageurs should be careful to establish positions with balanced coupons so that the long positions do not underperform the short positions in a substantial rally. It is often advisable to set up a bull arbitrage with a par-priced security long and a premium-priced security short to exploit the drag on premium prices in a rally. High coupon issues lag against par or discounted securities in a low interest rate market because the substantial coupon income must be reinvested at the low yielding short-term interest rate.

Each market environment sets different penalties on premium-priced issues, but Exhibit 8–5 demonstrates perhaps the most extreme penalty on record. Following the summer and early fall bull market of 1982, all coupon issues on the curve except the recent two-year note were at a premium of 4 to 24 points. The October 29, 1982, yield curve reflects the new three-year, ten-year and thirty-year when-issued (wi) securities announced as part of the mid-quarter financing. Until the auctions determined the coupon rates, the wi securities were by definition par or near-par securities. As such they show as dips in the upward sloping yield curve. The yield spreads of the old three-year, ten-year, and thirty-year issues to the new wi issues were 27 basis points, 50 basis points, and 47 basis points, respectively. The market, starved for par securities, put totally irrational valuations on their worth. More normal market circumstances might price a premium issue 5 to 7 basis points more in yield for each full percentage point the coupon rate exceeds the current interest rate. These valuations of coupon disparity can change erratically and arbitrageurs must beware.

BALANCING YIELD CURVE TRADES
FOR VOLATILITY

Exhibit 8–4 shows the Treasury yield curve on October 1, 1982. The curve is quite steep from three months to two years and quite flat from two years to longer term issues. A yield curve arbitrageur would be tempted to buy two-year notes and sell short ten-year notes, hoping that the back end of the yield curve would catch up with the steep front half. The two positions would have to be balanced, however. A move of 10 basis points in the two-year position would have to generate the same profit or loss as a change of 10 basis points in the ten-year position.

If an arbitrageur buys $10 million of 12 1/8 9/30/84 at 101 24/32, yielding 11.12 percent, and several days later the issue rises in price to 101 29 + /32 or 11.02 percent, he will have made 5 + /32 on $10 million notes or $17,187.50. His position in 13 3/4 5/15/92 should be of an appropriate size so that a change in yield of 10 basis points also equals $17,187.50. If he sells short $2.9 million of 13 3/4 5/15/92 at 110 26/32 yielding 11.83 percent and several days later they fall to 110 7/32 yielding 11.93 percent, he will have made 19/32 on $2.9 million of notes or $17,218.75, almost the same as his two-year note position.

Weighting By Yield Value of 1/32

The most common method of weighting trades uses the yield values ratio of 1/32 for each security. For example, let:

Y = par value of the 12 1/8 9/30/84

X = par value of the 13 3/4 5/15/92

V_y = yield value of 1/32 of issue Y

V_x = yield value of 1/32 of issue X,

then

$$\frac{Y}{V_y} = \frac{X}{V_x}$$

and solving for X:

$$X = \frac{Y V_x}{V_y}$$

Since the yield value of Y and X is .0177 and .0051, respectively, and X is $10 million, then

$$X = \frac{\$10(.0051)}{.0177}$$

$$= \$2.9 \text{ million (approximately)}$$

It should be noted that the yield value of 1/32 can be determined by simply changing the current price of the security for current delivery by 1/32 and noting the yield difference. The 1/32 yield value weighting method is the most common system used by arbitrageurs. An alternative system involves duration weighting the two positions.

The yield curve trade in our example is known as "buying the yield curve" since the arbitrageur has bought long the short-term position and sold short the longer maturity position. Buying the yield curve is usually a bullish trade since short rates are usually more volatile than long rates.

Returning to Exhibit 8–4, our yield curve arbitrageur might have been tempted to "sell the yield curve" by selling short six-month bills and buying long the two-year note, picking up the extraordinary spread of 187 basis points. To balance the positions he must first calculate the yield value of 1/32 for the six-month bill.

Compute the dollar value of $1 million of six-month bills at discount prices equidistant from the current discount price and determine the equivalent bond yields at those discount prices.

Since the current discount price is 8.72, decreasing it by 10 basis points to 8.62 gives a price of $956,421.11 and an equivalent bond yield of 9.138 percent. At a discount price of 8.82, which is an increase of 10 basis points, the price is $955,410.00 and an equivalent bond yield of 9.360 percent. Since $1,011.11 ($956,421.11 minus $955,410.00) changes the bond yield .222 percent, $312.50 will change the yield as follows:

$$\frac{\$312.50}{\$1,011.11} = \frac{X}{.222}$$

Solving for X:

    X = .0686

    = the yield value of 1/32 on the six-month bill at 8.72 discount.

If our arbitrageur now buys $10 million of two-year notes at 101 24/32, the amount of the six-month bills to sell short against it is determined as follows. Letting Y denote the two-year notes and X the six-month bills:

$$\frac{Y}{V_y} = \frac{X}{V_x}$$

$$X = \frac{Y V_x}{V_y}$$

Since Y is $10 million and V_x and V_y are .0177 and .0688, respectively, then

$$X = \frac{\$10(.0686)}{.0177}$$

$$= \$38.8 \text{ million six-month bills}$$

Our first yield curve trade was an example of "buying the yield curve." The arbitrageur bought $10 million of two-year notes and sold a weighted amount of ten-year notes. He expected the curve to steepen, so he was more bullish than bearish. Our second example trade was "selling the yield curve." The trader expected the front part of the yield curve to level off and the position implied a bearish leaning towards the market.

Butterfly Yield Curve Arbitrages

There are circumstances where an arbitrageur may perceive an issue on the yield curve to be cheap, but he has no strong opinion about whether the yield curve will flatten or steepen. In such a situation, if confronted with our yield curve dated September 27, 1982 our arbitrageur might do both trades—sell the front part of the curve out to two-years and buy the back part of the curve two years to ten years. Such a yield curve trade is known as a "butterfly."

Butterfly yield curve arbitrages are commonly used when the overall yield curve is stable and likely to remain so, but an issue seems especially cheap. An issue's inherent cheapness or expensiveness can be measured by netting the yield spreads from each wing to the middle and comparing that figure against spreads over recent weeks, months or even years. In the six-month to two-year to ten-year butterfly, the arbitrageur sold six-month bills and bought two-year notes to pick up 187 basis points. He also sold ten-year notes and bought two-year notes to give up 71 basis points. Therefore his net pick up to buy two-year notes and sell a weighted amount of six-month bills and ten-year notes was 187 minus 71, or 116 basis points. To decide whether plus 116 net basis points is extraordinary, compare that spread to past yield curves. In this case the two-year note had been at an extreme level of cheapness on September 21, 1982, of 141 net basis points (plus 191 basis points six-months to two-year and minus 50 basis points ten-year to two-year). Within six trading days the net spread moved to zero (plus 135 basis points six-months to two-year and minus 135 basis points ten-year back to two-year) because of the commercial banks' dramatic buying spree that was beginning.

Butterfly yield curve arbitrages involve some risks akin to simple two-sided yield curve arbitrages. Wider wings and spread from the middle mean more risk in the trade. A long two-year notes position versus a short thirty-year bonds position is much more risky than a long two-year notes position versus four-year notes position. The ratio of two-year to four-year is a little less than 2 to 1; the ratio of two-year notes to thirty-year bonds is approximately 4 1/2 to 1. We could conclude therefore that a two-year to thirty-year is roughly 2 1/2 times more volatile than a two-year to four-year arbitrage. Likewise a butterfly trade where we are long the two-year between six months and ten-years is more volatile than a trade where we are long two-year notes versus one-year bills and five-year notes. The weighting in our sample butterfly was almost 4 to 1 for six-month bills to two-year notes, and about 3 to 1 for the two-year note to ten-year note leg. A "tighter" butterfly would be a 2 to 1 ratio of one year bills to two-year notes and a 2.2 to 1 ratio of two-year notes to five-year notes.

Not only is our six-month to two-year to ten-year butterfly quite volatile, it is also lopsided. We have an approximate 4 to 1 ratio in six-month to two-year and 3 to 1 in the two-year to ten-year. We have more volatility in the front half of the trade than in the back half. A further measure of balance, or in this case imbalance, is to compare total long position with total short position. We are long only $20 million of two-year notes but short a total of $42 million ($39 million of six-month bills and approximately $3 million of ten-year notes).

Before leaving the subject of butterflies, let us examine a case where a butterfly can be most advantageously used. Exhibit 8–6 shows the yield curve on December 22, 1982, in the middle of a quarter-end financing. The four-year note had just been auctioned, establishing its coupon. The seven-year and twenty-year issues were trading on a when-issued basis still with undetermined coupons. The yield curve was historically quite steep for that period (a two-

EXHIBIT 8-6
Yield Curve on 12/22/82

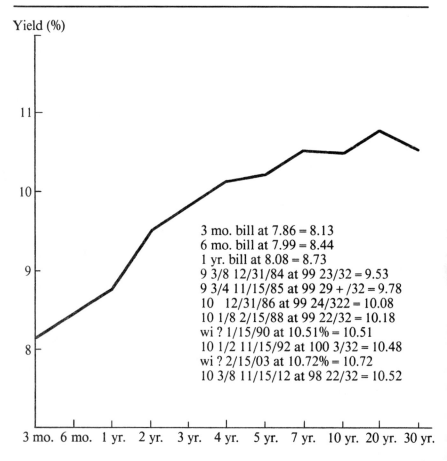

Yield (%)

3 mo. bill at 7.86 = 8.13
6 mo. bill at 7.99 = 8.44
1 yr. bill at 8.08 = 8.73
9 3/8 12/31/84 at 99 23/32 = 9.53
9 3/4 11/15/85 at 99 29 + /32 = 9.78
10   12/31/86 at 99 24/322 = 10.08
10 1/8 2/15/88 at 99 22/32 = 10.18
wi ? 1/15/90 at 10.51% = 10.51
10 1/2 11/15/92 at 100 3/32 = 10.48
wi ? 2/15/03 at 10.72% = 10.72
10 3/8 11/15/12 at 98 22/32 = 10.52

3 mo. 6 mo. 1 yr. 2 yr. 3 yr. 4 yr. 5 yr. 7 yr. 10 yr. 20 yr. 30 yr.

year to ten-year spread of + 95 basis points) because the Fed had been aggressively easing. Notice that all coupon issues on the yield curve were at approximately par dollar prices, making the curve "true" and not distorted by coupon disparities. There was little to indicate that the curve would change shape. Analyzing butterfly spreads, however, revealed that seven-year notes had never been so cheap between five-year and ten-year notes. Selling five-year notes and buying seven-year notes was + 33 basis points; selling ten-year notes and buying seven-year notes was + 3 basis points, for a net pickup of 36 basis points (33 + 3) to do the butterfly buying the middle issue.

In this case an arbitrageur would have bought $10 million wi seven-year notes (yield value of 1/32 = .0064) and sold $12.5 million of five-year notes (yield value of 1/32 = .0080). He would have also bought another $10 million wi seven-year notes and sold $8.1 million of ten-year notes (yield value of 1/32 = .0052). The ratios on both sides of the butterfly are approximately 1.25 to 1.0 for equal volatility. The arbitrageur is about as long as he is short ($20 million versus $20.6 million) for good position balance. Within ten days the net butterfly spread had returned to a more normal 17 basis points, netting the arbitrageur 19 basis points before transaction expense and carry costs.

STRATEGIES FOR TRADING THE YIELD CURVE

The most common yield curve trading strategy is to establish a position in preparation for new Treasury supply. If the Treasury is soon to announce a new five-year note, for instance, bond dealers and arbitrageurs will often sell short that area of the yield curve and hedge with a long position in bills or two-years (a bullish hedge) or a long position in ten-year or thirty-year issues (a bearish hedge).

Traders may also hedge an outright speculative position by establishing a contra position along the yield curve. A trader who has bought $20 million of two-year notes to speculate on a bull market move might later sell short approximately $6 million of ten-year notes to reduce his market exposure. Notice that our trader sells short an issue longer in maturity than his two-year position because he still has a bullish bias. If he turns slightly bearish he would sell out his long. If he turns still more bearish he might sell short $40 million of one year bills against his $20 million of two-year note long. Finally, if he is very bearish he might sell out his long and go short the market outright.

At times the relationship of two issues close to each other on the curve may seem in conflict with the rest of the curve. Arbitrageurs may try to profit from those apparent anomalies. The yield curve dated January 20, 1982 in Exhibit 8–1 suggests selling short thirty-year bonds and buying long twenty-year bonds. The yield curve in Exhibit 8–5 suggests selling ten-year notes and buying seven-year notes since the relationship is inverted in an otherwise steeply sloped yield curve. Arbitrages like these that are farther out the yield curve, involving issues next to each other on the curve, have less market direction risk and are more influenced by supply-demand pressures.

A fourth strategy for trading the yield curve is to center a butterfly arbitrage around a cheap or expensive issue as discussed earlier. Such trades can be very tight involving issues next to each other on the curve or stretched widely on the curve where the volatility (in this case "flap") can be extensive.

CARRY COSTS IN YIELD CURVE ARBITRAGE

Yield curve arbitrageurs, like all leveraged traders, finance their long positions by arranging repurchase agreements with the matched book departments of government securities dealers. An arbitrageur buys $10 million of two-year notes, for example 8 7/8's of 8/31/87 at 100-3/32 for settlement on 9/5/85 to yield 8.821. He owes

$10,009,375.00	principal
$ 4,903.31	accrued interest
$10,014,278.31	total

to the dealer from whom he bought the notes. That same dealer is likely to extend the trader a resale agreement (repo to the trader) whereby the dealer lends the trader $10,014,278.31 collateralized by the $10 million of two-year notes. The financing rate would likely be the standard repo rate or slightly higher to make a profit— a rate of say 7 3/4 percent. Deliveries flow as shown in Exhibit 8–7. Note that in practice these transactions are paired off with no delivery. The flows depicted above explain the theoretical deliveries or the actual deliveries if the outright trade and RP involve different dealers.

Our trader earns 8 7/8 percent each day on his $10 million of

EXHIBIT 8–7

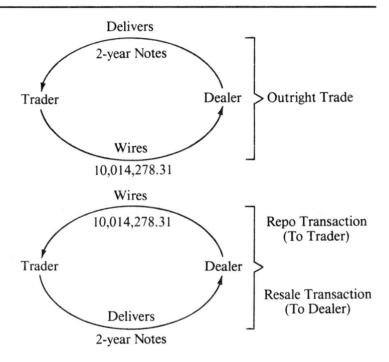

two-year notes or $2,451.66. He has committed $10,014,278.31 (principal of $10,009,375.00 plus accrual interest of $4,903.31). He is paying out 7 3/4 percent per day on the proceeds of his repo of $10,014,278.31 (for simplicity sake we will assume all repos and resales are in amounts equal to the proceeds of the outright purchases and sales) or $2,155.85 per day (.0775 times $10,014,278.31 times 1/360 days). The trader is earning $2,451.66 per day, paying out $2,155.85 per day in financing expense and therefore earning a net of $295.81 per day. For each $1 million face amount of two-year notes, he is earning $29.58 per day.

Arbitrageurs like to translate financing gains or losses into terms of basis points to determine how much yield they are gaining or losing by staying with the position. In this case the arbitrageur is earning $29.58 per day or 29.58/312.50 = .0947/32nds ($312.50 is

1/32 of 1 percent on $1 million of bonds). The arbitrageur calculates the yield value of 1/32 on the two-year note at 100 3/32 for September 5, 1985, settlement to be .0175. He multiplies the number of 32nds positive carry (.0947) times the yield value of 1/32 (.0175) and gets .00166, which is the net percentage he earns each day he carries his position with a financing rate of 7 3/4 percent. Multiplying that figure by 100 gives him the net basis points he earns per day (.166). Therefore, in ten days of those financing terms, he earns 1.66 basis points.

Suppose later that day the trader sells short $2.8 million ten-year notes at 102 6/32 to yield 10.143 (ten-year notes are 10 1/2's of 8/15/95 trading at 102 6/32 for 9/5/85 settlement with a yield value of 1/32 equal to .00492) to hedge his long position. To borrow the securities he is shorting, the arbitrageur will likely establish a resale agreement with the dealer (repo to the dealer) to whom he sold the notes. The trader, now an arbitrageur, will be receiving $2,878,027.17 proceeds from his sale ($2,861,250.00 principal plus $16,777.17 accrued interest). He is loaning the money to the dealer versus collateral but in this case he wants a specific piece of collateral, namely the 10 1/2's of 8/15/95. To entice the dealer to provide this specific collateral, the arbitrageur accepts a lower return on his money, say 6 3/4 percent, compared to the normal repo rate of 7 3/4 percent on nonspecified collateral. Deliveries on this transaction flow as shown in Exhibit 8–8:

Our arbitrageur is earning 6 3/4 percent each day on the $2,878,027.17 proceeds of his resale or $539.63 ($2,878,027.17 times .0675 times 1/360 days). He must pay out, however, 10 1/2 percent per day on the issue he is short or $798.91. He has a net carry loss of $259.28 per day on the $2.8 million short position or $92.60 per day per million ($259.28 divided by $2.8 million).

To translate that cash expense to basis points loss, we divide $92.60 by $312.50 (1/32 of 1 percent on $1 million bonds) which equals .2963 32nds. The yield value of 1/32 on ten-year notes at 102 6/32 for 9/5/85 settlement was .00492. Multiplying .2963 32nds times the .00492 yield value of 1/32 equals .00146, which is the percentage expense per day to be short 10 1/2's of 8/15/85 at a 6 3/4 percent resale rate. Multiplying that percentage expense times 100 gives us the basis points per day expense or .146.

EXHIBIT 8-8

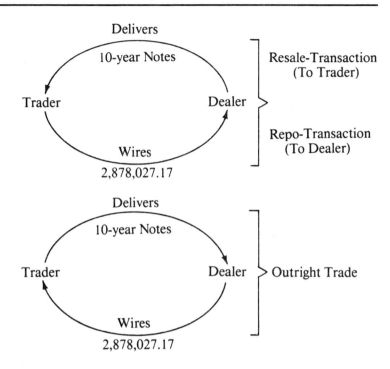

Remember the long position of $10 million two-year notes earned the arbitrageur .166 basis points per day; the short position of $2.8 million in ten-year notes cost him .146 basis points per day. Therefore the total position earns .166 minus .146 or .020 basis points a day. The arbitrageur has a small positive carry on his position.

Let us now examine the cost of carry analysis of a butterfly trade using the example of the five-year to seven-year and ten-year to seven-year butterfly discussed earlier. Remember that a butterfly arbitrage is two yield curve trades. We bought two lots of $10 million wi seven-year notes, selling $12.5 million of five-year notes against one $10 million lot of wi seven-year notes and selling $8.1 million of ten-year notes against the second $10 million lot of seven-year notes. We will analyze the cost of carry by dealing with each leg of the trade separately.

The wi seven-year note long position did not settle until January 4, 1983. Therefore until that date there was no carry gain from either of the two long positions. The proceeds of selling $12.5 million of five-year notes (10 1/8's due 2/15/88) are as follows for December 23, 1982, settlement:

$12,460,937.50   principal
      72,233.17   accrued interest
$12,533,160.67   total

To borrow these securities which we are shorting, we will establish a resale agreement with the dealer to whom we sold the notes (the agreement will bc a repo agreement from the dealer's standpoint). We will be receiving $12,533,160.67 from our sale of the five-year notes. We are lending that sum of money to the dealer, but we want a specific piece of collateral against this loan, namely 10 1/8's of 2/15/88. The dealer would normally pay us the standard RP rate of 8 1/4 percent on money we are lending to him, but because we want specified collateral which he must seek out in the RP market, we will receive something less than 8 1/4 percent, say 7 percent. We are short $12.5 million five-year notes with a 10 1/8 coupon costing us $3,439.20 per day or $275.14 per day per million ($3,439.20 divided by $12.5 million). We are earning seven percent per day on the proceeds of our resale agreement or $2,437.00 per day ($12,533,160.67 times .07 times 1/360) or $194.96 per day per million ($2,437.00 divided by $12.5 million). We are paying out $275.14 per day per million and earning $194.96 per day per million. Net, we are losing $80.18 per day per million ($275.15 minus $194.96) to be short the five-year note with a borrowing rate of seven percent. To translate that figure into 32nds per million of face amount of five-year notes we divide $80.18 by $312.50 to get .2566 32nds. The yield value of 1/32 for the five-year note at 99 22/32 for December 23, 1982 settlement is .0080. Therefore .2566 times .0080 equals .00205, which is the percentage per day we lose being short the five-year note on these terms. Multiplying by 100 gives us .205 or the number of basis points a day this short position costs us to carry.

Our next short position is $8.1 million in 10-year notes (10 1/2's

11/15/92 at 100 3/32) for December 23, 1982 settlement generating proceeds of

$8,107,593.75	principal
89,279.01	accrued interest
$8,196,872.76	total

To borrow these securities which we are shorting, we will also establish a resale agreement with the dealer to whom we sold the notes. This issue we will assume is harder to borrow so the dealer will only pay us 6 1/2 percent on our $8,196,872.76. We are paying out $2,349.45 per day to service the 10 1/2 percent coupon on $8.1 million of ten-year notes, or $290.06 per day per million ($2,349.45 divided by 8.1). We are earning $1,479.99 per day on our resale ($8,196,872.76 times .065 times 1/360) or $182.71 per day per million ($1,479.99 divided by 8.1). We are paying out $290.06 per day per million on our short and earning $182.71 per day per million on our resale. We are therefore losing $107.35 per day per million on our short position in ten-year notes on these borrowing terms. In terms of 32nds per million face amount of ten-year notes, that is $107.35/$312.50 or .3435 32nds. The yield value of 1/32 for 10 1/2's of 11/15/92 at 100 3/32 for settlement on December 23, 1982 was .0052. Therefore .3435 times .0052 equals .00179, which is the percentage per day we lose being short the ten-year note on these terms. Multiplying by 100 gives us .179 or the number of basis points a day that this short position costs us to carry.

We are short five-year notes at .205 basis points negative carry per day and short ten-year notes at .179 basis points negative carry per day. Our combined short position costs us .205 plus .179 or .384 basis points negative carry each day. Remember that the seven-year note long position we took on the butterfly settled on January 4, 1983. For the 12 days from December 23 to January 4 we will be accumulating negative carry of 4.61 basis points (.384 times 12), assuming the borrowing terms on our short positions stay constant. We established our butterfly position shorting five-years and ten-years versus long seven-years at + .36 basis points. For us to break even on the trade, the spread must move in our favor by 4.61 basis points, going to a net of 31.4 basis points by January 4.

After January 4, however, we will be earning positive carry on our position in seven-year notes. Let us examine what that positive carry will be beginning January 4, dealing with each $10 million long position separately.

On December 22, 1982, we bought $10 million in seven-year notes due January 15, 1990, at a yield of 10.51 percent. The auction results that day established the coupon on the issue to be 10 1/2 percent. The dollar price was determined to be 99.935 at a 10.51 percent yield. On settlement day January 4, 1983, we will establish a repurchase agreement with the dealer from whom we bought the seven-year notes. If the market prices have not changed materially, the amount of the repo would likely be the proceeds of our outright purchase, namely $9,993,500.00. (Remember for the moment we are treating the total $20 million purchase of seven-year notes as two separate $10 million purchases.) We are likely to receive the standard repo rate of 8 1/4 percent. (The actual RP rate on January 4, 1983, was 9 1/4 percent because of year-end money market strains and large Treasury note and bond settlements. Soon thereafter the more normal 8 1/4 percent rate prevailed.)

We are earning 10 1/2 percent per day on our $10 million seven-year notes or $2,853.26. Per million face amount of seven-year notes we are earning $285.33 per day ($2,853.26 divided by 10). We are paying 8 1/4 percent per day to borrow the $9,993,500.00 to finance our long position or $2,290.18 per day. Interest to finance $1 million of our seven-year notes is $229.02 per day per million. Our positive carry on one $10 million lot of our long position in seven-year notes is $285.33 per million per day minus $229.02 per million per day or $56.31 per day per million. That sum of money represents 56.31/312.50 32nds on $1 million face amount or .1802 32nds. We determined the yield value of 1/32 on wi seven-year notes assuming a 10 1/2 coupon maturing January 15, 1998, for January 4, 1983 settlement at 10.51 percent yield to be .0064. Multiplying the yield value of 1/32 (.0064) times the number of 1/32nds positive carry per day per million (.1802) gives us .00115 percent a day positive carry or .115 basis points per day.

We can now calculate the negative carry on our trade after January 4, 1983, assuming that the terms to borrow our two short positions and to finance our long position remain constant. Our short in five-year notes costs .205 basis points per day; our long in seven-year notes earns us .115 basis points per day. The front half of our butterfly therefore involves negative carry of .205 minus .115 or .090 basis points per day. Our short in ten-year notes costs .179 basis points per day; our other long in seven-year notes earns us .115 basis points per day net. The back half of our butterfly, therefore, involves negative carry of .179 minus .115 or .064. Our total trade has negative carry of .090 plus .064 or .154 basis points per day.

Positive or negative carry features of a trade are best expressed in this basis point evaluation system to determine how patient an arbitrageur can be with a trade and how much spread change must occur to make up the negative carry and still leave some profit.

ROLLING POSITIONS

At the outset of our discussion we had said that yield curve arbitrageurs tend to take positions only at points on the curve where the Treasury regularly finances. Those 11 points (10 points as long as the 20-year bond cycle is omitted) on the curve are the most liquid areas representing either recently auctioned securities or upcoming supply. Arbitrageurs avoid "dead spots" on the curve such as six years, eight years, and fifteen years.

When an arbitrageur has a position in say the seven-year note, and the Treasury announces a new seven-year note, the arbitrageur should usually roll the position into the new seven-year if he is long or reverse-roll his position if he is short. The new when-issued seven-year note more accurately represents the seven-year point on the curve; the old issue is beginning to drift into the "dead space" between five-years and seven-years. The new issue gets more market focus and is far more liquid.

Arbitrageurs try to estimate the roll spread between the outstanding issue and the when-issued security so that they can determine how that part of the yield curve will be reshaped. Certain factors affecting the roll spread lend themselves to mathematical calculation; other factors depend on the bullish or bearish market climate.

Quantitative Factors in the Roll Spread

The two main quantitative factors affecting the roll spread are (1) cost of carry and (2) extension on the yield curve.

Cost of Carry.   When short-term rates are lower than longer term rates, there is an advantage to owning a fixed-income security paying interest over one that is trading when-issued (wi). The owner of the outstanding two-year note earns say 9.00 percent; the owner of the wi two-year note only earns the RP rate which may be 7 1/2 percent until settlement date on the new wi two-year. The following example illustrates how this carry profit in owning the interest paying issue versus the wi can be calculated.

Consider the situation on the afternoon of September 11, 1985, in which the Treasury was to announce a new two-year note to be auctioned the next week, settling on September 30, 1985, and maturing September 30, 1987. The outstanding two-year note is the 8 7/8 8/31/87 trading at 99 20/32. We want to calculate the cost of carry component of the two-year roll.

We will first analyze the outstanding 8 7/8 8/31/87. At a dollar price of 99 20/32 for regular settlement 9/12/85 $1 million notes generate purchase proceeds of

Principal	$996,250.00
Accrued interest	2,451.66
Proceeds	$998,701.66

Each day we hold this position we earn 8 7/8 on $1 million or $245.16 (8 7/8 percent times $1 million divided by 362). Leveraged arbitrageurs would finance this position in the RP market by borrowing the $998,701.66 (note that a retail investor selling $1 million two-years at this price would generate the same $998,701.66 to place in the RP market). We may commit to a fixed rate RP from 9/12 to 9/30 or arrange separate RP's daily from 9/12 to 9/30 at varying RP rates. We will choose a fixed rate RP at 7 5/8 percent for purposes of our example. An RP rate of 7 5/8 percent on $998,701.66 equals $211.53 per day. Owning the outstanding two-year note earns $245.16 per day. The difference of $33.63 is our carry profit per day. Over the 18 day when-issued period that amounts to $605.34. We must now translate that dollar carry profit into an equivalent yield spread. This is done as follows. First, divide $605.34 by $312.50 (1/32 on $1 million notes) to obtain 1.937088. Next, multiply 1.937088 by the yield value of 1/32 on the 8 7/8 8/31/87 at 99 20/32 for 9/12 settlement which is .01775. The product of 1.937088 and .01775 equals .0344, which is the yield value of the carry profit to own the outstanding two-year note versus RP at 7 5/8 percent. If no other factors affected the roll and the markets behaved mathematically, the new wi two-year should yield 3.44 basis points more than the 8 7/8 8/31/87 immediately following the two-year announcement.

Notice that the carry profit declines as settlement date on the new issue approaches. Carry profit varies with the time to settlement date and the spread between the RP rate and the current yield on the outstanding issue. An arbitrageur who is *short* the 8 7/8 8/31/87 and is borrowing in the resale market at 6 percent has a carry *loss* in being short the 8 7/8 8/31/87. The short position is *costing,* not earning, 8 7/8 percent per day; the resale is earning only 6 percent a day. The carry expense in this position is $245.16 per day less $166.45 or $78.71 times 18 days or $1,416.78. The yield spread that results from these terms is $1,416.78 times (1/312.50) times .01775 or .0805. The break-even carry expense roll spread for the short seller is substantially different from that of the arbitrageur who is long the two-year note.

To summarize, the carry component of the roll spread is easily calculated mathematically and depends on the length of the when-issued period and the assumed repo or resale rate.

Extension on the Yield Curve.   Newly announced three- and six-month bills are one week longer than the old bills, the new one-year bill is four weeks longer, the new two-year note is one month further out the curve, and the remainder of longer coupons are three months longer than the respective outstanding issues. In a positively sloped yield curve, therefore, the new issues should usually trade at a higher yield than the outstanding issues. To determine how much higher in yield the new wi securities should trade, we shall look at the following situation.

On Wednesday, July 31, 1985, the Treasury was to announce a

mid-quarter financing package of three-year, ten-year, and thirty-year securities. Arbitrageurs are interested in estimating the roll spreads from the outstanding three-year, ten-year, and thirty-year issues to the new wi three-year, ten-year, and thirty-year so that they can forecast the change in the shape of the yield curve after the announcement. We will concentrate on the three-year note.

The yield curve consists of:

two-year note = 8 7/8 7/31/87 at 99^{25+} to yield 8.99%

three-year note = 10 5/15/88 at 101^{18} to yield 9.34%

four-year note = 9 5/8 6/30/89 at 99^{22+} to yield 9.71%

The new wi three-year note matures 8/15/88.

The yield spread between 7/31/87 and 5/15/88 is 35 basis points for 9 1/2 months or 3.7 basis points per month. A new issue maturing three months longer than 5/15/88 should theoretically yield 3.7 times three months or 11.1 basis points more than the 10's 5/15/88.

On the other hand the yield spread from 5/15/88 to 6/30/89 is 37 basis points for 13 1/2 months or 2.7 basis points per month. A new issue maturing three months longer than 5/15/88 should theoretically yield 8.2 basis points more than the 10 5/15/88.

Looking from two-years to three-years, the curve extension component of the roll should be 11.1 basis points, and from four-years back to three-years it should be 8.2 basis points. The truth lies somewhere in between or approximately 9.5 basis points. We have begun to confront some subjective elements in determining the roll spread.

Summarizing the Quantitative Aspects of the Roll Spread.   Let us assume that the term RP rate from 8/1 to 8/15 in the example above was 7 7/8 percent. The carry component of the roll spread for 10 5/15/88 into the wi three-year notes is then

10%/day earned =	$271.74
7 7/8%/day paid on RP proceeds of $1,015,625.00 + $21,195.65 or $1,036,820.65	226.80
Positive carry per day	$ 44.94

From 8/1/85 to 8/15/85 the carry profit equals $629.16. Then, $629.16 times (1/312.50) times .0130 (the yield value of 1/32 on 10 5/15/88 at 101 18/32) equals .026 or 2.6 basis points cost of carry component of the roll spread.

Theoretically the carry component of 2.6 basis points should be added to the yield curve extension component of 9.5 basis points to determine the roll spread. Experience shows that the 12.1 basis points resulting spread is about twice the spread that one should expect. Clearly other factors are influencing the roll spread. Let us now examine the qualitative elements of the roll spread.

Qualitative Elements of the Roll Spread

There are two qualitative elements of the roll spread: (1) coupon disparity and (2) when-issued volatility.

Coupon Disparity.   In the discussion of factors that shape the yield curve we had mentioned that issues trading at substantial premiums usually trade at higher yields than issues trading at par or discount prices. Exhibit 8–5 demonstrated an extreme case of this coupon disparity during the bullish climate in the fall of 1982.

The degree of coupon disparity varies with market climate. An outstanding issue with a coupon one percentage point above the prevailing interest rate can trade with a penalty of from 2 to 3 basis points or as much as 10 to 12 basis points depending on market conditions. In our example involving the roll from 10's of 5/15/88 into the wi three-year note, the 10s were 5/8 percent above the prevailing coupon rate and trading at a 1 18/32 premium. That coupon disparity may have been worth approximately 3 or 4 basis points.

When-Issued Volatility.   When-issued notes and bonds trading before an auction has set the coupon tend to be more volatile than outstanding notes and bonds with set coupons. During bull market moves before the wi is auctioned, a wi security is always a current coupon issue and does not rise in price premium as do other already set coupon issues on the yield curve. During bullish climates the wi issues are also in greater demand because they are current, par securities, and highly liquid. They therefore catch a lot of speculative demand. In bullish climates investors often prefer to focus their buying interest in new issues on the assumption, sometimes untrue, that the supply pressure of a new issue must mean that it is cheap. Customers like to buy what is offered.

In bearish climates the wi issue can sometimes trade cheaper than the cost of carry and yield curve extension factors would justify. Such occasions are rare and reflect a deeply depressed market atmosphere.

Investors interested in maximum liquidity and arbitrageurs will usually want to trade the wi issue. The issue that is "current" therefore commands some price premium in most market circumstances except in an extremely bearish environment.

To summarize, the more bullish the climate the more of a premium (lower yield) the wi issue will trade from the "logical" roll determination using cost of carry and yield curve extension factors. In our example above the roll spread from 10's 5/15/88 into the wi 8/15/88 should have been approximately 12 basis points using simple mathematics. The qualitative factors reduced that spread by approximately 4 basis points for coupon disparity and two basis points for being the "current, active" issue in a somewhat bullish environment. These qualitative factors reduced the roll spread to 6 basis points from 12 basis points, which was the actual roll spread for the first few hours of trading.

CHAPTER 9

MARCELLE ARAK is Vice President and Head of the Capital Markets Analysis and the Options and Arbitrage Units of Citicorp's North American Investment Bank. The CMA group analyzes developments in the fixed income markets and provides strategies for traders and investors.

Prior to joining Citicorp, she was Vice President in the Research area of the Federal Reserve Bank of New York. She has taught at Baruch College, a unit of the City University of New York, and at M.I.T.

Ms. Arak has written on a wide variety of financial topics including financial futures, tax exempt bonds, and original issue discount bonds and is especially known for her analysis of tax structure effects on financial markets.

Ms. Arak earned her doctorate in economics from M.I.T. and her B.A. from the University of Rochester.

LAURIE GOODMAN is a Vice President in the Capital Markets Analysis Unit of Citicorp's North American Investment Bank. She specializes in research and analysis of fixed income financial instruments, with an emplasis on futures and options. She also develops trading, hedging, and arbitrage strategies for Citicorp's customers as well as for internal purposes.

Prior to joining Citicorp, Ms. Goodman was a Secior Economist at the Federal Reserve Bank of New York, researching issues involving the interest rate risk management of financial institutions. She has also served on the finance faculty of the Graduate School of Business at New York University.

Ms. Goodman holds a Ph.D. in economics from Stanford University, and a B.A. from the University of Pennsylvania. She has published extensively in both academic and practitioner journals. Her recent publications have included articles on debt options, mortgage-backed securities and portfolio management techniques.

JOSEPH SNAILER is an Assistant Vice President in the Capital Markets Analysis Unit of Citicorp's North American Investment Bank. He specializes in research and quantitative analysis in fixed income financial instruments.

Prior to joining Citicorp, Mr. Snailer was an economist in the financial markets area of the research department at the Federal Reserve Bank of New York.

Mr. Snailer holds an M.S. in Statistics from New York University and a B.S. in Economics and Applied Mathematics from the State University of New York at Stony Brook.

DURATION EQUIVALENT SWAPS

Marcelle Arak, Ph.D.
Vice President
Citicorp North American Investment Bank

Laurie Goodman, Ph.D.
Vice President
Citicorp North American Investment Bank

Joseph Snailer
Assistant Vice President
Citicorp North American Investment Bank

In recent years, "duration" measures have become increasingly popular tools for portfolio immunization and hedging. However, duration can also be used as the basis of profitable trading and arbitrage strategies. In this chapter, we describe a methodology which we developed to select cheap securities to buy and expensive securities to sell while avoiding interest-rate risk. We show (1) how to select the most profitable way of achieving a given duration on a given day, (2) how to evaluate the risks involved in achieving the duration one way rather than another, and (3) how to spot arbitrage opportunities.

THE CONCEPT OF DURATION

We begin our discussion with an introduction to the concept of duration. Duration is a cash flow timing measure which is used to evaluate interest-rate risk. It is the time at which the cash flows, present valued, are centered. More importantly, duration measures the price responsiveness of an outstanding note or bond to changes in its yield. In fact, any series of cash flows, regular or irregular, can be characterized by a single duration number. For example, an instrument with a duration of four years will lose (approximately) 4 percent of its value if the required yield rises 100 basis points, whereas an instrument with a duration of eight years will lose (approximately) 8 percent of its value if the required yield rises 100 basis points.

The duration or center of the cash flows can be quite different from the maturity of a security. The duration of a zero-coupon bond will always be equal to its maturity since there is only one cash flow—at the end. However, the duration of a coupon-bearing bond will be less than its maturity since some of the cash flows (the coupons) are received before the bond matures. When interest rates are very low, the duration of a long bond was fairly close to its maturity. When rates are high, however, the coupon flows are large relative to the principal and pull the duration down. For example, in an 11.75 percent yield environment a twenty-year 11.75 percent bond will have a duration of about eight years, giving the twenty-year bond about the same price risk (relative to dollars invested) as an eight-year zero. That is, a 10 basis point rise in interest rates will cause the price of the two bonds to fall by an equivalent percentage.

Technically, the relationship between (Macaulay) duration and price sensitivity is given as follows:

$$dP/P = \frac{D \; dr}{(1 + r/2)} \tag{1}$$

where dP = change in price of bond

D = duration of the instrument (in years)

r = the interest rate (in decimal form)

dr = the change in the interest rate

Besides measuring the price sensitivity of securities, duration also tells us at what point in the future a portfolio's value is "immunized" against a change in interest rates. Clearly, the face value and the rate of return on an eight-year zero-coupon bond are locked in for eight years. However, in an 11.75 percent yield environment the same is true for an 11.75 percent, twenty-year coupon bond, since it also has a duration of close to eight years. If interest rates rise, the inflows for the first eight years will get reinvested at a higher rate thereby cumulating to a greater sum; however, the bond will have a lower market price at the end of the eighth year because it must yield a higher rate from then until maturity. Suppose, in contrast, interest rates fall. Then at the end of eight years the reinvested inflows will accumulate to less but the bond will have a higher market price. In either case, the plus and minus effects just balance if the asset is evaluated at its duration.

This is illustrated in Table 9-1. Let us assume $100 was invested on April 15, 1985, in a twenty-year bond with a coupon of 11.75 percent, priced at par. This bond has a duration of almost exactly eight years, and will be worth $249.28 on April 15, 1993, assuming that interest rates are unchanged and that the coupons are reinvested at a 11.75 percent rate. If interest rates go up to 12.25 percent immediately, the interest payments will cumulate to $152.39 eight years from now. The market value of a bond with a remaining maturity of twelve years and a coupon of 11.75 percent would be $96.90 in a 12.25 percent yield environment. This twenty-year bond will therefore have a liquidation value of $96.90 in April 1993. The total value of interest plus sale proceeds will be $249.29, virtually the same as in the constant interest rate scenario. If the position is liquidated prior to eight years, the fall in the bond price will be larger than the gain from reinvestment. (This is because the bond has a longer remaining maturity—and so more loss—while the coupon interest has less time to accumulate.) For example, if interest rates rose and liquidation occurred immediately, the value of the bond would be $96.30 and there would be no gains from the higher reinvestment rate. For liquidation dates beyond eight years, the price drop in the bond will be less because of its shorter remaining maturity, while the reinvestment of coupons will cumulate to more.

TABLE 9-1
Dollar Value of 11 ¾ Percent Bond Plus
Cumulated Interest at Various Future Dates*

	Interest Rate (%)		
Time Elapsed	11.25	11.75	12.25
An instant	0	0	0
	103.95	100.00	96.30
	103.95	100.00	96.30
2 Years	25.56	25.65	25.75
	103.82	100.00	96.40
	129.38	125.65	122.15
4 Years	57.37	57.89	58.41
	103.67	100.00	96.53
	161.04	157.84	154.94
6 Years	96.97	98.34	97.84
	103.48	100.00	96.69
	200.45	198.34	196.53
8 Years	146.25	149.28	152.39
	103.25	100.00	96.90
	249.50	249.28	249.29
10 Years	207.60	213.23	219.04
	102.96	100.00	97.16
	310.56	313.23	316.20
12 Years	283.96	293.59	303.59
	107.59	100.00	97.50
	386.55	393.59	401.09
14 Years	379.00	394.56	410.84
	102.14	100.00	97.92
	481.14	494.56	508.76

*Top number denotes value of reinvested coupons, middle number is resale value of bond, bottom number is total.

Thus the effect in interest earnings will exceed the effect on bond values. Similarly, if rates decline to 11.25 percent, the market value of the bond, eight years hence, rises. Due to lower reinvestment rates, however, total proceeds from liquidating after eight years remain at roughly $249.

The reader should note that to maintain an immunized portfolio for a particular future date, the holdings will usually need to be adjusted over time. For long coupon bonds, the duration measure is relatively insensitive to the passage of time. That is, the price sensitivity is roughly the same one year from now as at the present time. For example, on April 15, 1986, if yields remained at their 1985 levels, the 11.75 percent, twenty-year bond in the above example would still have a duration of about eight years. Thus, if the coupons were invested in additional quantities of that bond, the immunization date would be eight years after April 1986, which is beyond the April 1993 target date.

Calculating Duration

The duration of a stream of payments is roughly equal to the average term of the stream, where each flow is weighted by its contribution to the total present value. Thus, duration, as defined by Frederick Macaulay, is given below:

$$D = \sum_{i=1}^{N} \frac{tC_t/[2(1+r/2)^t]}{P} \qquad (2)$$

where:

C_t is the cash flow t semi-annual periods from now

C_N is the coupon plus principal flow N semi-annual periods from now

P is the price of the instrument

This can also be expressed in terms of price responsiveness as follows:

$$D = \frac{\frac{dP}{P}}{\frac{dr}{1+r/2}} \qquad (3)$$

Equation (3) is simply a restatement of equation (1), and is equivalent to (2).

Modified Duration

Many market participants prefer to think of price sensitivity as being linearly related to changes in interest rates. Rather than using Macaulay duration, they use "modified duration" which is Macaulay duration divided by $(1 + r/2)$. Thus, modified duration linearizes the relationship between changes in yield and changes in price as follows:

$$\frac{dP}{P} = D_{mod} \cdot dr \tag{4}$$

The other change which market participants make in Macaulay duration is that, since the actual amount which must be paid is not the price, but rather the price plus accrued interest, this is used as the market value.

When discussing duration, it is important to know whether the duration measure used is Macaulay or modified duration and whether or not the calculations incorporate accrued interest. The differences can be substantial as shown below for the $11\frac{5}{8}$ of 2004 on April 4, 1985 for settlement on April 8, 1985.

	Duration	
	Macaulay	Modified
Without accrued	8.038	7.589
With accrued	7.640	7.213

The methodology for these calculations is straightforward. The price of the bond on 4/4/85 was 98-12(in 32nds). This was translated into decimal form (98.375). The accrued interest was 5.130 per $100 face. The change in price for a one basis point move in rates can be calculated as: 1/32 divided by the yield value of 1/32. The yield value of 1/32 on this bond is .4186 basis points which enters the formula as .00004186. Thus modified duration with accrued is calculated as shown below:

$$D_{mod} = \frac{1/32}{\frac{P+A}{YV \text{ of } 1/32}} = \frac{.03125}{\frac{103.505}{.00004186}} = 7.213$$

In order to calculate Macaulay duration, the above would have been multiplied by $(1 + r/2)$ or (1.0592).

In our duration equivalent swap calculations we use modified duration with accrued. Neglecting accrued interest distorts duration calculations, particularly for high coupon bonds near a coupon drop. It does not matter if we use Macaulay or modified duration, providing we know which one is used.

Duration of a Combination

The duration of a combination of two securities is a weighted average of the two durations, with the weights determined by market values. Let us assume one purchased $10 million par of the $10\frac{3}{8}$s of 2/15/88 and $20 million par of the $11\frac{5}{8}$s of 11/15/2004. The market value (price plus accrued) of the $10\frac{3}{8}$s of 88 was about 100-17 at the close on 4/4/85; its duration was 2.380. The market value of the $11\frac{5}{8}$s of 04 was 103-16 on 4/4/85, while its duration was 7.213. The duration of the combination is given by:

$$\frac{(1.0053)(\$10)(2.380) + (1.0350)(\$20)(7.213)}{(1.0053)(\$10) + (1.0350)(\$20)} = 5.633$$

We should point out one other important fact at this point. In an 11.75 percent rate environment, long-term Treasury instruments have a modified duration of under $8\frac{1}{2}$ years or so (thirty-year coupon instruments have a duration only slightly longer than twenty-year instruments). Shorter term Treasury instruments have a modified duration a bit shorter than their maturity. Thus, if one is trying to use a combination of a thirty-year and a three-year security to replicate a seven year, the weights will be far more equal than one would have anticipated based on maturity.

DURATION EQUIVALENT COMBINATIONS

We have developed programs which identify duration equivalent swaps. Each day we examine these swaps to see where the most profitable opportunities exist. Appendix 9–A provides a technical description.

Table 9–2 shows the duration equivalent swap table based on April 3, 1985, closing prices. The maturity, duration, price plus accrued (in 32nds) and yield to maturity of the most actively traded Treasury securities are listed in the first row; the first column gives the combinations. In order to duplicate the duration of a target security with a combination of two other instruments, one of the instruments must have a duration higher than the target security, while the other must have a duration lower than the target security. For example, a ten-year security and a four-year security cannot duplicate the duration on a twenty-year security, so that square of the matrix is blank.

Where duration equivalent swaps are possible, the numbers on the right half of each square tell you how much face value of each security in the combination to buy, while the number in the left half of the square tells you the yield on the duration equivalent combination. For example, a twenty-year/seven-year combination will have the same duration as a ten-year security if .352 face value of the twenty-year and .631 face value of the seven year is purchased for each $1 face value of the ten year. Put differently, rather than purchasing $100 par of the ten year, you would purchase $35.20 par of the twenty year and $63.10 par of the seven year. The duration and dollars invested would be identical to those of the target security, but the yield on the combination would be 11.74 percent, above the 11.71 percent yield on the target security.

On April 3, 1985, there were many profitable swaps from combinations into single issues. For example, you could have picked up 37 basis points by selling the current thirty-year bond and the current two-year note ($.930 million face of the thirty year and $.095 million face of the two year) and buying $1 million of the twenty-year bond. The combination had a yield of 11.56 percent whereas the twenty-year bond yielded 11.93 percent. Or, you could have sold a combination of the twenty-year bond and the three-year note ($.447 million face of the twenty-year and $.554 million face of the three year) and bought $1 million of the seven-year note. The yield would have then been 11.65 percent instead of 11.28 percent and the duration would have been identical.

We denote by an asterisk cases where the combination yield is higher than that of the duration equivalent target issue. Absence of an asterisk means the single security provides a yield pick-up.

Bullets vs. Barbells

You may notice from Table 9–2 that a combination generally has a lower yield than a single instrument. This is due to the fact that in a normal upward sloping yield curve environment, the yield curve is "concave" when looked at from below. This means that the line connecting any two points on the yield curve (i.e., a weighted average of two different maturities) will, in general, lie below the yield curve. (See *Figure 9–1.*) Thus a combination with a higher yield than a

---

FIGURE 9–1
General Shape of Duration Yield Curve

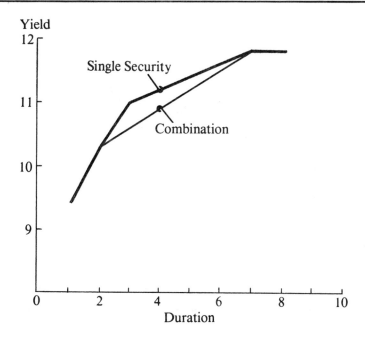

TABLE 9–2
Duration Equivalent Swaps for Treasuries*

Maturity	30	20	10	7	5	4	3	2
Duration	8.175	7.561	5.724	4.701	3.760	3.143	2.388	1.748
Price + Acc.	97.29	100.20	98.28	100.18	101.05	100.14	100.14	100.21
Yield to Mat.	11.685	11.926	11.706	11.649	11.351	11.149	10.766	10.445
Maturities								
30–10		11.69 .771 / .255						
30– 7		11.68 .847 / .177	11.66 .298 / .693					
30– 5		11.64 .885 / .138	11.50 .449 / .543	11.42 .219 / .782				
30– 4		11.62 .903 / .122	11.42 .518 / .479	11.31 .318 / .691	11.21 .127 / .884			
30– 3		11.58 .919 / .106	11.29 .582 / .417	11.13 .411 / .601	10.98 .245 / .768	10.88 .134 / .870		
30– 2		11.56 .930 / .095	11.21 .625 / .375	11.01 .472 / .540	10.83 .324 / .690	10.71 .223 / .781	10.56 .102 / .899	
20– 7			11.74** .352 / .631					
20– 5			11.64 .508 / .472	11.49 .247 / .748				
20– 4			11.60 .574 / .409	11.42 .352 / .648	11.25 .141 / .866			

Maturity					
20–3	10.60 .100 .888	10.93 .146 .854	11.07 .267 .740	11.28 .447 .554	11.51 .634 .350
20–2		10.80 .239 .759	10.95 .348 .657	11.19 .508 .492	11.45 .672 .310
10–5				11.52 .487 .518	
10–4			11.28 .245 .766	11.48 .614 .397	
10–3		10.97 .230 .774	11.15 .421 .593	11.41 .705 .307	
10–2	10.64 .163 .837	10.88 .356 .648	11.08 .518 .496	11.38 .755 .257	
7–4			11.34 .399 .608		
7–3		11.05 .326 .674	11.29 .597 .410		
7–2	10.70 .216 .782	11.01 .472 .527	11.26 .686 .320		
5–3		11.08 .546 .450			
5–2	10.73 .316 .681	11.07 .688 .306			
4–2	10.77** .459 .540				

* As of 4/3/85.
** Equivalent duration combination has a higher yield for equivalent investment than simple instrument.

target security is a rare occurrence and should be considered an excellent buy.

A combination of two securities is often referred to as a "barbell," whereas a single security is called a "bullet." Some astute readers are probably wondering why, if a barbell and a bullet have equivalent interest-rate risk, i.e., equivalent duration, the bullet will have a higher yield. Portfolio theory teaches that instruments of equivalent risk should have equivalent returns or the security with the lower return would be strictly dominated by the security with the higher return. No one would buy the inferior security at the stated yield and there would be excess demand for the superior security. The price on the inferior security must fall and the price on the superior security must rise until the yields are identical. At this point, both markets would clear.

Applying this argument, a duration equivalent combination should have the same yield as the target security. Stated differently, there should be a linear relationship between yield and duration. We don't, however, observe this relationship. The reason is that the single duration number does not capture the complexity of interest-rate risk. Simply matching the duration of assets with that of liabilities will guarantee immunization only for parallel shifts in the yield curve. If the yield curve moves up or down in a non-parallel fashion—flattens, steepens, or develops a hump—this assumption will obviously be violated.

A non-parallel shift of the yield curve in which short rates change more than long rates will usually cause a smaller change in price in a combination than in a single security. And short rates do, in fact, change more than long rates, as measured by the standard deviations shown in Table 9–3.

The impact of such non-parallel shifts on barbells and bullets can best be illustrated by positing a hypothetical combination—50 percent of a security with a duration of two years and 50 percent of a security with a duration of six years. Both securities are selling at par. This combination has the same duration as a single security with a duration of four years. We assume, hypothetically, that interest rates rise 50 basis points for the two-year duration security and 10 basis points for the six-year duration security. The change in price per $100 of the combination is approximately $.80. If the

TABLE 9-3
**Standard Deviation of One-Month Changes
in Rates on Various Treasury Securities**

Maturity (in Years)	March 77 to February 85	January 82 to February 85
30	.44	.40
20	.46	.43
10	.51	.45
7	.55	.46
5	.61	.48
3	.70	.52
2	.79	.54

yield on the four year duration security moved by the average shift— $(.5)(50)+(.5)(10)$ or 30 basis points—the change in price would be \$1.20, which is greater than the change on the combination.[1] Thus the bullet is, in general, more sensitive to the typical type of non-parallel shifts in the yield curve. That is, its risk is higher. Consequently, we would normally expect a configuration where the bullet has a higher return than the combination. Where we do not find this configuration, or, alternatively, where we find the situation where the return on the combination is substantially

[1] We can figure the breakeven change in the target security (t) as follows:

$$dr_t = \frac{W_L dr_L D_L P_L + W_H dr_H D_H P_H}{D_t P_t}$$

where W_L and W_H = the weights on the low and high duration securities, respectively

D_L, D_H, D_t = the durations of the low, high, and target duration securities

dr_L, dr_H, dr_t = the yield changes of the low, high, and target securities

P_L, P_H, P_t = the prices plus accrued interest on the low, high, and target securities

In the example above, the breakeven dr_t is roughly 20 basis points.

lower than is warranted by the reduced risk, we can capitalize on the misalignment.

Taking Advantage of Misalignments

The duration equivalent swap table, Table 9–2, can be used to suggest that certain bonds are overpriced relative to a combination. Consider the four-year/two-year combination in order to achieve the same duration as a three-year note. Even though the yield pick-up is extremely small, we would expect the combination yield to fall relative to the single instrument as the rates move back to the normal scenario where the single instrument has the higher yield. At the point when the normal configuration is reestablished, and the single instrument has become cheaper, the swap can be reversed. The holding period return on the combination will consist of the initial yield pick-up (which may be small) plus the realignment gain.

Here is a real life illustration. On December 31, 1984, a duration equivalent combination of a twenty year (the $11\frac{5}{8}$s of 2004) and a seven year (the $11\frac{1}{8}$s of 1/15/92) had a slightly higher yield than the then active ten year (the $11\frac{5}{8}$s of 11/15/94). The yield was 11.54 percent versus 11.523 percent. The weights reported in the table constructed for that day suggested that one purchase .348 of the twenty year and .671 of the seven year. The total initial cost of the combination would have been 102-06 (price plus accrued, in 32nds). The cost of the ten year was also 102-06. By February 6, 1985 the relative yields had realigned—the ten year was yielding 11.30 percent while the combination was yielding 11.26 percent. At this time, the ten year was selling for 104-18, for a gain of $2\frac{12}{32}$. However, the sale price on the combination was:

$$.348(104\tfrac{30}{32}) + .671(103\tfrac{5}{32}) = 105\tfrac{23}{32}.$$

for a gain of $3\frac{17}{32}$, larger than the gain on the ten-year security by $1\frac{5}{32}$.

Not every "misalignment" is a desirable arbitrage, however. The combination of a twenty year and a seven year to duplicate a ten year shown in Table 9–2 looks attractive. That is, investors can pick up 3 basis points in yield and achieve less risk through the combination. However, since the ten-year note (the $11\frac{1}{4}$ of 2/15/95) commands a premium because its coupons are Fed-wireable, it is not clear that one can count on a realignment. The combination is, nevertheless, attractive for buy and hold investors.

Arbitrage

The concept of duration equivalent swaps can be used for arbitrage purposes. For example, if a combination is more attractive, one could go short the simple instrument and go long the combination.

Let us consider the example above as an arbitrage strategy. On December 31, 1984 one could have bought the combination at the ask price of 102-06 and sold short the ten year at the bid price of 102-04. On February 6, the short position could have been closed out at the ask price, 104-18, and the long position could have been closed out at the bid prices:

$$.348(104\tfrac{28}{32}) + .671(103\tfrac{3}{32}) = 105\tfrac{21}{32}$$

Thus the gain on the long position would have been 105-21 minus 102-06 or $3\tfrac{15}{32}$, the loss on the short position would have been 102-04 minus 104-18 or $-2\tfrac{14}{32}$, and the gross gain would have been $\tfrac{33}{32}$. Assuming that the "haircut" for short selling was 50 basis points per annum, the cost over the period in question would have been about 5 basis points or $\tfrac{2}{32}$. The arbitrage would have produced a net gain of $\tfrac{31}{32}$— about 1 percent of the gross position. As you can see, large arbitrage profits were possible and the investor did not take on a net position in that duration category.

ADVANCED APPLICATIONS

Evaluating Yield Pick-Up Versus Risk

As was stressed earlier, a combination is usually more expensive than a bullet. This reflects, in a general sense, the lower risk of the combination when short rates move more than long rates. Is the premium paid for this lower risk fair? Or, would one be better off with the high yielding bullet? We now develop a methodology to evaluate the extra risk of a bullet, and compare it to the yield pick-up achieved by holding it rather than a barbell.

Because the combination is less sensitive to shifts in the yield

TABLE 9–4
Standard Deviations of Twelve-Month Changes
in Treasury Yield Spreads

Spread	March 77 to February 85	January 82 to February 85
30–20 Year	.14	.13
30–10	.29	.27
30– 7	.44	.38
30– 5	.64	.51
30– 3	.95	.69
30– 2	1.21	.79
20–10	.24	.27
20– 7	.38	.37
20– 5	.58	.51
20– 3	.89	.69
20– 2	1.16	.78
10– 7	.17	.11
10– 5	.37	.26
10– 3	.68	.44
10– 2	.96	.54
7– 5	.22	.16
7– 3	.54	.34
7– 2	.81	.45
5– 3	.33	.20
5– 2	.62	.31
3– 2	.32	.13

curve when short rates change by more than long rates, we first ask how much of a yield curve twist is likely. For each combination, we computed the spread between the yields on the two securities and the changes that the spread underwent over various twelve-month periods. Standard deviations of twelve-month changes in yield spreads between securities are shown in Table 9–4.[2] Thus the stan-

[2] The data used were monthly averages from the Federal Reserve series on constant maturity yields. A four-year constant maturity series was not available.

dard deviation of the change in the yield spread between a thirty-year and a three-year security was 69 basis points since January 1982. Assuming that twists are normally distributed, this standard deviation suggests that only one-third of the time are the absolute values of the twists larger than 69 basis points and only $\frac{1}{6}$ of the time does the short end move more than the long end by an amount exceeding 69 basis points. This information will help us evaluate the relative risk of holding the bullet versus the barbell.

An attractively priced bullet should be able to withstand large non-parallel yield curve shifts and remain cheap to the barbell. We consider a non-parallel yield curve shift in which the yield on the short security in the combination rises by the standard deviation of the change in the short-long spread. The yield on the long security is assumed not to change at all. This is, of course, the situation that is most favorable to the barbell. The yield on the bullet or target security rises by the standard deviation of the change in the target-long spread.[3] In order to illustrate our methodology for taking into account non-parallel shifts in the yield curve, we choose an example: a combination of a thirty-year and a three-year security in order to replicate a seven-year instrument.

Step 1. Using the duration definition given in equation (4), the price drop on the short security can be calculated from:

$$s_{(30,3)}D_3P_3 = dP_3$$

where $s_{(30,3)}$ is the standard deviation of changes in yield spreads between the thirty- and three-year securities.

[3] There are two other conceptual possibilities for non-parallel shifts in the yield curve which we considered and rejected. The first possibility was to treat the barbell the same as above (the yield on the short security in the combination rises by the standard deviation of the change in the short-long spread, while the yield on the long security remains constant). The yield on the target security, however, would rise by the duration weighted average. Thus, if the standard deviation of the 30-3 spread was 69 basis points, the seven year would fall in price by the amount .0069 $[D_7 - D_3]/[D_{30} - D_3]$. We felt this methodology produced numbers that were much too low as it did not take into account the possibility that the target security may rise disproportionately. The second possibility was to have yields on the barbell remain constant and have yields on the bullet rise by one standard deviation of the target-long spread. This type of yield shift was felt to be totally unrealistic.

We can evaluate this price drop by inserting appropriate values for each of the variables:

$$(.0069)(2.388)(100.4375) = 1.655$$

The weights on the (30,3) combination indicate that .601 par of the 3 year would be purchased. Thus, the loss would be .601 × $1.655 or $.995.

Step 2. We now calculate the price drop on the target security. Note the standard deviation of changes in the (30,7) combination is 38 basis points. Using

$$s_{(30,7)} D_7 P_7 = dP_7$$

we obtain

$$(.0038)(4.701)(100.563) = \$1.796$$

The difference between the price changes on the seven-year security and on the combination would be $1.796 minus $.995 or $.801. That is, $.801 measures the additional risk of holding the bullet vis-a-vis the combination.

Step 3. If the barbell and bullet had the same risk, they should have the same yield. However, the bullet has a greater risk than the barbell and so it should have a higher yield. We have quantified the price risk as $.801 and we must now translate this into yield. We can translate from price to yield using equation (1).

$$D_7 P_7 dr = \text{Risk Premium} = \$.801$$

$$dr = \frac{(\$.801)}{(100.563)(4.701)} = .0017$$

Thus a 17-basis point premium in the seven year would be consistent with a price premium of $.801. We can interpret this 17 basis points as one measure of the fair compensation for the increased risk from non-parallel changes in the yield curve.

Thus if the yield on the bullet is more than 17 basis points above the yield on the combination, we can say the bullet is cheap relative to the combination. In this instance, the yield pick-up was 51 basis points—a very profitable opportunity to buy the bullet.

TABLE 9-5
Yield Premium on the Target Security to Provide Protection
against Additional Risk (in Basis Points)

Combination	20-Year (7.181)	10-Year (5.732)	7-Year (4.68)	5-Year (3.755)	4-Year (3.139)	3-Year (2.406)
30-10	8	—	—	—	—	—
30- 7	9	5	—	—	—	—
30- 5	9	8	6	—	—	—
30- 4	10	11	10	7	—	—
30- 3	11	15	17	18	14	—
30- 2	11	18	22	26	26	17
20- 7	—	8	—	—	—	—
20- 5	—	11	6	—	—	—
20- 4	—	13	11	8	—	—
20- 3	—	17	18	19	15	—
20- 2	—	19	23	27	27	18
10- 5	—	—	0	—	—	—
10- 4	—	—	2	4	—	—
10- 3	—	—	4	10	9	—
10- 2	—	—	6	14	16	11
7- 4	—	—	—	3	—	—
7- 3	—	—	—	7	8	—
7- 2	—	—	—	9	12	8
5- 3	—	—	—	—	6	—
5- 2	—	—	—	—	8	5
4- 2	—	—	—	—	—	4

The general formula for calculating the maximum yield premium on the bullet is given in Appendix 9-B. It is important to realize that the value of this is in the approach, not in the specific calculations. Our standard deviations are calculated over the past three years. Some users may feel a longer history is in order. The choice of a twelve-month yield curve change standard deviation is also arbitrary. If readers are more comfortable with longer terms (24 or 36 month), the standard deviations of these changes may be substituted in the calculations.

Based on our assumptions, Table 9-5 shows the yield premium on the target security necessary to offset its disadvantage under non-parallel shifts in the yield curve.[4]

Comparing Tables 9–2 and 9–5, one sees the desirability of various swaps. Consider first the combination of the seven-year security and the three-year security to replicate the five year. Using the standard deviation over the January 1982 to February 1985 period, a 7 basis point premium in the three-year yield is necessary in order to compensate for non-parallel shifts in the yield curve. The actual yield pick-up is only about 6 basis points in this case—not enough to compensate for the risk. By contrast, using the thirty year and the two year to duplicate a ten year would seem attractive as the yield pick-up is close to 41 basis points—much more than the 18 basis points needed to compensate for non-parallel shifts in the yield curve.

Although the volatility of yield spreads, weights and relative prices all affect the values shown on a day to day basis, the changes will be small. Unless there are wide swings in interest rates, the numbers in Table 9–5 can be used as a rough guideline.

Let us illustrate this type of trade with an example. On December 31, 1984, a combination of the then current twenty year and two year in order to duplicate the then current 10 year was yielding 11.13 percent. The ten year was yielding 11.52 percent. If you had purchased the 10 year bond, the $11\frac{5}{8}$s of 1994, at 102-04 and sold it on April 3, 1985, at a yield of 11.71 percent or a price of 104-04, your profit would have been 2 points. By contrast, if you had purchased the combination—.687 of the twenty year and .322 of the two year—your initial cost would have been identical. The twenty year (the $11\frac{5}{8}$s of 2004) would have been sold for a yield of 11.84 percent and a price of 103-16. The two year (the $9\frac{7}{8}$s of $\frac{12}{86}$) would have been sold for a yield of 10.28 percent and a price of 102-01. Thus, on April 3, 1985, the yield on the combination was 11.35 percent and the price was:

$$.687(103\tfrac{16}{32}) + .322(102\tfrac{1}{32}) = 103\tfrac{31}{32}$$

---

[4] For a four-year security, as no comparable data exist, we used one-half the standard deviation of the five year and the other security in the combination plus one-half the standard deviation of a three year and the other security in the

Thus your profit would have been $1\frac{27}{32}$, $\frac{5}{32}$ less than on the bullet. In short, by selecting the proper alternative your annualized return is 60 basis points higher. Note, however, that your profitability was higher partly because the differential narrowed from 11.52 percent–11.13 percent or 39 basis points to 11.71 percent–11.35 percent or 36 basis points and partly because the current income was higher. Of the $\frac{5}{32}$ pick-up roughly $\frac{2}{32}$ was due to the narrowing of the differential and $\frac{3}{32}$ was due to the high initial yield.

Arbitrage

If the yield premium on the bullet is much wider than justified based on risks of non-parallel shifts in the yield curve, we would, in general, expect yields to come back somewhat into line. That is, the yield on the bullet would be expected to decline relative to the barbell.[5] The maximum differential that is sustainable is the risk premium plus the short selling "haircut." If rates widen close to this point, the bullet is an excellent buy relative to the combination. That is, even in the absence of retail interest, dealers would short the combination and go long the bullet in order to bring rates further into line. In general, we would expect that there are enough sophisticated investors so that the differential will stay well below the maximum. For instance, in the example above, rates were not far enough out of line to make the arbitrage worthwhile.

As a rule of thumb, we would suggest the arbitrage when the yield on the combination plus the risk premium plus 30 basis points is less than the yield on the bullet. As of the writing, for example, if you purchased $10 million par of the $11\frac{3}{4}$ of 4/15/94 and sold $5.40 million par of the $10\frac{3}{4}$ of 3/31/87 and $4.72 million par of the $11\frac{1}{4}$ of 2/15/15 your duration would be the same, but your yield would be 11.65 percent rather than 11.01 percent. The risk premium was

___

combination. Thus, if one wanted to find the standard deviation of a 20-4 year combination it would be $\frac{1}{2}(.58) + \frac{1}{2}(.89)$ or .74 for the period 1977–1985. The 5-4 and 4-3 standard deviations were assumed to be the same as the 3-2.

[5] An investor who has strong expectations about future changes in the yield curve should evaluate the arbitrage in terms of his expectations. For example, an investor who expects a further flattening of the yield curve in the long end would not take advantage of a short barbell/long bullet combination.

roughly 20 basis points. The "adjusted" rate, $11.01 + .20 + .30 = 11.51$ percent, was less than 11.65 percent and this was therefore a good arbitrage.

CONCLUSION

Analysis of yields on duration equivalent swaps can help in portfolio selection (security choice) as well as for arbitrage strategies. Watching for and acting on profitable opportunities can increase portfolio returns substantially.

APPENDIX 9–A

Computing Duration Equivalent Combinations

In order to compute the yield pick-up inherent in a duration equivalent swap, we impose two conditions:

1. The duration of the combination is equal to the duration of the target security

$$W_H P_H D_H + W_L P_L D_L = P_t D_t$$

2. The dollar amount invested in the combination is the same as in the single instrument

$$P_T = W_L P_L + W_H P_H$$

where W_L, W_H = face value in the low duration security and the high duration security, respectively, per dollar of face value of the target security.

P_T = price plus accrued interest of target security.

P_L = price plus accrued interest of low duration security.

P_H = price plus accrued interest of high duration security.

D_T = modified duration of target security.

p(3).
D_L, D_H = modified duration of low duration and high duration security, respectively.

We can solve for the face value weights as follows:

$$W_H = \frac{(D_T - D_L)P_t}{(D_H - D_L)P_H}$$

$$W_L = \frac{(D_H - D_t)P_t}{(D_H - D_L)P_L}$$

A duration equivalent swap is profitable if (3) holds:

3. $W_L P_L Y_L + W_H P_H Y_H$ greater than $P_t Y_t$ where Y_L, Y_H and Y_t are the yields on the low, high, and target security, respectively.

APPENDIX 9–B

General Formulation for Evaluating Non-Parallel Shifts in the Yield Curve

We can use this methodology to develop a general formulation for the risk from a non-parallel shift in the yield curve. Let us assume we are considering a duration equivalent swap involving security t versus a combination of x and y, where x is the longer maturity instrument. We are trying to achieve the target duration of instrument t. The change in the price of y is given by equation (1).

$$s_{(x,y)}D_y P_y = dP_y \qquad (1)$$

Thus the price change is, as above, the standard deviation of the yield spread, multiplied by the duration and price of security y.

The change in the price of the portfolio consisting of securities x and y is given by equation (2).

$$dP_c = dP_y W_y \qquad (2)$$

where P_c is the value of the portfolio consisting of x and y and W_y is the par amount of y purchased.

Thus the price change on the combination is simply the weighted amount in security y.

The price change on the target security is given by equation

$$s_{(x,t)}D_t P_t = dP_t \qquad (3)$$

The difference in the price changes is given by $(dP_t - dP_c)$. The yield differential must be large enough to compensate for this. Thus, the yield premium on the target security must be given by:

$$YP = \frac{(dP_t - dP_c)}{D_t P_t} \tag{4}$$

Substituting (1), (2) and (3) into (4) we obtain:

$$YP = \frac{[s_{(x,t)} D_t P_t - W_y s_{(x,y)} D_y P_y]}{D_t P_t}$$

or

$$YP = s_{(x,t)} - \frac{[W_y s_{(x,y)} D_y P_y]}{D_t P_t} \tag{5}$$

The first term in (5) is the standard deviation of the yield spread between securities x and t, while the second term corrects for the price movements in security y.

CHAPTER 10

MARCELLE ARAK is Vice President and Head of the Capital Markets Analysis and the Options and Arbitrage Units of Citicorp's North American Investment Bank. The CMA group analyzes developments in the fixed income markets and provides strategies for traders and investors.

Prior to joining Citicorp, she was Vice President in the Research area of the Federal Reserve Bank of New York. She has taught at Baruch College, a unit of the City University of New York, and at M.I.T.

Ms. Arak has written on a wide variety of financial topics including financial futures, tax exempt bonds, and original issue discount bonds and is especially known for her analysis of tax structure effects on financial markets.

Ms. Arak earned her doctorate in economics from M.I.T. and her B.A. from the University of Rochester.

LAURIE GOODMAN is a Vice President in the Capital Markets Analysis Unit of Citicorp's North American Investment Bank. She specializes in research and analysis of fixed income financial instruments, with an emplasis on futures and options. She also develops trading, hedging, and arbitrage strategies for Citicorp's customers as well as for internal purposes.

Prior to joining Citicorp, Ms. Goodman was a Secior Economist at the Federal Reserve Bank of New York, researching issues involving the interest rate risk management of financial institutions. She has also served on the finance faculty of the Graduate School of Business at New York University.

Ms. Goodman holds a Ph.D. in economics from Stanford University, and a B.A. from the University of Pennsylvania. She has published extensively in both academic and practitioner journals. Her recent publications have included articles on debt options, mortgage-backed securities and portfolio management techniques.

JOSEPH SNAILER is an Assistant Vice President in the Capital Markets Analysis Unit of Citicorp's North American Investment Bank. He specializes in research and quantitative analysis in fixed income financial instruments.

Prior to joining Citicorp, Mr. Snailer was an economist in the financial markets area of the research department at the Federal Reserve Bank of New York.

Mr. Snailer holds an M.S. in Statistics from New York University and a B.S. in Economics and Applied Mathematics from the State University of New York at Stony Brook.

BUTTERFLY AND CATERPILLAR STRATEGIES BASED ON FORWARD RATES

Marcelle Arak, Ph.D.
Vice President
Citicorp North American Investment Bank

Laurie Goodman, Ph.D.
Vice President
Citicorp North American Investment Bank

Joseph Snailer
Assistant Vice President
Citicorp North American Investment Bank

Forward rates are a topic routinely covered in finance courses and promptly forgotten by most students. But for those in the government securities markets, there are large profits to be made by using them to choose investments and develop arbitrages. In this chapter we show (1) how to spot hidden misalignments—not obvious from the yields on the securities themselves, (2) how to put on butterfly trades that capitalize on these misalignments, and (3) caterpillar strategies for the investor—how to use forward rates in selecting the most profitable maturities while limiting the risk involved in duration mismatches.

243

FORWARD RATES: SOME BACKGROUND

Suppose you own a Treasury note that matures in two years and has a yield to maturity of 8.5 percent. That "average" yield could represent receiving the same yield each year for the next two years or it could represent receiving a different yield in each of the two years which "average out" to 8.5 percent. How can you tell how to apportion the rates over the two years? If rates on one-year securities are 8 percent, you can assign 8 percent to the first year of the two year security. Then the return for the second year is the rate needed to bring the average yield to 8.5 percent. In this case, it is 9.05 percent. This implied rate for the second year out is a "forward" rate—it measures the rate of return between two points in the future. A yield to maturity, in contrast, measures the average rate between now and some point in the future.[1]

Forward rates are useful because they represent breakeven reinvestment rates implicit in the yield curve. That is, if reinvestment rates are higher than the forward rate, a shorter term investment with a rollover would be more profitable, whereas if reinvestment rates are below the forward rate, a longer term investment would be more profitable.

Suppose, for example, an investor likes the duration of a two-year note. One obvious way for this person to invest is in the two-year security. However, the investor can also meet the desired investment horizon by investing in a one-year security and, when this security matures, investing the proceeds in another one-year security.

Let's assume coupon payments are annual, and introduce some symbols for the various rates:

r_{1a} = the annual yield on the first one-year security.

r_{1b} = the annual yield on the second one-year security; i.e., the yield on a one-year security 1 year from now.

r_2 = the annual yield on the two-year security.

---

[1] Technically, the yields on zero-coupon bonds which mature in each year or yields from a spot rate curve should be used to calculate forward rates. However, forward rates measured between yields to maturity are very close to those obtained from the spot rate curve.

Suppose that all three rates are known with certainty. Then the investor could evaluate the exact results of each investment alternative. If all bonds were at par, \$1 invested in the two-year security would pay a coupon payment of r_2 after one year and a coupon plus principal payment of $(1 + r_2)$ after two years. If the coupon was invested in the one-year security one year hence the return on the coupon would be $r_2(1 + r_{1b})$. Thus the total return on this investment option is $r_2(1 + r_{1b}) + (1 + r_2)$.

If \$1 was invested in the first one-year security the investor would have $(1 + r_{1a})$ in one year. This would be rolled into the one-year bond one year hence; this results in a return of $(1 + r_{1a})(1 + r_{1b})$. Thus, an investor can evaluate the relative desirability of the two investment alternatives:

- If $(1 + r_{1a})(1 + r_{1b}) > r_2(1 + r_{1b}) + (1 + r_2)$, then the investor would pick the 1 year–1 year investment.

- If $(1 + r_{1a})(1 + r_{1b}) < r_2(1 + r_{1b}) + (1 + r_2)$, then the investor would pick the 2 year security.

- If $(1 + r_{1a})(1 + r_{1b}) = r_2(1 + r_{1b}) + (1 + r_2)$, the investor could pick either alternative since the two investments would produce the same dollars.

Let's consider the following numerical example. Let

$$r_{1a} = 10\%$$
$$r_{1b} = 10\%$$
$$r_2 = 11\%$$

Then with the rollover strategy:

$$(1 + r_{1a})(1 + r_{1b}) = (1 + .10)(1 + .10)$$
$$= (1.10)(1.10)$$
$$= 1.210$$

That is, if the investor chose the one year–one year alternative, in two years he or she would have \$1.210 for each dollar invested. However, if the person invested in the two-year security, the final sum after two years would be:

$$r_2(1 + r_{1b}) + (1 + r_2) = .11(1 + .10) + (1 + .11)$$
$$= .121 + 1.11$$
$$= 1.231$$

Thus the investor would choose the two-year security, since it would yield more dollars at the end of the two-year investment horizon.

In practice, however, while one knows the rate on a current one-year security and the rate on a current two-year security, one does not know what the rate on a one-year security will be one year from now. Thus, an investor cannot be certain which of the two investment alternatives will be more profitable.

There is, however, a breakeven rate for the one-year security one year from now which results in the same number of final dollars regardless of whether the investor purchases a two-year security or consecutive one-year securities. This breakeven rate is called the *forward rate*. (The mathematics of forward rates are shown in Appendix 10–A.) In our example above, which is detailed in the appendix, the forward rate is 12.12 percent.

If the one-year rate, one year from now, exceeds 12.12 percent— the forward rate—the rollover strategy will be more profitable. If it turns out less than 12.12 percent, the longer term investment will produce more profits. The forward rate is thus a breakeven rate that can be used against the backdrop of interest rate expectations and uncertainty.

Forward Rates: What Do They Mean?

As has already been discussed, forward rates are the implicit rates being earned between any two points in the future. In an upward sloping yield curve environment, the forward rate will be higher than the yield to maturity. For example, if the five-year note yields more than the four-year note, the forward rate for year five will be higher than the yield on the four-year note. In a downward sloping yield curve environment, each forward rate will be lower than the yield to maturity. But the forward rates need not increase monotonically. Indeed, substantial misalignments in the pattern of forward rates can occur even when the yield curve itself has a perfectly normal shape.

One question that always arises in discussions of the term structure of interest rates is whether forward rates simply reflect interest rate expectations, or if there are additional explanations of the shape of the term structure. There is one school of thought which is called the "pure expectations theory." This theory holds that any long term rate of interest is an average of the current short-term rate and the future short-term rates expected to prevail during the life of the obligation.

For this theory to be valid, securities of different maturities must be perfect substitutes to at least some investors or issuers. That is, some investors with a five-year investment horizon are open to alternative choices without requiring a risk premium. For example, the five-year investor might consider buying a four-, five-, or six-year security: with the four-year security, a year of reinvestment would be necessary; with a six-year security, sale before maturity would be required. In comparing the four-, five-, and six-year investments, the investor would consider estimates of the appropriate reinvestment rates and determine the expected income produced by each alternative. The choice would be made on the basis of which alternative was expected to produce more dollars.

Clearly, however, most market participants do care about the maturity and risk characteristics of their holdings. Most investors do not know exactly when they will need the proceeds of their investment. Consequently, they prefer to make investments that will preserve principal if the investment must be liquidated on short notice. The longer the duration of a security, the more it will fluctuate in price for a given change in interest rates. Since short term investments have less price risk, a liquidity premium must be offered to longer term investors.

An additional factor which reinforces this effect is that borrowers would prefer to borrow long in order to lock in a rate for a longer period. If expectations were that rates would remain steady, and offered rates on long and short term investments were identical, investors would bid down the price (bid up the yield) at the long end. Thus, the liquidity premium would tend to make the yield curve upward sloping even when investors expect interest rates in the future to be what they are today.

CATERPILLAR STRATEGIES USING FORWARD RATES

Based on forward rates, an investor can decide whether to marginally expand or contract the duration of the portfolio relative to the desired duration. We call these marginal shortenings or lengthenings "caterpillar" strategies.

Continuing with the example in the previous section, suppose the investor likes the duration of a two-year note with an annual coupon, but is interested in maximizing his or her rate of return. Suppose the rate on the two-year security is 11 percent while the rate on a one-year annual coupon security is 10 percent. If short term rates rose significantly during the first year, a rollover strategy might provide a better rate of return.

The key question, therefore, is what is the likelihood of short term rates going up before the year is out? In particular, this investor should consider whether one-year rates are likely to go up more than 212 basis points—from 10 percent, the current one-year rate, to 12.12 percent, the forward rate—in the next twelve months. If they go up to 12.5 percent, for example, the rollover strategy would yield 11.24 percent whereas the two-year investment would produce only 11.07 percent. So, the question is how much of a rate rise is likely? If the rise is likely to be 212 basis points or less, the two-year investment is better. In contrast, if rates of $12\frac{1}{4}$–13 percent are regarded as likely, the rollover could be the better strategy. This is the kind of thinking a person with a horizon of about two years must engage in.

An investor with a shorter horizon should do similar thinking about the pros and cons of buying a two-year note with the intention of selling it prior to maturity.

For example, let's consider a savings and loan (S&L) with liabilities in the form of one-year certificates. Suppose you are investing the assets of such an S&L and you think it's possible 52-week bill rates will go up to 100-150 basis points, but not more. In this case, where the forward rate is 12.12 percent, it is safe to extend even though you may need your cash in twelve months. If, one year from now, rates are 150 basis points higher—that is, the new one-year rate is 11.5 percent—the two-year note with twelve months remaining could be sold at $99.55. It was purchased at $100.00 to yield 11 percent. Your holding period yield over the twelve months is then 10.55 percent. In contrast, had you simply bought a 52-week bill to start with, your yield would be only 10 percent.

Tables 10–1 and 10–2[2] are illustrations of forward rates from

---

[2] The forward rates between Treasury bills are calculated from "compound yields," which are explained in Appendix 10–B.

TABLE 10-1
Illustration of Forward Rates from Treasury Bills
Close: 7/8/85   Settlement: 7/10/85

Date of Maturity	Number of Semiannual Periods	Bond Equivalent Yield (%)	Compound Yield* (%)	Forward Rate (%)
7/11/85	0.01	6.95	7.07	7.07
7/18/85	0.04	6.94	7.05	7.05
7/25/85	0.08	6.84	6.95	6.84
8/1/85	0.12	6.57	6.66	6.05
8/8/85	0.16	6.66	6.75	7.03
8/15/85	0.20	6.72	6.81	7.05
8/22/85	0.24	6.83	6.92	7.49
8/29/85	0.27	6.90	6.99	7.40
9/5/85	0.31	6.98	7.07	7.63
9/12/85	0.35	6.98	7.06	7.01
9/19/85	0.39	6.99	7.07	7.12
9/26/85	0.43	7.00	7.07	7.11
10/3/85	0.47	7.11	7.18	8.43
10/10/85	0.50	7.14	7.20	7.53
10/17/85	0.54	7.15	7.21	7.28
10/24/85	0.58	7.13	7.19	6.80
10/31/85	0.62	7.14	7.19	7.27
11/7/85	0.66	7.15	7.20	7.26
11/14/85	0.70	7.16	7.20	7.29
11/21/85	0.73	7.17	7.21	7.30
11/29/85	0.78	7.19	7.22	7.50
12/5/85	0.81	7.22	7.25	7.86
12/12/85	0.85	7.26	7.28	7.85
12/19/85	0.89	7.28	7.29	7.62
12/26/85	0.93	7.18	7.19	4.81
1/2/86	0.96	7.31	7.31	10.36
1/9/86	1.00	7.34	7.34	7.95
1/23/86	1.08	7.33	7.33	7.21
2/20/86	1.23	7.34	7.34	7.42
3/20/86	1.39	7.36	7.36	7.50
4/17/86	1.54	7.41	7.41	7.92
5/15/86	1.69	7.47	7.47	8.08
6/12/86	1.85	7.52	7.52	8.10
7/10/86	2.00	7.60	7.60	8.52

*See Appendix 10-B for an explanation of compound yield.

TABLE 10–2
Illustration of Forward Rates from Active Treasury Issues
Close: 7/8/85   Settlement: 7/10/85

Coupon	Date of Maturity	Number of Semiannual Periods	Yield to Maturity (%)	Forward Rate (%)
$8\frac{1}{2}$	6/30/87	3.95	8.48	8.48
10	5/15/88	5.70	8.78	9.55
$9\frac{5}{8}$	6/30/89	7.95	9.17	10.38
$9\frac{7}{8}$	8/15/90	10.20	9.41	10.38
$10\frac{3}{8}$	7/15/92	14.03	9.85	11.53
$11\frac{1}{4}$	5/15/95	19.70	10.00	10.65
$10\frac{3}{4}$	8/15/05	40.20	10.42	11.57
$11\frac{1}{4}$	2/15/15	59.20	10.28	8.80

Treasury bills and Treasury notes and bonds, respectively, on July 8, 1985. This information can be used to help you choose between investment alternatives.

To illustrate how to use these tables, let's consider an example. In Table 10–1, we see that the compound yield on the 10/3/85 bill was 7.18 percent while the yield on the 9/26/85 bill was 7.07 percent. The forward rate between these bills was 8.43 percent, which was considerably higher than neighboring forward rates. If an investor expected one-week rates to remain below 8.43 percent, the investor should have purchased the 10/3/85 bill rather than the 9/26/85 bill regardless of whether the investment horizon was 9/26/85 or 10/3/85:

- If the investor had a horizon of 10/3/85, it would have been better to buy the 10/3/85 bill than to buy the 9/26/85 bill and roll into a one-week bill.

- If the investor's horizon was 9/26/85, it would have been better to purchase the 10/3/85 bill and sell it on 9/26/85 rather than purchasing the bill of desired maturity.

Thus forward rates such as those shown in Tables 10-1 and 10-2 are useful in evaluating the attractiveness of extending or contracting the maturity of your investments.

SPOTTING ARBITRAGE OPPORTUNITIES AND CREATING BUTTERFLY TRADES

On July 8, 1985, the yield curve was nicely upward sloping as shown in Figure 10-1. However, forward rates calculated from these yields, shown in Figure 10-2, were not smooth at all but rather zig-zagged from year to year. Good economic or financial reasons for this shape are hard to imagine. For example, it seems far-fetched

---

FIGURE 10-1
Active Issues: Yield to Maturity

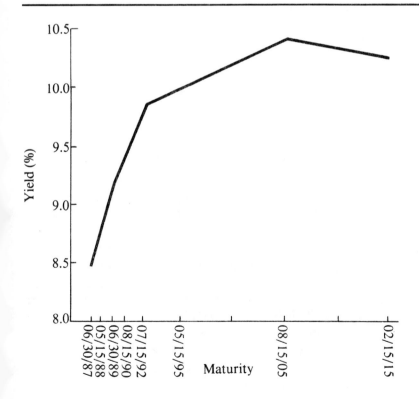

FIGURE 10–2
Active Issues: Forward Rates

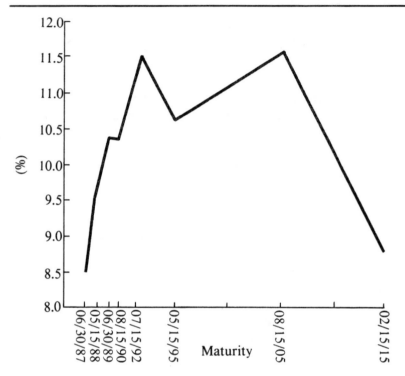

to assume that interest rates will rise through 1992, drop until 1995, rise until 2005, and drop in the subsequent ten years. Or that maturity preferences for years ten and thirty are so strong relative to years seven and twenty. In such cases where "Vs," inverted "Vs," or zig zags occur, there are frequently profitable arbitrages that will make money when a more normal configuration returns.

In order to illustrate the construction of the arbitrage strategy, we begin with a simple example of an inverted "V" pattern as shown in Figure 10–3. Note that the forward rate between years three and four is 11.5 percent. This is substantially higher than the 10 percent forward rate prevailing between years two and three and the 11 percent prevailing between years four and five.

How could one profit from this misalignment? Usually, it is logi-

FIGURE 10-3

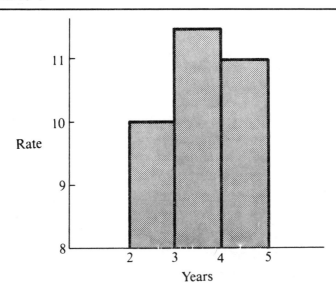

cal to expect that the three–four year rate will realign. One reasonable realignment would be the middle year declining to 11 percent so that the configuration would be 10 percent, 11 percent, 11 percent. Another reasonable pattern would be 10 percent, $11\frac{1}{2}$ percent, 12 percent where the outer year rate rises.

The difference between the middle rate and the average of the outer rates is a way to summarize the degree of misalignment. In this example, the rates in the two outer years average $10\frac{1}{2}$ percent, while the rate in the middle year is $11\frac{1}{2}$ percent. So the initial misalignment is 100 basis points. The $10\frac{1}{2}$ percent, 11 percent, 11 percent pattern has a misalignment of 50 basis points, considerably less. (A 10 percent, $11\frac{1}{2}$ percent, 12 percent also has a misalignment of 50 basis points.) A more "linear" arrangement would have a misalignment factor closer to zero. For example, 10 percent, $10\frac{1}{2}$ percent, 11 percent is exactly linear and has a misalignment factor of zero. So if we went from 10 percent, $11\frac{1}{2}$ percent, 11 percent to 10 percent, $10\frac{1}{2}$ percent, 11 percent, this would involve a 100 basis point change in the misalignment factor. But let's take the 50 basis point as a minimum realignment.

Now let's set up a trade that is positioned to benefit from a relative fall in the rate between years three and four. Basically, you would establish a long position in the low priced (or high rate)-year (between years three and four) and a short position both in the prior year (between years two and three) and the subsequent year (between years four and five), which are the high priced (or low rate) years. Step by step you would:

1. Create a short position between years two and three as follows:
   Go long the two-year note
   Go short the three-year note
2. Create a long position between years three and four as follows:
   Go short the three-year note
   Go long the four-year note
3. Create a short position between years four and five as follows:
   Go long the four-year note
   Go short the five-year note

Not all three positions should be the same size. The idea is to bet that the rate in year three-four falls relative to the *average* of the rates in year two-three and year four-five. Thus positions (1) and (3) should each be half as large as position (2). If you wanted to be long $100 million in position (2), you must be short roughly $50 million each in positions (1) and (3). (See Figure 10–4.) Adding up the positions for each piece, we have the following securities holdings:

Long $50 million two-year note (from step 1)
Short $150 million three-year note (from steps 1 and 2)
Long $150 million four-year note (from steps 2 and 3)
Short $50 million five-year note (from step 4)

When the securities are evenly spaced, a pattern of + .5, − 1.5, + 1.5, − .5 per $1 million bet is typical. (See Figure 10–5.)

Although the longs and shorts are roughly "balanced," there are net financing costs to arranging this position: for a long position, the cost of carry is the current yield minus the repo rate, while, for a short position, it is the reverse repo rate minus the current yield.

FIGURE 10–4
Amount in Each Piece

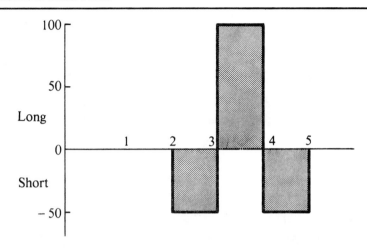

FIGURE 10–5
Setting up The Arbitrage: Market Value of Each Security

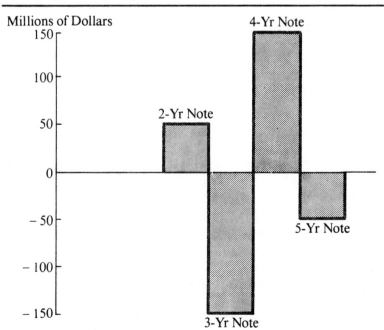

Assuming the reverse rate is 40-50 basis points less than the repo rate, the gross position of $200 million will cost 80-100 basis points per year. Let's use 100 basis points for computational ease. This financing cost is therefore:

$$\$100,000,000 \times .01 \times 1/12 \text{ or } \$83,333 \text{ per month}$$

Now the gain from a 50 basis point realignment in relative rates is the value of 50 basis points received for one year, four years in the future:

$$[.0050]\frac{1}{(1 + r/2)^8} \$100,000,000 = \$325,799$$

where r is the interest rate on the four-year note.

Notice that the realignment affects only the rate earned in that one year. One could, alternatively, figure its affect on the various yields to maturity, translate into price changes, and compute the net effect.

Comparing the per month carry cost to the arbitrage profit, you see that if the realignment takes place within a month, the arbitrage will be very profitable. If it takes place within four months, it will breakeven. If it takes longer than four months, it will lose money.

Real trades will be very similar in structure to that above. However, the securities may not be exactly one year apart. If not, the general .5, − 1.5, 1.5, − .5 (or 1, − 3, 3, − 1) arbitrage position will need to be modified. The example below shows how different dating can be taken into account.

A Real World Example

From Table 10–2 it is clear that the forward rate of 11.53 percent between 8/15/90 and 7/15/92 was very high relative to the rate of 10.38 percent between 6/30/89 and 8/15/90 and the rate of 10.65 percent between 7/15/92 and 5/15/95. Since you have no reason to expect a sharp interest rate peak in or around 1992, you expect that these three rates will realign—the middle rate will fall relative to the outer rates. (That is, either the middle rate falls, or the outer rates rise, or they all rise but the outer rates rise more, or they all fall but the middle rate falls more.) In any event, you are reasonably sure that the current misalignment—11.53 minus $\frac{1}{2}$(10.38 + 10.65) or $101\frac{1}{2}$ basis points—will narrow substantially.

You can set up for this realignment by taking a long position between 8/15/90 and 7/15/92—the high rate period—and short positions between 6/30/89 and 8/15/90 and between 7/15/92 and 5/15/95—the two low rate periods. Step-by-step, here are the trades:

1. Create a short position between 6/30/89 and 8/15/90:
   Go long the 9 5/8 of 6/30/89
   Go short the 9 7/8 of 8/15/90
2. Create a long position between 8/15/90 and 7/15/92:
   Go short the 9 7/8 of 8/15/90
   Go long the 10 3/8 of 7/15/92
3. Create a short position between 7/15/92 and 5/15/95:
   Go long the 10 3/8 of 7/15/92
   Go short the 11 1/4 of 5/15/95

Position (1) covers $13\frac{1}{2}$ months, position (2) covers 23 months, and the rate on position (3) is applicable for 34 months. If forward rates realign, you want the relative dollar gain to be roughly the same regardless of whether the realignment is achieved by a change in rates in position (1), position (3), or position (2). If all three positions covered the same amount of time, positions (1) and (3) should be half as large as position (2). However, since position (3) is for a longer time period, this symmetry can only be achieved by buying less of position (3) than half of position (2). You must short $23/(2 \times 34)$ or .338 times as much of position (3) as position (2). Similarly, since position (1) is for less time, you must short more of position (1) than an amount equal to half of position (2). More precisely, you must short $23/(2 \times 13.5)$ or .852 times as much of position (1) as you buy of position (2).

Assume you wanted to be long $100 million of position (2). The price plus accrued interest on the $10\frac{3}{8}$ of 7/15/92 was $102\frac{27}{32}$ or 102.854 on July 8, 1985, for settlement July 10. Thus the market value of a $100 million position is $102,854,000. You must short this same market value of the $9\frac{7}{8}$ of 8/15/90. Position (1) requires a market value of $.852 \times \$102,854,000$ or $87,616,370. Thus, you go long this amount of the $9\frac{5}{8}$ of 6/30/89 and short this market value of the $9\frac{7}{8}$ of 8/15/90. Position (3) requires a market value of $34,788,853. Thus you must go long this market value of the $10\frac{3}{8}$ of 7/15/92 and short this amount of the $11\frac{1}{4}$ of 5/15/95. Total positions are as follows:

Long $87,616,370 market value of $9\frac{5}{8}$ of 6/30/89
Short $190,470,370 market value of $9\frac{7}{8}$ of 8/15/90
Long $137,642,853 market value of $10\frac{3}{8}$ of 7/15/92
Short $34,788,853 market value of $11\frac{1}{4}$ of 5/15/95

These are illustrated in Figure 10–6.

FIGURE 10–6
Setting up The Real World Arbitrage:
Market Value in Each Security

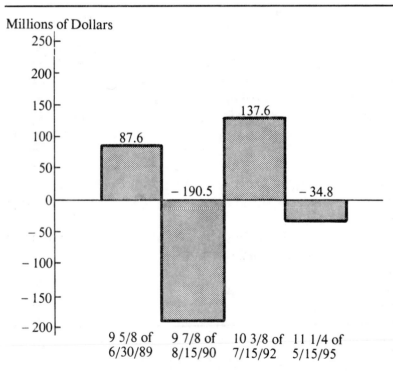

Millions of Dollars

In order to determine if the arbitrage pays, we must take into account the gain or loss from financing. This can be done by subtracting the repo rate from the current yield for a long position. For a short position, the reverse rate less the current yield is the net carry. In this example:

	Weight[3]	Current Yield	Rp or Reverse Rate	Net Carry
Long 9 5/8 of '89	.876	9.46	7.38	+ 2.08
Short 9 7/8 of '90	1.904	9.60	6.88	− 2.72
Long 10 3/8 of '92	1.376	10.09	7.38	+ 2.71
Short 11 1/4 of '95	.348	10.28	6.88	− 3.40

The total net carry is the net carry of each position multiplied by its weight:

$$\text{Total net carry} = [.876(2.08) + 1.904(-2.72)$$
$$+ 1.376(2.71) + .348(-3.4)]$$
$$= 1.822 - 5.179 + 3.729 - 1.183$$
$$= -.81$$

Thus the net carry is 81 basis points per annum.

If the forward rate from position (2) stays out of line by an equivalent amount over the arbitrage period, there would be no gain on the arbitrage position. You would have lost the net carry amount.

If forward rates move back into line, your gross gain would be given by:

$$\text{m.v. in position } 2 \times \frac{\text{\# months in Position 2}}{12} \times \text{Narrowing} \times \frac{1}{(1 + r/2)^b}$$

where r is the interest rate on the 10 3/8 of '92,
and b is the number of semiannual periods until 7/15/92.

Notice that the dollar gain includes three scaling factors: the narrowing in basis points, the length of the middle period, and the discount factor. Let us assume in the example above that rates re-

---

[3] Weights are the relative market values in each security.

align partially—that is the middle forward rate moves down by 40 basis points. Then the dollar gain can be computed as follows:

$$(\$102,854,000)\frac{23}{12}[.0040](1 + \frac{.0985}{2})^{-14.028} = \$401,439$$

The net carry on this position is

$$\$102,854,000 \times .0081 \times 1/12 \text{ or } \$69,426 \text{ per month.}$$

These monthly costs can be compared to the total dollar gain in order to compute the breakeven period. In our example, the breakeven period is close to six months. Since an arbitrage strategy will pay if the user feels that there is a good likelihood that the realignment takes place within the breakeven period, this case looks particularly attractive.

Calculations for a general case are shown in Appendix 10–C.

CONCLUDING REMARKS

Forward rates can be a powerful tool for improving the rate of return on a portfolio. First, they can be extremely useful for judging whether or not it pays to extend or shorten the maturity of one's holdings relative to one's desired duration. In addition, forward rates can suggest profitable arbitrage strategies that are often not obvious by simply looking at yields to maturity.

APPENDIX 10–A

How Do You Calculate Forward Rates?

Consider first the simple situation discussed in the chapter—we have two options: buying a two-year annual-coupon security versus buying a one-year annual-coupon security and rolling into another. The first one-year security has a yield r_{1a}, the second has a yield r_{1b}, and the two-year security has a yield r_2. The two-year security is selling at par. The forward rate is the value of r_{1b} which satisfies the following equation:

$$(1 + r_{1a})(1 + r_{1b}) = r_2(1 + r_{1b}) + (1 + r_2) \tag{1}$$

where r_{1a} and r_2 are the known rates on the current one-year and two-year securities, respectively.

Rearranging equation (1) leads to an expression for the forward rate, r_{1b}.

$$r_{1b} = [(1 + r_2)/(1 + r_{1a} - r_2)] - 1 \qquad (2)$$

Once we know the values of r_{1a} and r_2 we can solve explicitly for the forward rate, r_{1b}.

For example, let the rate on the current one-year security (r_{1a}) be 10 percent and the rate on the current two-year security (r_2) be 11 percent. Then, using equation (2):

$$r_{1b} = [(1 + .11)/(1 + .10 - .11)] - 1 = 12.12\%$$

Thus the one-year forward rate one year out is 12.12 percent.

This example is very simplistic. In general an investor will not be dealing with par securities that mature in exactly one and two years but with securities maturing at various times in the future, some of which will have prices different from par. Moreover, coupon payments are actually semiannual rather than annual and we are usually not at the very beginning of a coupon cycle. Thus, it is necessary to have a formula to calculate forward rates between any two securities, regardless of their maturities, price, and position in the current coupon cycle.

Note that the forward rate is always that yield which will make the investor earn the same amount from (1) buying and holding the longer term security and (2) buying the shorter term security and, when it matures, rolling into another security that meets the investment horizon.

The general case can be best illustrated by considering the cash flows involved in calculating the forward rate between two bonds, bond 1 and bond 2. Bond 1, the shorter instrument, has a yield to maturity of y_1 and bond 2 has a yield to maturity of y_2.[4] Bond 1 has $m + 1$ semiannual coupons left: m full semiannual periods plus the

---

[4] A spot interest rate measures the interest rate on a single payment security such as a zero-coupon bond. When many people speak about forward rates, they are referring to the forward rate between two spot rates. That is, the forward rate between years five and six is calculated from the five-year spot rate and the six-year spot rate; it is the rate such that when the five-year security is reinvested

fractional period until the receipt of the first coupon (j). Bond 2 has
n + 1 semiannual coupons left: n full semiannual periods plus the
fractional period until receipt of the first coupon (k). Bond 1 matures at m + j, bond 2 matures at n + k.

If k > j, we can illustrate the cash flows from the two bonds—
cash flows from bond 1 are above the time line, while those from
bond 2 are below the time line. Bond 1 pays coupons $C_1/2$. Bond 2
pays coupons $C_2/2$.

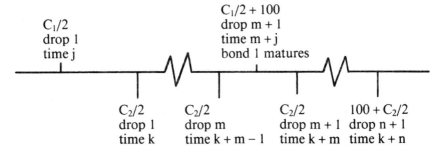

To compute the forward rate between m + j and n + k, we discount the cash flows on the second bond by the yield to maturity on
the first bond prior to the first bond's expiration. Cash flows after
the maturity of the first bond are discounted by the unknown forward rate back to the maturity of the first bond and are then discounted by the yield to maturity on the first bond. The cash flows,
discounted in this manner, should be equal to the price plus accrued
interest on the bond. Thus, given price plus accrued, we can find
the forward rate, f, which satisfies the following equation:

$$P + A = \sum_{i=0}^{m-1} (C_2/2)/(1 + y_1/2)^{i+k}$$
$$+ \sum_{q=0}^{n-m} (C_2/2)/[(1 + y_1/2)^{j+m}(1 + f/2)^{k+j+q}]$$
$$+ 100/[(1 + y_1/2)^{j+m}(1 + f/2)^{k-j+n-m}] \quad (3)$$

where P + A is the price plus accrued interest on bond 2.

---

for one more year, one will obtain the same return as on a six-year security.
There is not a unique set of spot rates: (1) if one uses only actively traded
securities, it is necessary to fill in the holes; (2) if one uses all issues, it is
necessary to smooth the curve. If one is using primarily current coupon bonds in
the analysis, calculating the forward rates using yields to maturity will produce
results very close to the forward rates calculated using spot rates.

The first summation on the right hand side of (3) discounts the coupons received on bond 2 prior to the maturity of bond 1. The second summation on the right hand side of (3) discounts the coupons received after the maturity of bond 1. The final term discounts the principal repayment. Rearranging (3) we obtain equation (4).

$$[P + A - \sum_{i=0}^{m-1}(C_2/2)/(1 + y_1/2)^{1+k}] [(1 + y_1/2)^{j+m}]$$

$$= \sum_{q=0}^{n-m}(C_2/2)/(1 + f/2)^{k-j+q} + 100/(1 + f/2)^{n+k-m-j} \quad (4)$$

The left hand side of (4) is known. The right hand side of (4) contains the unknown forward rate and looks like a standard yield to maturity calculation.

If bond 1 pays its first coupon after bond 2 (i.e., $k < j$), bond 2 will have an extra coupon drop before bond 1 expires. We can illustrate this with another time line:

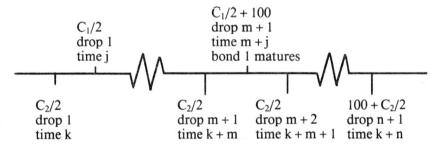

Thus we must solve for f from equation (5):

$$P + A = \text{price plus accrued on bond } 2 = \sum_{i=0}^{m}(C_2/2)/(1 + y_1/2)^{k+i}$$

$$+ \sum_{q=0}^{n-m-1}(C_2/2)/[(1 + y_1/2)^{j+m} (1 + f/2)^{1+k-j+q}]$$

$$+ 100/[(1 + y_1/2)^{j+m}(1 + f/2)^{n+k-m-j}] \quad (5)$$

(5) is very similar to (3). The only difference is in the timing of the coupons. We can rearrange (5) to resemble a standard yield to maturity calculation:

$$[P + A - \sum_{i=0}^{m}(C_2/2)/(1 + y_1/2)^{k+i}] [(1 + y_1/2)^{j+m}]$$

$$= \sum_{q=0}^{n-m-1}(C_2/2)/(1 + f/2)^{1+k-j+q} + 100/(1 + f/2)^{n+k-m-j} \quad (6)$$

This is again a standard yield calculation, where the left hand side of (6) is the present value of a bond expiring on $n - m + k - j$, and making its first payment on $1 + k - j$.

Slight modification in these equations are necessary to take account of short or long coupons—the first coupon payment differs from $C_2/2$, the normal payment. Additional modifications are necessary if one bond drops two coupons before the other bond drops its first coupon.

Let's use these expressions to calculate the forward rate between the current two-year and three-year Treasury notes, the $8\frac{1}{2}$ of 6/30/87 and the 10 of 5/15/88, respectively. The closing yields on 7/8/85 for settlement 7/10/85 on the two-year was 8.48 percent and on the three-year was 8.78 percent. The next coupon paid on the first bond is on 12/31/85; on the second bond on 11/15/88. Thus $j = .9457$ and $k = .6957$, and $k < j$. Using equation (6), we compute the forward rate to be 9.55 percent.

In order to calculate forward rates between zero coupon instruments such as Treasury bills, we can simplify equations (3) and (5) to obtain equation (7):

$$f = 2\{[(1 + y_2/2)^{n+k}/(1 + y_1/2)^{m+j}]^{1/(n+k-m-j)} - 1\} \qquad (7)$$

This formula was used to perform the calculations in Table 10–1.

APPENDIX 10–B

A Note on "Compound Yields"

The forward rates from the Treasury bills report (Table 10–1) are calculated using "compound yields" rather than bond equivalent yields (BEY). The reason for this is that the street formula for calculating a BEY for bills with more than 182 days to maturity assumes semiannual compounding while the street BEY formula for bills with 182 days or less to maturity ignores compounding entirely. Calculating the implied forward rate between one bill with less than 182 days to maturity and another with more than 182 days to maturity using BEYs will therefore lead to incorrect and misleading results. "Compound yields" are the result of converting the BEYs for bills with 182 days or less to maturity to a semiannual com-pounded basis. (Since bills with more than 182 days to maturity are already on a semiannual compounded basis, their compound yields equal their BEYs.) Thus, forward rates calculated with compound yields are consistent across all maturity combinations.

The securities reported in the note and bond forward rate report (Table 10–2) all have more than 182 days to maturity (i.e., at least two coupons to drop). Therefore the BEYs assume semiannual com-pounding and the compound yields are equal to the BEYs.

APPENDIX 10–C

Arbitrage Strategies For the General Case

We can calculate the potential gains from forward arbitrage for any three adjacent forward rates. In order to construct a forward position we need four bonds; for simplicity call these bonds A, B, C, and D in increasing order of maturity. We must first create the forward position.

1. Create the short position between the maturity date of bond A and the maturity date of bond B:
   Go long bond A
   Go short bond B
2. Create the long position between the maturity date of bond B and the maturity date of bond C:
   Go short bond B
   Go long bond C
3. Create the short position between the maturity date of bond C and the maturity date of bond D:
   Go long bond C
   Go short bond D

The market value of positions in each bond are given as follows:

Long bond A:

$$MV_A = \left[.5 \times \frac{\# \text{ of months of position 2}}{\# \text{ of months of position 1}} \right] \times P_C$$

Short bond B:

$$MV_B = \left[1 + .5 \times \frac{\text{\# of months of position 2}}{\text{\# of months of position 1}}\right] \times P_C$$

Long bond C:

$$MV_C = \left[1 + .5 \times \frac{\text{\# of months of position 2}}{\text{\# of months of position 3}}\right] \times P_C$$

Short bond D:

$$MV_D = \left[.5 \times \frac{\text{\# of months of position 2}}{\text{\# of months of position 3}}\right] \times P_C$$

where P_C is the market value of bond C for the desired par amount of the trade.

Your dollar gain on the position if rates realign is given as follows:

$$\text{Realignment Gain} = \frac{\text{\# of months of position}}{12} \cdot$$

$$\begin{matrix}\text{Narrowing over average} \\ \text{of positions (1) \& (3)}\end{matrix} \cdot \frac{1}{(1 + r/2)^b} \cdot P_C$$

where r is the yield to maturity on bond C,
    b is the number of semiannual periods until the maturity of bond C.

The cost of the trade is given by the net carry. This is calculated as follows:

$$\text{Total Net Carry} = [MV_A \cdot (CY_A - rp) - MV_B \cdot (CY_B - rev)$$
$$+ MV_C \cdot (CY_C - rp) - MV_D \cdot (CY_D - rev)] \times t$$

where rp = the repurchase agreement rate
    rev = the reverse rate
    cy_i = the current yield of bond i
    t = the proportion of the year in which the realignment is expected

The arbitrage will pay if the realignment gain is greater than the total net carry.

CHAPTER 11

THOMAS KLUBER received a B.A. and M.B.A. from Southern Illinois University and began his career in 1977 as a financial analyst with American Telephone and Telegraph. He joined American National Bank in Chicago in 1980 as an investment officer in the Bond Department. In 1982, Tom joined Belvedere Securities as general partner and trader. The firm specialized in the development and marketing of zero coupon treasury bonds and receipts. He is currently a Senior Vice President and zero coupon trader for William E. Pollock & Co.

THOMAS STAUFFACHER. After receiving an M.B.A. from Drake University in 1971, Tom began his business career in the Bond Department of the First Wisconsin National Bank. He was manager of the trading desk until 1978 and subsequently was named manager of the bank's Investment Portfolio.

Mr. Stauffacher left the First Wisconsin in 1981 to become managing partner of Belvedere Securities, a brokerage firm specializing in zero coupon treasury securities. In 1985 he joined William E. Pollock & Co. as Senior Vice President and Manager of the Chicago office.

ZERO COUPON TREASURY SECURITIES

Thomas J. Kluber
Senior Vice President
Wm. E. Pollock & Co., Inc.

and

Thomas Stauffacher
Senior Vice President
Wm. E. Pollock & Co., Inc.

The zero-coupon Treasury market has evolved rapidly since the early 1980s, as it became apparent that investor appetite for zero-coupon bonds was growing. Although zero-coupon securities existed for numerous years in the corporate and municipal markets, it was not until 1981 that zero-coupon Treasuries were created in a meaningful way. The zeros were created to fill a particular need of money managers, institutional investors, and individuals in a way that could not be previously satisfied. The zero-coupon Treasury offered investors an opportunity to "lock in" historically high rates of return without the credit risk associated with other types of zero-coupon securities. Thus the process of "coupon stripping" (separating the interest payments of a bond from the principal amount due at maturity) was initiated in order to satisfy the demands of investors for high quality zero-coupon bonds. Once separated, each coupon payment as well as the principal amount becomes a new security represented by a single payment due from the issuers of the security. Each single-payment claim becomes tantamount to a zero-coupon bond.

HISTORY OF COUPON STRIPPING

The process of coupon stripping has been used for many years, but it was not until the early 1980s that the market for "strips" was developed in earnest.

Prior to that time, the use of zero-coupon Treasuries was sporadic and limited in scope to specialized situations which required the Treasury zero's particular investment characteristics, but did not require an active secondary market to exist. A municipality refunding an outstanding obligation could, for example, utilize stripped coupons to replicate the cash flow of bonds being refunded. These stripped would remain in an escrow account until they matured, and the proceeds used to pay the bondholders who own the refunded bonds. Thus no liquidity was required and no secondary market necessary.

Commercial banks also began using stripped Treasuries in the late 1970s as a means of tax planning. At that time the cost basis for tax purposes of all bonds was allocated to the principal portion or "corpus" of the bond. Thus a bank or other taxable entity could physically remove the coupons from bearer Treasury securities that it owns and sell the corpus in order to book a tax loss (the loss being the difference between the book basis of the bond and the present value of the corpus). Conversely, a bank may prefer to accelerate income by selling off bearer coupons from Treasury securities and retaining the corpus (the taxable gain being equal to the present value of the coupons sold).

It was during this time that the Federal Reserve Bank of New York became aware of the possible tax ramifications associated with coupon stripping, and the possibility of investor misunderstanding and confusion if the market for stripped Treasuries was to grow. In a strongly worded letter from the New York Federal Reserve Bank, Peter Sternlight stated "in our view trading in Treasury securities stripped of coupons, or trading in the detached coupons themselves, is not a desirable market practice and should be discouraged." The letter was sent to all primary government security dealers and at the time closed the door on the possible development of the market.

It was not until 1981 that a handful of non-primary dealers began developing the market in the physical components of Treasury securities. Belvedere Securities of Chicago and Union Planters Bank of Memphis were two dealers that were instrumental in developing an active market for Treasury strips, where buyers and sellers could interact through dealers and dealers were willing to make active markets in the component pieces of Treasury securities.

During this time, coupon stripping required the use of physical securities — securities in bearer form, with coupons attached. A dealer would physically take possession of a particular Treasury security in bearer form and separate each coupon payment date from the corpus. An investor who purchased a specific coupon payment would receive the physical coupon attesting his ownership of that payment. This lump-sum payment, due at some future date, is tantamount to a zero-coupon bond.

The market for stripped Treasuries continued to grow, albeit at a slow pace, until the middle of 1982, when the Treasury Department announced that it would seek to amend the Internal Revenue Code to deal with "coupon stripping." The amendment, a part of the Tax Equity and Fiscal Responsibility Act of 1982, was proposed to prevent unwarranted tax opportunities and thus eliminated one of the major concerns the Federal Reserve of New York raised in its 1979 letter to all primary dealers.

Shortly after the tax code change proposal, a number of primary government security dealers commenced market-making activity in the component parts of government securities, believing that the tax code change freed them from the informal restrictions placed on them by the Federal Reserve Bank of New York. During the first few months after the Treasury announcements, the market for physical stripped coupons and corpus grew dramatically. With more and more dealers offering the product, and more and more salesmen touting the virtues of zero-coupon bonds, a major market emerged from the first stages of slow growth.

Physical stripped coupons and corpus offered numerous investment characteristics of value to a variety of investors, i.e., no reinvestment rate risk, high price volatility. Yet they also suffered from a number of physical characteristics that limited their appeal and use. Treasuries used to create physical strips were all bearer, physical securities. The tiny coupons, when stripped away from the corpus, were susceptible to loss, theft, and mishandling. They could not be replaced like other bearer securities because the Treasury offered no such service to the holders of physical strips. All deliveries had to be insured, and a number of safekeeping institutions refused to handle physical strips because of risk of loss. Also, physical strips had to be traded in odd denominations, since each coupon represented a fixed income payment derived from the bond it was stripped from. For example, a 12 3/8 percent coupon bond would have coupons due serially of $61,875 per $1 million of bonds. Once this bond was stripped, no other multiple could be delivered. For the investor who was accustomed to purchasing securities in lots of $5,000, $10,000, $100,000 or $1,000,000 in registered or book entry form, with homogenous characteristics, the acceptance of the unusual denominations was a problem.

TREASURY RECEIPT PRODUCTS

To overcome the disadvantages of the physical strip market, dealers began to market Treasury zeros where delivery was made by substituting a receipt which represented the component parts of the Treasury securities rather than the physical coupon or the corpus. In August of 1982 Merrill Lynch offered the first receipt form of Treasury zeros, Treasury Investment Growth Receipts. TIGRs are receipts issued by a custodian (commercial bank) which represent the individual coupon payments or principal payments of a specific U.S. Treasury bond deposited by the dealer and held by the custodian.

The TIGRs overcame many of the disadvantages of physical strips. Each receipt could be purchased in multiples of $1,000 rather than the odd denominations of the physicals. Second, each receipt is registered with the custodian so that any lost or stolen security can be replaced by the custodian. But the new form of receipt presented two new problems which inhibited the growth of the new market. First, the product is a proprietary one, issued by an individual dealer with that dealer's name associated with the issuance and secondary market activity. As a result, other dealers are less inclined to actively make markets in another dealer's product. As more dealers recognized the opportunity to create their own proprietary receipt, more and more new names were added to the list. Salomon Brothers was next to market their Certificates of Accrual on Treasury Receipts (CATs); Lehman Bros. offered Lehman Investment Opportunity Notes (LIONs); A.G. Becker marketed COUGARS. There were GATORs, EAGLEs, STARs, and others issued by an individual dealer and rarely traded by others. The numerous forms of receipt caused confusion and restricted liquidity.

The second concern was the nature of the obligation. A question arose as to whether receipts are a direct obligation of the U.S. Government with direct recourse to the Treasury, or an obligation of the issuing bank with U.S. Treasury securities held in escrow to back the new securities. Legally, the question led to much debate. If the receipts were new securities and not direct obligations of the U.S. Treasury, numerous traditional buyers of Treasury securities would be precluded from participation in the market. The question has never been answered convincingly, and there remain certain classes of investors who continue to shun the receipt market.

To overcome the two major drawbacks of the new proprietary receipt market, a group of primary dealers banded together to issue a generic Treasury Receipt (TRs), the issuance of which could not be associated directly with any of the participating dealers. The objective of the program was to allow free entrance to the market of any dealer wishing to issue TRs, thereby increasing the number of dealers willing to make markets in all TRs issued. Goldman Sachs, Paine Webber, and First Boston were the first dealers to participate in the issuance of TRs. Shortly afterward, other dealers joined, broadening the market and increasing liquidity.

Like physical strips, TRs were issued in denominations which replicated the bond deposited into the trust. If a 12 percent bond was deposited, coupon TRs of $60, $600, $6,000, etc., could be created. This was done in order to provide a stronger argument that

TABLE 11-1
Outstanding Receipt Products as of March 1985
(Dollars in Millions)

Receipt Product	Par Value of Bonds Stripped	Percent of Market	Par Value of Receipt Products Outstanding
CATs	$12,483	37.1	$ 45,097
TRs	12,179	36.1	44,519
TIGRs	6,055	18.0	21,088
Others	2,979	8.8	9,111
Totals	$33,696	100.0%	$119,815

TRs represented the U.S. Treasury securities deposited with the custodian and not a new security backed by U.S. Treasury securities to insure payment. The other forms of receipts had been issued in $1,000 denominations, not a multiple of the coupon, thus each receipt could be construed as an undivided interest in a pool of securities, as opposed to a specific identifiable security.

Many investors felt that this small difference was enough to insure that the TRs did in fact represent the U.S. Treasury security deposited and were thus more acceptable than the other proprietary receipt. This change did, however, have other adverse consequences which affected the development of the market for TRs. Since the TRs were issued in odd denominations rather than multiples of $1,000, many traditional investors continued to prefer the CATs, TIGRs, and other animals.

Throughout 1983 and 1984 the battle continued to be fought between the various dealers as to which type of receipt would ultimately dominate the market. Salomon Bros. opened the issuance of CATs to other dealers, all of whom became market makers in CATs. The issuance of all forms of receipts mushroomed, but it became more and more obvious that CATs and TRs were becoming the most dominant form of receipt. Through March 1985, $33.696 billion par amount of Treasury bonds has been stripped to originate $119.815 billion par amount of receipt products (see Table 11-1).

U.S. TREASURY STRIPS

Throughout the early growth stages of the market for Treasury zeros, the Federal Reserve of New York monitored the growth of the market in all forms. As agent for the U.S. Treasury, the Fed continued to monitor the growth of the market in order to ascertain the impact on Treasury financing. As the market grew, the Treasury recognized the opportunity to reduce its own financing cost by directly issuing zeros in some form, and assisting in the growth of a large market for Treasury securities.

As time went on and the zero market grew, it became apparent that the Treasury could not avoid the direct issuance of zeros, the only question was the form. Would the Treasury issue zeros as a part of a routine package of Treasury offering, choosing the maturities and amounts based on their best estimates of market demand? Or would the Treasury offer the services of the Fed, to be the custodian for bonds deposited by the dealers in the same manner as receipts are created? Either method would accomplish the goals of the Treasury, reduce net interest cost on Treasury debt by meeting the demand of the zero-coupon bond buyer, and increase liquidity and control over the market by issuing, directly or indirectly, a book entry zero in a homogenous form.

In February 1985, the Treasury announced a new STRIPS program (Separate Trading of Registered Interest and Principal of Securities). The program offered any member of the Fed wire system the opportunity to deposit certain designated bonds which would then be converted in book entry form to coupon and principal strips. Only those bonds designated as eligible by the Treasury could be converted. Initially the Treasury restricted the conversion to the $11\frac{1}{4}$% notes due 2/15/95 and the $11\frac{1}{4}$% bonds due 2/15/15, both issued February 15, 1985. Since February, a limited number of outstanding Treasuries have been included in the program and all new Treasury issues of ten years and longer are convertible.

The market for new book entry strips has grown dramatically since February 1985. By the end of March, the outstanding had risen to $12.8 billion, as shown in Table 11-2. By the end of August 1985, the outstanding had reached over $45 billion.

TABLE 11-2
Book Entry Strips by Issue Outstanding as of August, 1985

Amount Stripped by Issue ($ Millions)			Par Value of Strips Produced
$11\frac{5}{8}$	11/94	$ 384	$ 808
$11\frac{1}{4}$	2/95	507	1,085
$11\frac{1}{4}$	5/95	802	1,704
$11\frac{5}{8}$	11/04	4,273	13,959
$11\frac{3}{4}$	11/14	1,150	4,460
$11\frac{1}{4}$	2/15	4,630	19,995
$10\frac{5}{8}$	8/15	734	3,073
Totals		$12,480	$45,084

THE MATHEMATICS OF COUPON STRIPPING

The mathematics of coupon stripping involves evaluating the spot yield curve for a series of zero coupon bonds and comparing the price of all component parts of a specific bond with the bond itself. Coupon stripping evolved because the price of the pieces of a whole bond, in many cases, add up to more than the whole. This occurs because each individual component possesses some unique characteristics that the bond market values at a price higher than the whole bond stripped.

When coupons are detached from a coupon bearing bond, a series of independent zero coupon bonds is created. Each payment represents a future lump sum payment, the present value of which is determined by the marketplace. Assume for example $1 million par amount of a 10 percent bond due in ten years is stripped. This would result in a series of 20 semi-annual zero coupon bonds, each with a par value of $50,000, and a ten year zero coupon bond (the corpus), with a par value of $1 million, as shown in Table 11-3.

As can be seen from Table 11-3, when each separate coupon is discounted at the yield to maturity of the whole bond, the sum of all

TABLE 11-3
**Value of a 10-Year, 10 Percent Bond and its Components at
10 Percent Yield to Maturity**

Receipt of Coupon	Face Amount of Payment ($)	Price (%)	Yield (%)	Proceeds ($)
6-Month	$ 50,000	95.24	10	$ 47,620
1- Year	50,000	90.70	10	45,350
1.5-Year	50,000	86.38	10	43,190
2- Year	50,000	82.27	10	41,135
2.5-Year	50,000	78.35	10	39,175
3- Year	50,000	74.62	10	37,310
3.5-Year	50,000	71.07	10	35,535
4- Year	50,000	67.68	10	33,840
4.5-Year	50,000	64.46	10	32,230
5- Year	50,000	61.39	10	30,695
5.5-Year	50,000	58.47	10	29,235
6- Year	50,000	55.68	10	27,840
6.5-Year	50,000	53.03	10	26,515
7- Year	50,000	50.51	10	25,255
7.5-Year	50,000	48.10	10	24,050
8- Year	50,000	45.81	10	22,905
8.5-Year	50,000	43.63	10	21,815
9- Year	50,000	41.55	10	20,775
9.5-Year	50,000	39.57	10	19,785
10.5-Year	1,050,000	37.69	10	395,745
Total proceeds				$1,000,000

component prices will equate to the total price of the bond. In the example above, the price of both is par or $1,000.00.

The marketplace, however, does not value each component piece of the bond at the same yield level as the bond. The whole bond is priced based on the concept of yield to maturity. The components are priced based on the concept of the term structure of interest rates.

Yield to maturity is the rate at which the current investment must grow in order to provide for all future payments of interest and

FIGURE 11-1
U.S. Treasury Yield Curve

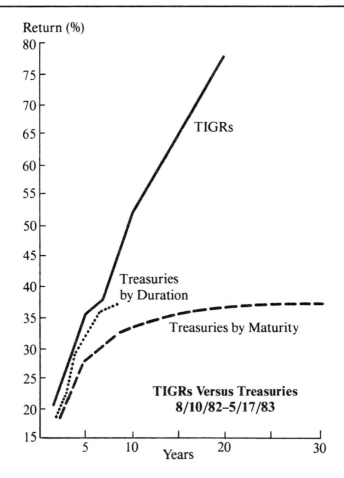

Return (%)

TIGRs

Treasuries
by Duration

Treasuries by Maturity

**TIGRs Versus Treasuries
8/10/82–5/17/83**

Years

principal. In the above example, that rate is 10 percent. The concept
of yield to maturity assumes each component piece is discounted at
the yield to maturity of the bond in order to determine the present
value of the entire bond. As long as each piece is evaluated in this
manner, the total price of all components will equal the price of the
bond stripped. When the yield to maturity of numerous Treasury

bonds of different maturities are displayed graphically, a yield curve can be constructed.

The marketplace values each par bond at a different yield level depending on maturity, and it does the same for all zero coupon bonds. A yield curve of zero-coupon bonds can be constructed showing the yield to maturity of zero-coupon bonds compared with their respective terms to maturity. Even though the zero-coupon bonds represent all the components of a specific bond, unlike the bond itself where one rate is used for all payments, the discount rate used to determine the value of the zeros is a function of the yield curve of each separate payment.

Assume that a six-month treasury bill currently has a yield of 7 percent and the one-year bill has a yield of $7\frac{1}{2}$ percent. The current price for $50,000 of such Treasury bill would be $48,310 and $46,450, respectively. Since the price of a like amount of six-month and one-year strips from a 10 percent bond discounted at the yield to maturity of the bond (Figure 11–1) was $47,620 and $45,350, investors would gravitate to the strips until the price was bid up to a level that approximates the Treasury bills.

The same process occurs for all other components from a ten-year bond, thus producing a "spot rate curve" or the term structure of interest rates.[1] Figure 11–2 depicts the rate for spot rate payments compared with the maturity of those payments.

The difference between the present value of each spot payment and the present value of the bond stripped is the value added from the stripping process and shows how the stripper of this bond can make money (see Table 11–4).

As long as the profits from stripping a particular bond are attractive, the stripper has an incentive to create more strips. In theory, at some point enough strips are produced to satisfy the demand at prices which in total are higher than the price of the bond, thereby driving the spot yield curve to a breakeven point with the price of the whole bond. This price level can be construed as the theoretical spot rate curve. (See Figure 11–3.)

---

[1] See Chapter 12 (pages 302–303) for how such a yield curve can be constructed.

FIGURE 11–2
Spot Rate Yield Curve

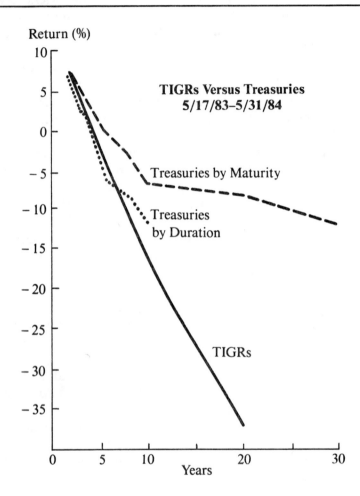

Return (%)

TIGRs Versus Treasuries
5/17/83–5/31/84

Treasuries by Maturity

Treasuries
by Duration

TIGRs

Years

TABLE 11-4
Price Difference of Spot Payments and Whole Bond on a 10 Percent Bond Due in 10 Years at Par

Years	Payment ($)	Present Value ($) at 10 Percent	Spot Yield Curve	Present Value of Spot Curve ($)	Difference ($)
.5	$ 50,000	$ 47,620	7.70	$ 48,140	$ 520
1.0	50,000	45,350	8.00	46,228	878
1.5	50,000	43,190	8.60	44,067	877
2.0	50,000	41,135	8.90	42,008	873
2.5	50,000	39,175	9.05	40,075	900
3.0	50,000	37,310	9.25	38,120	810
3.5	50,000	35,535	9.50	36,132	597
4.0	50,000	33,840	9.70	34,231	391
4.5	50,000	32,230	9.80	32,508	278
5.0	50,000	30,695	9.80	30,990	295
5.5	50,000	29,235	9.90	29,388	153
6.0	50,000	27,840	9.90	28,001	161
6.5	50,000	26,515	10.00	26,516	1
7.0	50,000	25,255	10.00	25,253	2
7.5	50,000	24,050	10.05	23,965	-85
8.0	50,000	22,905	10.05	22,818	-87
8.5	50,000	21,815	10.05	21,727	-88
9.0	50,000	20,775	10.05	20,687	-88
9.5	50,000	19,785	10.10	19,609	-176
10.0	1,050,000	395,745	10.15	390,123	-5622
Totals	$2,000,000	$1,000,000			+ $ 590

FIGURE 11–3
U.S. Treasury Curve and Theoretical Spot Rate Curve

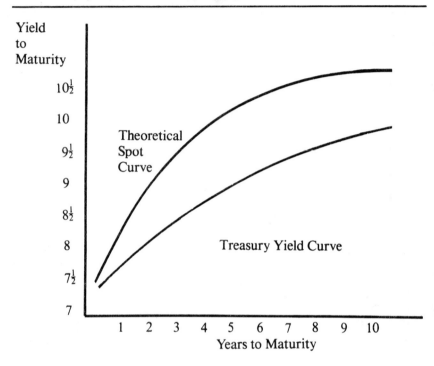

PRICING CALLABLE STRIPS

All zeros created by stripping a Treasury bond are priced by determining the present value of a lump sum payment due on a specific date in the future. But if the bond that is stripped is a callable bond, the callable portion of the bond takes on pricing characteristics that are unique and different from other non-callable corpus.

When a callable bond is stripped, all coupons that come due after the call date remain with the corpus. Coupons due after the call date are included with the corpus because some or all of them could prove worthless should the bonds be called prior to maturity. Callable corpus are typically priced to the call date regardless of the yield level in the marketplace.

Proper valuation of callable strips requires an examination of the probabilities of a call being exercised for the underlying callable Treasury securities. The higher the coupon on the callable bond, the more likely that it will be called. Conversely, the lower the coupon, the less likely the bond will be called. An investor who purchases a callable corpus priced to the call date will have a preference for a callable corpus from a high coupon bond because the probability of the bonds being called is greater. If the bonds are purchased at a yield to call and are not called, the effective yield to maturity will decline from the original yield to call by an amount which increases as the original coupon rate declines. (See Table 11–5.)

How can a price be determined for a callable corpus today based on an uncertain outcome in the future? Theoretically, for a 20-year bond with 15 years of call protection, the price should be based on a forward rate for five-year bonds 15 years in the future. Practically, this is difficult if not impossible to do. A more practical solution,

TABLE 11–5
Pricing Callable Corpus

Coupon	Maturity	Call date	Priced to Call at 10 percent	Priced to Maturity at 10 percent
10%	20 years	15 years	$23.13	$23.13

Date of Payments	Face Amount ($)	Price (%)	Present Value ($)
15.5 years	$ 50,000	22.04	$ 11,020
16.0	50,000	20.99	10,495
16.5	50,000	19.99	9,995
17.0	50,000	19.04	9,520
17.5	50,000	18.13	9,065
18.0	50,000	17.27	8,635
18.5	50,000	16.44	8,220
19.0	50,000	15.66	7,830
19.5	50,000	14.91	7,455
20.0	1,050,000	14.20	149,100
Totals	$1,500,000		$231,335

TABLE 11-6
Pricing a Callable Corpus

Payment Date	Face Amount ($)	Current Five-Year Yield (%)	Price (%)	Present Value ($)
15.5 years	$ 50,000	11	19.02	$ 9,510
16.0	50,000	11	18.03	9,015
16.5	50,000	11	17.09	8,545
17.0	50,000	11	16.20	8,100
17.5	50,000	11	15.35	7,675
18.0	50,000	11	14.55	7,275
18.5	50,000	11	13.79	6,895
19.0	50,000	11	13.07	6,535
19.5	50,000	11	12.39	6,195
20.0	1,050,000	11	11.75	123,375
Total present value				$193,120

and one that the market seems to have adopted, is to assume today's current rates will prevail on the call date 15 years from now. By discounting the callable corpus (and all coupon payments after the call date) by the current five-year rate and adding the results together, the total present value of the callable corpus can be determined. Using this price, a yield to call can be calculated. (See Table 11-6.)

Using the price of all discounted future payments, 19.312, the yield to the call date would be 11.27. These results would imply that a callable 15 year corpus with a coupon rate of 100 basis points less than the current five-year rate should be priced to call at 27 basis points higher in yield than a callable corpus with a coupon rate comparable to the current five year rate. All callable corpus with a coupon rate above the current market yield on five year Treasuries should trade at the same yield level.

PRICE BEHAVIOR

Price behavior of zeros, like all fixed income securities can be viewed in two ways, dollar price volatility and percentage price volatility.

FIGURE 11–4
**Dollar Price Volatility: The Value of an .05% for TRs
(Yields Fall from 12.05 Percent to 12 Percent)**

Change in Price
Per $1,000 (Dollars)

Maturity (Years)

Source: Goldman, Sachs Fixed Income Research, February, 1985

For both cases, zero-coupon bonds are unique. Zeros attain the maximum dollar price volatility for a given yield change in the intermediate maturity range. In the short maturities, zeros are priced at small
discounts, and even large changes in yield have only a small impact
on price movements. As the maturities are lengthened, the discounts
become greater and a given change in yield has a much more dramatic effect on price. This continues to be the case until approximately eight years. As maturities are lengthened beyond eight years,
the increasingly low dollar price diminishes the effects of a given
change in yields. (See Figure 11–4.)

    All zero coupon bonds produce greater percentage changes in
price for a given change in yield than do like maturity of coupon
bonds. This is true for all maturity of zeros. This greater percentage
price volatility is directly attributable to the high duration of zero-
coupon bonds. Since zeros do not pay periodic interest, the dura-

tion or time weighted present value is equal to the maturity. Coupon bonds, on the other hand, pay periodic interest, thus reducing duration and therefor reducing price volatility.

HEDGING ZERO-COUPON TREASURY BONDS

A classic definition of hedging is the assumption of equal sized positions on the opposite side of the market for the purpose of reducing exposure to market risk. The ideal or perfect hedge will move in identical and opposite increments to the related position being hedged. This pure type of hedge can be realized by selling short a position which is equal in all respects to the cash position which is being hedged, i.e., sell short the exact security that is held in the long position or sell short futures contracts for which the long securities are deliverable. Although the pure hedge is the most desirable, it is often not possible because either:

1.   The underlying security cannot be sold short for various reasons; or
2.   A futures contract does not exist for which the cash position is deliverable.

Both situations exist in the zero-coupon Treasury bond market. Although theoretically the securities could be sold short and borrowed to make delivery, the "real world" market does not currently have the liquidity to do so on a regular basis. In addition, no futures contract currently exists for which zero-coupon bonds are deliverable (although such a contract is reportedly being studied by the Chicago Board of Trade).

How then does one hedge a portfolio of zero-coupon bonds? To develop a model for hedging, it is helpful to reflect on how zero-coupon Treasuries are created. In February of 1985 the Treasury initiated the STRIPS program. This allowed security dealers to buy specific Treasury bonds and break down the bonds into the individual components of interest and principal payments. These components were assigned separate and generic CUSIP numbers so that each component could be treated as a new zero-coupon bond with a maturity date that corresponds to the interest or principal payment date.

Consider the position of a dealer who has made the decision to create STRIPS from the 10-5/8 8/15/15 T-bond. The dealer creates 60 interest payments of $53,125.00 and a single principal payment of $1,000,000. If the dealer has not traded any maturities and the portfolio is intact, it should be intuitively obvious that the portfolio is equal in all respects to the 10-5/8 of 8/15/15. (See Table 11-7.)

If the dealer sold short one million 10-5/8 of 8/15/15 to hedge the entire strip portfolio, this would be a nearly perfect hedge. The only risk taken is the "market basis" which will change as the aggregate present value of the zeros changes in relationship to the bond. The difference between the whole bond and the aggregate net present value of the strip is the profit that the dealer earns for creating strips from a whole treasury bond. If the Treasury allows repatriation of bonds, the process whereby the coupon flow and principal portion of the bonds are reunited and presented to the Treasury in return for the entire bond (a process which is currently under consideration), the theoretical difference could go no lower than zero and as high as market competition permits.

The real question is how the dealer hedges a portfolio of zeros which does not perfectly match the hedge in all respects. To address this, the concept of duration must be considered. Derived by Professor Frederick Macaulay in 1938, duration is the weighted average maturity of a bond in which the weight of coupon and interest flow are stated in present value terms. The mathematical notation of this is:

$$D = \frac{PVCF_1(1)}{PVTCF} + \frac{PVCF_2(2)}{PVTCF} + \cdots + \frac{PVCF_N(N)}{PVTCF}$$

where $PVCF_t$ = Present value of cash flow in period t discounted at current yield to majority

t = Period in which the cash flow is received

N = Remaining number of periods until maturity

$PVTCF$ = The aggregate present value of total cash flow from the bond (the bonds current market price plus accrued interest).

By calculating the duration of each individual serial zero, it is possible to begin formulation of an index of percentage price

TABLE 11-7
Cash Flow for 10 ⅝ of 8/15/15. Bond Maturity 8/15/15;
Settlement Date 9/15/85; Coupon 10.625; Quantity
1,000,000; Yield 10.625; Price $1,008,752

| Coupon | | | | Present |
No.	Date	Face ($)	Price (%)	Value ($)
1	2/15/86	$ 53,125	95.7694	$ 50,877
2	8/15/86	53,125	90.9552	48,320
3	2/15/87	53,125	86.3669	45,882
4	8/15/87	53,125	82.0102	43,568
5	2/15/88	53,125	77.8731	41,370
6	8/15/88	53,125	73.9448	39,283
7	2/15/89	53,125	70.2147	37,302
8	8/15/89	53,125	66.6727	35,420
9	2/15/90	53,125	63.3094	33,633
10	8/15/90	53,125	60.1157	31,936
11	2/15/91	53,125	57.0832	30,325
12	8/15/91	53,125	54.2036	28,796
13	2/15/92	53,125	51.4693	27,343
14	8/15/92	53,125	48.8729	25,964
15	2/15/93	53,125	46,4075	24,654
15	8/15/93	53,125	44.0665	23,410
17	2/15/94	53,125	41.8435	22,229
18	8/15/94	53,125	39.7327	21,108
19	2/15/95	53,125	37.7284	20,043
20	8/15/95	53,125	35.8252	19,032
21	2/15/96	53,125	34.0180	18,072
22	8/15/96	53,125	32.3019	17,160
23	2/15/97	53,125	30.6725	16,295
24	8/15/97	53,125	29.1252	15,473
25	2/15/98	53,125	27.6560	14,692
26	8/15/98	53,125	26.2609	13,951
27	2/15/99	53,125	24.9361	13,247
28	8/15/99	53,125	23.6782	12,579
29	2/15/00	53,125	22.4838	11,945
30	8/15/00	53,125	21.3496	11,342
31	2/15/01	53,125	20.2726	10,770
32	8/15/01	53,125	19.2499	10,227
33	2/15/02	53,125	18.2789	9,711
34	8/15/02	53,125	17.3568	9,221
35	2/15/03	53,125	16.4812	8,756

TABLE 11-7—*Continued*
Cash Flow for 10 ⅝ of 8/15/15. Bond Maturity 8/15/15;
Settlement Date 9/15/85; Coupon 10.625; Quantity
1,000,000; Yield 10.625; Price $1,008,752

	Coupon			Present
No.	Date	Face ($)	Price (%)	Value ($)
36	8/15/03	53,125	15.6498	8,314
37	2/15/04	53,125	14.8604	7,895
38	8/15/04	53,125	14.1107	7,496
39	2/15/05	53,125	13.3989	7,118
40	8/15/05	53,125	12.7230	6,759
41	2/15/06	53,125	12.0812	6,418
42	8/15/06	53,125	11.4718	6,094
43	2/15/07	53,125	10.8931	5,787
44	8/15/07	53,125	10.3436	5,495
45	2/15/08	53,125	9.8218	5,218
46	8/15/08	53,125	9.3263	4,955
47	2/15/09	53,125	8.8588	4,705
48	8/15/09	53,125	8.4091	4,467
49	2/15/10	53,125	7.9849	4,242
50	8/15/10	53,125	7.5821	4,028
51	2/15/11	53,125	7.1996	3,825
52	8/15/11	53,125	6.8364	3,632
53	2/15/12	53,125	6.4916	3,449
54	8/15/12	53,125	6.1641	3,275
55	2/15/13	53,125	5.8532	3,109
56	8/15/13	53,125	5.5579	2,953
57	2/15/14	53,125	5.2775	2,804
58	8/15/14	53,125	5.0113	2,662
59	2/15/15	53,125	4.7585	2,528
60	8/15/15	53,125	4.5185	2,400
		$3,187,500		$ 963,567
Corpus		$1,000,000		$ 45,185
TOTAL		$4,187,500		$1,008,748

Whole bond: 10 ⅝ 8/15/15 at 10 ⅝ yield to maturity
Settlement date 9/15/85 = Principal $ 999,808.49
                    Accrued interest   8,950.41
                                          $1,008,758.90

Error due to rounding

TABLE 11-8
Product of Present Value and Duration

	A Price (%)	B Present Value per Million ($)	C Duration	B × C ($)
8/86	90.9552	$ 909,552	.916	$ 833,150
8/87	82.0102	820,102	1.916	1,571,315
8/88	73.9448	739,448	2.916	2,156,230
8/89	66.6727	666,727	3.916	2,610,902
8/90	60.1157	601,157	4.916	2,955,288
8/91	54.2036	542,036	5.916	3,206,685
8/92	48.8729	488,729	6.916	3,380,050
8/93	44.0665	440,665	7.916	3,488,304
8/94	39.7327	397,327	8.916	3,542,568
8/95	35.8252	358,252	9.916	3,552,427
8/96	32.3019	323,019	10.916	3,526,075
8/97	29.1252	291,252	11.916	3,470,559
8/98	26.2609	262,609	12.916	3,395,694
8/99	23.6782	236,782	13.916	3,295,058
8/00	21.3496	213,496	14.916	3,184,507
8/01	19.2499	192,499	15.916	3,063,814
8/02	17.3568	173,568	16.916	2,936,076
8/03	15.6498	156,498	17.916	2,803,818
8/04	14.1107	141,107	18.916	2,669,180
8/05	12.7230	127,230	19.916	2,533,913
8/06	11.4718	114,718	20.916	2,399,442
8/07	10.3436	103,436	21.916	2,266,903
8/08	9.3263	93,263	22.916	2,137,215
8/09	8.4091	84,091	23.916	2,011,120
8/10	7.5821	75,821	24.916	1,889,156
8/11	6.8364	68,364	25.916	1,771,721
8/12	6.1641	61,641	26.916	1,659,129
8/13	5.5579	55,579	27.916	1,551,543
8/14	5.0113	50,113	28.916	1,449,068
8/15	4.5185	45,185	29.916	1,351,754
Whole bond		$1,008,758	9.384	$9,466,185

volatility for zeros. Because the zero has the same duration as term to maturity, the percentage volatility of a zero increases with its duration. However, the absolute volatility of the zero is greatest in the 8 to 12 year range as calculated by using the yield value of 1/32 point for a fixed change in yield.

The characteristics of percentage and absolute volatility are correlated to the price changes of the underlying security by utilizing the net present value of the zero discounted at market rates. Table 11–8 shows these relationships for the 10-5/8 of 8/15/15 as a strip of zero-coupon bonds (using 9/15/85 as a settlement date). The relationship is linear and the February maturities can be calculated by extrapolation.

The product of the flat price and the duration gives an index of volatility which can be compared to the volatility index of the entire bond, as shown below.

	Present Value	*Duration*
Strips 8/15/95	358,252	9.916
10-5/8 8/15/15	100.8758	9.384

$$\frac{358,252 \times 9.916}{100.8758 \times 9.384} = \frac{3,552,427}{9,466,185} = .375275$$

This calculation indicates that to hedge $1 million face value of zero-coupon bonds, $375,275 par amount of 10-5/8 8/15/15 must be sold short.

The volatility index can be used with securities other than the underlying security which was used to create the strip, creating an interesting "cross hedge." The hedge for $1 million 11/15/88 strips using the 9-1/2 8/15/88 is shown below.

Security	A Yield to Maturity	B Price per Hundred	C Duration	B×C× 1,000
11/15/88 strip	9.75	$ 73.978	3.166 yrs.	$234,214
9½ 8/15/88	9.10	101.790 (w/accrued interest)	2.597 yrs.	264,349

$234,214 ÷ $264,349 = .886 or sell $886,000 of 9½ 8/88 to hedge $1 million 11/15/88 strips.

Because strips trade at a spread over bonds of a similar maturity, it is probably wiser to sell short an actively traded security of a similar maturity. This hedge will have a fairly good performance, however, nothing can be done to hedge the basis risk between the zero and the security of the same maturity. (Recently, shorter term strips have traded as rich as even yield with similar maturity bonds and as cheap as plus 40 basis points to similar maturity bonds.) Although a good case can be made for hedging the zero with a whole bond of identical duration, an additional risk is added which is the relationship between the bond sold short and the bond from which the zero is spread.

When hedging the zero portfolio, as with any bond portfolio, it is important to match the average duration and cash flow of the cash side to the average duration and cash flow of the short. By matching these characteristics, both sides of the ledger are equally affected by changes in rates and changes in the shape of the yield curve. Because of the marginal liquidity in the strip market, there are certain factors which can cause a spread relationship for particular maturities to change quickly. Some of these factors are typically caused by a large professional buying or selling program, a change in the shape of the yield curve, specific retail demand, or other exogenous factors. When demand for a particular sector increases dramatically, the price for that specific maturity will increase quickly because of the demand imbalance. As this sector of the curve becomes more expensive, other parts of the curve will cheapen because of the markets efficiency and competitive pressures. As a result, over time, it would be possible for a portfolio to be long only those maturities which are getting cheaper or wider on spread. Irrespective of rate direction, the portfolio will lose value because the hedge will not increase in value as the cash portion is getting cheaper on an absolute basis. Conversely, the portfolio could be long strips which are becoming more expensive or narrow on spread. In this case, the portfolio will outperform the hedge. One obvious way to eliminate this sector risk is to own all possible maturities. Since it is not practical to have a portfolio of strips which can perfectly replicate the underlying security, sector basis risk can be minimized by having an equal cash flow within some set time interval. In other words, if the short security has a coupon flow of $53,125.00 per million every six months, and the time interval is set as two years, the portfolio should be long an average of $212,500 per million within that two-year period. Obviously, the shorter the time interval, the better the hedge. However, an interval of two years or less should give a fairly good correlation.

The portfolio of strips can be hedged with bonds other than those which were used to create the strip. This strategy can be utilized when:

1. The original security is difficult to borrow to make delivery on the short sale; or
2. The original security is trading cheap or at a wide yield spread to its historical level.

To determine the number of bonds required to hedge the portfolio, the volatility index for each bond is determined by the product of price plus accrued interest and duration. These indices are compared to determine a ratio for the hedge. The example below shows a comparison of 10-5/8 8/15/15 to 12.00 8/15/13.

		Price Plus Accrued (%)	Duration	Volatility Index
$10\frac{5}{8}$	8/15	106.280	8.909	946.849 (1)
12	8/13	116.143	8.505	987.796 (2)

Hedge = 1 ÷ 2 = $958,547 12.00 8/15/13 to hedge $1 million $10\frac{5}{8}$ 8/15

Note that a cross hedge of this nature might allow a hedge to be accomplished for less money. It is certainly axiomatic to the bond business to sell what is expensive and buy what is cheap. This strategy will allow the flexibility to do just that. However, an additional basis risk is introduced. Not only is there a basis risk between the strip and the underlying bond, there is a basis risk between the underlying bond and the bond chosen as a hedge. This can be minimized by choosing a bond which is very similar in coupon and duration. Historical performance, a knowledge of the markets, and plain common sense are the only way to determine what constitutes a good hedge.

The futures market represents another possibility for hedging the strip portfolio. Recognizing that the Chicago Board of Trade T-bond futures contracts represent the hypothetical $100,000 per 8.00 percent 20-year bond, the conversion of the hedge to futures contracts is very straightforward. The Chicago Board of Trade issues a list of conversion factors for each outstanding long bond which indicates the numbers of contracts to be sold per $100,000 per individual bond. For the 10-5/8 8/15/15 the December 1985 bond conversion factor was 1.2957 or sell 13 December bond contracts to hedge $1 million 10-5/8 8/15/15.

Once again, the hedge has added an additional basis risk, the cash/futures basis risk. However, thc spread over parity of the individual security gives a very good indication of the relative value of the cash bond. To calculate the hedge simply determine the required amount of 10-5/8 8/15/15 to sell short (from the earlier calculation) and multiply times the conversion factor (Table 11–9). A very simplified rule of thumb is to sell cash when the basis is historically wide (cash price over parity is large), sell futures when the basis is historically narrow (cash price over parity is small).

Options of futures present an interesting hedging alternative for positions which are to be held for a relatively short time. In a futures hedge, movement on the underlying position are offset by opposite movement on the futures position. When the position is hedged, the only upside potential that exists is when the long side moves up in value more quickly than the short side moves down. Thus, the profit potential is limited to this change in spread relationship. In contrast, buying a put option protects the portfolio if rates rise and allows the trader to preserve upside potential (less the premium) if rates fall.

Delta hedging refers to a technique whereby the trader not planning to hold options to maturity can calculate the hedge size. The delta of the option is the change in the price of the option for the change in price of the underlying instrument. The delta of the option can be calculated using the Black-Scholes option pricing formula, however, as a rule of thumb an at-the-money option will usually have a delta of .5, i.e., a one dollar change in the value of the security will have a fifty cent change in the value of the option. A

TABLE 11-9
Future Contracts to Hedge $1 Million Strips

Maturity	10 5/8 8/15/15 Required to Hedge $1 Million Bonds Face Amount of Strips ($)	Futures Contracts to Hedge $1 Million Face Amount of Strips
8/86	$ 88,013	1.1
8/87	165,992	2.2
8/88	227,782	2.9
8/89	275,814	3.5
8/90	312,194	4.0
8/91	338,751	4.4
8/92	357,066	4.6
8/93	368,501	4.8
8/94	374,234	4.8
8/95	375,275	4.8
8/96	372,492	4.8
8/97	366,627	4.8
8/98	358,718	4.6
8/99	348,087	4.5
8/00	336,408	4.4
8/01	323,659	4.2
8/02	310,164	4.0
8/03	296,193	3.8
8/04	281,969	3.7
8/05	267,680	3.5
8/06	253,475	3.3
8/07	239,473	3.1
8/08	225,773	2.9
8/09	212,453	2.8
8/10	199,568	2.6
8/11	187,163	2.4
8/12	175,269	2.3
8/13	163,904	2.1
8/14	153,078	2.0
8/15	142,798	1.9

deep in-the-money option will have a delta approaching 1, and a deep out-of-the-money option will have a delta approaching zero. For this example, an at-the-money option which has greatest market liquidity will be used to determine the hedge as follows:

1. Calculate the hedge ratio for the underlying security;
2. Translate the hedge ratio to the futures position;
3. Calculate the number of contracts required.

For example, to hedge $1 million 8/15/94 strip using at-the-money (December 76) put options or futures:

	Flat Price	Duration	
1. 8/15/94 strip	39.598	8.916	= 353.05 = 372,962 10-5/8 8/15
	100.875	9.384	946.61

2. Hedge ratio 10-5/8 8/15 vs. December bond contracts = 1.2957

3. $(1.2957 \div .5) \times .373 = .967$ contracts per $100,000 or 9.6726 December 76 put contracts to hedge $1 million 8/94 strips

When the position has been traded or closed out, it is always prudent to calculate the resultant profit/loss to evaluate the hedge.

SUMMARY

In this chapter we have discussed the coupon stripping process, the various products, pricing behavior of zero-coupon Treasury securities and technique for hedging a portfolio of these securities. In Chapter 12, techniques for analyzing zero-coupon Treasuries and portfolio applications are presented.

CHAPTER 12

JAMES L. KOCHAN is the manager of the Fixed Income Research Department of the Securities Research Division of Merrill Lynch. This department is responsible for analyzing the creditworthiness of all domestic and foreign issuers of dollar-denominated fixed income securities, and for all research sent to clients regarding investment strategy recommendations for managers of fixed income portfolios. Mr. Kochan served as the firm's Senior Fixed Income Strategist prior to becoming Department Manager. He continues to contribute to the Department research publications, including the weekly *Bond Market Comment* and the quarterly *Fixed Income Strategy Report.*

Prior to joining Merrill Lynch in 1980, Mr. Kochan served as a money market economist at Chase Manhattan Bank, and was the principal author of the bank's weekly *Money Market Letter*. He began his professional career as a research economist specializing in the money and bond markets at the Federal Reserve Bank of Cleveland.

Mr. Kochan holds undergraduate and graduate degrees from the University of Wisconsin.

MAUREEN MOONEY, since joining Merrill Lynch in June 1982, has been responsible for market analysis and special projects in addition to zero coupon bonds. At Wertheim & Co., she was the co-author of the weekly *Fixed Income Market Letter* and produced special bond market studies. During three years at A.G. Becker she was active in new computer product development.

Ms. Mooney received a B.A. in mathematics from LeMoyne College and an M.B.A. in finance from Fordham University. She is a member of the Fixed Income Analysis Society.

ANALYSIS OF AND PORTFOLIO STRATEGIES WITH ZERO-COUPON TREASURIES

James L. Kochan
Manager and Vice President
Fixed Income Research Department
Merrill Lynch Capital Markets

and

Maureen Mooney
Senior Fixed Income Research Analyst
Fixed Income Research Department
Merrill Lynch Capital Markets

The market for zero-coupon instruments backed by U.S. government securities has become a large and vital sector of the world capital markets. This chapter presents an analytical framework for analyzing these instruments. The theoretical and empirical characteristics of these instruments are examined in an effort to provide a guide to the benefits and costs of investing in these instruments in a volatile interest rate environment. Although there have been several proprietary zero-coupon instruments backed by U.S. government bonds, when examining proprietary instruments in this chapter we shall focus on the Treasury Investment Growth Receipts created by Merrill Lynch. A discussion of the other proprietary instruments is presented in Chapter 11.

THE FIRST TREASURY ZEROS

Merrill Lynch introduced the concept of zero-coupon Treasury instruments with the creation of Treasury Investment Growth Receipts (TIGR's) in August of 1982. The goal was to fill a void in the mix of safe, top-quality investments available to institutional and individual investors. Numerous corporate zero-coupon issues had already been issued successfully, but the U.S. Treasury and the Federal Reserve had a long-standing policy opposed to the so-called stripping of coupons from Treasury bonds for the purpose of selling the individual coupons as zero instruments.

In an effort to stay within those official guidelines and offer clients zeros absent of credit risk, Merrill and other dealers chose to create receipts of ownership of the payments that comprise a government bond. That is, a dealer purchases the underlying Treasury bonds, places these securities in an irrevocable trust with a custodian bank, and then the custodian bank issues the growth receipts that evidence ownership of each of the semiannual coupon payments plus the final principal payment of the bonds. The actual Treasury securities that are used to create a TIGR issue are held in book-entry form at the Federal Reserve Bank of New York.

This structure for the trust has several advantages. A receipt based upon book-entry securities was chosen to facilitate secondary market trading in the zero coupon instrument. The custodial arrangement whereby the Treasury securities are held at the Federal Reserve Bank of New York provides an additional margin of safety to the owner of the TIGR. In less than two years, Merrill Lynch underwrote and sold approximately $20 billion face amount of TIGRs. Other dealer firms also sold large volumes of zero-coupon instruments. Clearly, this innovation filled a major void.

That void was, in large part, a by-product of the extraordinarily high yields and the unprecedented volatility of interest rates that emerged during the decade of the seventies. Prior to 1973, bond yields were relatively low and quite stable. As a result, the so-called reinvestment risk inherent in a bond was not regarded as a serious problem. Back then, the yield to maturity (YTM) provided a reasonably close approximation of the total return an investor could expect from a bond.

In recent years, however, the yield to maturity of a bond at the date of purchase has been far less helpful in predicting the actual return from owning the security over a long holding period. In order for the realized total return from a bond to equal the time-of-purchase quoted YTM, each of the semiannual coupon payments must be reinvested at that purchase-date yield. When bond yields reached the 14 to 17 percent range, the YTM lost much of its earlier value. Investors recognized that achieving such exalted reinvestment rates on a consistent basis would be virtually impossible. They began to search for alternative investments that promised true returns closer to prevailing (generous) market yields, i.e., investments with little or no reinvestment risk.

Zero-coupon notes and bonds were ideally suited to this problem. The introduction of the TIGR's was a major step forward in the evolution of this investment product, as they allowed a portfolio manager to eliminate both reinvestment risk and credit risk. While no investment vehicle entirely eliminates market risk, for a portfolio manager seeking to fund a well-defined earnings objective, the TIGR's were near-perfect. Consequently, they were received enthusiastically by the marketplace and they have multiplied far beyond original expectations.

THE TREASURY STRIPS

The introduction in early 1985 of the Treasury's book-entry zeros, or STRIPS, (Separate Trading of Registered Interest and Principal of Securities) was a second milestone in the evolution of the market for zero-coupon instruments. Producing the earlier Treasury-related zeros entailed costs such as custodial, legal and insurance fees, which served to limit the number of institutions creating these products. The Treasury's innovation allowed STRIPS to be created more efficiently which, in theory, expands the list of producers of Treasury zeros. Most of the primary dealers soon began to create and make markets in the STRIPS.

The Treasury facilitated the creation of this new product when it decided to allow trading, via the Federal Reserve's book-entry system, of the individual interest and principal payments of some of its securities. In other words, the Treasury will, from time to time, conduct conventional auctions of notes and bonds that will have the special feature of allowing separate trading of each of the coupon payments and the corpus. The successful bidders in the auctions of these designated issues can then exchange the coupon issues for the component parts (which will be in registered form) and reoffer to investors each of the separate interest payments and the corpus. These reoffered instruments are, of course, zero-coupon securities and are called STRIPS by market participants.

In several respects, this process of creating a zero-coupon Treasury instrument is identical to the creation of TIGRs. Someone, such as a dealer firm, must bid for the complete note or bond, i.e., the full complement of coupon and principal payments, and then offer for resale the individual payments as zero-coupon securities. The investor becomes the registered owner of a direct Treasury obligation.

TRADING CHARACTERISTICS OF ZEROS

Theoretical Spot Rate Curve

The theoretical spot rate curve derives an implied yield curve for zero coupons from the Treasury yield curve. The starting points for the theoretical curve are the two active Treasury zeros—the six-month and one-year bills. Using these issues, it is possible to define the implied yield of an eighteen-month zero, and then use that yield to find the implied yield for a twenty-four-month zero, and so on, along the full maturity schedule. The cash flows from a note due in $1\frac{1}{2}$ years can be duplicated by using a six-month T-bill, a year bill, and a zero coupon due in $1\frac{1}{2}$ years, with par amounts equaling the coupon principal payments. The present values of a current $1\frac{1}{2}$-year note and a synthetic note should be identical. That value is the sum of the prices of the six-month, twelve-month, and eighteen-month components. As the first two components are known, a unique solution for the price of the final component is possible. The discount rate that produces that solution is the theoretical spot rate for an eighteen-month zero. That eighteen-month discount rate is then used in conjunction with the six- and twelve-month rates to produce a solution for the two-year spot rate.

Yield Spread Relationships

The theoretical spot rate curve may be viewed as defining an equilibrium between yields on zeros and Treasury notes and bonds. Consequently, variations in zero yields away from the spot rate curve would signal trading or investment opportunities in the zeros or the equivalent coupons. These should be superior decision rules than those that rely solely upon historical spread relationships between zeros and comparable coupons, as these historical relationships may become irrelevant if the yield curve changes abruptly. For example, a yield curve that is very steep between one and seven years, produces a spot rate curve that rises even more rapidly than the coupon curve, and rather wide equilibrium yield spreads between TIGR's and coupons in the two- to seven-year maturities. In contrast, zero-to-coupon yield spreads would be expected to be quite narrow if the yield curve were flat to inverted. In that instance, the theoretical spot curve would be very close to or even below the Treasury curve.

To be sure, yields on zeros have deviated from those implied by the spot rate curve, particularly when yields were unusually high or when the yield curve had a strange configuration. During the summer of 1984, yields on two- to seven-year zeros were consistently 10- to 30-basis points *below* the levels suggested by the spot curve. During that period, the relatively high level of yields prompted strong demand for zeros because of their inherent absence of reinvestment risk. Later, as yields fell, TIGR yields were equal to or only slightly below those implied by the spot curve in the two- to five-year range. Yields on Treasury STRIPS are generally 10- to 15-basis points below those on TIGRs.

The theoretical rates provide a measure of relative value for the long-term zeros, with durations of ten to thirty years, where there are few issues of the same volatility or duration. Table 12–1 suggests that recently the market on average values the twenty- and thirty-

TABLE 12–1
Yield Spreads between STRIPS and Theoretical Spot Rates by
Maturity from 7/85 to 10/85 (in Basis Points)

Spreads	2 Years	3 Years	5 Years	7 Years	10 Years	20 Years	30 Years
Average	– 12	– 12	– 15	– 10	– 9	36	34
Maximum	0	0	17	– 2	2	68	60
Minimum	– 28	– 26	– 25	– 19	– 21	17	2

year STRIPS 35 basis points below the yield that the theoretical curve would imply. Strong demand for the long zeros often reflects preferences of foreign investors for issues with low dollar prices and/or investors' expectations of lower interest rates.

Zero-Coupon Yield Spreads

The most relevant yield comparisons are between coupons and zeros of the same duration rather than maturity. If the five-year Treasury notes are matched against zeros of similar duration (3.5 to 4 years) the average zero-coupon spread from July 1985 to October 1985 has been approximately 10 basis points. Whereas, the five-year maturity matched zero/coupon spread averaged 30 basis points. Table 12–2 demonstrates that the duration-matched spreads are considerably tighter than maturity-matched spreads. Consequently, it would appear that the market evaluates zeros relative to coupon issues of the same duration.

The ten-year Treasury notes should be paired with zeros maturing in six years. The average zero-coupon spreads in these sectors has been approximately 5 basis points, with a range of – 15 to 20 basis points. Thirty-year bonds should be paired with zeros maturing in the eight- to nine-year range. The average STRIP-to-Treasury spread has been roughly 10 basis points, with a range of 0 to 20 basis points.

In the shorter coupon maturities, durations and maturities are not significantly different. In the two-year area, the STRIP-coupon spreads have averaged 5 basis points over the past three months.

TABLE 12-2
Yield Spread Comparisons between Treasuries and STRIPS
from 7/85 to 10/85 (in Basis Points)

Treasury Issue	Maturity-Matched Spreads			Duration-Matched Spreads		
	Avg.	High	Low	Avg.	High	Low
2 Year	5	22	− 5	5	22	− 5
3 Year	17	28	5	0	8	− 15
5 Year	30	40	20	10	20	− 5
7 Year	30	40	20	− 12	− 2	− 24
10 Year	30	45	10	5	20	− 14
20 Year	30	48	− 10	− 8	2	− 19
30 Year	− 50	− 15	− 85	10	20	3

Performance Characteristics of Zeros and Coupon Issues

The total returns from TIGRs and Treasury coupons of similar maturities are shown in Exhibits 12–1 and 12–2. These two exhibits demonstrate quite dramatically a fundamental principle of bond strategy. Students are taught very early in their introductory courses in finance that price volatility increases as term to maturity increases and as coupon levels decline. It follows that long, zero coupon instruments will be the most price volatile of any of the fixed income securities. Since, over relatively short holding periods, price changes will generally account for the bulk of any differential in total returns, the measured performance of zeros is also likely to be the most unstable.

An examination of total returns over a bullish and bearish market environment illustrates the extraordinary volatility in performance of the long TIGRs. In the strong market of August 1982–May 1983, the twenty-year TIGRs produced total annualized returns of almost 80 percent, compared with returns of around 30 percent for the long coupons. (See Exhibit 12–1.) In the bear market of May 1983 through June 1984, returns on long TIGRs were near − 40 percent

EXHIBIT 12–1
Annualized Returns TIGR'S versus Treasuries
8/10/82–5/17/83

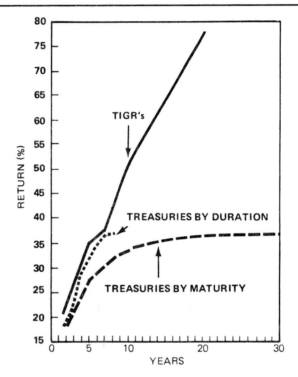

compared with − 10 percent on the coupons. (See Exhibit 12–2.) This seemingly asymmetrical relative performance of the bonds and TIGRs in bull and bear markets stems from the elimination of the unusually large negative spread between TIGRs and coupons during the 1982 rally. At the onset of that rally, TIGR yields were far below bond yields, so they declined less than the coupon yields during the 1982–83 period. Without those distortions, which reflected the market's inexperience with this new product, the relative performance of TIGRs and bonds should be more uniform during bull and bear markets.

The total returns from the intermediate maturities were not as

EXHIBIT 12-2
Annualized Returns TIGR's versus Treasuries
5/17/83–5/31/84

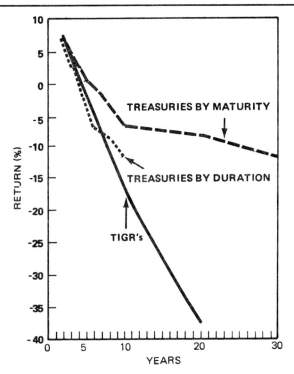

volatile and were far more favorable to the TIGRs over the full two-year period. Despite the sharp rise in yields during the final months of the August 1982 to June 1984 period, the two- to ten-year TIGRs produced total returns in the 12 percent to 14 percent range. However, even in these maturities, the TIGR's performed considerably better in 1982–83 and then considerably worse in the 1983–84 period.

Another important result of the performance comparisons is the much closer correlation of returns when TIGR's are paired with coupons of similar duration. The duration statistic is designed to provide a more realistic measure of the *economic* maturity of an income stream.[1] Securities of equal duration should have similar performance characteristics. Thus the total returns are far closer among TIGR's and coupons of similar duration than if these issues are matched by term to maturity. For most portfolio managers formulating investment strategies, the more relevant comparisons are between TIGR's and coupons of similar durations.

Performance over Rate Cycles

The asymmetrical relative performance of the long-term TIGRs and the Treasury bonds during the bull market of 1982 and the bear market of 1983–84 reflects the shifts in the TIGR yield curve that accompany cyclical changes in the Treasury curve. Table 12–3 shows that if both yield curves were to shift upward or downward in a parallel fashion, price changes on the thirty-year zeros would be approximately three times (29.75/9.47) larger than on the Treasury bonds. However, cyclical changes in the shape of the curves would be expected to have a slight dampening effect upon the price volatility of the zeros.

During a cyclical decline in rates, the yield curve typically shifts from an inverted to a positively sloped configuration. When the curve is inverted, the zero yields would be expected to be well below those on Treasury bonds.

However, as yields fall and the Treasury curve assumes a positive slope, long zero yields should move into closer alignment with the Treasury bond yields. The consequent narrowing in the zero-to-Treasury spread would limit the price gain in the zeros to somewhat less than three times the price gain in the bond. Conversely over a cyclical rise in bond yields, as the yield curve moves from a steep

[1] The standard term to maturity concept treats all cash flows equally. Duration expresses maturity as a weighted average of the present value of each of the cash flows of a bond. Table 12–3 shows the durations of coupons and STRIPS of similar maturities.

A very useful attribute of duration is that it describes the relative price volatility of a set of securities. For example, durations of thirty years for the STRIPS of 8/15/15 and 9.47 years for the Treasury $10\frac{5}{8}$ of 8/15/15 imply that the price response of the STRIPS (to equal changes in yields) will be $29.75/9.47 = 3.14$ times greater than on the Treasury bond.

TABLE 12-3
Durations on Treasuries and STRIPS

Treasury Issue	Duration	STRIPS	Duration
$9\frac{1}{2}$s '88	2.44	8/15/88	2.75
$9\frac{5}{8}$s '89	3.05	8/15/89	3.75
$9\frac{5}{8}$s '90	3.90	11/15/90	5.00
$10\frac{3}{8}$s '92	4.84	8/15/92	6.75
$10\frac{1}{2}$s '95	6.25	8/15/95	9.75
$10\frac{3}{4}$s '05	8.50	8/15/05	19.75
$10\frac{5}{8}$s '15	9.47	8/15/15	29.75

positive to an inverted configuration, the emergence of a large, negative spread between yields on long zeros and on the bonds would keep the drop in the price of long zeros from being as large, relative to the Treasury bonds, as the duration statistics would suggest.

ZEROS AND ACTIVE PORTFOLIO MANAGEMENT

For a substantial number of portfolio managers, the investment objectives of the portfolio can usually be achieved with a variety of alternative strategies. The successful manager adds value to the investment process by developing strategies that meet these objectives at the lowest cost consistent with quality and maturity constraints. When choosing between zeros and alternative investments, the key considerations are the tax status of the portfolio, the investment objectives (the target rate of return and the investment horizon) and the degree of variability in periodic returns that is acceptable.

Tax status is particularly relevant in the case of zero-coupon issues, as the owner must report as interest income the price accretion as the issue moves toward par. These instruments create tax liabilities but provide no cash flow for those tax payments. Consequently, the zeros have been used in portfolios with cash income well above the tax liability: tax-exempt or low-tax portfolios such as pensions and retirement funds, life insurance portfolios and personal IRA accounts, or similar tax-advantaged situations.

In an era of extraordinary volatility in market interest rates, intermediate and long zeros are not well suited for portfolios with short investment horizons. However short-term zeros may be suitable for these investors. The zeros are mathematically the most price volatile of all issues in a maturity class. Hence, they are inappropriate for portfolios that might be liquidated on short notice in order to meet a sudden cash need. Commercial banks, therefore, generally limit their portfolio purchases to the very short zeros. However, even for these accounts, the STRIPS typically provide yields that are considerably higher than on comparable Treasury bills, though the two issues are virtually identical instruments.

The intermediate and long zeros are best suited for meeting a well-defined total return objective over a specific investment horizon. Typically, this horizon would be measured in years rather than months or quarters. To be sure, zeros can be matched with liabilities of any maturity, including those that are quite short. But for purposes other than the exact matching of short-term asset/liability streams, potential returns on intermediate zeros should best be considered over longer holding periods.

In assessing the potential advantages of zeros over alternative instruments that would also be expected to meet the minimum investment objectives of the portfolio, the absence of reinvestment risk is perhaps the most compelling feature of the zeros. For longer holding periods, the reinvestment rate, which determines the interest on interest component of total return, is not a trivial matter. As an example of the power of the reinvestment assumption, consider the following example.

On June 8, 1984, an investor could choose between the active ten-year Treasury note, the $13\frac{1}{8}$ percent of 5/15/94 at a YTM of 13.41 percent, or a ten-year TIGR at a YTM of 13.64 percent. Assuming that an investor were able to reinvest the semi-annual coupon payments on the note at 13.41 percent, the realized annualized total returns over a ten-year holding period would equal the initial YTM, and the dollar proceeds from the two issues would be nearly the same. If, however, the reinvestment rate for the coupons were to average 10 percent, the annualized total rate of return on the notes would drop to 12.02 percent, and the dollar proceeds from a $1 million purchase of this security would be $513,000 less than from the TIGR over the ten-year holding period. Total income realized from a $1 million purchase would be $2.68 million for the TIGR versus $2.17 million from the coupon issue. A relatively conservative reinvestment rate assumption results in a significant decline in total return. The elimination of reinvestment risk becomes a particularly important feature of the zero-coupon issues whenever yields reach unusually high levels. The prospect of achieving generous reinvestment rates implicit in the high YTMs for standard coupon maturities becomes more remote as market yields move well into double-digit territory.

Breakeven Reinvestment Rates

One method of comparing the relative values of zeros and coupon issues is to calculate the reinvestment rate that would be required for the coupon stream in order for the coupon issue to produce the same total rate of return as the zero. We have labeled this "threshold" rate the Breakeven Reinvestment Rate (BRR). Clearly, if a zero and a coupon issue were each available at the same yield to maturity, the BRR would equal the YTM's i.e., the total returns would be equal if the reinvestment rates for the coupons were equal to the YTM. However, the zeros rarely trade at the same YTMs as coupons of comparable maturity. Moreover, most portfolio managers are interested in comparing zeros and coupons with similar durations, and such issues usually offer significantly different yields to maturity. Thus, it would be very unusual if the BRR were to equal the YTM for any combination of zero's and coupons.

The BRR is the reinvestment rate that must be earned on the coupon stream in order to produce equal total returns from a coupon issue and a zero. Relatively low breakeven reinvestment rates suggest that the coupon issue would produce better total returns. Relatively high BRRs suggest that it would be very difficult for the coupon issue to perform as well as the zero over the holding period.

The BRR will be higher as the date-of-purchase yield spreads between the zero's and the coupon issues become greater in a positive direction. Alternatively, the BRR declines as that spread becomes

TABLE 12-4
**Breakeven Reinvestment Rate Analysis: Reinvestment Rates that Equate
Total Returns of Zeros and Coupon Issues of the Same Maturities**

Coupon Issues	Yield(%) 6/29/84	TIGR Issues	Yield(%) 6/29/84	Breakeven Reinvestment Rates Holding Periods (%)		
				2 Yr.	5 Yr.	10 Yr.
U.S. 13%, '86	13.16	5/15/86	13.50	15.80	—	—
U.S. 12 ½%, '87	13.40	5/15/87	13.70	16.25	—	—
U.S. 13 ⅝%, '88	13.65	5/15/88	13.75	14.35	—	—
U.S. 13 ⅞%, '89	13.75	8/15/89	13.80	14.20	13.95	—
U.S. 12 ⅜%, '91	13.80	5/15/91	13.85	14.25	14.00	—
U.S. 13 ⅛%, '94	13.85	5/15/94	13.80	13.35	13.70	13.75
U.S. 12 ⅜%, '04	13.75	5/15/04	13.25	9.10	11.80	12.60

smaller or becomes negative. As the holding period increases, the importance of a positive initial date-of-purchase yield spread diminishes—the BRRs become smaller. However, if the initial yield spread was negative, the BRRs become larger as the holding period increases.

The BRRs presented in Table 12-4 show that on June 29, 1984, investors would have had to assume reinvestment rates of 13.35 percent to 16.25 percent if the total returns from the active Treasury notes were to equal total returns on TIGR's of similar maturity. The required reinvestment rates for the bonds are lower because of the negative spread between the bonds and the long TIGR's, but reach 12.60 percent for a ten-year holding period and would be approximately 13 percent for a twenty-year holding period.

For many portfolio managers, the more relevant comparisons are between issues of equal duration rather than equal maturities. The BRRs for issues of equal duration, presented in Table 12-5, are particularly impressive for the TIGR's with durations matching those on the long Treasury notes and bonds. The TIGR yield curve often reaches its peak in the five- to seven-year maturity segment, which roughly matches the duration of the long bond. Achieving

TABLE 12-5
Breakeven Reinvestment Rate Analysis: Reinvestment Rates that Equate Total Returns of Zeros and Coupon Issues of the Same Duration

Coupon Issues	Duration	Yield(%) 6/29/84	TIGR Issues	Duration	Yield(%) 6/29/84	Breakeven Rates (%) Holding Period 2 Year	5 Year
U.S. 13%, '86	1.82	13.16	5/15/86	1.89	13.50	15.80	—
U.S. 13$\frac{5}{8}$%, '88	3.21	13.65	8/15/87	3.15	13.75	14.30	—
U.S. 13$\frac{7}{8}$%, '89	3.65	13.75	2/15/88	3.65	13.75	13.75	—
U.S. 12$\frac{3}{8}$%, '91	4.59	13.80	2/15/89	4.65	13.80	13.80	—
U.S. 13$\frac{1}{8}$%, '94	5.63	13.85	2/15/90	5.65	13.85	13.85	13.85
U.S. 12$\frac{3}{8}$%, '04	7.16	13.75	8/15/91	7.15	13.85	14.65	14.15
U.S. 13$\frac{1}{4}$%, '14	7.70	13.65	5/15/92	7.89	13.80	15.05	14.25

reinvestment rates of 13.50 percent to 15 percent on a consistent basis has not been possible even during the past five years, when market yields were the highest of the postwar era.

Changes in Yield Spreads between Zeros and Coupon Issues

The breakeven reinvestment rates (BRRs) presented in the previous section show that for relatively short holding periods (two to five years), the initial yield spreads between zeros and comparable coupons will have a significant impact upon the relative performance of the alternative investments. If, at the time of purchase, the zero's offer significantly greater YTMs than the coupon issue, the BRRs tend to be very large. In other words, the coupon stream would need to be reinvested at extraordinarily high rates in order for the total return on the coupon issues to match the total returns on the TIGRs. If the date-of-purchase differentials in YTMs are substantially higher on the coupon issue (as may be true if one is comparing TIGRs with corporates of the same maturity) the BRRs tend to be very low. Low BRRs suggest that the coupon issues would very likely produce greater total returns than the TIGRs. Consequently, for performance-oriented portfolios, the pattern of yield spreads between the zeros and comparable Treasury coupons is a relevant consideration in formulating investment strategy.

As with most issues that trade in step with the active Treasury coupons but trade less actively, short-run variations in yield spreads arise in part because the STRIP yields respond with a lag to movements in the active governments. That is, when yields on the active Treasury issues are moving rapidly upward, yields on STRIPS tend to rise but at a much slower pace. As a result, most zero-to-coupon yield spreads tend to shrink. Similarly, when yields on the active issues are declining, the zero-to-coupon spreads tend to increase as the zero yields fall more slowly. However, the zero-to-coupon spreads tend to revert to the recent averages once the markets have time to adjust to the new (higher or lower) yield levels. Generally, it has taken only two or three weeks of relatively stable markets, following a sharp move in yields, for the yield spreads to move back to near the average levels.

For a portfolio manager seeking to time his purchase of zeros, this pattern suggests some general guidelines. During a market retreat in which yields are rising rapidly, purchases of zeros should be delayed until the markets have had time to adjust to the higher yield levels. If, as yields rise, the zero-to-coupon spreads have narrowed considerably, zeros are not a good purchase. However, once the spreads have moved to near the averages of the prior several weeks, the zeros again represent good value. During the initial stages of a market rally, the zeros are good buys because the zero-to-coupon spreads are likely to become quite large. These spreads can be expected to shrink again if the market yields remain at the new, lower levels for several weeks.

Of course, such decision rules are never infallible. For example, during very severe market declines such as May 1984, when yields are pushed to exceptionally high levels, prices and yield spread relationships become very unstable. At such exalted yields, the zero's absence of reinvestment risk becomes unusually valuable, and the equilibrium zero-to-coupon spreads would be expected to shrink somewhat. In this situation, waiting for the return of average spreads may not prove successful and the investor may miss an opportunity to capture zeros at very cheap prices. The markets usually become extremely volatile as bond yields move above 12 percent, so the period of stable prices needed for the zeros to "catch up" with the coupons may not emerge. Thus, the zero yields that surface during very sharp market declines are often short-lived.

Finally, portfolio managers must always assess these short-run variations in spreads in light of the tendency for the average spreads to change in response to cyclical changes in the yield curve. Parallel shifts up or down in the curve would not be expected to materially change the central tendency of the zero-coupon spreads. However, if the yield curve is changing shape as yields rise or fall, the portfolio manager must incorporate new average spreads implied by the theoretical spot curve into his strategic plans.

ZEROS AND PASSIVE PORTFOLIO MANAGEMENT

Because they have no coupons to reinvest, zeros are particularly well suited for most passive portfolio management applications.

Zeros have a locked-in rate of return to their maturity date compared to coupon issues where the return will vary depending on the available reinvestment rate for the coupons. This property of zeros can be used to offset a liability due in several years or to target an amount of money for some future date by acquiring a zero with a maturity date or duration equal to the target date.

Immunization

In the case of any zero-coupon bond, the duration is always equal to the time left to maturity. For coupon bonds, duration is a function of the coupon, maturity and price. Duration is the time-weighted average of the present value of the future cash flows divided by the present value, expressed in years. In other words, it is the average life weighted by the present value of the future cash flows. Immunization is a technique that makes a portfolio behave as a single, zero-coupon bond. It locks in a rate of return, although with a lesser degree of certainty than the zero coupon, and there is only one payment made which is at the target date (or maturity date). All coupon payments are put back into the portfolio. To immunize, the portfolio must have a market-weighted average duration equal to the target date. As long as the portfolio has an average duration equal to the time left to the target date, the portfolio will closely maintain its original yield. This calls for periodic adjusting in the portfolio because its duration will not move linearly toward its target date. Zeros, in an immunized portfolio, can minimize the amount of adjusting that is needed and thereby add stability to the portfolio.

In addition, zeros can extend the length of time that a portfolio can be immunized. In today's market, the longest duration on a coupon bond is between seven and ten years, which limits immunized portfolios to that horizon. Zeros, on the other hand, have durations beyond twenty years. They can be incorporated into a portfolio to extend the average duration and thereby extend the time the portfolio can be immunized. A simple way to immunize is to use only a zero and achieve a guaranteed yield with no adjusting necessary. However, an immunized portfolio that includes zeros, Treasuries, agencies, and corporates will be more diversified and can have whatever quality rating the investor seeks.

Dedication

Zeros are also effective in another passive management strategy, dedication. A dedicated portfolio is one in which the cash outflows from the portfolio (coupon and principal payments) are matched to a stream of liability payments. Most commonly, this stream is the retired lives portion of a pension fund. The benefit of a dedication program to the company is the difference between the cost of the portfolio and the present value of the future liabilities using an actuary's conservative discount rate (which is usually well below today's yields). This difference can reduce the contribution the company must make into the fund. As the outflows from the portfolio must be predictable, low coupon and noncallable bonds are frequently used. There is a scarcity of these types of issues with maturities in 1996–2005. Zeros, because they are available in a wide range of maturities, can fill this gap. The more closely the timing of the cash flows are matched to the liabilities, the less reliance upon an uncertain reinvestment rate and the more efficient the portfolio becomes. Zeros can also be used to offset a balloon payment in a dedicated portfolio or to dedicate an increasing liability stream since they have no coupon payments to impact the earlier years.

Defeasance

Defeasance is a specialized dedicated portfolio that is used to retire outstanding debt. This is accomplished by creating a portfolio of Treasury notes and bonds (or their equivalent such as STRIPS or TIGRs) in which the cash flows match those of the outstanding debt. These securities are then placed in an irrevocable trust. They allow the client to remove the debt from their books for financial reporting purposes and thus improve their debt-related ratios. Often, the cost of assembling the portfolio is likely to be below the par value of bonds being retired, so the issuer can realize a one-time increase in reported earnings. It is difficult to match the coupon and principal payments of a discount bond using current-coupon Treasuries. Zeros can facilitate this process and, in some cases, at a higher yield.

Low Cost Synthetic Notes

Zero coupons can be used to create a synthetic Treasury note or bond, sometimes at a lower cost than actually buying the equivalent Treasury note. To create the synthetic note, the cash flows of the note must be duplicated with a series of zero coupons. For example, the cash flows of $1 million of the Treasury $9\frac{1}{2}$ s of 8/15/88 are listed in Table 12–6 along with a schedule of matching zeros. The amount of the coupon and principal received from the Treasury note becomes the par value of the zero coupon.

The $1 million of the Treasury $9\frac{1}{2}$s of 8/15/88, at a price of 100.90625 (9.11 percent YTM) would cost $1,028,276. The zero portfolio, with the same cash flows, costs $1,020,180—a savings of $7,986, roughly $\frac{3}{4}$ of a point or 32 basis points. While there is a savings in this example, this is not always the case. The yield spread between the Treasury note and the zero coupon of the same matu-

---

TABLE 12–6
Creation of a Synthetic Treasury 9 $\frac{1}{2}$% '88 with a Par Value of $1 Million Price Yields as of 10/25/85

Par ($)	Maturity	STRIP Price	STRIP Yield (%)	Cost ($)
47,500	2/15/86	97.678	7.95	46,397
47,500	8/15/86	93.781	8.20	44,546
47,500	2/15/87	89.472	8.75	42,499
47,500	8/15/87	85.280	9.05	40,508
47,500	2/15/88	80.963	9.40	38,458
47,500	8/15/88	77.123	9.50	36,633
1,000,000	8/15/88	77.123	9.50	771,225

			Total	$1,020,276

	Cost ($)	Yield (%)	
	1,020,276	9.44	Synthetic
	1,028,166	9.12	Treasury note
Cost/yield advantage of the synthetic	$ 7,890	+ 32 Basis points	

rity influences the profitability of creating a synthetic Treasury. Another factor is the steepness of the zero yield curve in the shorter maturities. A steeper curve in those maturities will result in a lower profit than will a flatter curve. If the zero yield curve becomes inverted, creating a synthetic note with zeros could become very profitable. Investors should be prepared to take advantage of any anomalies in the zero-to-coupon yield spreads and enhance yield through replacing Treasuries with zeros.

THE TRADING MARKET FOR ZEROS

The depth and efficiency of the secondary or trading market in an instrument is of considerable importance to potential investors in that security. An active and efficient secondary market imparts liquidity which, in turn, attracts the broad spectrum of buyers necessary for market breadth and resiliency. Broad investor acceptance of any new financial instrument often hinges upon the timely development of the secondary market.

The traditional method of judging the adequacy of a secondary market is to monitor the trading volume and the bid/offered spreads. A sizable volume of trading activity implies a deep and liquid market, while relatively narrow bid/offered spreads imply an efficient trading market. Almost since their introduction, trading in zeros has been very active. The typical spread on institutional trades in STRIPS is 10 basis points in yield in the intermediate and long maturities, roughly the same as for actively traded corporate bonds. For the callable TIGRs, the spread is usually one-quarter of a point in price.

An efficient trading market must also have the ability to handle large-scale transactions. Though several variations of zero-coupon Treasury securities have been introduced, few trade in the size required to be considered truly liquid. STRIPS and TIGRs, by virtue of the large volume of issues outstanding, the ease of settling a trade (no physical delivery is required), and dealers' policy of making strong secondary markets, fulfill this requirement.

CHAPTER 13

H. GIFFORD FONG is president of Gifford Fong Associates.

A graduate of the University of California, he earned his B.S., M.B.A. and law degrees.

Mr. Fong is on the editorial boards of *The Journal of Portfolio Management* and *The Financial Analysts Journal;* contributor to the Chartered Financial Analysts text, *Managing Investment Portfolios; A Dynamic Process;* member of the Board of Directors of the Institute for Quantitative Research in Finance; Institutional Director, Financial Management Association; and a contributor to a number of other publications.

Mr. Fong is also co-author of *Fixed Income Portfolio Management* (Dow Jones-Irwin).

FRANK J. FABOZZI is currently a Visiting Professor in the Alfred P. Sloan School of Management at MIT, on leave from Lafayette College. A magna cum laude graduate from the City College of New York with bachelor's and master's degrees, he is a member of Phi Beta Kappa. Dr. Fabozzi earned a doctorate in economics from The City University of New York and is a C.F.A. and C.P.A. He is the managing editor of *The Journal of Portfolio Management* and has authored, coauthored, and edited several widely acclaimed books in investment management.

RETURN ENHANCEMENT FOR PORTFOLIOS OF TREASURIES USING A NAIVE EXPECTATIONS APPROACH

H. Gifford Fong
President
Gifford Fong Associates
and
Frank J. Fabozzi, Ph.D., C.F.A.
Visiting Professor
Alfred P. Sloan School of Management
Massachusetts Institute of Technology

Active bond portfolio strategies basically attempt to achieve the maximum return for a given level of risk. That is, this approach pursues the highest possible return while controlling risk. This is different from passive bond portfolio strategies, in which risk aversion is more important and less than maximum return is acceptable. Managers who pursue an active strategy use expectations to achieve higher returns. Basic to all passive strategies, on the other hand, is the minimal expectational input required. In fact, this difference in

323

the role of expectations is the main distinction between passive and active strategies.

Over the past sixteen years, a considerable amount of research has focused on the efficiency of the equities market. The preponderance of evidence suggests that the equities market is efficient. That is, investors should not expect to realize incremental returns after adjusting for additional transaction costs and management fees without incurring additional risks. This evidence has led to the increased use of the passive strategy of indexing to manage equity portfolios.

In recent years, some research has suggested that the bond market also may be sufficiently efficient so that active management may not provide added value. Several institutions have been taking a close look at applying the indexing approach to the management of fixed income portfolios, particularly portfolios of U.S. Treasury securities. Moreover, there is interest in the possibility of return enhancement within an indexing framework. The objective of this chapter is to demonstrate that within an indexing strategy, return enhancement is indeed possible. The first part of the chapter explains how the indexing approach can be applied to track a bond index.

INDEXING

The objective of indexing is to duplicate the performance of the bond market using a proxy that is frequently a designated index. In the equities market, the Standard and Poor's 500 Composite Index is generally the designated index. Typically for the fixed income market, one of the indexes constructed by either Salomon Brothers or Shearson/Lehman is used.

The index fund approach is supported by modern portfolio theory which indicates how portfolios can be constructed so as to maximize return for a given level of risk. Such portfolios are called efficient or optimal portfolios. The theory indicates that a *market* portfolio offers the highest level of return per unit of risk in an "efficient" market. By combining securities in a portfolio with characteristics similar to the market, the efficiency of the market is captured. The theoretical market portfolio consists of all risky assets. The weight of each risky asset in the market portfolio is equal to the ratio of its market value to the aggregate market value of all risky assets. That is, the market portfolio is a capitalization-weighted portfolio of all risky assets.

Practical Considerations

A fundamental issue in constructing a bond index fund is the identification of the appropriate index, which should be representative of the overall market and have a well-defined and stable composition. The broader the representation, the closer the replication of the market and, consequently, the greater the opportunity for efficiency. At the extreme, holding every security outstanding in the portfolio in proportion to its market value would be ideal, but in deference to the number of issues necessary, a sampling technique is sensible. This may take the form of a statistical selection which provides a representative cross section of securities, or perhaps, be based upon defined market characteristics which are achieved in the portfolio. Alternatively, segmenting the market can be pursued. As in the case for equities, there can be an emphasis on that part of the market representative of institutionally oriented securities. Use of the Salomon Brothers or Shearson/Lehman indices is an example. However, this segmentation has potential problems.

There will be a trade-off between desired practical considerations and the ability to replicate the market as a whole. Because the fixed income market is both larger and broader in security type than the equity market, an all-inclusive index tends to be unwieldy. For example, some indices have over 4,000 securities and still represent only fairly high quality corporate bond issues. The breadth of the fixed income market is such that manageable indices with comprehensive coverage are a significant problem. Without the ability to represent all relevant segments of the market, the risk-return efficiency theoretically achieved among stocks cannot be achieved in the bond market. In effect, by not capturing all the relevant segments of the market, considerable residual risk (unsystematic or diversifiable risk, which investors should not be compensated for bearing in an efficient market) may be assumed to frustrate one of the basic rationales of indexing. However, indices can be selected on the basis of maturity, coupon, issuing sector, quality, or combinations thereof. Due to the variation in return for various market cycles, the correct selection of the sector to index for a particular time period can make a sizable difference. However, broad replication of the market is not difficult. While more diverse than the stock market in types and number of issues, the dominance of the systematic risk component for institutional-grade fixed income securities provides a fairly homogeneous universe from a return-risk standpoint.

The implication is that total indexing may not be practical. However, there may be value in identifying a particular segment or segments, such as the Treasuries sector, as the desired index or *bogey*. Again, the basic assumption is that the segments or segment are efficient and will provide the return with minimum risk. Just as the S&P 500 does not represent the entire stock market, but is still valuable, a narrower bond index may serve a similar function.

A METHODOLOGY FOR TRACKING A BOND INDEX

If it were possible to buy the whole universe of bonds that is used in the calculation of the index to be duplicated, in amounts proportional to the amount outstanding of each bond, then the performance of the index could be replicated exactly, at least before transactions costs. In reality this is not feasible. Even small indices, such as the Shearson/Lehman Treasury Index, contain hundreds of securities, and some indices may actually be based on universes of several thousand bonds. An actual portfolio has to be limited to a much smaller number of securities. Moreover, the portfolio needs to be rebalanced each month to reinvest interest income and to reflect changes in the index composition, and that cannot be accomplished in practice if the portfolio were as large as to contain the whole universe.

The question then arises as to the construction and maintenance of an actual portfolio that would replicate the given index as closely as possible in actual operating conditions. Specifically, the following are typical conditions for a feasible strategy:

1. The portfolio should not contain more than a given number of securities (for example, 50).
2. The portfolio should not be rebalanced more often than monthly.
3. Any interest income should be kept as cash until the next rebalancing date or reinvested at a specified rate.
4. There should be a minimum amount for any purchase or sale (for example, $100,000 of face value).
5. All purchases or sales should be in round lots of a given size (for example, $10,000 of face value).
6. Transaction costs should be included in the portfolio returns.

In addition to these requirements, there are two desiderata that make the investment strategy practical. First, the strategy should be flexible enough to allow the portfolio manager to be involved in the selection of the securities for the portfolio. Second, the strategy should include a quantitative algorithm that determines exactly the holdings in each security selected for the portfolio, as well as the transactions necessary to maintain the portfolio.

Recently, Gifford Fong Associates developed a methodology to track the returns of an index as closely as possible, subject to the requirements discussed above.[1] The methodology consists of three steps.

The first step is to define the classes into which the index universe is to be divided. The number of classes should be made equal to the number of securities to be held in the portfolio. The classes should be as homogeneous as possible. This could be accomplished by dividing the universe into issuing sector-quality, maturity range, and coupon range. For instance, suppose that the objective is to track the Shearson/Lehman Treasury Index with a portfolio of, at most, 36 bonds. The classes can be defined by distinguishing Treasuries and agencies, breaking the maturity range into, say, nine intervals and separating the securities with coupons of, say, 10 percent or less from

[1] The system is called BONDTRAC.

those with coupons over 10 percent. The total number of classes will then be 36 ($2 \times 9 \times 2$). Each class is reasonably homogeneous, since it contains only one type of security in a narrow maturity range and with similar coupon levels.

The second step is the selection of securities. On the initial date, as well as on each rebalancing date (typically monthly), one security is chosen from each class for inclusion in the investment portfolio. The methodology places no requirements on the selection of the security from the class. This gives the portfolio manager complete freedom to exercise personal judgment. The portfolio manager may review the list of bonds in the class and select the one which has the most appeal in terms of availability, liquidity, etc. To keep turnover down, the portfolio manager will probably choose a security that is already held in the portfolio (if any), unless there are reasons to prefer a new security within the class. As will be discussed later in this chapter, it is even possible to base the selection on a valuation model.

The third and final step is the determination of the amount held in each security selection. This step does not involve any judgmental input and is done completely by quadratic programming. This mathematical programming technique constructs the portfolio to be as representative of the index as possible. The quadratic programming technique accomplishes the following:

1. Ensures that the duration of the portfolio is equal to that of the index;
2. Ensures that the distribution of maturities of the portfolio is equal to that of the index;[2]
3. Ensures that the amount held in each of the selected securities is as close to being proportional to the total weight of that class in the index as is possible given the above constraints.[3]

---

[2] This measure evaluates the extent to which the payments on the portfolio are dispersed in time. For instance, if the maturities in the index are more or less laddered, matching this measure of the portfolio to that of the index would avoid ending up with a portfolio (of the same duration) that is of a bullet type, or one which is a barbell type, etc.

[3] The first two conditions are the constraints in the quadratic program. The objective function is to minimize the sum of the square of the difference between the relative weights in the portfolio and the weights in the class.

After the quadratic programming solution is obtained, the solution can be modified to satisfy the round lot requirements and the minimum trade requirements. The residual amount of cash at the rebalancing date can also be minimized.

Application to Tracking a Treasury Index

Using the methodology for tracking described above, Exhibit 13-1 (page 330) shows a $50 million U.S. Treasury portfolio that would be constructed to replicate the Shearson/Lehman Treasury Index on September 9, 1985. Summary data comparing the characteristics of the portfolio and the index are presented in Exhibit 13-2 (page 331).

RETURN ENHANCEMENT USING A NAIVE EXPECTATIONS APPROACH

A naive expectations strategy takes the form of an approach which excludes judgmental information such as forecasts of interest rates. We investigated a naive expectations strategy to determine if increases in return in comparison to actual returns of the Treasury index could have been realized over the six-year period, January 1, 1979, to December 31, 1984.

The naive expectations strategy investigated used the following naive interest rate forecasts for a one-year horizon:

1. A market-implicit or market-consensus forecast.
2. Forecast based on historical relative yield shifts—one scenario for rising rates and one for falling rates.

The forecasts are naive in the sense that no specific information about future market conditions is used. A composite naive interest rate expectation for the one-year horizon was found by computing an equally weighted average of the three scenarios (rising, market-implicit forecast, and falling). The procedure for obtaining these naive interest rate forecasts is discussed next.

EXHIBIT 13–1
Portfolio of Treasuries to Track Shearson/Lehman Treasury Index on 9/6/85

Face Value ($000)	Concentration (%)	CUSIP Number of Treasury	Coupon Rate (%)	Stated Maturity Date	Price (% Par)	Yield to Effective Maturity (%)	Duration (Years)	Market Value ($0000)
3,200.	6.5	912827SF	9.125	5/31/87	100.156	9.031	1.7	3,254.
790.	1.6	912827PF	9.875	5/15/88	100.969	9.472	2.5	814.
220.	0.4	912827SK	9.625	6/30/89	99.500	9.782	3.3	221.
130.	0.2	912810CB	8.625	8/15/93	89.812	10.534	5.6	122.
510.	0.9	912810BV	8.375	8/15/00	81.594	10.889	7.8	436.
1,500.	2.5	912810CE	8.750	11/15/08	82.469	10.826	9.0	1,264.
9,710.	20.5	912827RX	10.000	2/28/87	101.562	8.919	1.4	10,272.
5,710.	12.2	912827RV	10.375	2/15/88	102.000	9.472	2.2	6,096.
4,130.	9.1	912827QF	11.375	2/15/89	104.344	9.893	2.9	4,525.
3,220.	7.6	912827QW	13.875	8/15/89	112.210	10.118	3.1	3,818.
1,930.	4.4	912827QZ	13.750	7/15/91	113.750	10.581	4.3	2,207.
2,090.	4.9	912827NE	13.750	5/15/92	114.719	10.651	4.7	2,458.
660.	1.4	912827PD	10.875	2/15/93	101.875	10.509	5.1	705.
1,220.	2.8	912827QU	13.125	5/15/94	113.125	10.778	5.5	1,414.
1,780.	4.1	912827RC	12.625	8/15/94	110.687	10.749	5.5	2,073.
2,970.	7.7	912810CZ	14.250	2/15/02	123.719	11.090	7.2	3,869.
1,430.	3.3	912810CS	12.750	11/15/10	113.625	11.129	8.5	1,663.
3,760.	9.6	912810CY	14.000	11/15/11	124.187	11.140	8.5	4,780.
								$49,989.

Total portfolio market value

EXHIBIT 13-2
Comparison of Tracking Portfolio with Index

	Number of Issues	Average Coupon (%)	Average Maturity (Years)	Average Duration (Years)	Payment Variance (Years^2)	Payment Standard Deviation (Years)	Yield to Effective Maturity (%)	Maturity Composition		
			Market Weighted Average Value					Short (0–5)Yrs	Intermediate (5–10)Yrs	Long (10–50) Yrs
Portfolio:	18	11.719	8.15	4.071	35.9	6.0	10.02	58.0	18.0	24.0
Index:	140	11.546	7.97	4.072	35.9	6.0	9.89	56.8	21.8	21.4

Market-Implicit or Market-Consensus Forecast

To obtain a market-implicit or market-consensus forecast of the term structure of interest rates for U.S. Treasury securities, term structure analysis was used. The term structure is defined as the spot rate or yield on a pure discount or zero-coupon security for each maturity for a homogeneous universe of bonds. The resulting term structure would consist of a series of spot rates representing the yield on a pure discount or zero-coupon default-free security for each maturity in the structure. That is, yields on U.S. Treasuries at any given point in time are adjusted to remove the coupon or tax effect and the residual spread between same-maturity Treasury yields that remains even after the coupon-tax effect has been adjusted for. Thus a market-equilibrium, default-free, pure-discount yield curve is, in effect, created.

It has been demonstrated that each of the theoretical spot rates located on this pure-discount yield curve can be mathematically converted into one-period spot and forward rates based on the pure expectations theory.[4] That is, every multiperiod spot rate in the term structure is equal to the compound average (nth root) of the current one-period spot rate times all the successive one-period forward rates mathematically implied into the future to the maturity of the multiperiod spot rate. In effect, each of the spot rates, and, taken together, all of the spot rates in the total term structure, implies a continuum of one-period future reinvestment rates that are expected at each future maturity date *if* the term structure created is assumed to remain constant.

Forecasts for Rising and Falling Rate Scenarios

We obtained the forecasts based on yield shifts for the rising and falling rate scenarios from a historical database of monthly yield curves. The forecast up (down) shift at each maturity in the term

---

[4] Oldrich A. Vasicek and H. Gifford Fong, "Term Structure Modeling Using Exponential Splines," *Journal of Finance* (May 1982), pp. 339–348.

structure is the root-mean square of all positive (negative) relative shifts at that maturity over the one-year projection horizon within the historical period. These two forecasts are naive since no specific information about present or future market conditions is used; only historical data are considered.

It should be noted that in order to choose the optimal maturity range one must subject model securities (discussed later in this chapter) of each range to a rate sensitivity analysis. Since there exists the possibility that rates may rise or fall over the next year, the question is what will be the magnitude of the rate changes. By analyzing historical experience one can establish a reasonable amount by which rates may change. The alternative is to simply make a guess which could be out of line with past experience. Implicit in the use of historic shifts in future forecasts is the assumption that the past performance of the market will tend to be repeated in the future. By including the market-implicit forecast in the composite expectation one is balancing the strict use of historical information with the market's current forecast of the future.

Methodology and Results

The creation of the portfolios to investigate the naive expectations strategy involved the following five steps. The first step, using the Shearson/Lehman Treasury Index as the universe for security selection, distilled the universe into the following nine maturity ranges: 1–2, 2–3, 3–4, 4–5, 5–7, 7–12, 12–17, 17–24, and 24–30 years. The procedure, as described earlier in this chapter, allows a description of a bond market index in terms of a few model securities. A model security is designed to homogenize a segment of the index into a single bond that represents the description, return characteristics, and market weights of the segment.

In the second step, we derived the interest rate expectations for the naive expectations strategy. We employed the term structure model developed by Vasicek and Fong to generate a one year horizon market-implicit forecast for the Treasury universe as of the beginning month date. Earlier we mentioned the procedure for obtaining the other two naive interest rate forecasts.

Third, we combined the model securities and interest rate expectations as inputs into a return sensitivity analysis.[5] This produced expected returns for each of the maturity ranges in the Treasury universe as represented by the model securities. Assigning an equal weight to each of the scenarios resulted in a probability-weighted composite return for each of the maturity classifications. The range of results represented by these three scenarios exemplify the distribution of possible returns over the projection period.

Once expected returns were determined, the fourth step employed a technique known as relative return analysis to identify the securities for the return enhanced portfolio.[6] Relative return analysis is a tool that allows a manager to compare alternative securities systematically. It recognizes that choosing the highest expected return security may be inappropriate, since it may not be the security with the highest realized return, or the level of associated risk may be undesirable. In this study, duration is used as a measure of risk.

Relative return analysis can be summarized as follows: The current date durations of each model security were regressed against total expected return under the interest rate forecast. A regression line was determined, and the model security located the greatest distance above the regression line was chosen for the return enhanced portfolio. This analysis is very similar to the security market line approach, which is used fairly widely in the analysis of equities.

In the final step of the procedure, we decomposed the model security into an equally weighted portfolio of every security in the universe in the maturity range chosen. A weighted average holding period return calculation of these actual securities was then used to track the performance of the enhanced portfolio created using each strategy.

---

[5] For a further discussion of return sensitivity analysis, see H. Gifford Fong and Frank J. Fabozzi, *Fixed Income Portfolio Management* (Homewood, IL: Dow Jones-Irwin. 1985), pp. 165–176.

[6] For a further discussion of return sensitivity analysis, see Fong and Fabozzi, *Fixed Income Portfolio Management,* pp. 177–179.

The simulation to investigate the naive expectations strategy involved a return sensitivity analysis run for each of the 72 months involved in the January 1979 to December 1984 simulation. The runs were completed as of the beginning of each month to determine the portfolio to be held over the subsequent month. In the historical simulations, it was imperative not to include any information that was unavailable at the actual date analyzed. Prices quoted as of these dates and the term structure derived from the prices were used for each historical date in the simulation. The empirical results thus represent a realistic measurement of the return that could have been achieved over the 72-month period.

In the simulation, the enhanced portfolio was turned over only when a new maturity range was expected to outperform the existing portfolio by a margin greater than transactions costs, estimated as 1/16 percent. As a proxy for risk, the duration of the model bond was used as a benchmark. Although there are some theoretical and practical limitations to this measure, it does provide a framework for differentiating securities based on their potential volatility. This is the basic postulation for choosing a portfolio through a duration versus expected return regression in the fourth step of the methodology. In this manner, selection is determined by the most favorable maturity sector of the Treasury universe; that is, the "best" ex ante risk return tradeoff as predicted by the methodology.

Exhibit 13–3 summarizes the year-by-year results for the naive expectations strategy investigated. The strategy outperformed the Treasury index. Compound annual average returns for the 72-month period were 13.67 percent before transactions costs and 13.51 percent after transactions costs, respectively. This translates into an impressive geometric average marginal return of 227 basis points per year over the Shearson/Lehman Treasury Index, before transactions costs. Most of the incremental return came in 1982, when the three-scenario forecast strategy outperformed the index by more than 950 basis points. The naive expectations strategy consistently picked a longer portfolio in 1982—an average duration of 6.02 years versus a 3.58 year duration for the Shearson/Lehman Treasury Index.

EXHIBIT 13–3
Summary of Results

	Returns			Durations	
		Naive Strategy			
Year	Shearson/Lehman Treasury Index (%)	Before Transaction Costs (%)	After Transaction Costs (%)	Shearson/Lehman Treasury Index	Naive Strategy
1979	5.73	8.72	8.66	3.71	1.31
1980	5.61	4.57	4.20	3.56	4.25
1981	9.24	9.71	9.58	3.41	4.07
1982	27.84	37.35	37.19	3.58	6.02
1983	7.05	4.73	4.66	3.76	5.75
1984	14.47	20.21	20.07	3.72	4.67
Total	11.40%	13.67%	13.51%		

Assumptions in computing returns: (a) rebalancing occurs monthly, (b) interest income reinvested at the 90-day Treasury bill rate until the next rebalancing date, (c) transactions costs calculated at the rate of 30 basis points per round trip of the transaction amount (i.e., 15 basis points each for a sale and purchase).

CONCLUSIONS

In this chapter we describe how a portfolio manager could construct a portfolio to replicate a designated index such as a Treasury index. In addition, we provide evidence that indicates it is possible to enhance the return on a Treasury portfolio using a naive expectations strategy.

CHAPTER 14

JOHN M. EZELL is currently a Vice President with Charter Atlantic Securities Corporation, a trading affiliate of Fischer, Francis, Trees and Watts which manages over ten billion dollars in fixed income assets. His association with derivative products began in Chicago at the Board of Trade in a regulatory capacity, then at the Chicago Board Options Exchange as Director of New Product Planning and Vice President in charge of marketing interest rate options. After six years at the Chicago exchanges, he moved to New York as National Sales and Marketing Manager for debt options and futures at Merrill Lynch and later as an arbitrage trader for Norden Government Securities. He has lectured extensively to groups such as the Mortgage Bankers Association, U.S. League of Savings and Loans, Institutional Investor's Bond Conference and the National Options Society, and has served as advisor to the Credit Division of the S.I.A. and to the Chicago Board Options Exchange. His education include a B.A. from Oberlin College with honors in history, and an M.B.A. in finance from the University of Chicago.

AN OVERVIEW OF OPTIONS AND FUTURES IN TREASURY MARKETS

John M. Ezell
Vice President
Charter Atlantic Corporation

INTRODUCTION

The 1970s and 80s have seen the development of derivative markets for Treasury instruments to the extent they have become an integral part of the overall market. Trading volume in 1985 has run around $30 billion principal per day in the derivative markets. Trades of $100 million principal are fairly common in these markets, and the value of open futures contracts runs easily into tens of billions. In some sectors, particularly the longer maturities, trading in derivatives exceeds trading in the actual Treasury instruments several fold.

It may seem odd that such an important innovation in the Treasury markets did not arise in the financial center of New York, but in many respects it would seem to have been inevitable that the development of markets for options and futures based on Treasury issues would occur in Chicago. Violent fluctuations in some commodity markets during the 1960s and early 1970s created a large pool of risk capital, a coterie of traders experienced in the use of leveraged instruments in sharply moving markets and institutional structures to effectively control the credit risk associated with exposure to large price fluctuations. The successful introduction of equity options and their rapid emergence as the most successful equity product of the 1970s diminished New York's dominance of the equity markets. The volatility of interest rates rose dramatically from increased issuance of private and government debt and the ongoing deregulation of domestic and international credit and currency markets. The elements for a successful market in financial futures were in place during the latter part of the 1970s.

Acceptance of the new instruments was neither immediate nor universal. Institutional reluctance and regulatory barriers would take more than two decades to be resolved. The taint of being "commodities" clung to the innovations in some financial circles. However, 30 percent annual movements in the Treasury bond market proved an irrefutable argument and the Chicago markets prospered, even as older, established financial institutions tottered.

The features of high leverage and relatively low cash flows characteristic of the derivative markets have proved to be a boon to the speculator and arbitrageur as well as the classical "hedger." Perhaps the most important contribution of the Chicago markets was to provide a mechanism for injecting a large pool of speculative, market-making capital into the Treasury markets at the same time government debt issuance was rising to levels which were previously unthinkable. Perhaps this could have been done with the introduction of more efficient lending practices in the government financing or repurchase markets, however, the continuing problems involving credit risk in these markets suggest that the Chicago solution was probably optimal. Apologists for the Chicago markets have stressed the benefits of the markets for hedging accounts, but the real benefit was the improvement of efficiency in government debt markets through the greater depth and narrower bid-ask spreads engendered by easier access to markets by speculative and arbitrage accounts.

One unfortunate aspect of the development of derivative markets away from established Treasury markets has been the growth of the options-futures expert or department at major broker dealers. This would seem to suggest some arcane science which can be divorced from underlying markets, but the separation of cash and derivatives in practice has often led to trades done in either the cash or derivative markets which would be more appropriately done in another market. That some naive participants have been dissatisfied with the results of their futures "hedge" would seem to be due at least in part to unfortunate marketing techniques required by the separation of cash from derivative markets. Until the two markets are joined on the marketing side with a view toward servicing the clients' real needs, management of interest rate exposure in the manner best suitable to a prescribed risk posture, there will continue to be incidents of improper usage. However, such problems should not be attributed to the highly useful tools provided by derivative markets, but to a lack of detailed understanding by many market participants.

TREASURY FUTURES

Futures on Treasury bonds and ten-year notes are traded on the Chicago Board of Trade and futures on 90-day T-bills are traded on the Chicago Mercantile Exchange. Expirations are set at three-month intervals. Payment for the underlying securities is deferred until actual delivery is made, but both the long and short positions post a good faith margin which is adjusted as market prices fluctuate. In practice, most futures contracts are closed out by taking on offsetting position rather than actually making or taking delivery. The exchanges should be consulted for up to date information on margin requirements and delivery specifications.

Futures markets differ from cash Treasury markets in three important respects. First, it is easy to take a short position in a future as it is to be long. Second, they are traded on exchange floors instead of "upstairs" by over-the-counter traders. Finally, futures contracts effectively introduce leverage into each transaction.

Maintaining a short position in futures does not require borrowing a specific security or negotiating rates of return on the proceeds of the sale as is necessary for short positions in the cash markets. In addition, contracts generally allow delivery of several different securities or a cash settlement rather than actual delivery. This minimizes the possibility of squeezes on individual securities, which would greatly increase the cost of maintaining a short position. As a result, selling futures has frequently been the preferred vehicle for establishing and maintaining short exposure to market fluctuations by both hedging and speculative participants in Treasury markets.

Exchange trading of futures contract has several ramifications. The existence of a large pool of risk capital available for easy access has been utilized often by the largest of the government dealers to speculate or to hedge inventories of Treasury issues, corporate issues, and mortgage-backed issues as well as other more esoteric exposures to interest rate fluctuations. Standardization of contracts, visibility, and easy access have resulted in the most liquid markets in the world where even very large trades have only a small impact on price levels. Like stock exchanges, the exchanges trading interest rate futures allow limit orders, stop orders, stop loss orders, and other types of orders which are not generally acceptable to Treasury dealers. Transactions in the trading "pits" are visible and prices are widely disseminated. Access to the floors of the exchanges is easily available to both individuals and institutions. The net effect of these factors has been to greatly enhance the efficiency not only of Treasury futures markets, but the underlying Treasury markets as well.

Futures Pricing

A futures contract generally calls for the delivery of a specified financial instrument at some point or period in the future, although recent contracts have increasingly allowed cash offsets instead of actual delivery. Because payment (other than "good faith" margin deposits and cash market-to-market payments) is required only upon actual delivery of the security, a futures contract is effectively a highly leveraged variant of the underlying security. Prices of futures contracts relative to the underlying security are primarily a function of the cost of financing the underlying position in the cash securities market. This difference between the futures price (adjusted for delivery specifications) and the underlying cash price is known as the *basis*. An understanding of the factors impacting the basis is fundamental to successful utilization of futures markets.

The principal determinant of the basis is the influence of the yield curve. In a positive or normal yield curve environment (short-term rates lower than long-term rates) futures will normally trade at a

EXHIBIT 14-1
Term Structure of Futures Market; Positive (Normal) Yield Curve

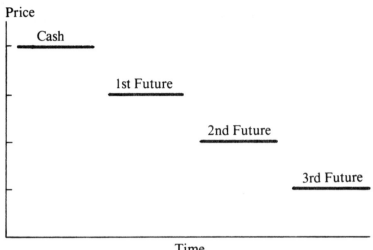

discount to cash prices and distant futures will trade at a discount to nearby futures (see Exhibit 14–1). This structure is enforced by arbitrage considerations. If the futures did not sell at a discount it would be possible to purchase a longer term security, hedge the interest rate risk by shorting the appropriate number of futures, finance the position at short-term rates, and the yield differential would produce an arbitrage profit. Therefore, futures will tend to trade at a discount sufficient to at least offset the positive carry in the markets. The futures may trade at discounts greater than this if there are uncertainties as to the financing rate until delivery, or if there are uncertainties with regard to the exact deliverable security. As time passes, the cost of financing the cash until the delivery date will decrease, as will the difference between cash prices and futures prices. At the time of delivery, cash and futures prices should be roughly equivalent. This process, called *convergence,* insures the viability of the contract as a hedging vehicle for the cash security.

In the case of a negative or inverted yield curve (long-term rates lower than short-term rates) futures markets will assume a different

EXHIBIT 14–2
Term Structure of Futures Market: Negative (Inverted) Yield Curve

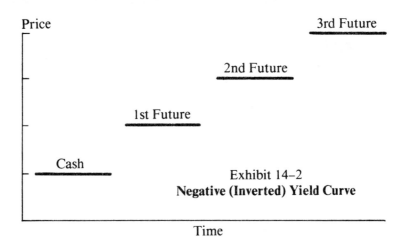

Exhibit 14–2
Negative (Inverted) Yield Curve

EXHIBIT 14–3
Shift from Positive to Negative Curve

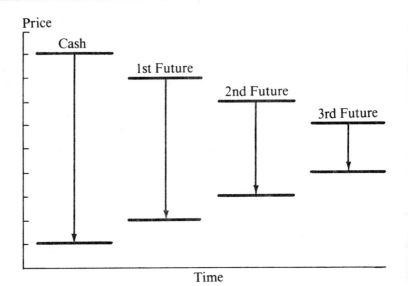

configuration. As shown in Exhibit 14–2, futures will trade at a premium to cash. Thus it is seen that yield-curve shifts can have a dramatic impact on the basis, and should be taken into consideration for hedging, investment, or speculative positions. In general, if it is expected that the yield curve will become more positive with short rates falling faster than long rates or long rates rising faster than short rates, then it is more desirable to have long positions held in the cash markets and short positions held in the futures markets. Conversely, if it is expected that the yield curve will become less positive (or more negative), this will increase the preference for holding long positions in the futures and short positions in cash markets. Exhibit 14–3 shows what would be expected to happen when a normal curve inverts in response to demands for short-term credit.

In addition to yield curve or financing considerations, factors peculiar to the individual contracts influence the basis. For example, the most important long-term futures, ten-year notes and Treasury bonds traded at the Chicago Board of Trade, both call for delivery of a hypothetical 8 percent coupon. In reality, any of a market basket of notes or bonds fitting certain standards can be delivered, but the futures price is adjusted by a *factor* which is designed to equate the bond to an 8 percent coupon. Table 14–1 illustrates a typical array of bonds and their prices.

Auctions, liquidity, stripping of coupons, extent of premium or discount as well as a myriad of other supply and demand factors will cause a fairly wide range of deliverable prices. Often an issue will emerge as *cheapest to deliver* and the futures contract will trade with a very close relationship to it, or with minimal risk of a

TABLE 14–1

Issue	Price	Factor	Converted Price	Implied Basis	Implied Repo	Futures Price
$7\frac{5}{8}$	2/15/07	74–10	0.9665	72–25	0.45	49/32	75–10
12	8/15/13	108–30	1.4144	106–17	0.40	77/32	75–10
$10\frac{3}{8}$	11/15/12	95–24	1.2427	93–19	0.16	69/32	75–10
$11\frac{1}{4}$	2/15/15	105–16	1.3645	102–24	– 1.66	88/32	75–10
$10\frac{5}{8}$	8/15/15	100–12	1.2957	97–19	– 2.61	89/32	75–10

dramatic change in the basis. Other Treasuries with different coupons and maturities will display wider fluctuations in the basis.
Corporate- and mortgage-backed issues with call and prepayment
assumptions impacting security prices can have very dramatic basis
movements, which provide trading opportunities but make hedging
these instruments an uncertain science at best.

Futures versus Cash Securities

Speculation on the relationship between the cash and futures markets
is known as *basis trading.* In its simplest form, the trader would buy
(or sell) a position in the cash markets and take an offsetting position
in the futures markets weighted by the factor. Based on Table 14–1 for
example, a $10 million short position in the 10 5/8 of 8/15 would be
offset by a long position of 130 contracts ($100,000 face per contract)
in the bond future. The *implied repo rate* is the financing rate at
which financing costs or gains incurred holding the cash position to
delivery will exactly offset the basis gain or loss from convergence,
and is useful in judging whether or not the futures are rich or cheap to
the cash securities. In this case with short rates around 8 percent, the
futures would seem cheap relative to cash issues.

The same considerations with regard to convergence and basis risk
apply with equal force to *hedging* with futures. Hedging uses futures
to offset price risks associated with positions in the cash Treasury
markets. In general, a hedged position in longer term instruments
will yield the same or less than short-term rates as illustrated by the
low implied repo rates in the example above. This is due to the
arbitrage mentioned earlier. Therefore, hedging long securities with
short futures positions may be very advantageous for the short period of time required to allow an orderly liquidation of the cash
security position, but in most cases is inappropriate as a long-term
strategy, unless implied repo rates are unusually high.

Conversely, if implied repo rates are lower than market rates, it
may make sense to substitute a long position in the future for a cash
position in long-term Treasuries, and to invest the money derived
from the sale of the Treasuries in short-term instruments. The income from the convergence of futures to cash plus the income from
the short-term investments should exceed that produced by the

longer term Treasury, but with approximately the same exposure to market risk.

Basis relations with long-term, non-deliverable securities, particularly if not Treasury issues, is a more difficult problem, and much of the "hedging" that takes place using Treasury futures against those markets would be more aptly described as a speculation on intermarket spreads. In practice, the most effective way to weight this type of trade is to construct a duration weighted hedge between the instrument to be hedged and the cheapest to deliver in the futures market and adjusting the resulting futures position by the factor. The liquidity of the futures markets become a major advantage in intermarket spreads as prepayments, call features or other special characteristics will necessitate frequent re-weighting or liquidation of the position. The risk of these positions can approach that of outright positions so they must be actively managed. Popular applications have included Treasury futures hedging corporates, municipals, preferred stock, and mortgage-backed instruments. *Spreading* between different contract maturities or between Treasury note futures and Treasury bond futures (the NOB) is also common among traders and includes essentially the same analysis that would be done for a basis trade and a yield-curve trade.

The most important Treasury futures for short-term instruments is based on 90-day T-bills and is traded on the Chicago Mercantile Exchange. The yield curve effects discussed above also apply to the short-term futures, however, there are some major differences between the T-bill contract and the note and bond contracts. The most interesting of these is the possibility of creating *synthetic securities.* For example, an investor who wishes to purchase a six-month T-bill might instead purchase a three-month T-bill and a future calling for delivery of another three-month T-bill ninety days hence. The *strip yield* of the combined cash and futures positions may be better than the six-month bill, and would offer incremental gains if the short-term yield curve gets less positive or more negative.[1] Longer strips of futures can be used to create synthetics for longer term securities. In this case, the futures may also be *stacked* in one contract month

---

[1] Note that the calculation of strip yields should include the compounding effect arising from three-month reinvestments.

if the trader has yield curve expectations. For example, a synthetic year-bill position, normally involving a three-month bill and one contract of each of three different deferred months, might be done with all futures contracts in the most distant month if it were expected that the yield curve would become less positive, as in Exhibit 14–3.

It should be noticed that it takes a 90-day bill plus three futures contracts to create a synthetic-year bill, and that it would take four futures to hedge a one-year obligation. Three months hence as the year bill had only nine months left, only two contracts plus the new three-month T-bill would form the synthetic or three contracts would hedge a nine-month obligation. This illustrates the principal difference between hedging in short-term markets and long-term markets. The rapid change in the value of a basis point in short-term maturities requires frequent changes in hedge ratios if a neutral position against an actual security is desired. Otherwise weighting by duration or value of a basis point is utilized very much in the same manner as for long-term futures.

TREASURY OPTIONS

Options on specific Treasury bonds, notes and bills are traded on the Chicago Board Options Exchange and the American Stock Exchange. Options on bond and note futures are traded on the Chicago Board of Trade and options on T-bill futures are to be traded on the Chicago Mercantile Exchange. Contracts on notes and bonds are for $100,000 principal, while T-bill options are based on $1,000,000 principal. All trade both puts and calls with striking prices above and below market prices. In general, expirations are set at three month intervals. Buyers of options must pay the premium, while sellers of options post margins in a manner similar to futures traders. The exchanges should be consulted for up to date margin requirements and specifications.

A prospective entrant into the options markets is faced with an overwhelming array of choices. In the over-the-counter options markets offered by some major dealers the number of possible option contracts is literally infinite due to variations in strike prices,

TABLE 14–2

	Expiration					
	December '86		March '87		June '87	
Strike Price	Calls	Puts	Calls	Puts	Calls	Puts
74	5.42	.18	5.00	.48	4.40	1.21
76	3.62	.36	3.40	1.14	3.24	2.04
78	2.33	1.07	2.30	2.04	2.35	3.00
80	1.28	2.01	1.35	3.08	1.44	4.10
82	.48	3.18	.63	4.24	1.15	5.26
Dec future	79.16			Prices in points and $\frac{1}{64}$s		
Mar future	78.17					
June future	77.19					

options maturity, underlying issues, and American or European exercise provisions.[2] Fortunately, there has been considerable standardization of option contract terms for those which are traded on exchanges whether based on futures or on the actual Treasuries. Normally, there will be both puts and calls at each of several different striking prices set both above and below the current market for the underlying security or future. In addition several option maturities, generally at three-month intervals, will be available. A partial array of available options on bond futures might appear as in Table 14–2.

Treasury options combine many of the attractive features of the futures markets with limited risk. The holder of an option has the right but not the obligation to purchase or to sell a security or futures contract at a specified price, the *striking price.* Thus, the money at risk to the purchaser of an option is limited to the fee or *premium* paid for the option while the potential gain is effectively unlimited. This is illustrated by the example in Exhibit 14–4. Whereas the gain or loss on the long future position is virtually

[2] American options can be exercised at any time while European options can be exercised only at maturity. Neither term has any relationship to where the options are actually traded or issued.

EXHIBIT 14–4
Comparison of Long Call Position with Long Future Position

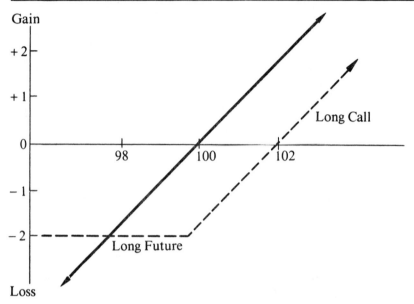

unlimited, the maximum loss on the call option is limited. However, it should be noted that the option will underperform the future in a rising market due to the payment of the premium.

Conversely, the seller or writer of an option can profit only to the extent of the premium received. In many respects, the position of the seller of options is similar to that of an insurance underwriter, willing to manage large risks in return for a fixed premium. In contrast to taking a position in the futures or cash markets the sale of an option does generate a positive cash flow. This provides opportunities to enhance cash flows and current yields on securities positions. In addition, premiums captured from selling calls can be used to cushion losses on long positions and premiums captured from selling puts used to cushion losses on short positions.

Basic Option Strategies

Exhibit 14–5 shows gain or loss configurations from the four basic options positions, if they are held to the expiration of the option. The

EXHIBIT 14–5
Basic Option Strategies

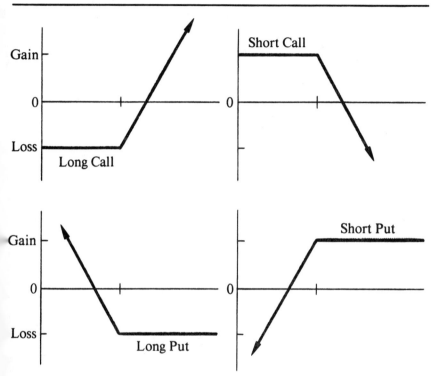

purchase of a *call* option gives the buyer a highly leveraged long position in markets where interest rates are falling but the premium paid is lost in markets that are stable or where rates are rising. Therefore, it would be an appropriate strategy if one believed that rates were going to fall, particularly if the economic scenario included some possibility of a sharp rate jump or if the call purchaser could not afford to risk a major capital loss.

While the purchase of a call is often considered to be primarily speculative, there are rather conservative applications as well. For example, the manager of a bond portfolio expecting violent fluctuations in the market should shorten the maturity structure dramatically and use a small fraction of his assets to purchase calls on bonds. In the event of a sharp increase in rates the option premium will be lost, but should be largely offset by the opportunity to roll the short-term investment to higher yields with little or no capital loss. However, if the market does rally and rates fall sharply the portfolio will perform as if it had been invested in long bonds, except the premium would be lost. In essence, the manager has positioned himself for a bear market, but purchased insurance against a rally. This type of strategy will work well if the market moves sharply in either direction; however, in a stable market performance is hurt by the loss of the premium. This illustrates the basic point that option purchases tend to work best in volatile markets.

The purchase of a *put* is the mirror image of a call purchase and conveys the right, but not obligation, to sell securities on futures at a specified price. It provides a highly leveraged exposure to rising rates, but only the premium is at stake if rates are flat or falling. Therefore, the purchase of a put becomes appropriate in environments with rising but fluctuating rates. It is also the ideal method for speculating on a rise in rates for investors who cannot absorb large capital losses.

The limited loss feature of the put makes it extremely useful for hedging purposes, for several reasons. First, the potential for upside gains on the securities being hedged is not eliminated as would be the case of a hedge placed in either cash or futures markets. As the market rallies, the value of the put will fall, but not as much as the underlying future or cash security. Second, since the purchaser of the put can lose only the premium paid for the purchase of an option, heavy negative cash flows resulting from margin calls are not encountered as they would be with futures or leveraged cash positions being used to offset a risk of rising rates. This would be critical to a business owner trying to protect against an increase in his floating rate obligations or a mortgage banker funding a development commitment since there would not be corresponding positive cash flows on the position being hedged. Finally, the purchase of puts is probably the vehicle of choice for hedging rate risks which may be only tangentially related to Treasury rates. Mortgages, bank rates, corporate and municipal obligations, as well as other rate sensitive areas will often tend to lag Treasury markets, and the short-term results of futures or cash security hedges can be extremely painful.

Sale of a call option provides the writer of the option with a positive cash flow from the premium received, which will prove to be profitable if interest rates rise or are unchanged. However, the gain is limited to the premium received. In the event of a rate decline, the leverage inherent in the call can produce very large losses for the writer. For this reason the holding of a short call position without any associated offsetting position (a *naked* or *uncovered call*) is considerably more risky than the purchase of a call. In addition to the disadvantages of being leveraged in adverse markets, and having only a limited profit potential in favorable markets, the seller of uncovered calls will be required to post margin in the event of unfavorable price action, without favorable cash flows in favorable markets. For this reason, call writing is often done in conjunction with the holding of the underlying security, where gains on the security will offset losses on the short call position. This might be done to enhance current yield (*covered writing* which is discussed later) or to enhance the sale price of the security by the premium received.

The sale of a put provides positive cash flow in the form of the premium received. This will be profitable in environments where interest rates are stable or falling, but the strategy leaves the seller of uncovered puts with exposure to large losses if rates rise sharply.

The sale of puts can sometimes be used to reduce the cost of acquiring a security. For example, an investor who has decided to increase his investment in bonds might sell puts on bonds. If the option is exercised the investor has reduced his cost of acquiring bonds due to the premium received. If rates fall and the put is not exercised, the investor has suffered an opportunity cost as he did not purchase bonds at the prevailing level; however, retention of the full put premium received from the sale of the option serves as at least partial compensation.

Combination Strategies

In addition to the straightforward purchase or sale of options, a number of different strategies can be implemented which utilize more than one option. Several of these are illustrated in Exhibit 14–6.

The purchase of a *straddle* involves buying both a put and a call with the same exercise price. This strategy will result in profits if rates move sharply in one direction either up or down. Consequently, this is most appropriate when there is a great deal of uncertainty with

---

EXHIBIT 14–6
Combination Option Positions

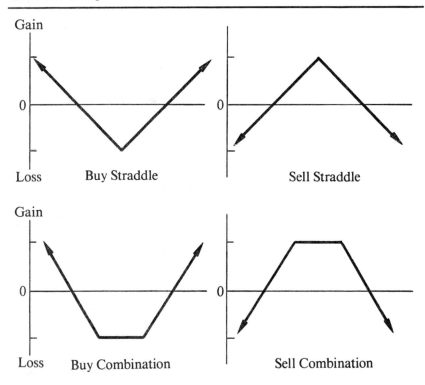

regard to the direction of rates, but large movements are expected. For example, an investor might spend 20 basis points[3] each for a put and a call on 9-day T-bills at 8 percent with the cash market also at 8 percent. If the market moves more than 40 basis points in either direction prior to the expiration of the options, the investor will have a profitable position.

Had the investor sold both the put and the call, the short straddle

---

[3] At $25 per basis point, this represents $500 per option or a total outlay of $1,000. The exercise price would be 92 (100-8) since the strikes are based on an index of 100 minus discount. A 75 basis point movement to either 7.25 or 8.75 results in a profit of $875 [$25 × (75-40)].

would produce profits as long as the T-bill rate remains between 7.60 and 8.40, but could be subjected to very large losses if the bill rate moves beyond this range. The maximum gain from selling a straddle is the sum of the two premiums and would be gained if the bill rate were precisely 8 percent at the expiration of the options and neither were exercised. The sale of straddles would be recommended if there is an expectation of a fairly narrow trading range.

If one purchases both a put and a call, but with different strike prices the resulting position is known variously as a *strangle,* a *combination* or a *combo.* In general, the most frequently seen trade will involve the purchase of *out-of-the-money* options, i.e., puts with striking points below the market price of the underlying security and calls with striking prices above the striking price of the underlying security. Like the buyer of a straddle, the buyer of a combination or strangle is hoping for large movements in the market. For example, if a put and a call on the bond future with striking prices of 78 and 80, respectively, and a premium of 1 point each were purchased, a profit would be recognized if the futures were trading either above 82 or below 76 at expiration. Conversely, the sale of the combination would be appropriate if a trading range between the two striking prices were expected. As can be seen, combinations follow the general rule for options that they should be bought if the market is expected to move greatly, or sold if the market is expected to be particularly stable.

Straddles and combinations can be given a market bias by using either a put or call closer to the money or in-the-money in the direction of the bias. Thus buying a 78 straddle would have a bullish bias and buying an 80 straddle or bearish bias if the bond futures were trading at 79. Alternatively, *spreads* between calls or between puts with different striking prices provide limited risk for trades with a bullish or bearish attitude. Exhibit 14–7 illustrates a *bull call spread,* which involves the purchase of the lower striking price and the sale of a call with a higher price. The maximum loss is the net debit, while the possible gain is limited to the value of the distance between the strikes less the net debit. A *bear call spread* would involve the sale of the lower striking price. If the spread is done in puts instead of calls, a *bull put spread* occurs when the lower striking price is bought and a *bear put spread* occurs when the lower strike is sold.

EXHIBIT 14–7
Bullish Call Spread

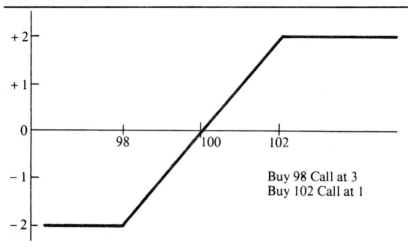

Buy 98 Call at 3
Buy 102 Call at 1

Options versus Treasury Securities

It is also very common to combine options with positions in the underlying security. The most frequent applications of this type are the put hedge and covered call writing, where a long position in the underlying security or a similar security is offset to some extent by either a long put or a short call. To implement these strategies it is necessary to observe how options prices move given changes in the price of an underlying security or future. In general, in-the-money options[4] should capture a high percentage of the movement of the underlying security, while out-of-the-money options will capture much less of the movement. As a good rule of thumb, an at-the-money option will move about half as much as the underlying security.[5] The difference in movement between options and securi-

---

[4] An in-the-money option has intrinsic value. This means an in-the-money put has a striking price above the market price of the security, while an in-the-money call has a striking price below that of the underlying security. Similarly an out-of-the-money put has a striking price below the market and an out-of-the-money call has a striking price above the market.

[5] In the parlance of the options models which have become increasingly popular, the movement of the option with respect to the underlying security can be

ties or between options with a different striking price is encompassed in the concept of time value.

Option premiums can be divided into two components, *intrinsic value* and *time value.* Intrinsic value represents the amount by which the strike price exceeds market price of the underlying for puts, and time value is the remaining excess premium, if any. Thus if a call option on a Treasury bond with a strike price at par was selling for 3 points with the price of the bond at 102, then that option has 2 points of intrinsic value and 1 point of time value.

Time value erodes with the passage of time, and represents the true cost of insurance in a put hedge or the maximum incremental yield for a covered writer. It is greatest for at-the-money options. Exhibit 14–8 illustrates the results of hedging with a put at various strike prices. Some or all of the put premiums may be offset by interest income from the underlying security, but this is not taken into account in Exhibit 14–8. In an efficient market, however, put premiums will be high enough to offset gains arising from extensions out on the yield curve.

The 98-put provides the least protection in a rising rate environment, but due to the relatively low premium, would be appropriate for an investor who was fundamentally bullish but wanted to purchase disaster insurance. Note that out-of-the-money put hedges are also the best performers in bull markets. The 102-, in-the-money put actually provides the best protection in a bear market. It is important to notice that the real cost of the put hedge is only the $2\frac{1}{4}$ points of time value. The at-the-money hedge will perform between in- or out-of-the-money hedges in rising or falling markets; however, it is the most expensive hedge if the markets remain unchanged because the at-the-money option suffers the most from decay of time value.

Covered call writing involves selling calls against a holding in the

---

expressed as a derivative of the option pricing equation. This is known as the delta. As it goes further into the money an option's delta approaches 1, or in other words, moves very much like the underlying security. As the option moves out-of-the-money the delta approaches 0 and movements in the underlying security have very small impacts on the option. The delta of an at-the-money option is about .5. Over time, delta for out-of-the-money options decline and deltas for in-the-money options increase, as time value decays.

EXHIBIT 14–8
Put Hedge at Option Maturity

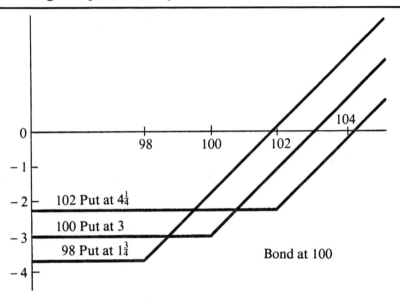

underlying security. Table 14–3 illustrates why this has been a very popular strategy for the enhancement of current yield.

The option premium received by the covered call writer serves not only to enhance current yield in flat markets but also provides a limited amount of protection in rising rate environments. As Ex-

TABLE 14–3

Buy $1,000,000 10 Percent 30-year bonds at 100

Sell 10 six-month 100 calls at 4

Six months later

Bond Price	Gain on Bond	Coupon	Gain on Option	Total	Compounded Return (%)
100	—	$50,000	$40,000	$90,000	18.8%
104	40,000	50,000	—	90,000	18.8
96	(40,000)	50,000	40,000	50,000	10.25

EXHIBIT 14–9
Covered Call Position at Option Maturity

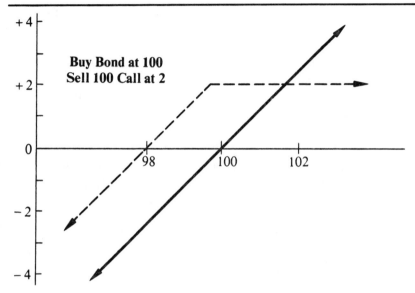

Buy Bond at 100
Sell 100 Call at 2

hibit 14–9 shows, a covered write will outperform a position in the underlying unless the market is rising sharply. The only drawback is that upside potential is limited by the possibility of having the security called away. If incremental yield is the primary objective of the covered write, an at-the-money option is usually chosen, since time value is maximized.

If additional protection is felt to be more desirable than the incremental yield then an in-the-money option would be used since its greater premium would provide more of a cushion. Finally a bullish investor engaged in covered call writing would probably chose an out-of-the-money call which allows for more profits before the security would be called away.

Other Option Pricing Considerations

The basic strategies outlined for options in this chapter have been presented in a static format so that they might be more easily understood. However, a great many other factors enter into the pricing options and these factors are constantly in a state of flux. For example, the value of options are affected by interest rates. The value of a put on a Treasury relative to a call on a Treasury increases as the yield curve gets more positive and declines relative to a call as the curve gets more negative. This arises due to a process known as *conversion.* A position consisting of a long call and short put is actually a synthetic version of the underlying security without the interest flows. The synthetic is priced relative to the security in the same manner as described for futures. For a flat yield curve, the time value of both the put and call should be the same. In a positive yield curve environment, the put premium paid in a synthetic short position must be greater than the premium received for the call by an amount sufficient to offset any positive carry. This is the principal difference between options on securities and options on futures where carry is not a consideration.

Market expectations of volatile markets will also increase the value of options, while expectations of narrow trading ranges will tend to diminish option premiums. Volatility is often measured in terms of an annualized standard deviation of returns for the purpose of estimating option values through various models. An excellent way to ascertain the relative value of options is to compare *implied volatilities* either between options or against historical volatilities. Implied volatilities are derived through an option model using market prices to derive volatilities instead of estimating volatilities to provide a price.

Finally, the passage of time also erodes the value of an option. Therefore, longer term options will almost always have higher premiums.[6] However, the decay of time premium is not a linear function but tends to accelerate as expiration approaches. Therefore, unless high volatility is expected sellers of options tend to prefer selling nearby option contracts to maximize decay while hedgers would prefer more distant contracts to minimize decay. However, if a large move is expected each would take the opposite position. This

---

[6] Exceptions can arise for European options and for options on futures where yield-curve effects can dominate the time value of option premiums, particularly in distant contracts.

is caused by the loss of time value is greater in the deferred contract as it moves either into or out-of-the-money.

SUMMARY

The increased volatility of interest rates beginning in the 1970s led to the development of new financial instruments to deal with financial risk. First were futures which provided a high degree of leverage combined with liquidity. Next were options which added a limited risk "insurance" like feature and the opportunity to generate current income from the sale of options. Taken together, these instruments have opened a wide variety of risk management techniques as well as providing an even wider array of investment or speculative opportunities. Given the uncertainties relating to the future course of the economy, and the banking system both internationally as well as domestically, growth in the markets would seem very likely.

CHAPTER 15

MARK PITTS is First Vice President and
Director of the Futures Division's Quantitative
Strategies Group at Shearson Lehman Brothers. His
specialties include pricing and hedging strategies for
derivative products in general, and fixed income
futures and options in particular. Mr. Pitts also uses
quantitative methods to create new financial
products for his firm, as well as his firm's clients.
Mr. Pitts serves on the editorial board of several
financial publications and frequently contributes
articles to the financial press. He holds a Ph.D. from
Duke University.

MANAGING THE INTEREST RATE RISK OF TREASURY SECURITIES

Mark Pitts, Ph.D.
Vice President
Shearson Lehman Brothers, Inc.

Futures on fixed-income securities are now widely used throughout the debt markets. Banks, savings institutions, pension funds, money managers, security dealers, and corporations of every description are active users of fixed-income futures contracts. While an impediment for many potential users has been regulatory and policy constraints, these constraints are now vanishing in many sectors. Other potential users have been deterred by a lack of knowledge and understanding of the futures markets. However, as more and more institutions learn about the futures markets and put them to effective use, those who remain outsiders find themselves at a competitive disadvantage. This chapter addresses the primary concern of many institutional users: how the futures market can be used to hedge the interest rate risk of Treasury securities.

THE PRELIMINARIES

Before a hedge is ever initiated, there are several steps which the prudent manager should take in order to be completely comfortable with the hedging process. By taking these steps *before* the hedge is set, the potential hedger gains an understanding of what a hedge can and cannot accomplish, and ensures that if the hedge is set, it is set in the proper manner. Briefly, the preliminary steps are as follows:

- Determine which futures contract is the most appropriate hedging vehicle.

- Determine the target for the hedge—that is, the rate or price which the manager should expect to lock in with the hedge.

- Estimate the effectiveness of the hedge, i.e., the risk of a hedged position relative to an unhedged position.

- Estimate the absolute (as opposed to relative) risk of the hedged position.

- Determine the proper hedge ratio, i.e., the number of futures contracts needed to hedge the underlying risk.

A primary factor determining which futures contract will provide the best hedge is the degree of correlation between the rate on the futures contract and the interest rate which creates the underlying risk that the manager wants to eliminate. For example, a long-term Treasury bond portfolio can be better hedged with Treasury bond futures than with Treasury bill futures because long-term Treasury bond rates are more highly correlated with T-bond rates than with T-bill rates. Similarly, an anticipated purchase of short-term Treasury securities could generally be more effectively hedged using T-bill futures than Eurodollar time deposit futures. Using the right delivery month is also important. Naturally, a manager trying to lock in a rate or price for June will use June futures contracts since June contracts will give the highest degree of correlation. Correlation is not, however, the only consideration if the hedging program is of significant size. If, for example, a manager wants to hedge the purchase of $500 million of short-term securities in a single month, liquidity in the futures market becomes an important consideration. In such a case, it might be necessary to spread the hedge across two or more different contracts. Consequently, a buyer of short-term securities might hedge by buying some T-bill futures and some Eurodollar time deposit futures.

Having determined the right contract and the right delivery months, the manager should then determine what is to be expected from the hedge—that is, what rate will, on average, be locked in by the hedge. Obviously, if this rate is too high (if hedging a sale) or too low (if hedging a purchase), hedging is perhaps not the right strategy for dealing with unwanted risk. Determining what to expect—i.e., calculating the *target rate* for a hedge—is not always simple. However, the pages that follow explain how the manager should approach this problem for both simple and complex hedges.

Hedge effectiveness tells the manager what percentage of his risk is eliminated by hedging. Thus, if the hedge is determined to be 90 percent effective, over the long run a hedged position will have only 10 percent of the risk (i.e., standard deviation) of an unhedged position. However, for any single hedge, it is possible that the hedged position will show more variation than the unhedged position.

The *residual hedging risk,* i.e., the absolute level of risk in the hedged position, tells the manager how much risk remains after hedging. While it may be comforting to know, for example, that 90 percent of the risk is eliminated by hedging, without additional statistics the hedger still does not know how much risk he still faces. The residual risk in a hedged position is expressed most conveniently as a standard deviation. For example, it might be determined that the hedged position has a standard deviation of 10 basis points. Assuming a normal distribution of hedging errors, the hedger will then obtain the target rate, plus or minus 10 basis points, 2 times out of 3. His probability of obtaining the target rate, plus or minus 20 basis points, is 95 times out of 100, and his probability of obtaining the target rate, plus or minus 30 basis points, is greater than 99 times out of 100.

The target rate, the hedge effectiveness, and the residual hedging risk determine the basic trade-off between risk and expected return. Consequently, these statistics give the manager the essential facts needed in order to decide whether or not to hedge. Using these figures he can construct confidence intervals for hedged and unhedged positions. Comparing these confidence intervals he can then determine whether hedging is the better alternative. Furthermore, if hedging is the right decision, his level of confidence in the hedge is well defined in advance.

The manager should also be aware that the effectiveness of a hedge and the residual hedging risk are not necessarily constant from one hedge to the next. Hedges that will be lifted near a futures delivery date will tend to be more effective and have less residual risk than those lifted on more distant dates. The life of the hedge, i.e., the amount of time between when the hedge is set and when it is lifted, also generally has a significant impact on hedge effectiveness and residual hedging risk. For example, a hedge held for six months might be 90 percent effective, while a hedge held for one month might be only 25 percent effective. The intuition behind this is that the security to be hedged and the hedging instrument might be highly correlated over the long run, but only weakly correlated over the short run.

Similarly, residual hedging risk usually increases as the life of the hedge increases. The residual risk on a six-month hedge may be 85 basis points even if the residual risk for a one-month hedge is only 35 basis points. It may seem surprising that the longer hedges have more risk if they are also more effective. However, hedge effectiveness is a measure of *relative* risk, and since longer time periods exhibit greater swings in interest rates, a greater percentage reduction in risk for longer hedges does not necessarily mean that there is less risk left over.

This concept is demonstrated in Figure 15–1, which shows the typical patterns of risk associated with hedged and unhedged positions. Because interest rates and spreads are generally less predictable further into the future, the risk (i.e., standard deviation) increases for longer holding periods for either position. Thus, residual hedging risk will tend to increase for longer holding periods. However, the effectiveness of the hedge is measured by the relative risk of the two positions. As shown, for shorter hedges the risk of the hedged position may be half as much as the risk of the unhedged position, leading to 50 percent hedge effectiveness (AB = 1/2 × AC). For longer periods, the risk of the hedged position is only about one-third as much as the risk of an unhedged position, giving 66.7 percent effectiveness (DE = 2/3 × DF). Consequently, effectiveness increases as the length of the hedge increases even though the total risk of the hedged position also increases with the length of the hedge.

FIGURE 15-1

Risk as a Function of the Length of a Hedge

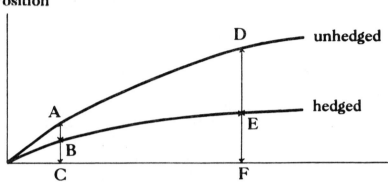

Length of Hedge

Note: $AB = \frac{1}{2} \times AC$ and $DE = \frac{2}{3} \times DF$

The target rate, residual risk, and the effectiveness of a hedge are relatively simple concepts. However, since these statistics are usually estimated using historical data, the potential hedger should be sure that these figures are estimated correctly. Statistics can be tricky business. Well-intentioned amateurs and not-so-well-intentioned professionals have been known to produce statistics that lead to overly optimistic estimates of what a hedge can do. Consequently, the potential hedger should not necessarily judge the skill of his broker by how much he promises to accomplish with a hedge.

The final factor that must be determined before the hedge is set is the hedge ratio, or the number of futures contracts needed for the hedge. Usually the hedge ratio is expressed in terms of relative face amounts. Accordingly, a hedge ratio of 1.20 means that for every $1 million face value of securities to be hedged, the manager needs $1.2 million face value of futures contracts to offset his risk. As the following pages demonstrate, hedge ratio calculations run the gamut from trivial to esoteric. Furthermore, the hedge ratio may change from one hedge to the next. Like the other statistics, the best hedge ratio is also a function of the life of the hedge, generally increasing for those hedges with longer lives.

THE CONTRACTS

Futures contracts are financial products created by futures exchanges. Subject to approval by the regulatory agencies, the exchanges are free to create virtually any contract they please. Not surprisingly, not all contracts offered by the exchanges are successful. Due to lack of interest by commercial accounts, speculators, or local traders, sufficient volume may never develop in a contract and it will eventually be dropped from trading. In other cases, a contract trades well for several years but then falls from favor due to changes in the economic environment or from increased competition from other contracts. Consequently, futures contracts come and go.

This section highlights some of the more important features of the futures contracts that are currently available on Treasuries securities. (The exchanges will gladly provide more detailed information.) Undoubtedly, as economic conditions change new contracts will be introduced and will flourish, while some of the currently popular contracts will eventually die out.

Interest rate futures contracts based on Treasury securities can be divided into two primary groups: those based on long- and intermediate-term instruments, and those based on short-term instruments. In the former category, the contracts are the Treasury bond contract and the Treasury note contract. In the latter category, the only contract is the Treasury bill contract. There are significant similarities in the contract specifications for the intermediate- and long-term contracts. Furthermore, both the long and intermediate-term contracts are traded on the Chicago Board of Trade (the Board or CBOT) while the short-term contract is traded on the International Monetary Market (IMM) of the Chicago Mercantile Exchange (the Merc or CME).

The Treasury Bond Contract

The T-bond contract is by far the most successful of the interest rate (or commodity) futures contracts. Prices and yields on the T-bond contract are always quoted in terms of a (fictitious) twenty-year 8 percent T-bond, but the CBOT allows many different bonds to be delivered in satisfaction of a short position in the contract. Specifically, any Treasury bond with at least fifteen years to maturity or fifteen years to first call, if callable, qualifies for delivery. Consequently, there are usually ten to twenty outstanding bonds that constitute good delivery.

The T-bond contract calls for the short (i.e., the seller) to deliver $100,000 face value of any one of the qualifying Treasury bonds. However, since the coupon and maturity vary widely across the deliverable bonds, the price that the buyer pays the seller depends upon which bond the seller chooses to deliver. The rule that the Chicago Board of Trade has adopted adjusts the futures price by a *conversion factor* which reflects the price the bond would sell for at the beginning of the delivery month if it were yielding 8 percent. Using such a rule, the conversion factor for a given bond and a given delivery month is constant through time and is not affected by changes in the price of the bond. To illustrate, consider the delivery price for the Treasury 12 percent bonds of August 15, 2013, if delivered on the June 1985 contract. At the beginning of June 1985 this bond had twenty-three years, $2\frac{1}{2}$ months to call. To calculate the conversion factor, the term to call is rounded down to the nearest quarter year, in this case giving an even twenty-three years to call. Since a twenty-three-year, 12 percent bond yielding 8 percent sells for 141.77, the conversion factor for the 12 percent bond for the June 1985 contract is 1.4177 (i.e., 141.77 ÷ 100).

The seller has the right to choose when during the delivery month delivery will take place and which qualifying bond to deliver. The buyer is then obligated to pay the seller the futures price times the appropriate conversion factor, plus accrued interest on the delivered bond. Paradoxically, the success of the CBOT T-bond contract can in part be attributed to the fact that the delivery mechanism is not as simple as it may first appear. Implicit in a short position in bond futures, there are several options. First, the seller chooses which bond to deliver. The seller has a "swap option." If the seller is holding Bond A for delivery, but Bond B becomes cheaper to deliver, he can swap Bond A for Bond B and make a more profitable delivery. Second, within some guidelines set by the CBOT, the seller decides when during the delivery month delivery will take place. He has a "timing option" which can be used to his advantage. Finally, the short retains the possibility of making the "wildcard" play. This potentially profitable situation arises due to the fact that the seller can give notice of intent to deliver for several hours after the exchange has been closed and the futures settlement price has been fixed. Thus, in a falling market the seller can use the wildcard option to profit from the fact that the delivery price is fixed even if the market if falling. A detailed example of the wildcard play is given in Appendix 15–A.

Each of the seller's options tend to make the contract a bit more difficult to understand, but at the same time they make the contract more attractive to speculators, arbitrageurs, dealers, and anyone else who believes they understand the contract somewhat better than other market participants. Thus, in the case of the bond contract, complexity has helped provide liquidity.

The Treasury Note Contract

The CBOT Treasury note contract was modeled after the CBOT Treasury bond contract and resembles it in many respects. The T-note contract allows delivery of any note that has a maturity of $6\frac{1}{2}$ to ten years on the first delivery day of the month. To qualify for delivery the instrument also must have been issued as a Treasury note; thus, old Treasury bonds with a remaining life of $6\frac{1}{2}$ to ten years do not qualify.

The T-note contract offers the seller the same flexibility that the T-bond contract offers. By giving proper notice, the seller can deliver at almost any point he chooses during the delivery month. He also chooses which of the qualifying notes to deliver and receives an amount equal to the futures price times the conversion factor for the delivered note (also based on an 8 percent yield), plus accrued interest. There has not, however, been as much of a play concerning the most deliverable issue for the T-note contract as there has been for the T-bond contract. It has usually been obvious well in advance which note (or when-issued note) would be delivered by the seller. The note contract offers the seller the same wildcard play that is offered by the bond. Thus during the delivery month, this idiosyncrasy in the contract specifications can be particularly profitable when prices fall after the exchange has closed.

The Treasury Bill Contract

The Chicago Mercantile Exchange's futures contract on Treasury bills was the first contract on a short-term debt instrument and has been the model for most subsequent contracts on short-term debt. The contract is based on three-month (i.e., ninety-day) T-bills with a face value of $1,000,000. The contract is quoted and traded in terms of a futures "price," but the futures price is, in fact, just a different way of quoting the futures interest rate. Specifically, the futures price is just the annualized futures interest rate subtracted from 100. For example, a futures price of 91.00 means that T-bills are trading in the futures market at a rate of 9.00 percent. The actual price that the buyer pays the seller is calculated using the usual formula for Treasury bills:

Invoice Price = $1,000,000 × [1 − Rate × (Days to Maturity ÷ 360)]

where the rate is expressed in decimal form. As can be easily verified by this formula, for a ninety-day instrument each .01 change in the quoted futures price (i.e., each basis point change in yield) leads to a $25 change in the invoice price.

The T-bill futures contract is considerably simpler than the intermediate and long-term futures contracts. First, since all T-bills of the same maturity are economically equivalent, there is effectively only one deliverable issue, i.e., T-bills with three months to maturity. The fact that the three-month bills may be either new three-month bills or older T-bills that currently have three months of remaining life makes little difference since the new and old issues will trade identically in the cash market. Thus, all the subtleties surrounding conversion factors and most deliverable issues are absent from the T-bill futures market. Furthermore, there is little uncertainty or choice involved in the delivery date because delivery must take place during a very narrow time frame, usually a three-day period. The rules of the exchange make clear well in advance the exact dates on which delivery will take place. Finally, since there are no conversion factors, there is no wildcard play in the Treasury bill futures market.

Although the T-bill contract is simple and thus may not provide as many speculative and arbitrage opportunities as the more complex long and intermediate-term futures contracts, the T-bill contract does provide a straightforward means of hedging or speculating on the short end of the yield curve. Since the T-bill rate is the benchmark off which other short-term rates are priced, the bill contract fills a well-defined need of many market participants.

HEDGING PRINCIPLES

Hedging is one of the primary ways that institutional accounts use interest rate futures contracts. While it is difficult to state the general principle that underlies futures hedging concisely, a one line attempt might be as follows: do in the futures market today what you anticipate needing (or wanting) to do on a future date. For instance, if a portfolio manager owns a long Treasury bond that he anticipates selling in six months, he hedges by selling T-bond futures for delivery six months hence. If the same manager does not anticipate an actual sale but wants to hedge the value of the bond six months forward, then the manager in a sense would like to sell the bond (as evidenced by the fact that he no longer wants the volatility of a long bond position), but may be constrained from doing so. His course of action should be the same; he should sell bond futures to hedge his position.

An asset manager can also use futures to hedge the rate at which anticipated cash flows will be invested. A manager expecting a cash inflow in one year might plan to buy long-term Treasury bonds when the cash is available, but he would like to hedge the rate at which that investment will be made. Anticipating a future purchase of bonds, the manager hedges by buying bonds in the futures market today. If, on the other hand, the manager plans to invest the cash in short-term securities, he would hedge by buying T-bill futures instead of T-bond futures.

Liability managers can apply the same hedging principles. The liability manager who funds his operations by continually rolling over short-term debt tied to the T-bill rate faces substantial risk arising from the uncertainty of future rate levels. Since the manager anticipates having to sell new short-term debt in the future, he hedges by selling futures contracts on Treasury bills.[1]

The liability manager who plans to sell long- or intermediate-term debt closely tied to the Treasury bond rate faces the risk that rates will rise before the anticipated bond issuance. To hedge, he will enter into a trade in the futures market to mirror the trade he anticipates having to do on a future date; namely, he sells futures on Treasury bonds or notes to hedge the subsequent sale of his own debt.

In each of the foregoing examples, the managers follow essentially the same rule. Whatever action they expect or want to take in the cash market, but are constrained from taking, they take instead in the futures market. At the risk of oversimplification, this rule can be followed by most, if not all, asset and liability managers.

EXPECTED RETURN AND RISK IN A HEDGE

When one enters into a hedge, the objective is to lock in a rate for the sale or purchase of a security. (Or, if hedging floating rate payments, the objective is to lock in future interest rate payments.) However, there seems to be much disagreement as to what rate or price one can expect to lock in when futures are used in a hedge. One view is that the hedger can expect to lock in the current spot rate for the security. The opposing view is that the hedger should expect to lock in the rate at which the futures contracts are bought or sold. As it turns out, the truth usually lies somewhere in between these two positions. However, as the following examples illustrate, each view may be correct in certain special cases.

---

[1] A manager who funds with floating rate debt tied to the T-bill rate does not actually roll over short-term debt, but his interest rate expense is determined by future short-term rates. Consequently, his best hedge will be to sell T-bill futures.

The Target for Hedges Held to Delivery

Hedges that are held until the futures delivery date provide an example of the hedge that locks in the rate implied by the futures contracts. A hedge with T-bill futures contracts is a straightforward illustration of this. Suppose an investor buys a $1 million six-month T-bill at 8.50 percent and expects to sell it three months hence, at which time the bill will have three months of remaining life. To hedge his sale, the investor sells one $1 million three-month T-bill contract for delivery in three months. Suppose further that when the hedge is set, spot three-month bills are at 8.18 percent and three-month bill futures are at 9 percent. What rate does the hedger lock in for the sale of his T-bill three months hence (on futures delivery date)?

The process of *convergence* guarantees that the hedger locks in 9 percent (the futures rate) for his sale, while the spot rates of 8.18 percent and 8.50 percent are all but irrelevant. Convergence refers to the fact that at delivery there can be no discrepancy between the spot and futures price for a given security (or commodity).[2] If the futures price were higher than the spot price, one could buy in the cash market, immediately sell in the futures market, and take out money at no risk. If the futures price were lower than the spot price, one could buy in the futures market and immediately sell in the cash market, again taking out cash at no risk. Thus arbitrage between the cash and futures market forces the cash and futures price to converge on the delivery date.

To see how convergence guarantees the hedger a price equal to the futures price on the day the hedge is set, consider the cash flows associated with a T-bill contract sold at 9 percent (quoted as 91.00). For each basis point increase in the futures yield above 9 percent (or .01 decrease in the quoted futures price below 91.00), the investor receives a margin inflow of $25. Now, if the investor targets 9 percent as the expected sale rate for his T-bill (which will then have three months to maturity) every basis point above 9 percent at which he sells his T-bill will cost him exactly $25 (from

---

[2] In the case of more than one deliverable, this is true only for the cheapest to deliver.

TABLE 15-1
T-Bill Hedge Held to Delivery*

Actual Sale Rate (%)**	Actual Sale Price ($)	Gain/Loss ($) from Futures**	Effective Sale Price ($)	Effective Sale Rate (%)***
5.00	987,500	− 10,000	977,500	9.00
6.00	985,000	− 7,500	977,500	9.00
7.00	982,500	− 5,000	977,500	9.00
8.00	980,000	− 2,500	977,500	9.00
9.00	977,500	0	977,500	9.00
10.00	975,000	2,500	977,500	9.00
11.00	972,500	5,000	977,500	9.00
12.00	970,000	7,500	977,500	9.00
13.00	967,500	10,000	977,500	9.00
14.00	965,000	12,500	977,500	9.00
15.00	962,500	15,000	977,500	9.00

*Rate on futures contracts when sold = 9%; target rate = 9%; target price = $977,500.

**By the process of convergence, the actual sale rate equals the final futures rate.

***Transaction costs and the financing of margin flows are ignored.

$1,000,000 × .0001 × 90/360). Thus, ignoring transaction costs, any short-fall relative to the targeted rate is just offset by gains on the futures contract. Conversely, if the hedger is able to sell his T-bill at a price higher (or yield lower) than the target, losses on the futures contract just offsets any windfall he experiences in the cash market. This guarantees that he does no worse than, and no better than, the target.[3] Table 15-1 illustrates this fact in more detail. (It must be emphasized, of course, that while a hedge may be perfect, futures losses—if any—must be met immediately, and in cash.

[3] For this to be exactly true, one must ignore the fact that net margin inflows from the futures contract can be invested over the life of the hedge, and net margin outflows must be borrowed (or paid out at an opportunity loss) over the life of the hedge. To adjust for this fact, the total futures position should be reduced by the factor $(1 + r)^t$, where r is the rate for borrowing or lending margin flows, and t is the time until delivery.

Consequently, the institution should be very aware of the cash flow considerations implicit in a futures position.)

As the example above shows, the rate on the securities in the cash market does not affect the price that can be locked in. However, it must be noted that while the hedge guarantees a sale price equal to the futures price, futures prices are often lower than cash prices. This is frequently referred to as the "cost of convergence."

The same principle holds in the market for intermediate- and long-term debt, only the situation is a little more complicated because the hedger doesn't know for sure when delivery will take place or which bond will be delivered. For the sake of simplicity though, consider the T-bond contract and assume for now that it is obvious which bond will be delivered, and that delivery will take place on the last day of the delivery month (frequently the most advantageous day to make delivery). Consider the 7 5/8 percent Treasury bonds maturing on February 15, 2007. For delivery on the June 1985 contract the conversion factor for these bonds was .9660, implying that the investor who delivers the 7 5/8 percent bonds would receive from the buyer .9660 times the futures settlement price, plus accrued interest. Consequently, at delivery, the (flat) spot price and the futures price times the conversion factor must converge. Otherwise, arbitrageurs would buy at the lower price and sell at the higher price and earn risk-free profits. Accordingly, a hedger could lock in a June sale price for the 7 5/8 percent bonds by selling T-bond futures contracts equal to .9660 times the face value of the bonds. For example, $100 million face value of 7 5/8 percent bonds would be hedged by selling $96.6 million face value of bond futures (966 contracts). Furthermore, the sale price that the hedger locks in would be .9660 times the futures price. For example, if the futures price is 70–0 when the hedge is set, the hedger locks in a sale price of 67.62 (or approximately 67–20) for June delivery, regardless of where rates are in June. Table 15–2 shows the cash flows for a number of final prices for the 7 5/8 percent bonds and illustrates how cash flows on the futures contract offset losses or gains relative to the target price of 67.62. In each case the effective sale price is very close to the target price (and, in fact, would be exact if enough decimal places were carried through the calculations). However, since the target price is determined by the futures price, the target price may be lower than the cash market price.

TABLE 15–2
T-Bond Hedge Held to Delivery*

Actual Sale Price for 7 $\frac{5}{8}$ Percent T-Bonds**	Final Futures Price***	Gain/Loss on 966 Contracts ($10/.01/Contract) ($)	Effective Sale Price ($)****
62–0	64.182	5,620,188	67,620,188
63–0	65.217	4,620,378	67,620,378
64–0	66.253	3,619,602	67,619,602
65–0	67.288	2,619,792	67,619,792
66–0	68.323	1,619,982	67,619,982
67–0	69.358	620,172	67,620,172
68–0	70.393	– 379,638	67,620,362
69–0	71.429	– 1,380,414	67,619,586
70–0	72.464	– 2,380,224	67,619,776
71–0	73.499	– 3,380,034	67,619,966
72–0	74.534	– 4,379,844	67,620,156
73–0	75.569	– 5,379,654	67,620,346
74–0	76.605	– 6,380,430	67,619,570
75–0	77.640	– 7,380,240	67,619,760

*Instrument to be hedged: 7 $\frac{5}{8}$% T-bonds of 2/15/07; conversion factor for June 1985 delivery = .9660; price of futures contracts when sold = 70–0; and target price for 7 $\frac{5}{8}$% T-bonds = .9660 × 70 = 67.62.

** By convergence, must equal final futures price times the conversion factor.

*** Bond futures trade in even increments of 1/32. Accordingly, the futures prices and margin flows are only approximate.

**** Transaction costs and the financing of margin flows are ignored.

When we admit the possibility that bonds other than the 7 5/8 of 2007 can be delivered, and that it might be advantageous to deliver other bonds, the situation becomes somewhat more involved. In this more realistic case the hedger may decide not to deliver the 7 5/8, but if he does decide to deliver them, he is still assured of receiving an effective sale price of approximately 67.62. Whether he delivers the 7 5/8 or not should, of course, depends upon whether another bond can be delivered more cheaply.

In summary, if an investor sets a risk minimizing futures hedge *that is held until delivery,* he can be assured of receiving an effective sale price for his bond that is dictated by the *futures* price (and *not* the spot price) on the day the hedge is set.

The Target for Hedges with Short Holding Periods

Let us return to a variant of our original example of purchasing a $1 million six-month T-bill at 8.50 percent. Now, however, we want to assume that the investor has no intention of holding the T-bill for an extended period of time but intends to sell it in the very near term, say within a day. The investor still faces the risk that rates will rise and the sale price of the T-bill will fall, and so he decides to hedge this risk by selling two of the nearby T-bill futures contracts, currently trading at 9 percent and calling for delivery in three months. (Two three-month T-bill contracts are required since at the time of sale the T-bill will be approximately twice as volatile as a three-month T-bill.) What rate should the hedger expect to lock in: the futures rate of 9.00 percent or the spot rate of 8.50 percent?

Since the hedge is lifted before delivery the hedger can no longer be assured of locking in a rate, spot or future. However, the effective rate that he receives in this example is much more likely to approximate the current spot rate of 8.50 percent than the futures rate of 9.00 percent.

The critical difference between this hedge and the earlier examples is that the hedge is not held until delivery and, therefore, convergence will generally not take place over the life of the hedge. In fact, since the futures delivery date is three months from the day the hedge is set and the hedge will be lifted in one day, it is much more realistic to assume that rates on the spot six-month T-bill and the three-month T-bill futures will move in a parallel fashion for the one-day period, rather than converge.

This example is not unique to the T-bill. Whether the hedger is hedging with one of the other short-term contracts or with the intermediate and long-term contracts, he should expect the hedge to lock in the spot rate (or more exactly, the one-day forward rate), rather than the futures rate for very short-lived hedges (unless, of course, the short-lived hedge ends on a futures delivery date). For example, returning to the simplified example in which the 7 5/8 percent T-bonds of February 15, 2007 were the only deliverable bonds on the T-bond futures contract, suppose that the hedge is set three months before delivery date and the hedger plans to lift the hedge after one day. It is much more likely that the spot price of the bond will move parallel to the converted futures price (i.e., the futures price times the conversion factor), than that the spot price and the converted futures price will converge by the time the hedge is lifted.

A one-day hedge is, admittedly, an extreme example. Other than underwriters and money managers who reallocate assets very frequently, few investors are interested in such a short horizon. The very short-term hedge does, however, illustrate a very important point: the hedger should not expect to lock in a futures rate (or price) just because he is hedging with futures contracts. This would be true only if the hedge is held until delivery, at which point convergence must take place. If the hedge is held for a very short time period and is lifted before delivery, the hedger should expect to lock in the one-day forward rate, which will very nearly equal the spot rate. Generally, of course, hedges are held for more than one day, but are not necessarily to delivery. The proper target for these cases is examined in the next two sections.

How the Basis Affects the Target Rate for a Hedge

The *basis* is a concept used throughout the futures markets. The basis is defined as simply the difference between the spot price of a security (or commodity) and its futures price, that is:

$$\text{Basis} = \text{Spot Price} - \text{Futures Price}$$

In the fixed-income markets two problems can arise when one tries to make practical use of the concept of the basis. First, the quoted futures price does not equal the price that one receives at delivery. In the case of the intermediate and long-term contracts, the actual futures price equals the quoted futures price times the conversion factor. In the case of the short-term contracts, the quoted futures price is actually 100 minus the annualized interest rate. The actual invoice price must be derived using the applicable yield to price conventions for the instrument in question. Consequently, to be useful, the basis in the fixed-income markets should be defined using actual futures delivery prices rather than quoted futures prices.

A second problem arises due to the fact that fixed-income securities (unlike most other commodities and securities) age over time. Thus, it is not exactly clear what is meant by the "spot price." Does the spot price mean the current price of the actual instrument that can be delivered in satisfaction of a short position, or does it mean the current price of an instrument that currently has the characteristics called for in the futures contract? For example, when the basis is defined for a three-month T-bill contract maturing in three months, should the spot price refer to the current price of a six-month T-bill, which is the instrument that will actually be deliverable on the contract (since in three months it will be a three-month T-bill), or should the spot price refer to the current three-month T-bill (which will mature on or near the delivery date)? Obviously, how this problem is resolved depends upon the purpose one has in mind. The purpose here is to see how the basis affects the results of a hedge. For hedging purposes, the only basis that really matters is the basis defined by the difference between the futures price and the current price of the security that can be held and actually delivered into the contract (i.e., the six-month bill in this example).

For hedging purposes, it is also frequently useful to define the basis in terms of interest rates rather than prices. Using the spot interest rate of the instrument to be hedged and the interest rate for that instrument implied in the futures delivery price (as opposed to the quoted futures price), the *rate basis* is defined as:

Rate Basis = Spot Rate – Implied Futures Rate

The rate basis is particularly useful for analyzing hedges of short-term instruments because it nets out any effects due solely to the aging process. For instance, if spot one-year T-bills and three-month T-bill futures maturing in nine months are both trading at 12 percent, the rate basis is zero since cash and futures are at the same interest rate. However, a one-year T-bill at 12 percent has a price of 88, while a three-month T-bill at 12 percent has a price of 97, giving a price basis of − 9. Furthermore, because the cash security ages, a change in the price basis does not necessarily imply that there has been a change in the rate basis, or vice versa. Accordingly, the relationship between the price basis and the rate basis is not always an obvious one.

Both rate and price bases are helpful in explaining the two kinds of hedges examined in the preceding sections. The first hedge was a hedge of six-month T-bills for a sale date three months in the future. By selling three-month T-bill futures for delivery in three months, the hedger was able to lock in a rate equal to the rate at which the contract was sold (9 percent in the example). The second hedge was a hedge of the same T-bill for a sale date only one day in the future. In this case, the hedger sells the nearby T-bill contract (assumed to mature in three months) and expects to lock in a rate approximately equal to the current rate on his six-month bill (8.50 percent in the example). To illustrate why the two hedges are expected to lock in such different rates, we define the *target basis* as the expected rate basis on the day the hedge is lifted. In the former case, a hedge lifted on the delivery date is expected to have, and by arbitrage activity will have, a zero-rate basis when the hedge is lifted. The target rate for the hedge should be the rate on the futures contract. In the latter case, one would not expect the basis to change very much in one day and so the target rate basis approximates the current rate basis. Accordingly, the target rate for the hedge should be the futures rate plus the current rate basis, i.e., the current spot rate.

To generalize this concept, the hedger can set the target rate for any hedge equal to the futures rate plus the target basis:

Target Rate for Hedge = Futures Rate + Target Basis

This definition of the target rate is applicable to the intermediate- and long-term contracts as well as to the short-term contracts. (A numerical example is given in the next section.)

The target basis concept also explains why a hedge held until the delivery date locks in a rate with certainty and the very short-lived hedge does not. It is often said that hedging substitutes basis risk for price risk, and the examples show that this is true. For the hedge held to delivery, there is no uncertainty surrounding the target basis; by convergence, the basis on the day the hedge is lifted is certain to be zero. For the short-lived hedge the basis will probably approximate the current basis when the hedge is lifted, but its actual value cannot be known in advance. Thus, the uncertainty surrounding the outcome of a hedge is directly related to the uncertainty surrounding the basis on the day the hedge is lifted, i.e., the uncertainty surrounding the target basis.

A More General Approach to the Target

The discussion so far has centered on two special cases, the very short-term hedge and the hedge held to delivery. Many hedges fall somewhere between these two extremes. The problem then is to choose a target rate for hedges that are held for more than a few days, but are closed out prior to delivery. This is essentially a question of deriving the target basis since, as before, the target rate for the hedge should equal the implied futures rate plus the target basis.

To show how this approach can be implemented in a general context, let us examine a simplified case in which we believe that the rate basis will decline linearly over time. The basis is thus expected to change by the same amount each day until, at delivery, the basis is zero. To show how this assumption affects the target rate for the hedge, assume that the hedger who invests in six-month T-bills at 8.50 percent plans to resell the bills in 30 days, i.e., one-third of the way between the purchase date and the futures delivery date. To account for the relative volatility of five-month T-bills and three-month T-bill futures, the investor should sell 1.67 contracts per $1 million invested. In these circumstances, what rate should the hedger target if the nearby T-bill contract is selling at 9.00 percent?

The rate basis at the outset of the hedge is − .50 percent. Assuming a linear decline in the basis, after thirty days the rate basis will equal − .33 percent. The target basis for the hedge is therefore − .33 percent. Using the formula for the target rate given in the last section, we have:

$$\text{Target Rate for Hedge} = \text{Futures Rate} + \text{Target Basis}$$
$$= 9.00\% - .33\%$$
$$= 8.67\%$$

As expected, since the hedge is lifted closer to the day the hedge is set than to the delivery date, the target rate is closer to the spot rate of 8.50 percent than to the futures rate of 9.00 percent.

The actual outcome of the hedge will be determined by how realistic it is to assume that the basis will decline linearly over time. However, as Table 15–3 shows, if this assumption is accurate, the target rate and price will be locked in by the hedge.

In the intermediate- and long-term markets it is somewhat easier (but not necessarily more accurate) to define the target for the hedge in terms of a price rather than an interest rate. Accordingly, in a hedge one might assume that the price basis, rather than the rate basis, will decline linearly over time. For example, suppose that eighty days before the assumed delivery date for the June 1985 T-bond futures contract a hedger wants to lock in a sale price for $100 million face value of 7 5/8 percent T-bonds of February 15, 2007, for a sale date twenty days in the future. (To simplify, assume the 7 5/8 is the only deliverable bond.) These bonds, for example, may be selling at 67 in the cash market while the bond futures contract is at 68. Since the conversion factor for these bonds for the June 1985 contract was .9660, the price basis is calculated as $67 - (.9660 \times 68) = 67 - 65.688 = 1.312$. If the price basis does indeed decline linearly through time, on the day the hedge is lifted the basis will equal .9840. Thus, the target basis, in terms of price rather than yield, is .9840. Using a formula similar to the earlier one, the target price for the hedge is given by:

$$\frac{\text{Target Price}}{\text{for Hedge}} = \frac{\text{Futures Price} \times}{\text{Conversion Factor}} + \frac{\text{Target Basis}}{\text{(in Price)}}$$

Or, in this example,

$$\text{Target Price} = 65.688 + .984$$
$$= 66.672$$

As in the earlier example, if the actual price basis on the day the hedge is closed out equals the target basis, and the hedger shorts the appropriate number of futures contracts (966 in this case), the effective sale price for the hedged security will closely approximate the targeted price. (The effective sale price would exactly equal the

TABLE 15-3
T-Bill Hedge Held for 30 Days

Actual Sale Rate for T-Bill (%)	Actual Sale Price for T-Bill ($)	Futures Rate When Hedge Is Closed Out (%)*	Gain/Loss ($) from 1 2/3 Futures	Effective Sale Price for T-Bill ($)	Effective Sale Rate for T-Bill (%)**
5.00	979,167	5.33	-15,292	963,875	8.67
6.00	975,000	6.33	-11,125	963,875	8.67
7.00	970,833	7.33	-6,958	963,875	8.67
8.00	966,667	8.33	-2,792	963,875	8.67
9.00	962,500	9.33	1,375	963,875	8.67
10.00	958,333	10.33	5,542	963,875	8.67
11.00	954,167	11.33	9,708	963,875	8.67
12.00	950,000	12.33	13,875	963,875	8.67
13.00	945,833	13.33	18,042	963,875	8.67
14.00	941,667	14.33	22,208	963,875	8.67
15.00	937,500	15.33	26,375	963,875	8.67

* Rate on futures contracts when sold = 9%; target rate = 8.67%; and target price = $963,875.

** By assumption, equals the T-bill rate + .33%.

*** Transaction costs and the financing of margin flows are ignored.

TABLE 15–4
T-Bond Hedge Held for 20 Days

Actual Sale Price of Bonds	Future Price When Hedge Is Closed Out**	Gain/Loss on 966 Contracts ($10/.01/Contract)***	Effective Sale Price****
60–0	61.093	$6,672,162	$66,672,162
61–0	62.128	5,672,352	66,672,352
62–0	63.164	4,671,576	66,671,576
63–0	64.199	3,671,766	66,671,766
64–0	65.234	2,671,956	66,671,956
65–0	66.269	1,672,146	66,672,146
66–0	67.304	672,336	66,672,336
67–0	68.340	– 328,440	66,671,560
68–0	69.375	– 1,328,250	66,671,750
69–0	70.410	– 2,328,060	66,671,940
70–0	71.445	– 3,327,870	66,672,130
71–0	72.480	– 4,327,680	66,672,320
72–0	73.516	– 5,328,456	66,671,544

*Instrument to be hedged: $7\frac{5}{8}$% T-Bonds of 2/15/07; conversion factor = .9660; price of futures contracts when sold = 68–0; and Target price for $7\frac{5}{8}$ = .9660 × 68 + .984 = 66.672.

**By assumption, when closed out, the futures price equals (cash price – target basis) + conversion factor.

***Bond futures trade in even 32nds. Thus the futures price and the gains and losses are approximate.

****Transaction costs and the financing of margin are ignored.

target if enough decimal places were saved.) Table 15–4 demonstrates this fact.

Basis Risk

For a given investment horizon, hedging substitutes basis risk for price risk. Thus one trades the uncertainty of the price of the hedged security for the uncertainty of the basis. Consequently, when hedges don't produce the desired results, it is customary to place all the blame on *basis risk*. However, basis risk is the correct explanation only if the target rate for the hedge is properly defined. Basis risk should refer only to the *unexpected* or *unpredictable* aspect of the relationship between cash and futures prices or rates. The fact that this relationship changes over time does not in itself imply that there is basis risk. If, for example, the rate basis between a T-bill futures contract and the deliverable T-bill is 1 percent, we know for certain that the basis will decline to virtually 0 percent on the delivery date. Thus, with respect to delivery date, there is no basis risk. The basis will change by 1 percent, but this change is completely predictable and there is nothing risky about it.

Basis risk, properly defined, refers to the uncertainty associated with the target rate basis or target price basis. Accordingly, it is imperative that the target basis be properly defined if one is to correctly assess the risk and expected return in a hedge.

Risk and Expected Return

We have, until now, taken the minimum variance hedge as our point of departure and assumed that this is the desired hedge. In so doing, we have ignored expected return in our desire to minimize risk. This approach can be altered to achieve different targets (i.e., different expected returns), but only at the cost of increasing risk.

A simple example is when the hedge ratio is set equal to zero, that is, when there is no hedge. The risk is then the risk of holding an unhedged cash security, and the target is the expected price of the security on the anticipated sale date. Futures prices in this case are irrelevant.

Alternatively, one can define the target and work backwards to find the hedge ratio that gives the desired target. For example, a hedger may want to hedge a deliverable security for a sale date corresponding to the delivery date (meaning that he could lock in the sale price with no risk), but he wants the target to be the current price of the security. This may be possible: there is frequently some hedge ratio that on average (at least, historically) offsets changes in cash prices with changes in futures prices, thus making the current price the appropriate target. However, if the hedger uses a hedge ratio that makes the current price the target price, he must take on more risk than he would if he chose a hedge ratio that equates the target price to the futures price.

The important point is that it is imperative that the target and the risk be correctly defined, and both the target and the risk level depend upon the hedge ratio. If the manager uses the minimum variance hedge ratio, then the target and risk level are determined as described in earlier sections. If, on the other hand, the target is set equal to the current price, a hedge ratio can usually be found to give this expected return, but the hedge will not generally be the minimum variance hedge. (The exception being very short-lived hedges and those cases in which the futures price equals the current price.) Thus the hedger may obtain a more desirable target rate for the hedge, but does so only by assuming incremental risk. In subsequent sections, we will continue to assume that risk minimization is the primary concern of the hedger and set up hedges accordingly.

MONITORING AND EVALUATING THE HEDGE

After a target is determined and a hedge is set all that is left is to monitor the hedge during its life, and to evaluate it after it has been lifted. Most hedges require very little active monitoring during their life. In fact, overactive management poses more of a threat to most hedges than does inactive management. The primary reason for this is that the hedger only infrequently receives enough new information during the life of the hedge to justify a change in the hedging strategy.

There are, however, exceptions to this general rule. As rates change, volatilities (i.e., PVBPs) change and the discounting for margin changes over time. Accordingly, the hedge ratio may change slightly.

Normally, a hedge can be evaluated only after it has been lifted. Evaluation involves, first, an assessment of how closely the hedge locked in the target rate, i.e., how much error there was in the hedge. To provide some meaningful interpretation of the error, the hedger should calculate how far from the target rate the sale (or purchase) would have been had there been no hedge at all. For example, a hedger might set a target of 10 percent for a subsequent sale of bonds. Even with the hedge, he might find his effective sale rate to be 10.50 percent—a significantly higher rate than expected. However, it may be that without hedging, the bonds would have sold at 13 percent. Consequently, the hedge, although far from perfect, saved the seller 250 basis points.

SUMMARY

There are many different ways to go about hedging and in the interest of prudence it is best to do some preliminary work before the hedge is ever initiated. Besides determining the appropriate number and type of contract to use, we suggest that managers also obtain an estimate of the effectiveness of the hedge (i.e., risk reduction relative to an unhedged position), and the residual hedging risk (the absolute level of risk in a hedged position). While these are simple concepts, the subtleties of certain statistical procedures may make it difficult to derive reliable estimates of hedge effectiveness and residual hedging risk. The manager should be able to depend upon his broker to help assess these parameters of the hedge.

The target of the hedge, i.e., the expected rate or price which the manager hopes to lock in, is another important number that should be considered before the hedge is set. The target of the hedge depends upon how long the hedge is held, the projected value of the basis, and the projected relationship between the security to be hedged and the deliverable security.

APPENDIX 15–A

The Wild Card Delivery

The wild card delivery play offers potential profits to sellers of T-bond and T-note futures contracts traded on the Chicago Board of Trade. During the delivery period for these contracts, the seller can give notice of intent to deliver up until 8:00 P.M. (Chicago time). The price that the seller receives from the buyer equals the conversion factor for the instrument delivered, times the futures settlement price (determined shortly after the close of the futures market at 2:00 P.M. Chicago time), plus accrued interest. Profit opportunities arise from the fact that up until 8:00 P.M. sellers can choose to make deliveries at prices determined at 2:00 P.M.

To see how the wild card play can work to the advantage of the seller, suppose an investor buys the 12 1/2 percent T-bonds of 8/15/14 and uses the bond futures contract to hedge for an anticipated sale date in September of 1985. Since the conversion factor for the 12 1/2 percent bonds for September 1985 was 1.4749, the hedger would sell 14.75 bond contracts for every $1 million face amount of underlying bonds.

During the delivery period, the hedger may profit from the wild card delivery play if spot market prices fall after the futures market closes. To illustrate, suppose the hedger holds $100 million face amount of the 12 1/2 percent bonds and is short 1475 bond contracts. Assume that one day during the delivery period futures close at 78 with the bond simultaneously trading at 115.25. The investor can lift his cash-futures position in either of two ways. He can buy back his futures position and sell the bonds in the cash market. His net position would then be $115,250,000 in cash, plus the gains (or minus the losses) on 1475 futures contracts. Alternatively, he could deliver bonds in satisfaction of the short futures position. However, in order to make delivery on the futures position, the investor must purchase an additional $47.5 million face value of bonds. If this purchase is made at the close of futures trading, the cost will be $54,743,750 (i.e., 115.25 percent × $47.5 million). From the buyer, he receives $169,687,245 [from $147.5 million (face value) × 1.4749 (the conversion factor) × 78 percent (the futures price)]. This gives a net position of $114,943,495 in cash, plus the gains (or losses) on 1475 futures contracts.

Obviously, the second alternative is inferior to the first. However, consider what happens if the investor takes no action and bond prices fall after the futures market closes; say, for example, that by 7:00 P.M. the price of the 12 1/2 bonds fall two points to 113.25. The investor then gives notice of intent to deliver. As before, additional bonds must be purchased, but now the cost is only $53,793,750 (from 113.25 percent × $47.5 million). Receiving $169,687,245 from the buyer, the investor's net position is $115,893,495 in cash, plus the gain (or loss) on 1475 futures contracts. Of course, if prices do not fall after the close of futures market (or do not fall sufficiently far), the investor will not give notice of intent to deliver and not buy bonds in the cash market. Consequently, the seller has the option to make delivery if profitable, or carry the position another day if not profitable (unless, of course, the end of the delivery period has been reached).

In essence, the seller has an option. The option gives him the right to sell at a fixed price (the futures settlement price) for a period of six hours, regardless of the price of the underlying asset. In this sense, the wild card play is much like a daily put option.

CHAPTER 16

JACK BERNARD is presently with the Financial Futures and Options Group of Merrill Lynch (Chicago office), where he is involved in the sale of mortgage-backed securities.

In 1984, he received his MBA from Stanford University. Prior to his career with Merrill Lynch, Mr. Bernard served in the United States Navy.

YIELD ENHANCEMENT OPPORTUNITIES WITH TREASURY FUTURES

Jack Bernard
Financial Futures and Options Group
Merrill Lynch Capital Markets

Treasury futures have been highly touted by practitioners as offering an efficient means for speculation, risk management, and yield enhancement. Speculation and risk management (hedging) have been discussed in previous chapters; the focus of this chapter is on yield enhancement opportunities.

YIELD ENHANCEMENT DEFINED

Yield enhancement is nothing more than buying something cheap or selling something expensive. Put in the context of portfolio management, the portfolio manager must first decide how to apportion his portfolio amongst the different sectors of the yield curve. This decision is expounded in modern portfolio theory as the mean-variance tradeoff. Simply put, because of increasing price volatility along the yield curve, if the manager is bullish, he will extend on the yield curve (increase portfolio duration); if bearish, he will shorten up. The degree of confidence in his market forecast will determine how far he extends or shortens up. Once he decides where to be on the curve, he can then look for yield enhancement. Note that if he is successful in enhancing yield in the given sector of the yield curve but his market forecast is wrong, i.e., he is in the wrong sector, he may not achieve a superior return relative to a manager who put himself into the correct sector.

WHERE "SHOULD" FUTURES TRADE?

If we know at what price futures should trade, we can observe if futures are cheap or expensive and then make our yield-enhancement strategy based on some additional analysis. To see where futures should trade, look at the trade from the standpoint of an arbitrageur:

1. Buy the cheapest-to-deliver bond, finance (reverse repo) the bond to the last delivery day of the deliverable month. Note that *no money is put up.*
2. Sell futures at the same time the bond is purchased.
3. Deliver the bond into the futures receiving effectively the price at which the futures were sold (converted to the bond being delivered).

Because no money was put up, no money should be received when the transaction is unwound. By owning the bond over the holding period, the current yield minus the financing rate (reverse repo) is earned (in a positive yield curve environment this carry is positive). To make up for this positive carry, the futures must be sold below the converted bond price; this difference should be the amount of carry earned on the bond. For example, on November 18, 1985:

*   Buy the 12.5 percent of 8/15/14 at 119–8

*   Finance the bond at a term reverse repo rate of 8 percent for 132 days

*   Sell the March T-bond futures

*   On March 31, 1986—Deliver the bond into the futures

Over 132 days, the trader earned 10.037 percent current yield on the bond, but must pay 8 percent to finance it for a positive carry of 2.037 percent. This positive carry is worth $9,148 per million par on 29/32nds (0–29). On November 18, the futures price (multiplied by the bond conversion factor) *should* therefore trade 29/32nds below the cheapest-to-deliver bond price. If it is, the trader makes nothing, which is fair because nothing was put up. Let's see how cheap futures were on November 18, 1985:

Nov. 18—12.5 of 11/15/14 bond price = 119–18

Nov. 18—Theoretical *converted* futures price = 119–8 minus 0–29 = 118–11

Nov. 18—Theoretical futures price (conversion factor for the 12.5's is 1.4714) = 118–11 ÷ 1.4714 = 80–14

Nov. 18—Actual futures price = 79–22

"Cheapness" of futures = theoretical price minus actual price

= 80–14 minus 79–22

= 0–24

DO FUTURES TRADE AT THEIR "FAIR VALUE?"

Futures are a natural sell by institutions speculating on interest rate movements and using them as a risk management tool (to hedge Treasuries, corporates, mortgages, municipals, etc.) because it is often easier and more efficient than shorting bonds. With more people wanting to sell, the futures price is offered down below its *fair* value. For many complex reasons, arbitrage interest is not sufficient to get futures to their *fair* value; however, arbitrage does work to limit the "cheapness" of the contract.

TAKING ADVANTAGE OF THE "CHEAPNESS" OF FUTURES

Given that futures are cheap, yield enhancement can be attained by buying futures. The portfolio manager should have already made his decision to be in the 30-year, 10-year or 3-month sector because the only interest rate futures that exist are, respectively, the T-bond, T-note and T-bill futures which correspond to those sectors. By buying the futures in the correctly weighted proportion, the investor is still exposed to the same price volatility (i.e., interest-rate risk) as would be experienced if the corresponding bond position was held.

The Trade

A manager who owns long Treasury bonds would execute the trade by:

1. Selling the Treasury bond;
2. Putting the proceeds into a short-term instrument (T-bill, CD, or money market) maturing in the futures delivery month;
3. Buying the T-bond futures using a dollar volatility weighted hedge ratio.

A portfolio manager who wants to buy a long Treasury bond should instead:

1. Put the intended investment into a short-term instrument (T-bill, CD, or money market) maturing in the futures delivery month;
2. Buy the T-bond futures using a dollar volatility weighted hedge ratio.

The trade would be reversed in the delivery month giving the manager ownership of the bonds (or the trade would be rolled which would again take advantage of the cheapness of futures). Let's look at a trade opportunity that existed on August 27, 1985.

The 12s of 8/15/13 were sold, the proceeds put into a CD expiring in December, and T-bond futures were bought. The cheapest to deliver was assumed to be the 12.5s of 8/15/14.

The basis is sold at the current level of 84/32nds. By selling the bond, the investor is giving up a current yield of 10.50 percent but earning 7.96 percent on the CD for a net giveup of 2.54 percent; this will cost the investor 28.5/32nds over the $3\frac{1}{2}$-month holding period. The most critical assumption in the analysis is the estimate of the basis on the swap bond on the last trading day. This can be found by assuming a yield spread to the cheapest to deliver which itself has an assumed basis of 4/32nds reflecting just over the estimate of carry to the end of the month. The 3-month yield spread history of the swap issue to assumed cheapest to deliver is used to get a range of the predicted basis on last trading day; this varies from 4/32nds to 20/32nds. To find the net gain per million, subtract what the basis was bought at from what the basis was sold for to give the pick up from the basis collapse, and then subtract the current yield giveup. This is summarized in Exhibit 16–1.

In order to improve our analysis, we must be sensitive to a key assumption, the assumed cheapest to deliver bond. In a low rate environment, as existed on August 27, 1985, premium bonds are cheapest to deliver. As the market falls off, the longer maturity securities will become cheapest because of the maturity bias in the conversion factor. Finally, in high rate environments, the discount coupons become cheapest because reinvestment of coupon proceeds is of greater importance, giving premiums more value over discounts.

For our analysis we used, for the assumed cheapest, two characteristic premiums (12.5 of 8/15/14 and 11.75 of 11/15/14) at the current rate environment, a longer maturity security (11.25 of 2/15/15) at a higher rate environment (85 basis points), and a discount (7.625 of 2/15/07) at an even higher rate environment (120 basis points).

Exhibit 16–2 gives the predicted pickup in the refined analysis which changes the assumed cheapest to deliver with a corresponding change in level of long-end interest rates.

What actually happened on December 18, 1985? As we originally predicted, the cheapest to deliver remained the 12.5s of 8/15/14. The 12s cheapened up slightly to the 12.5s and ended up at a basis of 9/32nds. Total pickup turned out to be 46.5/32nds over the 113 day holding period. Note that this 46.5/32nds is a pickup *in addition* to the gain (or loss, if rates had instead increased) realized if the 12s alone had been held over the period; this is an incremental gain of $14,531 per million dollars par of the 12s held!

EXHIBIT 16–1
Sell Cash Bond—Buy Futures Basis Swap

---

(1) Sell: 12 of 8/15/13. Buy: Dec T-bond futures. Settlement dates: 8/28/85 to 12/19/85

	Three-Month History CTD-Bond Spread (B.P.s)	Cash Bond YTM (%)	Sell Basis 8/27/85 (32nds)	Current Yield Giveup (32nds)	Buy Basis 12/19/85 (32nds)	Net Gain per $MM Par (32nds)
Present	− 2	10.73	84.0	28.5	11.0	44.5
Low	− 5	10.70	84.0	28.5	20.0	35.5
Average[2]	0[3]	10.75[4]	84.0[5]	28.5[6]	5.0[7]	50.5
High	7	10.82	84.0	28.5	4.0	51.5

A. Assumed cheapest to deliver	: 12.5 of 8/15/14
YTM of cheapest	: 10.75[8]
Implied repo	: 4.33
B. Value of one B.P.	
in yield spread (32nd)	: 3[9]
C. Current yield giveup	
CY of bond	: 10.50[10]
Return on proceeds	: 7.96
Net giveup	: 2.54

Explanation:
1. The trade and holding period.
2. Yield-spread history between the swap bond and assumed cheapest to deliver.
3. Cash bond yield-to-maturity at assumed spread.
4. Current market for selling the basis on the swap bond: basis = price of swap bond − (futures price × conversion factor) rounded to the nearest 32nd.
5. Current yield giveup:
   (overnight repo equivalent of current yield of swap bond − CD rate) × (holding period ÷ 360) × (price + accrued interest for $1mm of swap bond) ÷ 312.5.
6. Assumed basis of swap bond on last trading day. This is determined by spreading the yield of the swap bond off the assumed cheapest (with an assumed basis of 4/32nds); spreads are from historicals.
7. Net gain per million par of the swap bond. Sell basis − buy basis − current yield giveup.
8. Assumed cheapest to deliver with assumed yield on last trading day and implied repo. Different levels of assumed yield on the cheapest do not make a major difference in the analysis because convexities are similar.
9. Value of one basis point of yield-spread change between swap bond and cheapest to deliver: as the spread changes by one basis point this is the change in 32nds in net gain per million par.
10. Current yield give up.

EXHIBIT 16-2
**Pickup (in 32nds Per MM) under Given Yield Spreads
and Cheapest-to-Deliver Assumptions
(Swap Issue: 12 percent of 8/15/13)**

Yield Spread	Assumed Cheapest to Deliver			
History	12.5	11.75	11.25	7.625
Present	45	47	51	52*
Low	36	47	26	4
Average	51	52*	48	38
High	52*	52*	52*	52*
		Pickup (32nds per mm)		

*Indicates swap issue becomes cheapest to deliver at spread.
Assumed cheapest to deliver: 12.5   of 8/15/14
                             11.75 of 11/15/14
                             11.25 of 2/15/15
                             7.625 of 2/15/07

RISKS OF THE TRADE

The primary risk of this trade is that the yield spread between the swap issue and cheapest to deliver could noticeably narrow. If the spread becomes narrower than historics, less pickup will be realized. It is easy to calculate a breakeven spread between the swap issue and cheapest to deliver.

Another risk exists in the delivery month. This trade assumes that the position stays on to the last trading day of the month (December 18, 1985) when the futures position is subsequently liquidated. Being long futures, the investor may have to take delivery of a bond anytime during the month. In most cases, it is optimal for the short to deliver at the end of the month (in a positive yield-curve environment). A look at the bond delivery sheets show that bonds are rarely delivered before the last trading day. The only time it may be optimal for the short to deliver early is if the market takes a big plunge between the end of futures trading (3 P.M., EST) and the close of the bond market, and the short was already set up to deliver a premium coupon. This is known as the *wildcard* option. This risk can be mitigated if the investor takes the trade off before the last trading day; however, the benefit of full convergence would not be realized.

APPLICATIONS TO OTHER MARKETS

The swap issue could be other than a government bond. A bond thought to be expensive to governments would be an especially attractive swap bond; however, it should be realized that due to credit considerations, supply/demand, convexity etc., these issues do not move in concert with bond futures as much as governments do, so the yield-spread risk between the swap bond and cheapest to deliver will be much greater. Also, bid-ask spreads on bonds in other markets may eat up some of the gain if the swap bond is sold and bought back at a later time.

CONTRASTS WITH BASIS TRADING

The yield-enhancement trade looks similar to *trading the basis;* however, it is motivated by different factors. The yield enhancer has a time horizon of several months, taking advantage of the full convergence of the futures with the underlying instrument. The basis trader has a much shorter time horizon, anywhere from a few hours to several weeks. This short term movement of the basis is most affected by financing (repo) rates and short-term market movements, so the basis trade is a play on repo and market direction. If a bond is in heavy demand to be borrowed, it *goes on special,* meaning the repo rate declines which caused the basis to widen out. Although it may seem like a good opportunity to sell the bond and buy futures against it (i.e., "sell the basis") it will most likely cost the trader a lot in current yield giveup because most basis traders finance the bonds in the overnight repo market. Market direction also frequently affects the basis. The futures market often (but not always) reacts faster to factors affecting the government bonds; if the market rallies, the basis often narrows, if the market falls off the basis often widens.

The basis graph shown as Exhibit 16–3 illustrates the difference in perspective between the yield enhancer and the basis trader. The yield enhancer's objective is to capture the general trend in the collapse of the basis. The basis trader looks to take advantage of the short term ups and downs of the basis on its way to full convergence.

EXHIBIT 16–3
Basis Graph

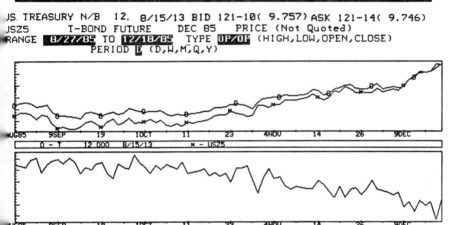

```
US. TREASURY N/B   12.  8/15/13 BID 121-10( 9.757) ASK 121-14( 9.746)
USZ5        T-BOND FUTURE      DEC 85    PRICE (Not Quoted)
RANGE  8/27/85  TO  12/18/85   TYPE  OP/OP  (HIGH,LOW,OPEN,CLOSE)
            PERIOD  D  (D,W,M,Q,Y)
```

APPENDIX

Frank J. Fabozzi is currently a Visiting Professor in the Alfred P. Sloan School of Management at MIT, on leave from Lafayette College. A magna cum laude graduate from the City College of New York with bachelor's and master's degrees, he is a member of Phi Beta Kappa. Dr. Fabozzi earned a doctorate in economics from The City University of New York and is a C.F.A. and C.P.A. He is the managing editor of *The Journal of Portfolio Management* and has authored, coauthored, and edited several widely acclaimed books in investment management.

TAXATION OF TREASURY SECURITIES

Frank J. Fabozzi, Ph.D., C.F.A., C.P.A.
Visiting Professor
Alfred P. Sloan School of Management
Massachusetts Institute of Technology

All interest income from a Treasury coupon security is taxable as ordinary income at the federal income tax level; however, interest income is exempt from income taxation by state and local governments. A portion of the income realized from the sale or redemption of a Treasury issued security or zero-coupon Treasury security (that is, stripped Treasury) may be in the form of a capital gain. The Internal Revenue Code (IRC) provides for a special tax treatment of any capital gain in the hands of a qualified investor. The tax rules for determining whether a capital gain has resulted and would qualify for this preferential tax treatment are discussed in this chapter.[1]

CAPITAL GAIN OR LOSS DETERMINATION AND TAX TREATMENT

To understand the tax rules for Treasury securities, we must define the tax *basis*. In most instances, the *original basis* of a Treasury

---

[1] At the time of this writing, legislation has been proposed to eliminate the preferential capital gains treatment.

409

security is the investor's total cost on the date it is acquired. For Treasury securities, the *adjusted basis* is its original basis increased by any amortization of a discount or decreased by any amortization of a premium.

To determine whether a capital gain or loss is realized from the sale, exchange,[2] or redemption of a Treasury security, the proceeds received are compared to the adjusted basis. If the proceeds exceed the adjusted basis, the investor realized a capital gain; on the other hand, a capital loss is realized when the adjusted basis exceeds the proceeds received by the investor. It should be noted, however, that while traders and investors are entitled to realize capital gains and losses, generally, dealers are not.[3] In the case of dealers, the securities held are considered inventory, and any gains or losses are treated as ordinary gains or losses rather than capital gains or losses.[4]

Once a capital gain or loss is determined for a Treasury security, there are special rules for determining the impact on the investor's adjusted gross income.[5] To apply these rules, it is necessary to ascertain whether the sale or redemption has resulted in a capital gain or

[2] An exception to the general rule of recognizing a gain or loss as a taxable event is when the offering circular of the Treasury Department for a particular exchange declares that no gain or loss shall be recognized for federal income tax purposes.

[3] There is an exception. If a dealer (1) clearly designates that certain securities are being held for investment purposes when the securities are acquired, and (2) does not hold the securities primarily for sale to customers in the ordinary course of business after the designation, then gains or losses on the designated securities qualify for capital gain and loss treatment.

[4] For tax purposes, taxpayers are classified as either dealers, traders, or investors. A dealer in securities is a merchant of securities who is regularly engaged in the acquisition of securities with a view to the gains and profits that may be derived as a result of such transactions. A dealer may be an individual, partnership, or corporation. A trader is a person who buys and sells for his or her own account rather than the account of a customer, and the frequency of such transacting is such that the person may be said to be engaged in such activities as a trade or business. Investors, like traders, transact for their own accounts. However, transactions are occasional and much less than required in a trade or business.

[5] Gross income is all income that is subject to income tax. Adjusted gross income is gross income minus certain business and other deductions. For an investor, one such deduction is the long-term capital gain deduction that is explained later in this chapter. Taxable income is the amount on which the tax liability is determined.

loss that is long term or short term. The classification depends on the length of time the capital asset is held by the taxpayer. For capital assets acquired after June 22, 1984, the general rule is that if a Treasury security is held for six months or less, the gain or loss is short-term.[6] A long-term capital gain or loss results when the Treasury security is held for more than six months. For Treasury securities acquired before June 22, 1984, the holding period for a long-term capital gain is anything over one year.

For individuals, all short-term capital gains and losses are then combined to produce either a *net short-term capital gain* or a *net short-term capital loss.* The same procedure is followed for long-term capital gains and losses. Either a *net long-term capital gain* or a *net long-term capital loss* will result.

Next, an overall *net capital gain* or *net capital loss* is determined by combining the amounts in the previous paragraph. If the result is a net capital gain, the entire amount is added to gross income. However, net long-term capital gains are given preferential tax treatment. A deduction is allowed from gross income in determining adjusted gross income. The permissible deduction is 60 percent of the excess of net long-term capital gains over net short-term capital losses.[7] With a current maximum marginal tax rate for ordinary income of 50 percent for individuals, the maximum tax paid on the excess is 20 percent.

If there is a net capital loss, it is deductible from gross income. The amount that may be deducted is limited to the lesser of (1) $3,000 (but $1,500 for married taxpayers filing separate returns), (2) taxable income without the personal exemption and without capital gains and losses minus the zero bracket amount, and (3) the sum of net short-term capital loss plus half the net long-term capital

---

[6] An exception to this general rule applies to wash sales. A wash sale occurs when "substantially identical securities" are acquired within 30 days before or after a sale of the securities *at a loss.* In such cases, the loss is not recognized as a capital loss. Instead, the loss is added to the basis of the securities that caused the loss. The holding period for the new securities in connection with a wash sale then includes the period for which the original securities were held. The rule is not applicable to an individual who is a trader, nor to an individual or corporate dealer.

[7] A capital gain deduction taken by an individual could result in a minimum tax liability.

loss. The third limitation is the so-called "$1 for $2 rule" and is the basic difference between the tax treatment of net short-term capital losses and net long-term capital losses. The former is deductible dollar for dollar, but the latter requires $2 of long-term capital loss to obtain a $1 deduction.

Because of the difference in the tax treatment of net long-term capital losses and net short-term capital losses, the order in which these losses are deductible in a tax year is specified by the Department of the Treasury. First, net short-term capital losses are used to satisfy the limitation. Any balance to satisfy the limitation is then applied from net long-term capital losses using the $1 for $2 rule. Any unused net short-term or net long-term capital losses are carried over on a dollar-for-dollar basis.[8] When they are carried over, they do not lose their identity but remain either short term or long term. These losses can be carried over indefinitely until they are all utilized in subsequent tax years.

The procedure for determining a net capital gain or loss for a corporation is the same as that for individuals. However, the tax treatment of any net capital gain or loss differs from that of individuals in the following two ways. First, a corporation is not entitled to a net capital gain deduction for the excess of net long-term capital gains over net short-term capital losses. Instead the excess is subject to an alternative tax computation that limits the tax to 28 percent of the gain.[9] The tax attributable to the excess of net long-term capital gains over net short-term capital losses is the lesser of (1) the tax liability on the taxable income when the excess is included in taxable income (i.e., regular tax computation), and (2) the tax liability on taxable income that is reduced by the excess, plus a 28 percent tax on the excess. The latter tax computation is the alternative tax computation.

Second, no deduction is allowed for a net capital loss. However, net capital losses can be carried back to three preceding taxable

---

[8] However, in determining the amount of the net capital loss deduction in a future tax year, the $1 for $2 rule applies.

[9] The minimum tax can increase the effective tax rate on net capital gains to 29.7 percent.

years and carried forward five taxable years to offset any net capital gains in those years.[10] Although there are exceptions, the general rule is that any unused net capital loss after the fifth subsequent year can never be used by a corporate taxpayer. Net capital losses are not carried over in character. Instead, they are carried over as a short-term capital loss.

TAX TREATMENT OF TREASURY COUPON SECURITIES

Prior to the Deficit Reduction Act of 1984, any capital appreciation was treated as a capital gain. The 1984 act still allows this tax treatment for bonds issued on or prior to July 18, 1984; however, for bonds issued after that date, part of the capital appreciation is treated as ordinary income.

For Treasury coupon securities issued before July 18, 1984, any capital appreciation is treated as a capital gain. If there is a loss, it is a capital loss. For example, suppose that a Treasury *coupon* security was issued 25 years ago at par ($10,000) and 20 years later its price declined to $7,683 because of a rise in interest rates. If this issue is purchased by an investor for $7,683 and sold 2.5 years later for $9,000, the investor will realize a capital gain of $1,317. No amortization of the discount is required even though a portion of the capital appreciation really represents interest.

The 1984 act changed the tax treatment for *taxable* bonds issued after July 18, 1984. Any capital appreciation must be separated into a portion that is attributable to interest income (as represented by amortization) and a portion that is attributable to capital gain. The portion representing interest income is taxed as ordinary income when the issue is sold. This is called *accrued market discount*. The amount of the market discount that represents interest income (that is, amortization) is not taxed until the issue is sold. Accrued market

---

[10] There is a limitation on the amount that can be carried back. The amount cannot cause or increase a net operating loss in the taxable year it is carried back to. Net capital losses are applied to the earliest year as a carry-back or carry-over.

discount can be determined using either the straight-line method or the constant-yield method.[11]

Exhibit A–1 shows the tax consequences for five assumed selling prices for a hypothetical Treasury coupon issue. The results are shown assuming issuance before and after July 18, 1984. The results are also shown for the constant-yield and straight-line methods.

Two implications are evident from Exhibit A–1. First, from a tax perspective, Treasury coupon securities issued before July 18, 1984, and selling at a discount will be more attractive than those issued after that date and selling at a discount. This will be reflected in the market price of those issues. Consequently, investors that are in low marginal tax rates will find that they may be overpaying for Treasury coupon securities issued before July 18, 1984. The second implication is that it is not in the best interest of the investor to select the straight-line method to compute the accrued market discount because the capital gain will be lower than if the constant-yield method is elected.

When a Treasury security is purchased at a price greater than its par value, the issue is said to be purchased at a premium. For an issue purchased by a nondealer investor, he may elect to amortize the premium ratably over the remaining life of the issue. For example, suppose on January 1, 1981, a calendar-year taxpayer/investor purchased a Treasury issue for $10,500. The issue has a remaining life of 10 years and a $10,000 par value. The coupon rate is 7 percent. The premium is $500. The investor can amortize this premium over the 10-year remaining life. If so, the amount amortized would be $50 per year ($500 divided by 10).[12] The coupon interest received of $700 ($10,000 times .07) would then be effectively reduced by $50 so that $650 would be reported as interest income. At the end of 1981, the first year, the original basis of $10,500 is reduced by $50 to $10,450.

---

[11] With the constant-yield method, the interest each year is determined by multiplying the adjusted basis at the beginning of each year by the purchase yield-to-maturity.

[12] In this example the straight-line method is used to amortize the premium. An investor may use either the straight-line or constant-yield method. The former is preferred for Treasury securities since the adjusted basis would be lower, resulting in a greater capital loss or smaller capital gain if the issue is sold before maturity.

EXHIBIT A-1
**Tax Treatment of Treasury Coupon
Securities Selling at a Market Discount**

Characteristics of hypothetical Treasury
coupon issue:

Coupon	= 4 percent
Price	= $7,683
Par value	= $10,000
Years to maturity	= 5
Yield to maturity	= 10 percent
Market discount	= $2,317

Basis at time of purchase = $7,683
Issue sold after 2.5 years

Issued before July 18, 1984

Sale Price	Accrued Market Discount	Capital Gain (Loss)
$9,500	$ 0	$1,817
9,000	0	1,317
8,700	0	1,017
7,683	0	0
7,000	0	(693)

Issued after July 18, 1984, with amortization based on constant-yield method

Sale Price	Accrued Market Discount	Capital Gain (Loss)
$9,500	$1,017	$ 800
9,000	1,017	300
8,700	1,017	0
7,683	1,017	(1,017)
7,000	1,017	(1,700)

Issued after July 18, 1984, with amortization based on straight-line method

Sale Price	Accrued Market Discount	Capital Gain (Loss)
$9,500	$1,161	$ 656
9,000	1,161	156
8,700	1,161	(144)
7,683	1,161	(1,161)
7,000	1,161	(1,844)

By the end of 1985 the issue would be held for five years. The adjusted basis would be $10,250 ($10,500 minus $250). If the issue is held until retired at maturity, the adjusted basis would be $10,000, and thus there would be no capital gain or loss realized. If the investor does not elect to amortize the premium, the original basis is not changed. Consequently, at maturity the investor would realize a capital loss of $500.

The original basis and the remaining number of years to maturity were used in the preceding example to determine the amount of the premium to be amortized. In the case of callable Treasury bonds acquired after January 1, 1957, the investor must elect to compute the amortization based upon the earlier call date *if a smaller deduction results compared to using the number of years remaining to maturity.* For example, suppose an investor purchased a callable Treasury bond that has 10 years remaining to maturity for $1,300. The par value is $1,000; however, the bond may be called in six years for $1,150. The first election the investor must make is whether or not to amortize the premium. If the investor elects to amortize the premium, then he must base the amount of the amortization on the call price and date rather than on the par value if the deduction is less. If the amount amortized is based on the par value, then the annual amount deducted would be $30, since the premium is $300 and there are 10 years remaining to maturity. If the earlier call date is used, the amount of the premium is $150. The annual deduction is $25 per year, since there are six years to the call date.

Should a Treasury bond be called before its maturity date, any unamortized portion of the premium is treated as an ordinary loss in the year the issue is called. For example, consider our hypothetical 10-year Treasury issue that is callable in 6 years. If the issue is actually called in the sixth year, an investor who did not elect to amortize the premium would realize an ordinary loss of $150 (original basis of $1,300 minus call price of $1,150). Notice what happens if the premium is amortized. Amortization based upon the maturity date would result in a capital gain of $30.[13] Of course, amortization

[13] The adjusted basis would be the original basis of $1,300 minus the amount amortized over the six years of $180 ($30 times six). The capital gain is therefore the call price of $1,150 minus the adjusted basis of $1,120.

based upon the call date would have generated neither a capital gain nor loss.

TAX TREATMENT OF ZERO-COUPON TREASURY SECURITIES

Although the Treasury does not issue zero-coupon securities, dealers have issued zero-coupon securities collateralized by Treasury securities. These securities are discussed in Chapters 11 and 12. Special tax rules are applicable to zero-coupon Treasury securities because they are classified as original-issue discount securities. The tax law requires that for an issue with a maturity of greater than one year,[14] each year a portion of the original-issue discount, which is the difference between the redemption value and the purchase price, be amortized (accrued) and included in gross income. A corresponding increase in the adjusted basis of the security is made.

The tax treatment of an original issue discount issue depends on its issuance date. For securities issued prior to July 2, 1982, the original-issue discount must be amortized on a straight-line basis each month and included in gross income based on the number of months the bond is held in that tax year. For securities issued on or after July 2, 1982, the amount of the original-issue discount amortized is based on the constant-yield method and included in gross income based on the number of days in the tax year that the issue is held. With this method for determining the amount of the original issue discount to be included in gross income, the interest for the year is first determined by multiplying the adjusted basis by the yield at issuance. From this interest, the coupon interest is subtracted. The difference is the amount of the original-issue discount amortized for the year. The same amount is then added to the adjusted basis.

To illustrate the tax rules for original-issue discount bonds issued after July 2, 1982, consider a hypothetical zero coupon Treasury security, maturing in five years, that was issued for $6,139, and has a redemption value of $10,000. The yield-to-maturity for this hypo-

---

[14] The tax rules for zero-coupon Treasuries with an original maturity of less than one year are discussed in the next section.

thetical issue is 10 percent. The original-issue discount is $3,861 ($10,000 – $6,139). The constant-yield method is used to determine the amortization and the adjusted basis. The procedure is as follows. Each six months, the investor is assumed to realize for tax purposes 5 percent of the adjusted basis. The 5 percent represents one half of the 10 percent yield to maturity. The original investment is the purchase price of $6,139. In the first six months the bond is held, the investor realizes for tax purposes 5 percent of $6,139, or $307. Therefore, $307 is assumed to be realized (although not received) by the investor. This is the amount of the original-issue discount amortized and reported as gross income from holding this issue for six months. The adjusted basis for the bond at the end of the first six months will equal the original-issue price of $6,139 plus the amount of the original-issue discount amortized, $307. Thus, the adjusted basis is $6,456.

Let's carry this out for one more six-month period. If the security is held for another six months, the amount of interest that the investor is assumed to realize for tax purposes is 5 percent of the adjusted basis. Since the adjusted basis at the beginning of the second six-month period is $6,456, the interest is $323. Therefore, the amount of the original-issue discount amortized for the second six-month period is $323. The adjusted basis at the end of the second six-month period is $6,779—the previous adjusted basis of $6,456 plus $323. If this issue was purchased on January 1, and sold on December 31 of the same year, interest income would be $630 ($307 + $323), the original-issue discount amortized. If this issue is sold on December 31, for $7,800, there would be a capital gain of $1,021, the difference between the sale proceeds of $7,800 and the adjusted basis of $6,779.

Exhibit A–2 shows the amount of the original-issue discount that must be reported as gross income for each six-month period that the issue is held and the adjusted basis at the end of the period. Notice that amortization is lower in the earlier years, gradually increasing over the life of the bond on a compounding basis.

There are two more points the investor should be familiar with when dealing with zero-coupon Treasury securities. First, if a security is sold before maturity, subsequent holders must continue to amortize the original-issue discount. Second an investor must pay taxes on interest included in gross income but not received in cash.

EXHIBIT A–2
Tax Treatment for a Zero-Coupon Treasury Security

Characteristics of hypothetical issue:
Issue price   = $6,139
Redemption value   = $10,000
Years to maturity   = 5
Yield to maturity   = 10 percent
Original-issue discount = $3,861
Amortization based on constant-yield method

Held (Years)	Gross Income Reported = Original-Issue Discount Amortized [+]	Adjusted basis at end of period [*]
0.5	$307	$ 6,446
1.0	323	6,769
1.5	338	7,107
2.0	355	7,462
2.5	373	7,835
3.0	392	8,227
3.5	411	8,638
4.0	432	9,070
4.5	454	9,524
5.0	476	10,000

[+] By the constant yield method, it is found as follows:
Adjusted basis in previous period × .05

[*] Adjusted basis at the end of the period. The adjusted basis is found by adding the original-issue discount amortized for the period to the previous period's adjusted basis.

TAX TREATMENT OF TREASURY SECURITIES WITH AN ORIGINAL MATURITY NOT MORE THAN ONE YEAR

The original-issue discount rules that were discussed in the previous section are not applicable to securities issued at a discount with an original maturity of not more than one year. Treasury bills fall into this classification, as do short-term zero-coupon Treasury securities. For tax reporting purposes, the investor must determine

(1) when to report the acquisition discount (that is, the difference between the redemption value and the purchase price) if an issue purchased in one tax year is sold or redeemed in the next tax year, and (2) how to classify any gain or loss that results.

For an investor reporting on a cash basis who holds an issue until maturity generally, the acquisition discount is realized in the calendar year that the issue matures. The exception is when an investor deducts interest for carrying an issue. This is explained in the next section.

An investor who reports on an accrual basis and holds the issue to maturity must allocate a ratable share of the acquisition discount between the tax year that the issue was purchased and the tax year that it was redeemed based on the number of days that the issue is held in each year. The daily portion of the acquisition discount included in gross income may be determined by using the straight-line method or the constant method.[15] Using the straight-line method, the includible portion of the acquisition discount is found by dividing the amount of the discount by the number of days after the date of purchase up to and including the day of maturity. If the constant yield method is elected, the includible portion of the acquisition discount is computed by using the yield to maturity in the same manner as described in the previous section for determining the amortized portion of an original-issue discount for a zero-coupon Treasury with a maturity of more than one year. The adjusted basis of the issue is increased by the amortized portion of the acquisition discount computed by either method. No amount previously included in gross income is required to be included again.

For an issue held to maturity, the acquisition discount is treated as ordinary income. When an issue is sold prior to maturity, the acquisition discount must be partitioned between interest income and capital gain or loss in the same way that it is partitioned for Treasury coupon securities issued after July 18, 1984 and zero-coupon Treasuries with a maturity of more than one year.

[15] An irrevocable election must be made to use the constant-yield method.

LIMITATION ON DEDUCTIBILITY OF
INTEREST EXPENSES

The IRC imposes limits on the amount of current interest paid or accrued on debt to purchase or carry a market discount bond such as a Treasury coupon security selling at a discount. The deduction is limited to the amount of any income from the bond. Any interest expense that remains can be deducted in the current tax year only to the extent that it exceeds the amortized portion of the market discount. The amount of the interest expense that is disallowed can be deducted either (1) in future tax years if there is net interest income and an election is made or (2) when the bond is sold.

To illustrate this limitation, suppose that interest expense incurred to carry a Treasury bond selling at a discount is $5,000 for the current year, the coupon interest is $2,000 from that bond, and the amortized portion of the market discount is $1,400. The investor is entitled to deduct $2,000 (the amount of the coupon interest). In addition, since the remaining interest expense of $3,000 ($5,000 – $2,000) exceeds the amortized portion of the market discount of $1,400 by $1,600, an additional $1,600 may be deducted. Therefore, the total interest expense that may be deducted in the current tax year is $3,600. The $1,400 can be deducted in future tax years if it does not exceed the limit or when the bond is sold.

There is an exception to the above rule. An investor may elect to have the amortized portion of the market discount taxed each year. In that case, the entire interest expense to purchase or carry the bond is deductible in the current year. For example, if an investor elects to include the $1,400 of amortized market discount as gross income in the current year, he may deduct the $1,400 as current interest expense. If an investor elects to include the amortized portion in order to avoid deduction limits, the election covers all acquisitions on or after the first day of the first taxable year to which it applies and cannot be revoked without the consent of the Internal Revenue Service.

For an investor reporting on a cash basis, the same limitation applies to interest expense to carry a Treasury bill and a zero-coupon Treasury with a maturity of no more than one year. Interest expense paid or accrued to carry such securities is limited in that it must exceed the year's aggregate daily acquisition discount. The limitations can be avoided by making the election discussed in the previous paragraph.

INDEX